A BIOGRAPHY OF

Mrs. MARTY MANN

A BIOGRAPHY OF
Mrs. MARTY MANN

The First Lady of Alcoholics Anonymous

SALLY BROWN AND DAVID R. BROWN

HAZELDEN®

Hazelden
Center City, Minnesota 55012-0176

1-800-328-9000
1-651-213-4590 (Fax)
www.hazelden.org

Library of Congress Cataloging-in-Publication Data

Brown, Sally, 1923–
    A biography of Mrs. Marty Mann : the first lady of Alcoholics Anonymous /
Sally Brown and David R. Brown.
        p.   cm.
    Includes bibliographical references and index.
    ISBN 1-56838-626-5 (hardcover)
    ISBN 1-59285-307-2 (softcover)
            978-1-59285-307-6 (13-digit, softcover)
    1. Mann, Marty, 1904–   2. Women alcoholics—United States—Biography.
3. Alcoholics Anonymous—History.   4. National Council on Alcoholism—
History.   I. Brown, David R., 1923–   II. Title.

HV5293.M155 B76 2001
362.29'86'092—dc21
[B]

                                                                00-054050

Interior design by Elizabeth Cleveland
Typesetting by Stanton Publication Services, Inc.

Contents

Foreword by Stacia Murphy   VII
Foreword by William Cope Moyers   VIII
Acknowledgments   X
Our Gratitude List   XI
"Imagine Such a Disease" by Ruth Fox, M.D.   XIII

Part One

Prologue   3
Introduction   6

Chapter 1: Roots (1904–10)   12
Chapter 2: Chicago! (1910–18)   18
Chapter 3: Through the Wringer (1918–21)   26
Chapter 4: School Days, School Days (1921–25)   36
Chapter 5: The Sleeping Lion Stirs (1921–25)   46
Chapter 6: The Glory Years (1925–26)   53
Chapter 7: The Merry Marriage-Go-Round (1926–28)   58
Chapter 8: Rising and Falling Stars (1928–30)   65
Chapter 9: The Sleeping Lion Awakes (1930–35)   71
Chapter 10: In the Fury of the Storm (1935–36)   80
Chapter 11: The Lion Roars (1937–38)   85

Part Two

Chapter 12: Rebirth (1938–39)   97
Chapter 13: A Pioneer in the Making (1939)   111
Chapter 14: The Learning Curve Steepens (1939–42)   124
Chapter 15: Priscilla (1942–44)   138

Chapter 16: Dawn of a Vision (1944)   152
Chapter 17: The Entrepreneur (1944–46)   164
Chapter 18: Rocking the Boat (1946)   179
Chapter 19: Sowing the Future (1946–48)   187
Chapter 20: Life Happens (1948)   197
Chapter 21: Yale Files for Divorce (1948–50)   207

Part Three

Chapter 22: Unsettled Weather (1950–54)   217
Chapter 23: The Sun Breaks Through (1954)   233
Chapter 24: The Clouds Lift (1954–60)   239
Chapter 25: Leo Redux (1960–64)   252
Chapter 26: Letting Go (1964–70)   270
Chapter 27: A New Path (1970)   284
Chapter 28: Sorrow and Serenity (1970–79)   293
Chapter 29: Transcendence (1979–80)   311
Chapter 30: Afterward (1980–93)   321
Epilogue   324

Notes   327
Selected Bibliography   353
Audiotapes   359
Interviews   362
The Twelve Steps of Alcoholics Anonymous   364
The Twelve Traditions of Alcoholics Anonymous   365
Index   367
About the Authors   383

Foreword

ADDICTION TO ALCOHOL AND OTHER DRUGS continues to be a persistent public health threat. While we've come a long way in our scientific understanding of its complexity, one woman, in her wisdom more than fifty years ago, recognized that stigma would remain our most powerful foe when trying to influence public attitudes about a problem that too many people still consider to be moral, not medical. Her name was Marty Mann.

Through her work in educating the public and setting up local alcoholism information centers around the country, Marty helped shape the modern alcoholism movement. A visionary and a pioneer, she took on an unpopular cause during an era when women were supposed to remain silent. With her enormous public relations and communication skills, Marty began our long crusade to change the way America views those who are afflicted and affected by alcohol and other drugs. Yet very little has been written that tells of her life and courageous work.

This painstakingly researched biography finally gives Marty Mann her due place in history and proves how each of us owes this remarkable woman our gratitude. Sally and David Brown deserve our tremendous thanks for bringing out of the closet and into the light one of the twentieth century's most fascinating American women.

STACIA MURPHY
President
National Council on Alcoholism and Drug Dependence, Inc.

Foreword

OUR UNDERSTANDING OF THE DISEASE OF ADDICTION has markedly improved in the twenty years since Marty Mann died. Science is explaining how people become addicted. Pharmacology is coming up with new tools to improve outcomes. Treatment centers are meeting higher standards for licensing, and counselors are going back to school to improve their clinical skills. And hundreds of thousands of people and families are getting well and staying well.

Yet sadly, the shame and the stigma around addiction disease are stronger today than they were during the last years of Marty's life. Ignorance, intolerance, and indifference still drive America's so-called war on drugs. This national fight has cost billions upon billions of dollars and stuffed our prisons with inmates. It has polarized and paralyzed public policies so that our nation continues to do the same thing over and over again, with the same result. Supplies of legal and illegal drugs remain constant, as does the demand for them. If Marty were alive today, she would be disappointed that America is still stuck in the past on this issue.

But there are stirrings of change—what I call "the great awakening." And it is coming from people like Marty: alcoholics and addicts who have recovered. People who are now willing to stand up and speak out and share their firsthand experiences with addiction and with recovery. It is happening in places like Saint Paul and Dallas and Grand Rapids and Tallahassee—in forums like state legislatures, news conferences, and community meetings.

In telling their stories, these individuals shatter the myths that only bad or evil or "other" people are vulnerable to addiction disease, and that nobody recovers. By putting a human face on recovery, they promote the reality that people from all walks of life can and do get well, if given the chance. When addiction is viewed this way, it is easier for the public and the policy-makers to understand why America needs to stop fighting a war against people and start dealing with addiction disease as a public health crisis.

It is risky to share addiction and recovery with people who do not know or do not understand. The shame and the stigma are strong. But like Marty Mann, we are the fortunate ones, the ones who got well. And people in recovery have an opportunity, and a responsibility, to change the terms of the debate for the sake of those who still suffer. The risks are high. But so, too, are the rewards.

WILLIAM COPE MOYERS
Hazelden Foundation

Acknowledgments

Excerpts from *Alex: The Life of Alexander Liberman* by Dodie Kazanjian and Calvin Tomkins, ©1993 by Dodie Kazanjian and Calvin Tomkins, are reprinted by permission of Alfred A. Knopf, a division of Random House, Inc.

The excerpt from "Chicago" is from *Chicago Poems* by Carl Sandburg, copyright 1916 by Holt, Rinehart and Winston and renewed 1944 by Carl Sandburg, reprinted with permission of Harcourt, Inc.

Excerpts from the letters of Jane Bowles are reprinted from *Out in the World: Selected Letters of Jane Bowles 1935–1970* with the permission of Black Sparrow Press, ©1985 by Paul Frederic Bowles.

Excerpts from *The Dogs Bark: Public People and Public Places by Truman Capote* (New York: Random House, 1973) are reprinted with permission of Random House, Inc.

The excerpts from the book *Alcoholics Anonymous Comes of Age: A Brief History of A.A.* and the Twelve Steps and Twelve Traditions of Alcoholics Anonymous are reprinted with permission of Alcoholics Anonymous World Services, Inc. (AAWS). Permission to reprint these excerpts and the Twelve Steps and Twelve Traditions does not mean that AAWS has reviewed or approved the contents of this publication, or that AAWS necessarily agrees with the views expressed herein. AA is a program of recovery from alcoholism *only*—use of the Twelve Steps and Twelve Traditions and these excerpts in connection with programs and activities which are patterned after AA, but which address other problems, or in any other non-AA context, does not imply otherwise.

Our Gratitude List

WE HAVE BEEN TOUCHED and honored by the many, many people who contributed so unselfishly of their time, their records, and their goodwill. Like us, they believe Marty is the great unsung heroine of the alcoholism movement in this country, as well as the world, and that recognition of her contributions and accomplishments in the face of nearly insurmountable odds is long overdue. We would like to single out a few persons who were pivotal in our journey of discovery.

Barbara Brown Zikmund, D.Min., recent president of Hartford Seminary, planted the seed for Marty's biography when she suggested many years ago that a seminary paper of Sally's might warrant book-length treatment.

LeClair Bissell, M.D., was the first in the alcoholism field to give us the courage to undertake a biography of Marty. LeClair introduced us to innumerable resources and has been a steadying anchor and adviser throughout.

We are especially grateful to have known the only one of Marty's natal family still living when we began our research—her younger brother, Bill. This story would have been incomplete without his recollections. Sadly, he died on January 16, 1999, soon after reviewing and approving a near-final draft of the manuscript. One of Bill's sons, Ted Mann, and two others of Marty's nephews, Gregory and Tyler Miller (sons of Marty's sister Betty), have also been helpful.

We are indebted to the two living direct descendants of Priscilla Peck's forebears for their information, Lucia R. Anderson and her brother, W. Thwing Havens.

Felicia Gizycka Magruder's personal journals were of inestimable value.

We thank her grandson, Joe Arnold, for his help in enabling our access to this material. Felicia died on February 26, 1999, a few months after Sally met her.

Living members of the Blakemore family, especially Bruce L. Blakemore (Mrs. Hugh Jones) and John Blakemore, adult children of Marty's ex-husband by his third wife, graciously enlarged our understanding of Marty and John Blakemore's early brief marriage.

Hessie Kennedy Rubin, the daughter of R. Foster Kennedy, M.D., and Katherine Caragol de la Terga, cleared up some mysteries for us about Dr. Kennedy, a pivotal figure in Marty's life and in the history of Alcoholics Anonymous.

Paul Wood, executive director of the National Council on Alcoholism and Drug Dependence (NCADD) when we began, and Stacia Murphy, present president of NCADD, and their staffs, especially Jeffrey Hon, director for public information, have been very supportive of our endeavor. Former executive directors George C. Dimas and Walter J. Murphy and his wife, Debbie, former staff member George Marcelle, and Adele Smithers-Fornaci made major contributions regarding the history of NCADD as well as in their recollections of Marty.

Judit Santon, archivist at the General Service Office (GSO) of Alcoholics Anonymous (AA), and Gail La Croix, archivist of the Akron, Ohio, AA central office, shared generously of their resources.

Three professional historians of the alcoholism movement have provided exceptional information, insight, and perspective on our research—Ernest Kurtz, Ph.D.; William L. White, M.A.; and Ron Roizen, Ph.D. Ron Roizen was the first to introduce us to some of the important documents connected with Marty and the alcoholism movement in America.

Nancy Olson was a valuable guide to the history of the Hughes Act, and Lyn Harbaugh to that of High Watch Farm.

We are grateful to the many others who were themselves leaders in the alcoholism movement. They admired, respected, learned from, and loved Marty. If they hadn't shared their memories, this book could not exist.

Nearly all of the people above, plus others unnamed, have reviewed various drafts of the book and made helpful suggestions. They are not responsible for our interpretations or for any remaining errors of fact.

Finally, we honor and thank Bill Pittman, Kathryn Kjorlien, and Hazelden for their vision and persistence in bringing Marty's story to fruition.

Imagine Such a Disease[*]

by Ruth Fox, M.D.
President, American Medical Society on Alcoholism

IF SOME NEW AND TERRIBLE DISEASE were suddenly to strike us here in America—a disease of unknown cause, possibly due to noxious gas or poison in our soil, air, or water—it would be treated as a national emergency, with our whole citizenry uniting as a man to fight it.

Let us suppose the disease to have so harmful an effect on the nervous system that 6½ million people[†] in our country would go insane for periods lasting from a few hours to weeks or months and recurring repetitively over periods ranging from 15 to 30 years.

Let us further suppose that during these spells of insanity, acts of so destructive a nature would be committed that the material and spiritual lives of whole families would be in jeopardy, with a resultant 25 million persons cruelly affected.[‡] Work in business, industry, professions, and factories would be crippled, sabotaged, or left undone. And each year more than one and one-quarter billion dollars would need to be spent merely to patch up in some small way the effects of the disease on families whose breadwinners have been stricken.[§]

Finally, let us imagine this poison or disease to have the peculiar property of so altering a person's judgment, so brainwashing him that he would be unable to see that he had become ill at all; actually so perverting and so

---

[*] As it appears in Marty Mann, *Marty Mann Answers Your Questions about Drinking and Alcoholism* (New York: Holt, Rinehart and Winston, 1970).

[†] 17–20 million in the year 2000

[‡] 85–100 million in the year 2000

[§] Total direct and indirect cost in 1995=$428.1 billion

XIV — Imagine Such a Disease

distorting his view of life that he would wish with all his might to go on being ill.

Such an emergency would unquestionably be classed as a countrywide disaster, and billions of dollars and thousands of scientists would be put to work to find the cause of the disease, to treat its victims, and to prevent its spread.

The dread disease envisioned above is actually here. It is alcoholism.

Part ONE

"*History is not a luxury; it is a public-health necessity.*"

—Thomas Layton, anthropology professor
San Jose State University
San Jose, California

Prologue

LATE 1940S. The audience, several hundred strong, packed the ballroom. Hotel staff were hurriedly setting up extra rows of chairs in the back for standees holding up the walls on either side and those spilling out the rear doors into the hall. Noisy waves of talk and laughter swelled as people found their seats and greeted one another. Finally, the chairman moved to the podium and began his introduction of the speaker. The audience quieted.

This would be a tough audience—nearly all men, physicians attending a medical conference. Many were clinicians, others researchers and medical school faculty. Skeptical by training and natural inclination, they had read the speaker's brief bio in their programs and were probably not impressed. There were no college degrees, no professional credentials that they could see. What's more, she was a woman. The speaker's message was more or less discounted before she said a word. At least the audience could look forward to the next speaker, a bona fide medical researcher from Yale University.

So why were these people here instead of sight-seeing? Curiosity as much as anything, perhaps. But most of all, the frail hope of learning something new about a condition they saw discouragingly often in their practices and were helpless to treat successfully: chronic inebriety—drunkenness, in other words. They hoped the program committee for the conference had good reasons for featuring this particular speaker.

The chairman concluded his remarks: "And now it gives me the greatest of pleasures to present Mrs. Marty Mann." Onto the stage strode a tall (five-foot, eight-inch), handsome, elegant, self-assured woman, her carriage erect and graceful. As one reporter said, "Any woman would have known that her gown of soft gray wool combined with knit came straight from an exclusive designer."[1] Wearing a dramatic hat in the fashion of the day, her short blondish brown hair in a stylish cut, blue-green eyes snapping, Marty stepped to the microphone. She paused and looked out over the assemblage. A smile on her expressive face lit up the whole room. And something happened—an electricity, an indefinable connection with an audience that people call charisma—the gift that blesses every great speaker, actor, politician, or preacher. Before she said a word, most of the audience was hers.

"My name is Marty Mann, and I am an alcoholic."

The shock value of those words in the 1940s is indescribable, especially when they came from such an improbable source as this beautifully groomed, poised *woman*. Marty would go on to tell her personal story of what it was like as the disease of alcoholism took hold, what happened to propel her into recovery, and what her life had been like since. In her talk, she would explicitly, as well as by example, teach her audience about the early and middle signs of alcoholism. (They already knew the late-stage signs.) Among these earlier signs would be a family history of alcoholism, a high tolerance for alcohol, minimal negative consequences of drinking, often a slow progression of the disease, and an increasing loss of control over drinking. She would warn her audience of the dangers and consequences of denial, including their own as medical professionals. She would lay out a map of how to address the central issue of stigma. Speaking entirely without notes, pounding the podium for emphasis, she would enlist the minds and hearts of her audience with a passionate yet pragmatic approach to the *disease* of alcoholism (an as-yet uncommon and unaccepted medical concept). The audience sat transfixed.

At the conclusion of her dramatic hour-long presentation, delivered with humor, flawless timing and pacing, an educated yet straightforward vocabulary, and knowledge of their profession, the audience knew they had met a force of nature. They would return to their work energized with new information, inspired with new hope for their patients.

After such a session, Marty typically stayed up until after midnight, meeting with all comers. They were as charmed by her personal warmth as they had been by her address. More often than not, individuals felt they had made a lifelong friend even though they encountered her only that once.

Marty Mann met hundreds of such groups. She would spellbind audiences night after night, day after day, for months at a time, perhaps a gathering of lay and professional community leaders concerned to do something about the use of alcohol that was affecting their children and their families, perhaps a regional conference of Alcoholics Anonymous (AA).

People rarely forgot hearing Marty Mann speak. Decades later they could describe the occasion in detail. She permanently changed the lives of many. Inspired by Marty's example, large numbers flocked to recovery. Others devoted themselves to educating their communities about alcoholism. It is no exaggeration to credit Marty with being the leader in significantly reducing the public stigma about alcoholism and the alcoholic, thereby turning this country around in its attitude regarding chronic inebriety.

Where did this remarkable woman come from? What molded her early life and prepared her for such a mission? How did she become an alcoholic and how did she recover? And what happened after she recovered? The story is both simple and complex, as was the woman herself.

Introduction

THE NAME MARTY MANN IS scarcely a household word. Today, most people would say, "Who's he?" Yet among historians of public health care and many others, *she* was America's most effective public health care reformer of the twentieth century, the peer of such luminaries as Margaret Sanger, Jane Addams, and Dorothea Dix.[1] Important as these great reformers were, Marty successfully tackled the most serious endemic public health issue of all, alcoholism.

Most Americans are unaware that alcoholism is the country's major overall health problem, a primary social and economic drain that has no equal, as Ruth Fox described in the essay that opens this book.[2] If one looks at mortality alone, the death rates for cancer and cardiovascular disease exceed that from alcoholism, but numbers of knowledgeable researchers and clinicians in the field of alcoholism believe that alcoholism would really be classified as the number one killer if it were accurately identified as the underlying contributor to those diseases in many cases. (Among the addictive drugs, of which alcohol is one, nicotine presently has the highest known death rate, with alcoholism second, and all the street drugs combined a distant third.)

Alcoholism is considered a primary public health problem not only because of its prevalence over centuries, but also because of its terrible drain on many intersecting systems—the medical system, the economy, the judicial system, the workplace, the school system, social agencies, and the government, to say nothing of the families with an alcoholic member. No other disease, no other drug, has such broad negative societal impact. Then there are the sheer numbers of alcoholics themselves—a steady 7 to 8 percent of the population, or seventeen to twenty million Americans (in year 2000).

Marty's "personal courage in bringing alcoholism out of the shadows and into the mainstream of American life ignited a social revolution that is one of the most remarkable stories of the 20th century."[3] She pointed the way to resolving the tragedy that saps our strength as a nation and in the process laid the groundwork for important advances in community education, in prevention and treatment, in research, and in legislation. Before her death in 1980, she was renowned throughout the United States and abroad as a compelling and outspoken advocate on behalf of alcoholics and their hopeful options for recovery. Her name and activities were regularly in the media for thirty-five years. She received many professional honors. In addition, she was beloved throughout Alcoholics Anonymous as the first woman to come to AA and stay.

Many people and institutions before and after Marty have had a part in advancing knowledge about alcoholism and a humane response to it. Effective as many of the earlier programs were, they were local efforts and limited in time and scope to relatively few alcoholics. The general public, including most alcoholics, remained unaware of the massive national, even global, extent of alcoholism, what it was, and what could be done about it. The concepts of alcoholism as a disease and the alcoholic as a sick person worthy of help were largely foreign. The very word *alcoholic* was generally unknown except as a little-understood technical term among researchers, clinicians, and scattered providers of treatment services.

Most Americans today have never lived in the dark ages before the terms *alcoholic* and *alcoholism* were widely known, when there seemed no relief from a then-nameless killer. *Inebriate* (*ineb* for short) or *people like you* were the polite names. More common were *drunk, bum, stiff, losers.* All of the terms implied lack of moral character and willpower.

Marty's eminence in the history of the alcoholism movement rests on her initiating and successfully conducting a comprehensive national grassroots campaign of education to reduce the stigma surrounding alcoholism by countering fear, ignorance, and myth with facts. Her efforts vastly enhanced the possibilities for intervention and treatment that were already under way in a few locations.

With single-minded zeal, Marty set herself the tremendous task of

shifting public opinion regarding alcoholism to one of informed understanding that would enable alcoholics and their families to seek help and
treatment. Nobody had more to do with that enlightenment than Marty
Mann. It is an enormously significant development, particularly when judged
against America's temperance and Prohibition history.

The fact that alcoholism is now legitimized and accepted as a treatable
disease is due largely to Marty's unrelenting efforts to bring the information to everyone she could. Marty didn't invent the terms *alcoholic* and
alcoholism, nor did she conduct the research that supported scientific understanding and treatment. But she was a brilliant educator, a visionary organizer, and an effective catalyst who grasped that public understanding and
acceptance were essential prerequisites to addressing what to do about the
ancient scourge of alcoholism. During her lifetime, she aimed to educate an
entire country—and a good piece of the rest of the world—thereby making
possible recovery for millions of alcoholics and relief for their families, employers, and communities.

Marty's vehicle for this monumental accomplishment was the National
Council on Alcoholism (NCA), which she founded, directed, and repre-
sented for thirty-five years until her death in 1980. (NCA is now called the
National Council on Alcoholism and Drug Dependence—NCADD.)

Ironically, Marty's name is scarcely known in AA today among second-
and third-generation alcoholics. Even within her own lifetime thirty years
after she became sober, her name caused occasional confusion. Marty reported a time when she was asked to speak at the twenty-ninth anniversary
of the AA Northeast Group in Cleveland, Ohio. One local AA member objected, saying he'd "heard him many times before and he never had anything to say." The AA man obviously had Marty confused with someone
else, for if there was one thing predictable about Marty, it was her ability to
captivate an audience with both the content and the delivery of her
speeches.

Sometimes Marty is remembered as the author of *Marty Mann's New
Primer on Alcoholism.* When the first edition of this book appeared in
1950 (under the title *Primer on Alcoholism*), it was the first of its kind and
has had an enduring impact. The information remains fresh, relevant, and
accurate. It is still a classic reference.

Few AA members these days are aware that Marty's story appears in

Alcoholics Anonymous, AA's Big Book showing the way to recovery. In the second, third, and fourth editions, her account is among those of the twelve earliest pioneers of AA who joined the cofounders, Bill W. and Dr. Bob. (Her story begins on page 222 of the third edition of the Big Book.) These Big Book stories of recovered alcoholics are never signed, but most AAs back then knew by word of mouth who wrote those first stories. Moreover, Marty's national prominence as founder and director of NCA and the accompanying publicity wherever she went on her extensive travels crisscrossing the country (and many parts of the world) ensured her familiarity within AA.

So why isn't the name Marty Mann better known, either by the general public or within AA?

One reason is that Marty accomplished what she set out to do—to create an organization that would continue her mission of educating the world, but especially the United States, about alcoholism and alcoholics. While founders of important movements are remembered within their organizations, names often fade from public consciousness after they become inactive or die.

A second reason is that Marty herself, though she loved the spotlight and was a master at manipulating it, truly felt that she was only an instrument of the present in her chosen mission of serving humankind. What mattered was getting the job done. "It's amazing," she once said, "what you can accomplish if you don't care who gets the credit." Her attitude was that posterity would take care of itself. Susan B. Anthony II, grandniece of the great suffragist, said of Marty, "Self as subject bored her."[4] Though Marty may have wanted her biography written after her death, she refused to write her own autobiography or systematically to accumulate archives except as they related to her work. Even these archives are incomplete and must be supplemented from other sources. In addition, after her death many archival materials simply disappeared into untraceable private holdings. We hope this book may stimulate the recovery of some of these resources to NCADD.

Another reason probably has to do with the consequences of anonymity. Personal anonymity at the level of "press, radio, and films" is the cornerstone principle of Alcoholics Anonymous. Marty was anything but anonymous within AA during her lifetime, but except for the cofounders of AA, Bill Wilson and Dr. Bob Smith, even prominent deceased AA members generally drop off the screen.

Many have speculated that Marty's gender may have something to do with the neglect of her outstanding contributions to public understanding of alcoholism as a disease. She was a high-powered woman making waves in a male-dominated society. AA mirrored that society in its leadership. Its two founders were men, and for many years after AA's birth in 1935, it remained a largely male bastion. Bill W. and Dr. Bob supported and encouraged Marty, as did most of the men, but during her lifetime, some in and out of AA feared and resented her power and popularity.

Finally, as more and more women gradually entered AA and stayed sober—a goal Marty fervently worked for all her life—and as the membership overall expanded, her uniqueness in AA faded, and with it much of the controversy she provoked in her earlier years of sobriety.

Although a majority of Americans have come to accept alcoholism as an illness, political attitudes toward treatment of alcoholism and drug addiction have regressed in recent years from a focus on intervention and treatment to an emphasis on punishment.[5] As has happened in the past, a public health issue has been criminalized. Public funding for prevention and treatment has been neglected in favor of punishment alone, by far the least effective and most expensive of any approach.[6] The story of Marty Mann's life and accomplishments can help clarify public understanding and action, and renew the focus on her basic message:

> Alcoholism is a disease and the alcoholic is a sick person.
> The alcoholic can be helped and is worth helping.
> This is a public health problem and therefore a public responsibility.

Marty's story in this book is organized more or less chronologically along the lines of "what it was like before recovery, what happened, and what it was like after recovery," the same way talks in AA meetings are structured. Sometimes, however, chronology is temporarily displaced to emphasize a particular topic. The book is a true story, in which we have attempted to be honest, balanced, and complete to the best of our ability. Nevertheless, some holes remain in the story that future chroniclers may be able to resolve.

In general, we refer to Alcoholics Anonymous only by its well-known abbreviation—AA. Except for occasional popular idioms, unattributed quotes are Marty's and are taken from one or more of fifty-one audiotapes we collected or from articles and books she wrote. Second-person quotes of Marty are duly cited.

The tapes are listed in the back matter. It should be noted that while our tapes span Marty's sober career right up to immediately before her death, they are but a representative sample of the hundreds if not thousands of tapes made of Marty. Unfortunately, most of these tapes vanished from public archives.

To protect the anonymity of still-living AA members, we have used only first name and last initial if their membership in AA is mentioned. Deceased AA members are identified by full name.

We have selected the spelling *sanitarium* for institutions treating chronic disease such as tuberculosis, except when the actual name of the institution is spelled differently. Finally, we have adopted Marty's educational style of interweaving explicit facts about alcoholism with the material implicit in her life experiences. For example, she usually specified the early signs of alcoholism after describing her own experience.

A thorough history of NCADD and the alcoholism movement has not been our goal. However, the latter half of Marty's life is so entwined with NCA and the alcoholism movement that our intent has been to highlight certain developments in that organization as they affected and were affected by Marty.

We approached the telling of Marty's story with humility and awe that increased as we uncovered her life. Yet her magnificent potential might never have been released had she not been literally knocked to her knees by a Power greater than herself and forced at the age of thirty-five to make a 180-degree turn in her life. We believe you, too, will be inspired and motivated by her transforming story.

I

$\mathcal{R}$oots

1904–10

FEW PEOPLE IN EITHER AA OR NCA have known anything about the family into which Marty was born, even when her parents and sisters lived near her in New York City and she saw them often. Marty's reticence was due partly to her upbringing, partly to the very private side of her outgoing nature, partly to AA customs of the time. She seldom mentioned her parents and grandparents, her aunt and uncle, her three siblings, her nephews, or anyone else in the family in her speeches and talks or in conversation with nonintimate friends, so people had no way of appreciating the depth and constancy of her attachment to them—and their mutual influence on one another. Yet all her life she treasured and nurtured these family relationships.

Nor were the family relationships one-sided. Marty's immediate family not only blessed her with excellent genes, they surrounded her with bountiful love and appreciation despite all the turmoil she eventually put them through.

Marty's crusading spirit was a direct heritage of her American ancestors—Christy on her mother's side, Mann on her father's. Solid pioneer stock distinguished her legacy.

The ancestral Manns lived for generations in Braintree, Vermont. They descended from Richard Man, whose name appears in the colonial records as "one of the thirty-two persons who took the 'oath of fidelity' at Scituate, Mass., in 1644, and as one of twenty-six persons who received . . . the Conihasset grant of land in 1646."[1]

Both her mother's and father's sides included successful merchants. Among the Mann forebears were also educators and doctors. Most illustrious of these Mann ancestors may have been Horace Mann, America's greatest public-school reformer and educator. Horace was a distant relation at best, but he and Marty were directly connected through their passion for education. Living a hundred years before Marty, Horace Mann was responsible for almost single-handedly convincing America to adopt and fund a progressive public education system open to everyone—a solidly democratic educational system unique in the world at that time, and one that in retrospect prepared American citizens for the remarkable events, opportunities, and advances of the twentieth century.

Marty would be the first female Christy or Mann descendant to achieve national public acclaim. Her accomplishments unquestionably outshine all her forebears with the possible exception of Horace Mann, whom she may be said to equal.

Like Horace, Marty had a single-track mind when it came to education, in her case the challenge of educating everyone about the disease of alcoholism and what to do about it. Both of them had a national impact that has endured. And as with Horace, Marty's effectiveness derived not only from expressive and organizational genius, but also from a passionate concern for the welfare of others. The motivating principle of Horace Mann's life, expressed in his last commencement address as president of Antioch College (Yellow Springs, Ohio), also applied to Marty after she got sober: "Be ashamed to die until you have won some victory for humanity."[2]

Marty grew up hearing family stories about her ancestors. Her great-grandfather Elisha Mann was a Vermont physician who died when his children were young, leaving his widow without support. Believing that the West possessed opportunities not found in New England for her two sons, she moved with them to Fond du Lac, Wisconsin. One of those sons, Horace Edwin Mann, Marty's grandfather, became a doctor and surgeon himself, eventually settling in Marinette, Wisconsin. Marinette, on Green Bay, was lumberjack country. This is where Marty's father, William Henry Mann, known as Will, grew up.

Grandfather Mann was considered a self-made man of the Northwest. In a history of northern Wisconsin, he was noted as having acquired his medical practice and prosperity "unaided, by sheer manhood and manly effort."[3] This spirit of triumphant individualism, typical of the frontier, was an integral part of Marty's family's philosophy.

Before Marty's grandfather went into medicine, he worked briefly in the woods, ran the post office, then a hotel. He bought and later sold a drugstore. He owned and operated a meat market (excellent basic training in what became his medical specialty, surgery). After studying at Rush Medical College in Chicago and Long Island Hospital Medical College, he opened his practice in Marinette and married Marty's grandmother, Flora Ann Tracy. A few years later, Dr. Mann and two partners developed the Menominee River Hospital. His mother-in-law had operated the building as a boardinghouse and stayed on as matron.

Dr. Mann initiated the first industrial medical care in Marinette. At his hospital, patients were covered by both physician and hospital insurance. In the late 1800s, several Marinette doctors signed an agreement with the Peshtigo Company to provide its workers with medical care. To finance physician coverage, $1.25 ($30 in year 2000 dollars) was taken out of every family man's monthly paycheck, 75 cents for a single person ($18 in year 2000 dollars). Patients could choose any physician in the group to provide treatment. Dr. Mann's philosophy was, "If you're going to care for people, you have to care."[4] This attitude impressed the young Marty so deeply that decades later it resurfaced almost verbatim in her consciousness as a statement of her own philosophy.

The Mann children learned that because of Grandfather Mann, hospital care in Marinette was covered by the novel sale of a hospital ticket costing $10 ($240 in year 2000 dollars), which was sold in the lumber camps by a crew of agents. It entitled the purchaser, when injured or ill, to all the inpatient services needed plus an additional $1 ($24 in year 2000 dollars) per week during his stay. Thus, a discharged patient had a little stake to get him home or seek work after hospitalization.

> At first, only male patients were admitted, midwives attending expectant mothers at home. Since only the worst [maternity] cases went to the hospitals, many Marinette residents [women] were reluctant to seek treatment there, afraid they might not recover.
>
> Many victims of woods accidents arrived at the hospital by handcar on the rails across the street. One lumberjack with a broken thigh was brought in strapped to a tree, which proved an effective temporary splint.[5]

Another famous family legend concerned Marty's father, Will. When he was a boy, he accidentally chopped off his thumb while splitting wood in the backyard. The maid saw what had happened, pulled a rubber glove on him, and yelled for Dr. Mann. Fortunately, it was customary in those days for doctors to maintain offices in their homes. Dr. Mann sewed the thumb back on. Marty's father had a big scar ever after, but he could use his thumb.

Dr. Mann was known as a highly skilled surgeon until he himself had an ill-fated mishap. During a surgery he inadvertently cut through his glove, and the wound became infected. When it healed, Dr. Mann was left with a permanent tremor that ended his surgical career. However, he continued in general practice as a popular physician.

Dr. Mann's various businesses prospered, as did his large and successful medical practice. Will and his brother, Fred Eugene Mann (Marty's Uncle Fred), were raised in more than comfortable circumstances. Their father was a civic and political leader in his own community as well as the state of Wisconsin.

Dr. Mann's library was "one of the largest and best selected"[6] in the area. Always an advocate of education, he even served a three-year term as county superintendent of schools. Dr. Mann's mother, who had struggled so hard to give her boys an education and a future, lived with him until her death.

Following the example of their entrepreneurial, educated doctor father, Fred and Will Mann enrolled in college. Fred received an appointment to West Point, then dropped out in his senior year. He married but had no children. Marty's father graduated from the University of Wisconsin and later served on its board of trustees. Eventually, the brothers gravitated to Chicago to seek their fortunes.

Marty was eleven years old when her Wisconsin grandfather, Dr. Mann, died, so she never really knew him or her grandmother well on that side of the family. However, proud family stories sensitized her to the prestige and power of the medical field and especially to the practical idealism of her grandfather Mann.

Marty's maternal grandparents, on the other hand, she knew very well—Margaret (Deming) and Robert Curtis Christy. Marty (Margaret) was named for this grandmother. Robert Christy was a prosperous merchant who was born in Pennsylvania and grew up in Des Moines, Iowa, settling permanently in Chicago as a young man. He became vice president and general manager of A. Bishop and Company, hatters and furriers.[7] Bishop's was known as Chicago's finest fur store. Marty's knowledge of and taste for furs began early. Grandpa Christy was also a great reader, probably inspiring and nurturing Marty's lifelong love of books through both his example and her access to his personal library.

Lillian, nicknamed Lill, was the Christys' beautiful red-haired daughter, a precious only child. One may be sure that Lill's parents scrutinized each of her suitors carefully. Will and Lill were a tall, striking, head-turning couple. Both came from educated, highly regarded families. Will's charming, go-getter personality boded well for the couple's future. A successful advertising solicitor at the time he was courting Lill, Will had a promising career. There was no question he could support Lill in the manner to which she was accustomed. Indeed, within a few years he would exceed the riches of his wealthy father-in-law.

After Marty's parents were married in November 1903, they usually lived near the Christys in Chicago, often on the same street. At this particular time the two families resided on Magnolia Avenue in Sheridan Park, a newly developing upscale residential area of Chicago's North Shore.

Marty was born in her grandparent Christys' home on October 15, 1904, eleven months after her parents' wedding. Lill, attended by a nurse midwife and physician, was twenty-five; Will was twenty-eight. It was a pleasant fall Saturday, the temperature in the mild fifties. No trumpets blared, no earth shook, to announce the arrival of an infant whose life would become a blazing fire nearly extinguished by personal tragedy and degradation, and then would rise as a phoenix from the ashes to triumph amid the roaring flames of a passionate mission that powered a historic, unparalleled sea change in American society.

Marty was the first of four children born to Lill and Will Mann who grew to adulthood. A fifth child, a girl, born in 1906, died at thirty-six hours from intestinal hemorrhage. This infant, named Christy for Lill's family name, came between Marty and her six years' younger sister who was named Lillian Christy Mann—but was always known as Christy. This second Christy was usually called Chris. The last two children were twins, a boy and a girl, born fourteen years after Marty.

A nurse who specialized in infant care was engaged for Marty. Will called the nurse a policewoman, and she left within weeks. Thereafter, the first of many nannies to come was engaged. Each of the Mann children had a nanny through at least preschool. Marty's parents followed the upper-class British tradition of leaving most of the hands-on care of their children to the nannies.[8] When the Mann children were young, they usually saw their parents only at cocktail time for an hour or so every day.

At nine months of age, Marty was baptized in Sheridan Park's local Episcopal church, St. Simon's.[9] Before Marty started school, the Christys and the Manns moved to an even more fashionable neighborhood, Kenmore Park in north Chicago near Lake Michigan. The great mansions of Chicago's wealthiest were only a couple of blocks away on Lake Shore Drive. For some reason, Will Mann always rented, never bought. The Manns lived in several different homes on Kenmore Avenue, moving as their family grew.

For years, the Christy grandparents had a big house on Kenmore Avenue. The grandchildren were in and out all the time. After Grandpa Christy died in 1919, Grandma Christy continued to live in luxury in the same house for ten more years. Then she sold the property in the late 1920s and moved into Chicago's grand Edgewater Beach Hotel for the remainder of her life.

Chicago!

1910—18

MARTY WAS AS MUCH A PRODUCT of her social, cultural, and political environment as she was of her genes and her family upbringing. She had access to the multifaceted riches of Chicago's robust civilized society.

The pioneer city into which Marty was born was what the poet Carl Sandburg would describe twelve years later.

> Hog Butcher for the World,
> Tool Maker, Stacker of Wheat,
> Player with Railroads and the Nation's Freight Handler;
> Stormy, husky, brawling,
> City of the Big Shoulders.[1]

Following the Great Fire, which leveled huge sections of the city in 1873, Chicago was rebuilding with a vengeance. A city of nearly two million ambitious, hardworking European immigrants, American migrants, and numerous self-made millionaires, it pulsed with an energy and a rhythm that found expression in the thrusting skyscrapers and other architecture for which Chicago is famous. Chicago's motto, "I will," conformed perfectly to Marty's innate temperament.

Chicago had for decades been the premier transportation hub of the Northwest, its rail yards extending for miles. The stockyards were equally mammoth, the city's beefsteaks renowned. Only Detroit exceeded Chicago's love affair with the automobile. By 1925, six lanes of cars and one of double-decker buses created curb-to-curb traffic jams on Michigan Avenue, Chicago's "Main Street."

Marketing and industry weren't all that Chicago had to offer, however. The city was also becoming a dynamic cultural center. The University of Chicago, established in 1892, was well on the way to its position as one of the country's renowned centers of learning. The World's Columbian Exposition of 1893 provided the nucleus of Chicago's great parks and museums gracing the lakefront. Opera and symphony, jazz, swing, blues, and popular music all flourished. Marty's love of music, and especially jazz, was probably born here.

Chicago led the country in the creative use of radio, beginning in the 1920s. Soap operas and the concept of original radio scripts originated in Chicago. Chicago radio invented the talk show.

Advertising was a major industry. The city was crazy about movies, which could be viewed in any number of lavish movie houses.

Bohemianism, originally a European socio-politico-literary-artistic rebellion against Victorian conventions, found sturdy American roots in Chicago. Bohemian clubs mushroomed in Chicago's gusty climate. They hosted exciting poetry nights, drama nights, and rambunctious discussion and debate nights—well oiled by liquor, of course.

Many famous American writers besides Carl Sandburg lived and worked in Chicago when Marty was growing up—Theodore Dreiser, Ernest Hemingway, Upton Sinclair, George Ade, Ben Hecht, Richard Wright, Vachel Lindsay, Sherwood Anderson, Ring Lardner, James T. Farrell. Numerous writers and artists resided in studios in a small area around Chicago's old Water Tower on North Michigan Avenue known as Towertown. Chicago claimed that until about 1924, Towertown was "the geographical center of what was perhaps the most vital literary and artistic upsurge in the history of the country."[2] Marty, the nascent writer, could not help but be influenced by this yeasty ferment.

Chicago was a home not only of American literary greats but of experimental theater and avant-garde expressionism of all kinds. The most brilliant and influential of America's avant-garde magazines, the *Little Review,* was spawned in Chicago by the "Queen of the Chicago Boheme," Margaret Anderson. Eventually, the *Little Review* moved to New York. "When it finally ceased publication in 1929, it had published, long before their talent was acknowledged, most of the important new writers—American, English, and French—of its era."[3]

The *Chicago Tribune* was among the most powerful and influential newspapers in the country. Headed by the Medill-Patterson-McCormick families, it was staunchly Republican, conservative, and isolationist. One of Marty's dearest friends as an adult, Felicia Gizycka, one who followed her into recovery from alcoholism, was closely related to this great newspaper dynasty. Felicia was the only child of Eleanor "Cissy" Patterson, the flamboyant editor of the Washington, D.C., *Times.* Cissy and Robert McCormick of the *Chicago Tribune* were cousins.[4]

If commerce was the lifeblood of Chicago and culture its heart, politics was its muscle. Hard-hitting and combative, Chicago politics has always been a favorite spectator sport. Corruption and graft were accepted as more or less standard. With the arrival of Prohibition in the 1920s, however, the big money to be made in bootlegging and illegal liquor traffic attracted major gangsters and escalating crime. Chicago developed a reputation as home to Al Capone and the mob. A natural politician and networker like her father, Marty absorbed these lessons in civic relations.

Notorious as Chicago was for its brand of politics, crime, and corruption, the other side of the coin was represented by Jane Addams and Hull House, the neighborhood settlement house she founded. In 1931, her pioneer work in social reform was honored with the Nobel Peace Prize. Addams's energy, diplomacy, warmth, and bravery pushed Illinois to pass far-reaching laws benefiting children and labor and improving the schools and juvenile courts. She was deeply involved in women's rights, politics, and pacifism. She wrote hundreds of articles and books and lectured around the country. Decades later, Addams's service and educational approaches would inspire Marty as she entered upon her own life's work.

When Marty first came onto the scene, her father was at the beginning of his rapid rise in the merchandising world, being employed with the Frank A. Munsey Company as an advertising solicitor—and soon to become its general advertising manager. By the time Marty was seven, Will had moved to Marshall Field and Company, one of the nation's leading department stores, as vice president and general manager of its huge wholesale production and operations. Marshall Field's advertising won prizes and won business with fastidious ad art and copy. Marty's talent for advertising and public relations was in her genes, to say nothing of her advantages in learning the profession at her father's knee.

Department stores today are pale imitations of those early twentieth-century pacesetting emporia. Marshall Field, for example, had the first dome ever built of Tiffany iridescent glass. At the time, the dome was also the largest glass mosaic one in the world. Entire houses were set up in the furniture department, complete with lawns, trees, and formal gardens. The store's display of seventeenth- and eighteenth-century art objects, tapestries, and furniture was considered so fine that Chicago's Art Institute bought several of the interiors intact.

This incredible store offered almost every product and commodity imaginable, helping to make Chicago the great central market of the United States. Chicago residents demanded the latest styles, the latest fashions, the latest in everything. Hundreds of thousands of customers patronized the main Chicago department stores every day. They were cosseted with such added attractions as an aquarium, children's playrooms, tennis courts, restaurants, and cafés covering entire floors.

Marshall Field was good to its employees as well as its customers. The employees' library offered a splendid collection of books and magazines with a circulation of eight thousand a month. A junior academy for employees under sixteen years of age had a staff of six experienced teachers. The instruction offered a general and a commercial course.

The medical bureau for employees employed a staff of four physicians and four nurses. In 1922, the bureau cared for more than twenty thousand medical cases, plus almost a thousand home visits by nurses. Wards were maintained at local hospitals. In addition, the company had a part ownership in a sanitarium at Valmora, New Mexico, not too far from a ranch the Manns owned. Marty's father possibly had something to do with the establishment of this sanitarium, having grown up with his doctor father's enlightened approach to medicine.

The wholesale division that Will Mann ran was a mammoth distribution center occupying an entire city block. This division supplied not only its own huge retail store but thousands of other retail outlets unrelated to Marshall Field across the country. An enormous cadre of salesmen constantly fanned out to service these smaller firms. The Chicago wholesale center was also the focal point of the firm's foreign buying offices.

Part of Will Mann's responsibility was to oversee the fourteen major textile mills in Virginia and North Carolina that produced linens and other goods for Marshall Field. Factories in and near Chicago and elsewhere manufactured innumerable kinds of products for Marshall Field—from mattresses to candlesticks to shoes and phonographs.

The Mann family had unlimited access to the riches to be found at Marshall Field. Like a sponge, Marty absorbed the world of merchandising. She became schooled in the skills and techniques of advertising. Her elegant sense of clothing style had free rein to develop. From early childhood, she learned firsthand about quality. She knew the difference between a designer dress and one off the rack, between real Tiffany and a copy.

Funds for the very best private education were ample. Marty's first school was the Chicago Latin School for Girls, located about six miles from the Manns' Kenmore Avenue home. This was an outstanding private day school with high standards of scholarship for North Side girls. Marty's two younger sisters also attended the Latin School for Girls for several years.

The girls' school had its counterpart in the Chicago Latin School for Boys, which was the original of the two schools. Marty's younger brother attended here. Both schools emphasized a strong classical education. One catalog of the period assured parents: "Increased watchfulness will be exerted to insure the use of good English, to drill pupils in correct pronunciation, and to help them to articulate clearly, with refined and agreeable intonation."[5] Marty's speaking skills were honed early and well.

Eventually the two schools merged, remaining in the same North Side location. Now called the Chicago Latin School, it continues a fine academic reputation.

Marty described herself as an extremely bright, quick, and idealistic student, a bookworm who liked to read and study. She was a gregarious, precocious child, restless and energetic all her life, and with a keen, mischievous wit. Her competitive spirit drove her to excel. In England years later she was once told, "The trouble with you, Marty, is you've always got to be top shot."

From the age of ten Marty wanted to be a writer. At various times she wrote poetry. At least once she set out to pen the great American novel while living abroad as an expatriate. Her major talent, however, appeared to lie in lucid, pungent nonfiction prose. During her lifetime, she wrote voluminously—three books, innumerable articles, radio scripts, news re-leases, and various educational, public relations, and advertising materials. She was also a fierce editor with little tolerance for sloppy writing. Through-out her life, Marty was attracted to writers and artists of all kinds, many of them luminaries, and they to her.

Chicago offered numerous opportunities for extracurricular learning. Marty and Chris were good tennis players. They took up golf. They swam. They rode horses. Their parents were excellent bridge players, and all the children learned from them. Marty and her siblings were introduced at an early age to the symphony and the theater. All her life, she regularly attended both, finding many close friends among music and theater professionals.

When Marty was a child, her parents saw to it that she and her brother and sisters went to Sunday school at the family's church, Church of the Atonement. The handsome old Episcopal sanctuary was in the same upper-class neighborhood as the Mann residence. The children could easily walk the short distance from home. Marty's father was a church warden. Her mother's parents, Robert and Margaret Christy, were members. The memo-rial services for these grandparents were held at Church of the Atonement. Marty was confirmed at Church of the Atonement at the usual age of thir-teen, and her younger sisters and brother were baptized there as infants.

The Manns' choice of an Episcopal church was not surprising since both Will and Lill had grown up in Episcopal churches. However, the con-gregation of Church of the Atonement also included socially and financially prominent Chicagoans. The business contacts alone would have attracted Will and his father-in-law, the furrier. One of Mr. Mann's personal as well as business friends was James Simpson, later a president of Marshall Field—and thus Will Mann's boss. Jim Simpson and his wife, Jessie, were godparents to the Mann twins, Betty and Bill.

Another attraction of Church of the Atonement for upwardly mobile parents was the surety that their children would be introduced to the best circles in society. Some of Marty's extensive social connections probably began at Chicago Latin School for Girls and at Church of the Atonement.

Marty turned against all religion when she was seventeen. Sounding like a young Marxist, she labeled religion an illusion and an "opiate of the masses." Her attitude was that anyone with a brain would know better than to believe in God. She "wanted to be an atheist because it was the intellectual thing to do." In later years, however, Marty confessed, "I realize now that I had a spiritual nature as a child and I had deliberately tossed religion out of my life." As an adult she resumed a loose affiliation with the Episcopal Church, but also explored a number of other spiritual paths. One of her memorial services, however, was held at St. Bartholomew's Church (Episcopal) in New York City.

In addition to their favorable educations, the Mann children traveled widely in the United States and abroad. A favorite American vacation spot for a few years was New Mexico. Will Mann had bought a half-interest in a several-hundred-acre ranch on the Pecos River between Santa Fe and the little town of Las Vegas to the east (in New Mexico, not Nevada). Most of the property was open, rolling grassland located on both sides of the river. Hills and mountains lay to the west. One nearby mountain was dedicated to the Penitentes, Catholics who believed in mortification of the flesh as atonement for sins. Penitentes whipped and beat themselves as they toiled up the mountain on their knees, carrying a heavy cross. The Manns found this an alien, repugnant practice, antithetical to their standards of religious propriety.

The ranch was approached from the main road, actually a narrow, unpaved access. Outbuildings, stables, corrals, and staff quarters sprawled on one side of the river near the entrance from the road. To reach the large, concealed ranch house, people rode over a bridge across the river and up a long drive. The house had a big central *sala* with a tremendous fireplace at one end. This spacious area was surrounded by bedrooms and baths.

Best of all, there were horses and all kinds of outdoor activities to delight children. The twins each had a horse. All the children loved to ride. Will Mann brought the first rodeo to Chicago. The kids also learned about guns. They used to shoot prairie dogs for practice. The ubiquitous prairie dogs were a dangerous nuisance because of the holes they dug. "Step in one and break a leg," recalled Marty's brother, Bill.

Usually the family traveled by train between Chicago and New Mexico. One year, though, the chauffeur drove the car out West. It was nearly a disaster because the car kept breaking down. In the 1920s, even the highways were still primitive dirt or gravel and the tires on cars not at all durable. The trip took much longer than the train. It was at the ranch that Marty, like children whose parents worked on ranches, learned to drive before she was twelve or thirteen.

As Marty often said, she never lacked for any material thing. Yet accompanying this exceptional background was a paradox. Marty bore two significant attributes that would eventually overcome a self-centered insecurity that sought only the fulfillment of her own will—a strong innate sense of justice and a deep sympathy for the underdog.

Through the Wringer

1918—21

BY 1918, THE AGONIES OF WORLD WAR I were finally drawing to a close. A vast sense of relief settled over America. The stock market began its astronomical climb to new heights. Hope for fresh beginnings reawakened throughout the land.

In Chicago, the Mann household bustled with the exciting birth of twins. Additional nannies were engaged. The expanded family moved into a larger residence, still on exclusive Kenmore Avenue. Lill Mann's doting, wealthy parents lived a few blocks to the north, also on Kenmore Avenue.

The baby boy was named William "Bill" Henry for his proud father. His twin sister was christened Mary Elizabeth, after a great-aunt. But at an early age, little Mary Elizabeth insisted on being called Betty. Sweet-natured Chris, the middle sister, was eight, the pet of the family.

Marty was fourteen years old, a tall, lively, headstrong teenager. She'd come out of the womb with what her brother described as a whim of iron. Marty later agreed: "Anyone who knew me could testify that I had been afflicted with a little too much of that commodity known as willpower, in my case called willful." Her gentle, loving mother often didn't know what to do with her.

Marty was clearly the leader of the four children by virtue of her birth rank and her natural gifts. Through all the ups and downs of her life, she continued to dominate the sibling relationships. When younger, she could be insufferably bossy. However, the other three children were also strong-minded individuals. Marty and Betty, the youngest girl, often didn't get along. Nevertheless, the family and sibling bonds were strong despite the differences in the ages of the children. They might fight and argue among themselves, but let anyone outside the family criticize or attack one of them, and they closed ranks immediately. When Bill became an adult, the fourteen-year age difference with Marty wasn't as important, and they grew close despite living a thousand miles apart. Everybody loved Chris, the middle child. She and Marty had a special relationship. Their adult lives became significantly entwined.

Marty's father was a powerful influence on her character and outlook. Their temperaments were very similar. Will Mann had great charm coupled with a compelling managerial personality. He was domineering, opinionated, and certain of what he wanted. And Marty tested the limits. She and her father were frequently at loggerheads even before she grew into adolescence. Will was a Republican, so Marty naturally became a Democrat. (As an adult, she proclaimed herself an Independent.) Marty and her father clashed because they were so much alike, but deep down they loved each other.

Will was entering the peak period of his successful, affluent career with Marshall Field. Lill Mann remained a strikingly beautiful redhead, a traditional helpmate devoted to her children and their welfare. She loved to sew. A protected wife and daughter, Lill could not have imagined what disasters lay ahead and how drastically her life would change.

First, in the midst of all this good fortune, Marty's mother discovered she had breast cancer. Lill underwent a successful mastectomy. One can only imagine what that surgery must have been like in the year 1918 and so soon after giving birth to twins.

Then Marty, about to enter high school, was suddenly diagnosed with a serious case of tuberculosis (TB) of the lungs. As late as the 1920s, TB was associated with poverty, dirt, and inadequate sanitation. To contract the disease was a disgrace. Nice people didn't get TB, especially wealthy ones with routine access to the finest, most modern hygiene and medical care. How could this happen to a daughter whose family had money and social position, who traveled widely and had at their fingertips easy entrée to all kinds of knowledge?

In those days, however, vast ignorance about TB existed at every level of society. And ignorance breeds fear, which leads to terrible stigma. Stigma has always accompanied diseases not yet understood. Leprosy, cancer, mental illness, and alcoholism are historical examples.

Now that the ancient disease of TB has been brought under control, at least in the developed countries of the West, only older citizens may remember when the White Plague was pandemic—and synonymous with the Grim Reaper. In 1918, TB was America's greatest killer—a frightening scourge. Tens of thousands of Americans died every year. It was the major cause of death in Chicago. The city's public sanitarium (Municipal Tuberculosis Sanatarium) housed around four thousand patients, with many times that number still in the community. Only cases diagnosed early had a reasonable chance of cure. Advanced cases were generally hopeless. When Marty became ill, "few real cases of tuberculosis ever recovered and few of these remained well."[1] The outlook was usually hopeless, and "discouraging to doctor and to patient."[2]

Research into TB was in its infancy. Until 1882, people thought the disease was hereditary. Then the German physician Robert Koch discovered the cause of TB when he identified the tubercle bacillus. It became clear that the disease was transmitted through direct and close contact with family members and others with histories of the disease. "This revelation was coupled with a growing belief that in many cases infection took place in early childhood, remaining latent until later in life."[3] Marty did not mention a source of her infection, nor are there extant medical records. Perhaps a specific contact was never identified.

Modern drugs to control and cure TB were not developed until the early 1930s. Before then, the only known treatment was isolation in a TB sanitarium, where the patient was usually confined to bed for months and given the best possible nourishment, rest, and symptomatic care to restore strength and energy. In essence, the body had to heal itself against overwhelming odds.

Quantities of pure, fresh air and sunshine were considered essential for the damaged lungs to recover. Therefore, TB sanitaria were often located far away from the dirt and air pollution of big industrial cities. Unspoiled sites in mountains, the desert, or at the seashore were favorite areas. Most of the sanitaria were private. Many accepted indigent as well as full- and partial-pay patients. Not until the 1940s did federal and state governments begin to recognize tuberculosis as a public health problem and therefore a public responsibility in the crucial areas of education, prevention, research, and treatment.[4]

The fear that would have gripped Marty's parents must have been terrible. Their firstborn was walking in death's shadow. Her infection was well past the early stages. No reputable specialist could promise that Marty would survive, much less recover fully. Lill and Will Mann would have been frantic with worry about the three other children in the family, too, especially the vulnerable newborn twins.

Marty probably felt too ill, feverish, and weak to worry about the future. She was an intelligent girl who ordinarily wanted answers and tended to ask why, but the doctors and adults around her were protective about not frightening her with the known statistics of TB outcomes. As a matter of fact, Marty wasn't even told that she had tuberculosis.

She later said that the reason she wasn't told what was wrong with her was because her parents believed that children couldn't be trusted to keep their mouths shut. Marty might blab to her little friends. Then the neighbors would learn about this shameful thing that had happened in the Mann family. Stigma slammed shut the doors to protect the family name and standing in the community. Marty was informed merely that she'd grown too fast. She was obviously tall for her age, so the reason for her malaise didn't strike her as odd, nor that she should be shipped off to Barlow Sanatorium[5] in Los Angeles with a registered nurse.

California was a long way off, but money was no object. Moreover, the Manns had extensive national connections and would undoubtedly have screened their choices thoroughly to procure the very best medical treatment available.

Barlow Sanatorium was founded in 1902 as a nonsectarian institution by W. Jarvis Barlow, M.D., to serve "poor consumptives" but by Marty's time had expanded its service to include full- and partial-pay patients. Barlow Sanatorium enjoyed an enviable national and international reputation for excellence in research and treatment of TB. Dr. Barlow, a courageous, practical, and optimistic man, was a famous TB specialist.

To be close to Marty, the whole Mann household moved to Pasadena, nannies and all, renting an estate. Will and Lill were probably also anxious to get the family away from Chicago, the locus of infection. If one was going to come down with TB, Marty certainly picked the right parents.

In 1918, Los Angeles was already a city of half a million. Today's great movie industry was well under way, though the talkies would not arrive for another decade. The infamous eye-watering, bronchi-stinging smog of the Los Angeles basin lay in the future. Moreover, Barlow Sanatorium, located in Chavez Ravine adjacent to Elysian Park (and later a neighbor to Dodger Stadium, too), was blessed by its location in a pocket of exceptionally clean air even for those uncontaminated days.

Barlow Sanatorium, now a Los Angeles Historic Site, was a pleasant collection of main buildings and a few bungalows on a sprawling rural campus. Most of the patients were housed in a central infirmary near a combined recreation, occupational therapy, physical therapy building. Nurses had their own on-site residence. The staff was known for its successful team approach to treatment. From the hospital's beginning, Dr. Barlow had fostered the feeling of family among the staff and patients, "totally unlike the traditional one-way patient-hospital relationship."[6]

At the same time, there were strict rules.

> Patients must not expectorate anywhere except in cups provided for that purpose. Cloths are to be used as handkerchiefs and burned morning and evening. Patients must not discuss their ailments or make unnecessary noise. Patients must not put anything hot on glass tables. Lights out at 9 P.M. Cold plunge every morning; hot baths Tuesday and Saturday. Patients are forbidden to throw refuse of any kind on the ground. When doctors think them able, every patient must do some work about the Sanatorium or go away. Patients disobeying these rules will be dismissed.[7]

Dr. Barlow constantly crusaded for earlier diagnosis and treatment. Patients stayed an average of 221 days. "He was adamant that if they left before the medical staff said they should, they couldn't come back if the disease became active again."[8] His toughness and persistence paid off for those patients who understood what he was trying to do to help them.

Marty was admitted to Barlow Sanatorium as a private patient, living in a separate bungalow with her nurse. She had a moderately advanced case of TB, with both lungs affected. Most of the other patients were older, so she was additionally isolated because of her youth and student status. Marty's personal physician was Dr. Barlow. She had no idea he was a specialist in TB. His name meant nothing to her. Nor did she then know he had himself contracted a mild case of tuberculosis early in his career and recovered. Dr. Barlow soon became her friend and substitute father, a wise counselor who gave her far more than treatment for TB. Not only did he have a warm and optimistic bedside manner, but he also understood and related to the adolescent that Marty was.

When Marty arrived, priority in admissions had been granted to TB casualties among American troops in World War I. The hospital, stretched to the limits of its sixty- to seventy-bed capacity, had a distinctly military flavor. Suddenly, the worldwide flu epidemic hit hard at Barlow Sanatorium. This virulent strain of influenza seemed to have come out of nowhere. Tens of millions perished worldwide. The United States did not escape. Luckily, only one patient at Barlow died from flu. Both the military and flu crises placed a heavy extra load on the medical staff. The advantage for Marty, however, was that the young soldiers were nearer her own age.

Shortly after Marty's admission to Barlow, her condition grew steadily worse. The TB infection was undoubtedly exacerbated at least in part by the often "long-term treatment and the resulting boredom that encouraged mischievousness among the patients."[9]

One day Barlow took Marty into his office and said, "I must break my word to your family. You have to know what's wrong with you because you must cooperate. You must do what you're told. You must eat when you don't want to eat. You must drink those eggnogs [she'd been throwing them out the window because she didn't like them]. You must stay in bed [she'd been sneaking out]."

"Well," as Marty later said, "a kid of fourteen is likely to do things like that out of ignorance, but so is an adult of forty-four, out of ignorance. So is anyone who doesn't know any better." In a speech before the National Tuberculosis Association (NTA) in 1961, she commented further:

> There is no illness on the face of this earth from which a patient can recover if that patient either doesn't want to recover or won't do anything about it themselves. Ask your medical friends. The will to live and the will to recover which, in turn produces cooperation with those who are trying to help, is the key to getting well from anything. It is not just the doctor who treats, and the Lord who saves. It is also the

patient who determines whether or not, in the long run, that patient will recover. In my case I didn't know what I was fighting. I didn't realize what I had to do—so I didn't do it. But when I was told, when I was informed, when I was given the opportunity, young as I was, to make my own decision, I made it. And I made it on the side of life. It took a long while. It took 3 years before I could even begin to rejoin life—at least the kind of life that kids of my age were leading by then. But it was done.

At that same time a little girl who lived next door to me [in Chicago], and with whom I played quite a lot, and whose family were friends of my family, also got TB. And her family was as horrified and ashamed and disgraced as mine. But instead of sending her away they kept her at home. They hid her. And she died. All my life I have felt that stigma killed Catherine. And it nearly killed me. So I have a strong feeling about the elimination of stigma on illness.[10]

Much as Marty chafed at all the restrictions during the years of recovery from TB, she acknowledged in retrospect how grateful she was that her family loved her enough to see that she stuck to the prescribed regimen even after she was discharged to home in Pasadena.

Pasadena, on the outskirts of Los Angeles, was a quiet pastoral town with the same wonderful fresh air and sunshine as Barlow's a few miles away. In the late 1800s, it acquired a reputation as a prime winter resort, especially for wealthy easterners and midwesterners seeking the land of eternal sunshine. Many of them subsequently settled in or retired to Pasadena. Grand estates were built in the beautiful countryside. The growing town became known as an art, music, cultural, and intellectual center.

Pasadena had also attracted tubercular patients because of its healthful climate, but by the late 1800s they were no longer encouraged to come to the city. Publicity was spread to the effect that "many consumptives arrive here only to die within a few weeks."[11] As a matter of fact, the "early death statistics of Pasadena reveal that from the 1890s until at least into the 1920s one-third to one-half of all deaths reported in the city were due to TB. Plainly, the invalids came in great numbers, but not all were cured."[12]

Several of Pasadena's tourists and settlers were prominent Chicagoans—another reason, perhaps, for the Manns' selecting the town and for their knowing about Barlow Sanatorium nearby in Los Angeles. Among those who had moved from Chicago by 1918 were Andrew McNally of Rand-McNally Publishing; Henry Calvin Durand, who had amassed a fortune in the wholesale grocery business; Mrs. George M. Pullman, widow of the sleeping-car magnate; William J. Wrigley, of chewing gum fame; and Amos G. Throop, a prominent Chicagoan and the founder of Pasadena's Throop Institute, which grew into the famed California Institute of Technology.

By a curious quirk of fate, Pasadena later became the home of Tom and Katherine Pike, major benefactors and advocates of NCA and the alcoholism movement. The Pasadena affiliate of NCA was established very early, in 1949.

For at least the next two years, Marty lived in southern California. The first year, she underwent the standard rigid isolation/bed rest/nourishment/ fresh air/sunshine regimen as an inpatient at Barlow. The second year she was allowed to return home (in this case Pasadena) with a trained nurse, where she continued a strict schedule, for example, eating at least a light snack every hour. However, she was allowed to get up each afternoon for a couple of hours.

During this second year of Marty's recovery, her grandpa Christy died in Chicago—one more blow for Lill, in particular. Then at some point during either the inpatient or outpatient phase of her treatment, Marty had the misfortune to lose the big toe on her left foot to amputation because of complications from the TB. But the loss didn't slow her down once the TB had gone into remission. She was able to walk and run, to participate fully in the sports she loved, and to dance for hours. However, in Marty's later years, her balance was somewhat unreliable. The big toe is an important fulcrum of balance, and with age she may have been less able to compensate for its loss.

During the third year, Marty could stay up all day except for a mandatory two- to three-hour siesta. Marty's mother moved everyone back home to Chicago at this time. The 1920 census lists the whole family as living once more on Kenmore Avenue with three servants, Anna, Jessie, and Alice. It is possible that Marty was able to resume at least limited schooling, perhaps with private tutoring. At any rate, she was able to complete the equivalent of her freshman year of high school.

Marty was fortunate. She recovered. However, she knew that for the rest of her life, her TB was simply arrested, not cured, and that she would have to continue taking certain precautions such as getting adequate rest. She would also have to remain alert for danger signs, like a recurrent low-grade fever.

Marty's bout with tuberculosis was a pivotal point in her life. Clearly, TB was her introduction to the deadly dangers of stigma. It was a lesson burned into her very being. Twenty-five years later, it would power her life's work in combating the stigma of another disease, alcoholism. TB was also her trial by fire in confronting and understanding the consequences of a chronic illness that was in remission, not cured. In time, this gut-level understanding of TB helped her to grasp and accept the similarity to alcoholism. She openly acknowledged the debt, saying that her experience with TB had prepared her well for accepting the concept of alcoholism as a chronic disease that required certain lifelong behaviors for recovery. Marty once commented, however, that the difference in recovery between the two diseases was that AA recovery can be fun along the way. Apparently her memories of recovery from TB were not the happiest.

Young though she was, Marty absorbed the message of the growing public health movement of which the National Tuberculosis Association (NTA, now the American Lung Association) was a part. The heart of the message was that public health issues—for example sanitation, pure drinking water, and smallpox and polio vaccinations—were the concern of everyone, not only the individual. Infectious disease was no respecter of boundaries. Marty would later come to understand that alcoholism, though not an infectious disease like TB, was also a public health issue requiring a community-based response.

Marty personally observed the power of voluntary community support of a healing institution by families and friends of those afflicted. For most of its existence, Barlow Sanatorium was funded entirely by private donations, some of them very large and extending over the life of the donor and beyond. The emergence of NTA as an advocacy, fund-raising, and educational organization made a profound impression on her.

Marty saw how important were the efforts of Dr. Barlow, his staff, and voluntary support in educating the community at large with the facts about TB—its causes and its treatment. To the outer world, these leaders continually emphasized early diagnosis and treatment as essential for hopeful outcomes.

She learned firsthand the value of scientifically informed research and treatment of an illness. The high medical standards at Barlow would spoil her for anything less in the approach to alcoholism.

These early years in southern California also introduced Marty to a part of the country to which she would return decades later—with knowledge of the area, contacts, and affection, to enlist help in establishing NCA affiliates.

Finally, given Marty's naturally energetic, forceful temperament, she must have been a handful to control once she began to feel even a bit better. Couple with that the stresses of the onset of adolescence. One can only contemplate the long-term emotional and social effects of illness and isolation from one's peers at such a critical period of development as adolescence. Marty often remarked how difficult it used to be for her to meet strangers or to encounter unfamiliar situations. By the age of seventeen, just as she was returning to normal life, she quickly learned that a few drinks of alcohol would settle her social anxieties.

School Days, School Days

1921–25

IN 1921, MARTY WAS ABLE TO RESUME regular schooling. Considering that she lost three years of school while ill in her teens, it may seem remarkable that she was able to make up one of those years during that time. However, Dr. LeClair Bissell, a later friend of Marty's who also survived TB as a teenager, commented that in the days before TV, there wasn't much else to do except read during the long periods of enforced bed rest. TB patients could actually get ahead in some subjects. On the other hand, Marty was now permanently separated from her normal high school age group and would remain two years behind them. Bright though she was, she would henceforth be two years older than her fellow students—a considerable source of stress to a maturing adolescent, somewhat similar to that experienced by the student who has been held back.

She returned to California, enrolling as a seventeen-year-old sophomore boarder in the four-year-old Santa Barbara Girls' School, ninety miles up the Pacific Coast from Los Angeles. Long before Ronald Reagan made Santa Barbara famous because of his ranch in the lovely hills above the city, it was renowned as a resort town, artists' mecca, and the site of a historic Spanish mission. Probably most important for a recovering TB patient in Marty's day were the mild climate and clean sea air.

The Santa Barbara Girls' School was an exclusive, academically excellent school. The small boarding department accommodated twenty-five girls age seven to nineteen, who came from the East as well as the West. The school probably made special arrangements for students who had had tuberculosis. In fact, it became a TB sanitarium later on in the 1920s.[1]

36

Following the year at Santa Barbara, Marty's remaining high school years were spent at the Montemare School in Lake Placid, New York. The Montemare School, like Santa Barbara's, was also new, having opened in 1920. And as in Santa Barbara, the air was clean and pure. Montemare was a "migratory school." Students spent spring and fall on the Adirondack campus, and the winter term in the mild climate of Miami Beach. (Miami Beach in those days was a quiet town, the beautiful beach virtually deserted except for the Montemare students.)

Each girl had an individual course of training laid out along the lines of her particular needs. The school boasted a "remarkable health record"[2]— which surely caught the eye of Marty's parents. In addition to the rigorous academic curriculum, the girls were required to choose one among the following: an occupational course, home economics, mechanics, gardening, or business. French was taught in all grades, and Marty learned to speak and read French.

One of the undoubted attractions of Montemare for the Manns was the adjacent Lake Placid Club. The club was an elite, private health resort for the wealthy. There the Manns could visit Marty and take a vacation at the same time. No members or guests were accepted against whom "there is any fisical [*sic*], moral, social or race objection, or who would be unwelcome to even a small minority [presumably of one]."[3] Only prominent citizens recognized as leaders in their communities were accepted. Membership, as in many private clubs today, depended on personal recommendation by a current member.

Montemare emphasized what now is called physical education, made available through the adjacent Lake Placid Club as well as nearby facilities in Miami when the school migrated to Florida. In addition to the many outdoor activities, the Lake Placid Club offered a variety of artistic and recreational choices. Music was provided by the Boston Symphony Ensemble or a popular dance band eight times a week. Every September the club hosted a northern New York music week and festival.

Health maintenance was a major issue. The club maintained an infirmary, operating room, and contagious house, staffed by a year-round resident physician and nurses. Presumably the operating room was for emergencies such as broken bones. Tuberculosis and all other diseases were rigidly excluded, so Marty's infection must have been considered a thing of the past.

There were "no bar, no public cigar stand, no smoking in the dining rooms, library or ladies' parlors, no smoking by women, no stock ticker, and no gambling even 'when sugar coated as a chance in aid of charity.'"[4] Perhaps Marty's mother appreciated these restrictions with reference to her husband, who was developing an increasing problem with alcohol and gambling. And perhaps Will welcomed the chance to prove he could control his addictions by shelving them for a short period, something many addicted persons can do on occasion.

Nearly forty years later, Marty would hear a voice from her Montemare past. Jim Marsh was a new master at the school when Marty was a student. In 1963 he wrote Marty after first reading a *Reader's Digest*[5] article about her, then seeing her interviewed on David Susskind's TV show *Open End*. Another coincidence immediately followed those two events. Marsh's San Francisco sister told him that her husband, Dr. Donald A. Shaskan, had appeared with Marty at a meeting of the American Group Therapy Association.

In the opening sentences of Jim Marsh's letter,[6] he said, "I have always remembered you and wondered what you were doing and what had become of your life." He continues with the following reminiscences:

> You will recall Scovill Aspinwall, the tall handsome blond boy from Washington, DC, who was very much in love with you. . . . Scovill and I at once struck up a deep friendship which continued at least for that year, after which he entered Yale and not too long afterwards went abroad to Paris for study and I understand that he died there. I last heard from his father in 1953 after I had related to him an episode in which you, Helen McIlvaine, Scovill and I figured.
>
> I refer to the Sunday Scovill and I went over to meet you and Helen at the Lake Placid Club, although we had sworn to the school authority that we were going only to have lunch with Mr. and Mrs. Baker at the Baker Cottage, which you may recall was the residence of Robert Louis Stevenson the winter he stayed at Saranac.
>
> We did have lunch with old Mr. and Mrs. Baker and then we excused ourselves and hied over to Lake Placid not realizing we were being shadowed. We had a delightful afternoon with you and Helen, or "Mac" as we called her. I am not sure your mother and father were

there at the time, but I recall meeting them then or at some other time. I recall your father as a tall handsome man. Didn't he wear tortoise shell pince-nez held with a black ribbon? And you had a younger sister, didn't you? I also recall a snapshot you sent Scovill later of you in your Marmon phaeton with the top down, taken of you in Chicago. . . . Those were wonderfully exciting days when we held life and the world in our hands, or at least we believed we did. And the future stretched ahead like an emerald city that we must enter at last.

Do you recall the lorgnette you handled so expertly as a girl of 19? You don't mind my saying, do you, that you were one of the most striking girls I have ever seen? And from your recent pictures, both live and inert, I should say you are holding your own. You obviously have inherited the great organizing ability of your father. . . .

It has been delightful remeeting you, Marty. May you always live as abundantly as you have until now.

Marty was seventeen, nearly eighteen, when she entered Montemare, usually the age of graduation from high school. This is also the age she identified as the onset of her drinking career. Alcohol was already so much a part of her background, however, that she didn't remember when she had her first drink.

Marty grew up in a drinking family. Her parents educated her about wine, beer, and spirits as they did about the other fine things of life. She recalled that as a child she would have a little glass of wine on holidays at her grandparents'. For Sunday dinners, there was a small glass of beer with the family. Marty especially loved Thanksgiving and Christmas, when a tiny glass of crème de menthe would be served with a tiny straw after dinner. The liqueur tasted to her like a chocolate mint.

Marty's father maintained an excellent cellar. Anticipating Prohibition, Will Mann laid down a very large supply for the duration. Marty had unlimited access to her father's cellar from the time she was seventeen. A selection of wines and hard liquors was always available on the sideboard and elsewhere in the house.

Will and Lill enjoyed cocktails every evening. Marty's grandparents apparently drank moderately, and so did her mother. Lill had two cocktails each night her whole adult life. Marty saw her mother "tight" just once.

Lill was reading the newspaper upside down. Will, however, became both an alcoholic and a compulsive gambler, conditions which would impact the family severely not long after Marty graduated from high school.

Marty was a product not only of her family and her class. Her attitudes and behaviors around drinking were also formed by two major historical influences: America's drinking culture and the temperance movement. Both were in turn significantly influenced by what has become known as the Puritan ethic, a religiously based conviction that equated salvation with hard work, good works, right living, and success. Early in America's history, the Puritan ethic became the pervasive American ethic.

A major but little-known contribution of the original dominant Protestant culture in America, persisting today, was a strong bias in favor of voluntarism. The dissident Pilgrim and Puritan congregations were self-governing and self-supporting. Except for the minister, who was selected and paid by the congregation, all the church's tasks were performed by volunteers among that church's membership. From the practices of these early churches spread America's distinctive pattern of civic and social voluntarism as expressed in innumerable nonreligious settings, a pattern that continues to differentiate our society and culture from the rest of the world.

Marty may never have realized these historic roots of her passionate preference for the philosophy of voluntarism. The voluntary public health organization she eventually founded to serve alcoholics is thus indebted to America's earliest settlers.

The common daily use of alcohol is another contribution of those early colonists and has continued as a significant part of the American scene. The settlers brought their European customs, which included the drinking of wine and beer throughout the day, both as a safe alternative to impure water and as a pleasant addition to meals. Alcohol was additionally an anesthetic and medicine.

In general, social drinking was the rule. Hospitality customs required the host to offer a guest an alcoholic drink upon arrival. "Have a drink! What would you like?" (It is still the custom among the majority of Americans.) People drank to feel better, to feel good, to be sociable. Women were free to drink in the home, but they were expected to be moderate and definitely not to drink to excess.

The cocktail party of more modern times is an American invention. Besides the attraction of liquor itself, a cocktail party is an easy, relatively cheap way for a host to repay many social debts at once.

So the Manns and the Christy grandparents were not unusual in their social use of alcohol. Chicago, like the rest of the United States, was a drinking society. Marty embraced this cultural climate.

An important factor in America's attitude toward alcohol flows from the religious traditions embedded in American culture by the early colonists. Religious reformers and rebels, these early settlers were steeped in Judeo-Christian teachings and in the Bible. They believed that the bounty of all nature was a gift from God. Grapes, and by extension wine, were thus inherently beneficent. Asceticism was not typical, but people also frowned on drunkenness. They saw inebriation as a violation of the body as the temple of God. To be drunk was more than an individual or social perversity. It was a personal affront to God. Moderation was the goal.

In the New Testament, the Gospels contain no direct references to temperance in the use of wine. Of greater New Testament importance in relation to colonial and later American attitudes toward alcohol were the writings of St. Paul. While Paul agreed with his contemporaries two thousand years ago that wine was intrinsically good, he preached against its improper use. He classified drunkenness as a weakness of the flesh, associating it with bad moral conduct and a defiling of the body. Abstinence was advised, not for asceticism's sake, but in the interest of brotherly love. Paul recommended substituting the positive measures of righteousness, peace, and joy in Jesus Christ for the negative ones of drunkenness. The seeds of alcoholism as a sin were sown by this powerful missionary and convert to what became Christianity.

Like many, if not most, Americans of her day, Marty was acquainted with the Bible when she was a young person attending Sunday school and church. The New Testament lessons emphasizing perfection and self-mastery undoubtedly reinforced her natural bent. During her drinking career and for some years afterward, however, she maintained a firm distance from anything smacking of organized religion. In her later years, she returned to study of the Bible and found herself relearning the Gospels in particular.

The second broad historical influence on Marty was the temperance movement. This movement was a response to the increasing abuse of alcohol in the nineteenth century. It would have a marked effect on Marty's prerecovery attitudes toward drinking, as well as later when she organized NCA.

The introduction of hard liquor produced in America by Americans was an important milestone in the history of alcohol use in this country. Gin and other hard liquors were Marty's favorites. The ready availability of these beverages was a plus for an alcoholic. Between 1800 and 1850, the United States experienced an explosion in excessive drinking that seriously afflicted home and community.[7]

In the beginning, temperance meant moderation in the use of alcohol. Only later did temperance become equated with abstinence. The temperance movement has been a significant abiding dynamic in American history and culture, sometimes waxing to dominate society and never waning completely. It has profoundly affected politics, the early women's movement, social welfare, and education. Most abolitionists of the nineteenth century were also temperance supporters.

At first, the culprit was perceived as hard liquor, not beer or wine. Yet in a surprising foreshadowing of modern thought, a renowned Boston preacher, Lyman Beecher, stated in 1826 that intemperance was a disease as well as a crime. He aimed to influence public sentiment and morality through boycotts of vendors, through education, and through temperance associations. Instead of encouraging legislative action, he urged the churches to become involved, applying all their powers of moral suasion.

And become involved, the churches did. They grabbed the temperance banner and led the movement for the next one hundred years, right up to passage of the Eighteenth Amendment (Prohibition) to the Constitution in 1919. The church was slow, however, to educate itself about modern twentieth-century discoveries of the nature of alcoholism.[8] Its role in perpetuating the image of the alcoholic as fallen, sinful, and unworthy of compassion and understanding is not a happy one. A harsh, judgmental, moralistic attitude prevailed. The church as an institution, and its representatives in the clergy, were eventually perceived by alcoholics as irrelevant at best, and basically hostile to those who weren't of the flock. It is no wonder that Marty, like many, if not most, of her fellow alcoholics, had long since turned against religion by the time she found recovery in Alcoholics Anonymous.

On the other hand, the church opened up leadership opportunities to women participating in the temperance movement. From the beginning of the movement, women played crucial roles. They were attracted to the temperance movement because drink was seen to affect the home and family, a woman's domain. Many women were victims of alcohol abuse or had alcoholism in the family. Heretofore powerless over the ravages endured from alcoholic husbands and relatives, women recognized the value of banding together to bring about change.

Women became the power in pushing legislation for temperance education and later for Prohibition. They joined the movement in droves, mobilizing churches and communities. Their membership cut across social strata, at least in the earlier years. Later, the temperance movement was more characterized by middle-class, rural, Protestant, native-born whites.

The eventual breadth of the temperance movement offered a focus to interest almost any woman, from poverty issues to vocational training to safer working conditions for women to kindergartens, and later on to suffrage. And as they worked in the temperance movement, women discovered the uses and rewards of power in the public realm. The experience was a determining factor in the long, slow process of raising the consciousness of women and freeing them from an unrecognized tyranny that dictated their roles as wives and mothers.

Women, however, soon found they had two important problems. They could neither vote, nor could they speak about temperance from a public platform. When the great suffragist Susan B. Anthony, by that time an experienced orator at women's temperance meetings, was barred from speaking at a large Sons of Temperance gathering in Albany, New York, in 1852, she was so infuriated that she promptly formed the first Women's State Temperance Society (WSTS) so she would have a platform regardless of the audience.[9] (See chapter 19 for a twentieth-century account of Susan B. Anthony's grandniece and namesake, the second Susan B. Anthony.)

At first the temperance movement concentrated on the alcoholic. Pledge drives began, often sponsored by churches, in which the alcoholic man would sign a public pledge to refrain from alcohol. The goal now was total abstinence (teetotaling). Unfortunately, the men would backslide more often than not. Women became disillusioned and impatient and sought another recourse—namely, control of the manufacture, sale, and distribution of liquor.

An important precursor of Alcoholics Anonymous was the Washingtonian Society.[10] A pledge-signing variation of the temperance movement, it was founded in a Baltimore tavern by six workingmen, reformed drunkards, who had heard a temperance lecture and taken a pledge of abstinence. The Washingtonians believed in mutual support and self-help. There was no connection with organized religion as existed in the main temperance movement.

The Washingtonian movement swept through America like wildfire for five years in the 1840s, then abruptly vanished. In large part, its demise was due to a loss of focus on reclaiming the individual alcoholic. The Washingtonians became involved in all kinds of politics, exhibitionism about their recovery, competition with other organizations, and fruitless controversy. Also, the movement offended the social and cultural leaders of the day because it attracted common people, many of them uneducated.

One hundred years later, Alcoholics Anonymous was determined to organize itself in a way that would avoid a similar eclipse.

The Women's Christian Temperance Union (WCTU) was formed specifically to overcome the power of the liquor industry and its supporters. Its dynamic leader was Frances E. Willard, a leading feminist of the nineteenth century. She saw clearly that women needed the vote if they were to combat the liquor forces. For nearly thirty years the WCTU[11] was not only the ranking temperance organization; it was the ranking women's organization in the United States. It pioneered in local organization, providing a respectable bridge between the radical suffragists and the home. Marty would one day become well acquainted with the WCTU's leader of the time.

Other women's temperance and suffrage groups formed. By 1919 the temperance groups had spearheaded the adoption of Prohibition (the Eighteenth Amendment). A year later the suffragists had successfully promoted ratification of the Nineteenth Amendment, giving the vote to women.

Marty had no basis for appreciating how the temperance and suffrage movements contributed to her freedom as a woman, nor how they paved the way for her eventual life's mission and her very successful public leadership and advocacy roles in a society still dominated by men. In fact, she had unlimited scorn for teetotalers before she sobered up, even though she'd never known anyone who didn't drink. She vigorously resisted meeting any people in AA at first, because she feared they would be "gray, dull, do-gooder teetotalers with big, white teeth who lived narrow lives and never had any fun."

She certainly didn't want to be a drunk, either. Girls were socialized early not to drink too much. "Be a lady," they were told. To Marty, as to most of her contemporaries, drunks were mission stiffs and Bowery bums on skid row. She saw drunken derelicts on West Madison Street when she was growing up in Chicago and remembered their dirty, seedy appearance and "Oh my God, the smell." And they were always men "with an over-growth of whiskers, and feet tangled up in newspapers, sticking out filthy hands for a cuppa coffee. You hoped they wouldn't touch you."

As did most people at the time, Marty believed that a drunk chose to be the way he was. Why else would anyone live like that? "Or if by chance he had been born to better things, he had something missing, something that made him unable to take advantage of his opportunities. I would have said that there was nothing that could be done about it; and if there were, he wouldn't be worth salvaging anyway."[12]

Once in a while, Marty would hear her elders whisper about people they knew who drank too much. Marty was puzzled by the secrecy. One of the people whispered about was the father of a little friend of hers. She called him "Uncle." However, the fact that Marty's own father also drank too much was carefully concealed from the Mann children by their mother. Indeed, Marty did not recognize that her father was an alcoholic until she herself became sober in AA. Only then did she begin to realize how power-ful a dynamic is family denial.[13]

All these cultural, religious, family, class, and ethical norms led to the universal sentiment that the excessive use of alcohol was a matter solely of willpower—a choice that could be controlled by the person. The inebriate was therefore weak in character, lacking in moral fiber. Marty, too, believed this totally. In time, the belief would nearly kill her. It would also drive her desperately to seek answers.

The Sleeping Lion Stirs[1]

1921—25

SO HERE WAS MARTY AT MONTEMARE, seventeen years old, newly recovered from tuberculosis, and ready to jump back into life. It was the era of Prohibition immortalized by F. Scott Fitzgerald and John Held Jr.—a heady time for any young person with Marty's background. The flapper and the boyish bob symbolized the age. Sophistication was the goal. Marty set out to be "gay with the gayest." Her own inner urges led her to outdo them all.

Taboos surrounding women were falling everywhere. Women had the vote at last, and they'd made themselves heard loud and clear with the Prohibition Amendment. They were freeing themselves in all manner of other ways. Their short, loosely fitted shifts with the dropped waistlines and hems above the knees were a far cry from the tight corsets and long skirts of their mothers. It was reported that "the men won't dance with you if you wear a corset."[2] Cosmetics previously associated with loose women—face powder, lipstick, and rouge—became big sellers for the first time among ordinary women. Women took up smoking and drinking in public.

Marty became a chain-smoker, addicted to cigarettes the rest of her life. In the end they would contribute to her death. A reporter interviewing her in 1964 noted that Marty lit her fifth cigarette in forty minutes. She stopped once for a couple of weeks but had such psychological and physical difficulties in withdrawal that she went to her doctor. Since she claimed she smoked only a pack a day, the doctor reasoned it would be better for her to smoke if she could keep it to that. The stress of trying to quit seemed a greater risk. In those days, ignorance, denial, and rationalization went hand in hand for both patient and doctor.

Alcoholics whose disease is active have a very high incidence of smoking, which they tend to continue in sobriety. Only in recent decades has nicotine been recognized as an addictive drug as pernicious in its own way as alcohol. Until well after Marty died in 1980, most AA meetings were blue with cigarette smoke. George Marcelle,[3] an NCA staff member from 1975 to 1990, recalls being told by somebody in a bar that AA meetings were "full of cigarette smoke and bullshit." Alcoholics recovering in AA were discouraged from quitting cigarettes because it was feared the stress might cause them to relapse on alcohol. Newcomers were rarely advised to stop smoking. If they brought it up, they were told to wait at least a year. Marty was no different from her AA peers.

Years later, as physicians began to recognize the addictive nature of nicotine, a leading specialist in addictive medicine, Joseph Zuska, M.D., instituted a no-smoking policy in his pioneering treatment program at the Long Beach Naval Hospital in California, where Betty Ford would later be admitted for alcoholism and addiction to prescription drugs. One time when Marty was lecturing in Long Beach, Zuska told her she couldn't smoke. "Oh yes I can," she retorted, and proceeded to light up.

Dr. Zuska believes her fatal stroke was related to smoking. Yet she was only one of a multitude of recovered alcoholics adversely affected by nicotine. Two major leaders of AA and the alcoholism movement were also felled, not by "demon rum," but by nicotine—AA cofounder Bill Wilson and Senator Harold Hughes.

Joe Zuska was an early advocate of what is now beginning to take hold in treatment centers—tobacco cessation as an essential element of alcohol- and drug-treatment programs. This development would have caused Marty problems personally, though she might have supported it intellectually for other people. In any event, she would have considered attention to nicotine addiction a distraction from her focus on addressing alcoholism.

The generation of "Flaming Youth" set the pace of experimentation in other ways. Victorian sexual mores were already in decline. The doctrine of free love was in. In 1924, the sexual revolution was advanced by the advent of the closed car, which provided a private, movable room. One Chicago judge called the closed car "a house of prostitution on wheels."[4]

Marty drank because it was the thing to do, an accepted social custom. That's what her peers did. That's what 70 to 80 percent of Americans continue to do. In talking to groups years later, Marty would time and again remind her audiences that onset of this behavior is normal for American adolescents and young adults. Further, it was normal for young people who typically are unsure of themselves and, like their elders, find that alcohol eases social anxieties. Marty would also tell her audiences that most people who pick up a drink for the first time do not become alcoholics. After a period of experimentation, the majority can take it or leave it. Today it is believed that about 7 to 10 percent will go on to develop alcoholism.[5] The dilemma still is that when people begin to drink, there is no sure way to identify who will become an alcoholic.

Marty described herself as a shy, tongue-tied, awkward adolescent.[6] She had two dates before she started drinking and was so stiff and inarticulate that these boys never asked her out again. In her drive to be popular, she at first went to one of two extremes—either to "sit like a bump on a log or hog the whole show." Neither approach met her need for acceptance. She thought she was different, never realizing she was experiencing many of the normal insecurities of adolescence. She soon discovered that it always took three stiff drinks to get to a base comfort level before going out. Later she said that liquor did her growing up for her. With it, she became one of the gang. What Marty learned eventually was that alcoholic drinking stops emotional growth ("like a needle stuck in a record") but as a rule not physical or intellectual growth. So when she finally got sober, her emotional development and behavior were initially those of a teenager.

In 1921, Prohibition was in full swing. Neither Marty nor the crowd she traveled with let that detail stand in the way of their drinking. Liquor was readily available in her own home and the homes of her friends. On dates, "any boy would sooner go out without his pants than not have a flask"—a silver one at that. And no self-respecting young woman would turn down swigs from the flask. Access to liquor in the community was simple. She and her escorts frequented the many roadhouses that functioned as clandestine speakeasies. No questions were asked in Prohibition-defiant Chicago. The popular drink was a gin cocktail. It cost 75 cents ($7.50 in year 2000 dollars) for patrons and was free to the police.

Marty had an astonishing capacity for alcohol. From the start, she was able for years to outdrink everyone and not show it. It was a point of great pride both to her and to her dates. They boasted about her ability, but sometimes complained she made for an expensive date. At the end of a party, she was the designated driver to get her companions home. It wasn't until after she found recovery from alcoholism that she learned you don't have to be visibly drunk to be a dangerous driver. At the time, she was contemptuous about people who drank too much and couldn't hold their liquor. When Marty got sober, she recognized that her hollow leg was an important early indicator of alcoholism. In her talks, she seldom failed to make the point that alcoholics often exhibit this abnormal reaction to alcohol.

Among all Marty's hard-drinking crowd, only one person rivaled her legendary capacity for alcohol, a young married woman named Virginia (possibly a pseudonym since Marty also called her Grace). Marty and Virginia each had her own admirers and supporters. Marty's current beau belonged to the fast set. He and the other men decided to stage a contest to determine which of the two girls could drink more or better. Bets were placed totaling $5,000 ($50,000 in year 2000 dollars).

Virginia and her husband lived in her wealthy family's palatial home on Lake Shore Drive. The parents were away in Europe, so that house was chosen for the party-contest. An important consideration was that Virginia's father had a good supply of liquor. The party began at 6:00 P.M. The cellar was set up with a bar and a buffet. The servants were dismissed for the duration.

The group selected three judges. The judges were not allowed to drink. Their job was to make the drinks for the two contestants and monitor their consumption. The contest drink was a French 75, a highball consisting of homemade bathtub gin plus expensive champagne. The name of the drink referred to a French 75-mm cannon of World War I. The judges doled out measured drinks to Marty and Virginia, making sure none went into the potted plants or out the window. Everyone but the judges and the contestants could drink whatever and however much they liked.

The party grew rowdier and rowdier. A young man was supposed to be playing the piano upstairs, but he wanted to stay at the bar in the cellar. Marty scooped him up, lugged him upstairs, and plunked him down on the piano bench. At one point the guests, in high spirits, became curious about how far the dumbwaiter went, so Marty climbed inside and rode up to the attic and back.

By 2:00 A.M. the party began to dwindle, and by 5:00 A.M. only the three judges and two contestants were left on their feet. The judges declared the contest a draw, and the five of them went out for breakfast. After breakfast Virginia and Marty settled down for some really serious drinking.

Marty often wondered what happened to Virginia. After she herself got sober, she realized that her rival had had the same symptoms of alcoholism. Marty thought she might meet Virginia in AA one day, but she never did.

After Marty graduated from Montemare in 1924, she returned to Chicago to prepare for a long-planned year in Italy. In those days, privileged young women from wealthy families usually received a final educational flourish at a finishing school in a European city, often Florence, Paris, or Lucerne, Switzerland. This 1924 summer interim would be an exciting time of renewing family ties, partying with friends, and shopping for clothes and all the items dear to a rich young lady.

That same June, the whole country was gripped by a sensational murder that occurred in Chicago. Instantly labeled the "crime of the century," it commanded the public's attention much as did the O. J. Simpson story in Los Angeles seventy years later. Two sociopaths, Nathan Leopold and Richard Loeb, intellectually brilliant young men from millionaire Chicago families, believed they were so much smarter than anyone else, they could commit a perfect crime that no one could solve. To this end they deliberately kidnapped and murdered Bobby Franks, a fourteen-year-old boy picked at random from a neighboring wealthy family.

The cruel passionlessness of the crime, the rapid identification of the perpetrators, and the subsequent trial were front-page news for weeks. The defense attorney was none other than Clarence Darrow. Strongly opposed to capital punishment, he was able to deflect a certain death sentence to life imprisonment.

A lurid aspect of the trial was the revelation that Leopold and Loeb were homosexual men. The detailed testimony about their relationship by the consulting psychiatrists riveted even a city accustomed to journalistic extremes. The consequence of all the prurient publicity was that public opinion related homosexuality to criminal behavior.

Marty and the other Manns would have been especially interested in the murder for two reasons. First, Marty heard a distorted, inflammatory view of homosexuality that would impact her own life. Second, it is likely that Will Mann was acquainted with the prominent businessmen fathers of the three principals. All three of the shattered families were Jewish, though the Frankses had converted to Christian Science. The Jewish and Christian moguls of Chicago and their families may not have mixed socially, but Will's path and the paths of these particular fathers could have crossed through mutual business, political, and civic interests. And there were some additional intriguing possibilities.

Bobby Franks's father, Jacob, made his main fortune through real estate investments in the Loop, Chicago's dynamic and profitable central business district. Jacob's early career, however, had begun as head of an upscale pawnshop called the Franks Collateral Loan Bank. It catered to the city's gamblers, who knew Jacob as "Honest Jake." Jacob Franks was reported to have the respect of every man who made a loan, in some cases loaning 90 percent of the value of the items pawned.

> Chicago then was a wide-open gambling town. The gamblers would visit the Franks Collateral Loan Bank to hock their watches, rings, and diamond studs. Honest Jake offered generous allowances, so his customers multiplied. While the fortunes of the gamblers rose and fell, the fortunes of the Franks Collateral Loan Bank rose.[7]

Will Mann, the high-rolling compulsive gambler, would undoubtedly have known about and perhaps patronized Jacob Franks's and similar select pawnshops.

Albert Loeb, Richard's father, was an attorney who had joined Sears, Roebuck and Company, the huge mail-order firm headquartered in Chicago, in its earlier days. He became vice president, also serving as chief officer during World War I. The top leaders of Chicago's major merchandising marts, like Will Mann and Albert Loeb, would have been acquainted through their common business interests.

Nathan Leopold Sr. was the younger Nathan's father. Connected through his wife with several Illinois banks, he was independently wealthy through investments in shipping, mining, and paper. It is possible that Nathan Sr., along with Jacob Franks and Albert Loeb, were among those approached by Will Mann a few years later when Will sought backing for a gold-mining scheme.

Mercifully, the Leopold-Loeb trial and sentencing were over by August, coinciding with Marty's departure for Italy. She would have spent the last two weeks of summer in a frenzied round of farewell parties filled with drinking and fun. Then Marty was off on the train to New York where she would board a ship for Europe, dressed to the nines as always. She would study the next year at Miss Nixon's School in Florence.

Miss Nixon's no longer exists. Housed in the Villa Laugier, it was located behind a big gate at 10 Via di Barbacane, a long, winding, walled lane rising into the hills leading to the nearby town of Fiesole. The landscape was dotted with big villas. Miss Nixon's had the most spectacular view of all.

Italy, and especially Florence, the artistic heart and soul of the Renaissance, was a superb place to learn about art. Marty's interests were enlarged and sharpened in this historic city that had been home to so many great artists—Giotto, Donatello, Masaccio, Uccello, Botticelli, da Vinci, Michelangelo, Raphael, and Cellini, to highlight a few.

Italy was also perfect for expanding one's knowledge of wine. And by the end of the year, Marty was able to get along in Italian in addition to speaking and reading French.

As the year drew to a close, Marty's life looked as if only good fortune awaited her. The years of illness lay in the past. She would go home with the assurance that she belonged among the most polished of America's privileged daughters.

6

The Glory Years

1925—26

MARTY WAS TWENTY-ONE YEARS OLD when she returned from Florence to Chicago, traveling by ship and by train. She was anxious to get home after the yearlong absence. Despite the excitement of living in a foreign country, she was sometimes homesick, notably during the holidays, and especially at Christmastime.

The twins were now almost seven years old. How much had they grown in a year? And Chris, fifteen, how was she doing at the Latin School? Marty could hardly wait to find out what had happened when she was away, the sorts of things that didn't get into the long letters she'd received from home. She wondered about her friends. What had she missed?

Catching up on the past was only part of it. Marty was returning to enter a new phase of her life. Her formal education was now complete. She was ready to be introduced to society and thereafter spin through an endless upper-class social whirl with no particular goals for life except marriage and children. Her future as a conventional debutante and young matron was assured. How could such a popular, gregarious, intelligent heiress not gain whatever or whomever she wanted?

For the moment, Marty would enjoy her status as a desirable debutante. This was a transition time, the time from school graduation to the time of marriage and raising a family. In her social stratum, this period would be especially enjoyable. She would rejoin her circle of wealthy friends, visiting one another's homes, shopping, attending the theater, viewing exhibitions at the Art Institute, attending dinner parties and dances, and traveling to parts of the country she had never seen before.

Marty had everything money could buy. For her, the contrast in shopping venues between Renaissance Florence and 1925 Chicago could not have been greater. Chicago, the home of the first skyscrapers, had more department stores than any city in the world, and Marshall Field was the nonpareil. Will Mann was at the top of his form, managing Marshall Field's vast wholesale division. His advancement in the business world had been rapid and rewarding. In 1925, it promised to continue without end.

Marty returned to find the family already settled in the summer residence at Highland Park, near Chicago. It seemed as if the Mann family was blessed with success. Summer vacation in Highland Park would be leisurely, a welcome opportunity to readjust to family and social life without too many distractions. The end of summer, on the other hand, heralded the resumption of full schedules and expectations. The family returned to their elegant residence on Kenmore Avenue. Chris and the twins went back to school. The fall would be the busy prelude to Marty's debut, her bow to Chicago society.

The social season in Chicago was divided into distinct periods and began with the opening of the opera season in November. Around Christmas and New Year's, there was intense activity, highlighted by children returning on holiday to their families from schools both local and distant—boarding schools, finishing schools, colleges, and universities. A focus of this period was the debutante cotillion, a banquet and formal ball in which the debutante, or "bud," would make her bow to society.

A debut tacitly announced a young woman's readiness and availability for marriage, to the proper person, of course. A debutante always wore white at her cotillion and carried a lovely bouquet in the manner of brides. She chose her escort (date) for the ball. The young men considered it a great honor to be selected. Other eligible men and all of the parents could size up the suitability and desirability of individual "debs" for future contacts. The first dance was reserved for the deb's father or designated senior sponsor.

This was to be Marty's year, along with hundreds of other young women of Chicago in her social class. Events were carefully planned, including teas, dinner parties, nights at the theater, operas, dances, and formal balls. The 1925–26 season reached its peak just before Christmas, when debutante balls were almost nightly galas. The Crystal Ballroom of the

Blackstone Hotel, Chicago's finest, was a favorite place for the banquet and debutante ball, although other venues were also used. Sometimes the banquet would be at one place and the ball at another. The debutante balls often lasted all night. That year the weather was unseasonably frigid, the thermometer hovering at zero and below. One poor, homeless indigent was found frozen to a fence, but the party-goers, involved in their various affairs, were oblivious.[1]

By Epiphany, January 6, 1926, the debutante balls were over, but the parties didn't stop, not until Lent. After Epiphany, Marty traveled with her friends to New Orleans, where the partying was just beginning, leading up to Mardi Gras, the day before Lent. She was pleased to learn that an eye-opener was not unusual in New Orleans. The maid routinely brought guests a daiquiri first thing in the morning, not tea or coffee, while they were still in bed.

Two months later Marty was back in New Orleans to be a bridesmaid at the wedding of Kit Williams,[2] a close friend and former schoolmate at the Montemare School in Lake Placid. The wedding was the social event of the season, uniting two prominent, wealthy families. Attending the bride were eight bridesmaids, a maid of honor, and a matron of honor. The groom, Ted Simmons, had a best man and nine groomsmen. One of the groomsmen was a young man named John Blakemore.

Marty later said of Blakemore, "He was one of the most attractive men I've met, interesting, traveled, with a keen mind. His family was prominent socially and he was the town's worst drunk. He was on the wagon at the time and when people spoke of his terrific drinking, I treated it lightly. After all, didn't I drink, too, and enjoy it?"[3]

What with the wedding and that famous southern ambience, romance was in the air. It was "love at first sight," but Marty had to return home.

Blakemore had all the right credentials. He was a southern gentleman, educated, handsome, charming—and fairly rich. His father had made his money in the oil and gas fields of Louisiana. However, during the Depression, the Blakemore family lost their plantation when they were unable to make a go of cotton growing. Ironically, in the 1970s, the largest oil fields in Louisiana were discovered on that land.

John was associated with his father in the general contracting business, in particular the construction of huge waterworks at Slidell, Louisiana, and was regarded as one of the coming business leaders of the community. Mr. Mann immediately took a dislike to Marty's suitor and vigorously opposed Marty's intent to marry him.

After returning from the wedding festivities in New Orleans, Marty joined the Chicago Junior League, a usual affiliation for young women of her station. She was featured on the society page of the *Chicago Tribune* as "one of the girls who is to appear in the society girl skit for the Actors' Fund benefit performance at the Auditorium this afternoon."[4]

In the meantime, the Manns' fortunes continued to increase rapidly. One year, Will received a $100,000 bonus ($1,000,000 in year 2000 dollars). The volatile stock market of the 1920s also contributed to the family fortune. Marty's father asked her mother which she would rather have, a car for herself to drive, or a car with a chauffeur. Lill chose the car with chauffeur. Over the years the Manns owned Cadillacs, Lincolns, and Rolls Royces. As a special treat (and maybe to relieve the nannies!), Axel, the chauffeur, used to put the twins, Betty and Bill, in the backseat and take them out for a drive.

Up to a point, Will Mann was a shrewd investor of his wealth. However, he was addicted to gambling, whether on the horses, the numbers, cards, stocks, or land. "Easy come, easy go" might have been his motto. He could spend money as fast as he made it, and eventually faster—lots faster. Finally, his compulsive gambling led to conflict with his good friend and boss, Jim Simpson, the president of Marshall Field. Simpson objected to his senior associate's behavior, probably as much from personal concern for Will as for Marshall Field's reputation.

Will's escalating alcoholism fueled the situation. His reaction whenever confronted was, "What I do with my personal life is not your concern!" Despite Will's outstanding success in business, apparently the argument with Simpson became critical, and in early 1926, after fifteen years with Marshall Field, Marty's father resigned. He was fifty-four years old. However, he had ample assets to fall back on, and golden parachutes (unusually generous financial severance settlements) were not unknown.

Within a few years, Marty duplicated her father's pattern of addictive behavior. In this pattern, actions grow out of control and spill over onto others and into the workplace, but the individual affected believes the rest of the world doesn't understand. Instead of dropping the addiction or getting help for it, the person picks up his or her marbles and goes elsewhere, nursing a "justifiable resentment" all the while.

It was the beginning of the end for Will.

The Merry
Marriage-Go-Round

1926–28

WILL'S FIRST ACT IN RETIREMENT was to take Lill, Marty, and Chris to Europe for six months, traveling first class everywhere, of course. The eight-year-old twins were left at home in Chicago with their nannies and under the watchful eye of Grandma Christy.

Betty and Bill loved to go to Grandma's once a week for a manicure. The two children bit their nails, and the manicure was intended as a reward for refraining. Little Bill also loved the smell of the battery recharging on his grandma's "electric" (car). She kept it parked in the back of the garage. It was a model with an arm for steering instead of a steering wheel.

One good reason for Will's promoting the European trip, of course, would have been that he could thereby avoid the inevitable questions from his multitudes of business colleagues by getting out of town for a period. Also, Will needed time to strategize for the future. In addition, Chris would be ready in a couple of years for finishing school in Florence. It would be a good way to introduce her to the continent and Miss Nixon's. Probably another important reason for this extended tour was the hope that Marty would forget about John Blakemore. At the very least, she would be where her parents could monitor her.

The ploy didn't work with Marty. "Absence," as they say, "made the heart grow fonder." As soon as the family returned to Chicago, and Mardi Gras rolled around again, Marty was back in New Orleans with Blakemore. After a whirlwind courtship that took in the carnival ball and Mardi Gras, Marty and John fled across the Mississippi River to Gretna, Louisiana, and were secretly married there by a justice of the peace on March 12,

1927. They were both high on alcohol at the time. All the friends of the newlyweds were sworn to secrecy for six months. But then a group of them went to a house party at a beach resort in Pass Christian, Mississippi, and "Mr. Blakemore revealed the fact that Miss Mann was his wife."[1]

Once the news was released, Marty's parents issued a brief one-paragraph announcement of the elopement in the *Chicago Tribune,* with no picture of the couple. How different the newspaper account would have been had Marty followed the conventional path of a big society wedding uniting two leading, moneyed families. The New Orleans papers, on the other hand, sensationalized the secret marriage, reporting the wedding at length and running separate pictures of the couple.[2] New Orleans society was scandalized.

Sometime after the elopement, a church service was held at Trinity Church in New Orleans and was attended by both families. Following the service, John's grandparents hosted a reception at their home. The newlyweds then went on an extensive wedding trip to Chicago, New York, Virginia, Washington, Atlanta, and Pass Christian before settling into an apartment on Rue St. Louis in New Orleans.

John worked in his father's firm. Having married a southerner, Marty now became a "damnYankee"—all one word. She later observed there were two other words pronounced as one—"hopelessdrunks." Marty was no slouch in the drinking department, but John's alcoholism was considerably more advanced than hers. To Marty's dismay, he was also a violent, belligerent drunk. Her romantic illusions received a jolt. The man she'd married seemed to have one consuming ambition—to drink all the liquor in the South. John drank continuously, starting as soon as he got up in the morning.

One scene followed another. The couple made contracts for John to cut down or quit. He promptly broke them. Marty said, "He was a very bad actor when drunk—fighting mad and fighting jealous." Worse, he was "a falling-down drunk, a brawler, liar, cheater, and weakling." In short, he couldn't hold his liquor and was therefore "not a man."

Marty hadn't crossed the line into her own uncontrolled drinking yet. Like any family member living with an active alcoholic, she felt bitter resentment, even hate. She lost all faith in her alcoholic husband. Desperation drove her to try coping with the situation, but nothing worked. She tried everything she knew to change him. She was sure that if John would only stop drinking, all would be fine. She acted out of both ignorance and good intentions. Decades later she would reflect, "I showed neither patience nor understanding—I thought his drinking showed lack of character and will."[3]

It didn't take Marty long to realize she'd made a bad mistake. She stuck with John only three months before admitting defeat. Adding to Marty's distress, her tuberculosis flared up again. In mid-1927 she left to file for divorce and recover from the TB. Her father would have been justified in saying, "I told you so."

Little did Marty know at the time how common divorce would become by the end of the twentieth century for someone who marries while under the influence of alcohol and/or drugs.[4] Marty was unusual, however, especially for her day, in being willing to leave a marriage and as promptly as she did. For one thing, a divorced woman was not generally viewed with favor by society. Also, Marty hated to fail at anything she undertook. On the other hand, the Manns' and the Blakemores' money provided a cushion not readily available to most divorcing women, who often stayed in unsatisfactory marriages for economic reasons.

Between the recurrence of TB and the marriage fiasco, Marty could hardly return to her parents' home. To establish residency for a divorce and heal from the TB, she moved to familiar territory for a year—the New Mexico ranch and Santa Fe. In due course the divorce was granted on June 20, 1928.[5] There were no children, and Marty never remarried. The judge granted her request to resume her maiden name, and at some point she started to identify herself as Mrs. Marty Mann.

Marty certainly didn't waste her energies grieving the breakup of the marriage. Nearby Santa Fe offered plenty of opportunity for a good time. Stanley Gitlow, M.D., Marty's physician in later years and a longtime pilot, reported that he'd been told by the navigator both he and Amelia Earhart used, that at some point Marty went barnstorming with Amelia for a while. Barnstorming is just the kind of adventure that would have attracted Marty while she was awaiting her divorce. Given the records of both Amelia's and Marty's activities in 1927 and 1928 and subsequently, a few weeks during Marty's year in New Mexico would probably have offered the only chance.

More important for long-term impact on Marty than a brief fling with barnstorming was her meeting Leopold Mannes during the year in New Mexico. In his late twenties, and four years older than Marty, Leopold was already an accomplished musician, composer, educator, scientist, inventor, and man of wealth. Marty dived headlong into an affair with this extraordinary man. Leopold was married to his first wife at the time. Tall and handsome, with dark hair and dark eyes, he was urbane and perhaps a little reticent, but among friends he was noted for his sense of humor.

Leopold's background and accomplishments were a sure magnet for Marty. He personified what she most admired. Leopold was the son and grandson of famous musicians. He began playing the piano at the age of four. Leopold's father, David, a violinist, and his mother, Clara, a pianist, founded what was eventually called the Mannes School of Music in New York. Clara was the daughter of conductor Leopold Damrosch, for whom her son was named. Her brothers Walter and Frank were also conductors. Young Leopold's uncle Frank Damrosch founded the music school that would become the Juilliard School of Music.

When Leopold was fifteen, he took up photography as a hobby. The problems of color intrigued him. Leopold Godowsky, a schoolmate, had the same ideas about photography. They joined forces and created their own laboratory. Godowsky, too, had musical forebears. His father was the famous pianist Leopold Godowsky. His mother was Frances Gershwin, the sister of George and Ira Gershwin. The two junior Leopolds continued working on color photography; Leopold Mannes also earned his bachelor of arts degree from Harvard and began teaching at his parents' school, playing the piano, and composing.

In 1930 the director of the Kodak laboratory in Rochester, New York, became impressed with the work of the young men and persuaded them to work full time in Rochester's Kodak lab. Six years later, their invention, Kodachrome, was announced. Five years after that, Mannes patented a sound track of gold that improved the sound of colored motion pictures.

Leopold Mannes's enduring love, however, was music. He divorced, remarried, and returned to New York City to administer the family music school and to teach, perform, and compose.

The correspondence from Leopold that Marty saved began in October 1928.[6] They shared mutual interests in music, photography, literature, and philosophy. Several letters back and forth between them preceded the first extant letter from Leopold. In this letter, Leopold was very much the big-brother guru in a long philosophical discourse about the nature of music, personal environments, and literature. Clearly he enjoyed Marty's intellectual stimulus as much as she did his. He was also thrilled to receive a poem from Marty (the first of several); then he proceeded forthrightly to critique it. Marty would not be the first person to fall in love with someone's mind.

When Marty's divorce became final, all the Manns congregated at the New Mexico ranch. The twins were ten years old. Bill recalls that his big sister Marty, then twenty-four, had been living it up with some of her wealthy young friends while awaiting her divorce. She owned an old car. Bill was thrilled when she let him take the wheel on a trip into Santa Fe.

It was the last time all the Manns would be together as a family. Chris would be leaving shortly for Miss Nixon's School in Florence, and Marty was on her way to New York City to seek her fortune. After the reunion, everyone but Chris returned to Chicago to prepare. She stayed an extra day for the Santa Fe roundup.

At the time, the Manns were living in Chicago's elegant Belden Stratford Hotel. Lill and Will had a very large apartment. The twins, Betty and Bill, were in another apartment with their governess. Chris was in a third apartment. She came home from New Mexico to pack for the long-awaited year at Miss Nixon's. The twins told her good-bye and went off to school the day she was supposed to leave. When Betty and Bill returned, they were astonished to find Chris still there. She was deathly ill. In fact, she'd come down with polio.

In those days, polio epidemics were common in the United States, especially in the summertime. They struck terror into people's hearts. There was no vaccine then. Death or permanent paralysis were the usual outcomes. The disease was known to occur most often in crowded urban surroundings. Yet Chris had apparently picked it up out on the ranch, perhaps by unknowingly drinking some polluted water.

Once again Lill and Will were confronted with the possible loss of a daughter. One had died as an infant, Marty had nearly died from TB, and now here was Chris, just as an exciting future was starting to unfold for her. The doctors wanted to admit her immediately to Chicago's hospital for contagious diseases. Mr. Mann had political pull, however. He went to the mayor, whom he knew well. Chris was allowed to stay under isolation in the hotel apartment with medical care until she was over the acute phase of the illness and able to be moved to an orthopedic hospital in Los Angeles for rehabilitation.

Chris's legs were badly paralyzed, but at least she was alive. She could breathe on her own. After many weeks, she graduated to a wheelchair, still unable to walk. Her hands were a little crippled. When Chris was strong enough to travel, Lill moved with the twins to Pasadena, while Chris was admitted to Los Angeles Orthopedic Hospital.

Marty's father probably stayed in Chicago to pursue business interests and try to raise money for a gold-mining venture in Montana. He'd already lost heavily on several grandiose investments. The money was running out quickly, and he needed badly to recoup. Regardless, the family continued their opulent lifestyle.

Returning to Pasadena with a desperately ill daughter must have been a scary déjà vu experience for Lill. For the ten-year-old twins, it was a great adventure since they were too young the first time with Marty to remember anything. Lill rented one of Pasadena's palatial houses on Hillcrest Avenue, very near the elite Huntington Hotel. The house and large garden occupied a quarter-block. There was a big garage for the Cadillac limousine. Betty and Bill were enrolled in private school because Lill didn't discover until later that Pasadena, unlike Chicago at the time, boasted a fine public school system.

During the next six months in Los Angeles Orthopedic Hospital, Chris was confined to bed with straight leg and back braces. The physical pain of the braces and necessary treatments often reduced patients to tears. Every morning Chris would be taken out to the pool to swim. Since the function in some of her leg muscles didn't return, an operation was performed to re-attach one of the muscles and stabilize her ankle so she would have a usable range of motion. Like Marty years before, she worked hard at her recovery. As a result, she was able to resume an almost normal life. She walked and moved like other people. Although she would never play tennis again, she was a good golfer. She bicycled, swam, rode horses. She wanted children after she married but could never carry a child.

All the Mann children had strong inner reserves they could call on in the face of great adversity. Chris's illness and recovery profoundly affected both her family and her spirit. It was as if she had passed through a refining fire. She developed a strength and sweetness of spirit that drew people to her. Marty had always loved this younger sister and felt protective toward her. From then on, however, they shared a special, unbreakable bond forged by their mutual experiences with near-fatal illnesses.

Rising and Falling Stars

1928–30

WHILE CHRIS WAS IN THE ORTHOPEDIC HOSPITAL in 1928, Marty had borrowed money to get to New York and was moving ahead there. She shared a small Greenwich Village flat with two other young women. Though they may occasionally have been short of food, they were seldom without bootleg whiskey.

Chicago was a great metropolis, but New York was *the* greatest American city. Marty was no stranger to New York, of course. The Manns had periodically visited the city on their travels, and Marty was further acquainted with New York from her high school years at the Montemare School in Lake Placid. To actually live in New York City, however, as a young, single adult would have been exciting and full of youthful dreams for a confident, independent twenty-four-year-old like Marty.

During a brief period in the fall of 1928, Marty was associated with an interior decorating firm. Then, untrained for any specific career but having a talent for writing and being favored with important moneyed and social connections, she soon found work as assistant editor on William Randolph Hearst's *International Studio Magazine*. A costly production with glossy pages, excellent photography of gallery exhibits, and classy writing, the magazine was aimed at a leisure class that had lots of money to spend for art.

From this time forth, Marty considered her career to be basically journalism and public relations. For much of her life, she was the kind of writer who needed a deadline and relished having only a day or two to write an article of several thousand words.

Between October 1929 and October 1930, Marty wrote for the magazine a very knowledgeable signed column called "Seen in the Galleries." In her discussions of Waterford glass, silver, furniture, and paintings can be seen the flowering of youthful exposure to the treasures of Marshall Field and Chicago's great museums, her studies abroad, and the Mann family travels. The content of the articles is worthy of an art historian. Marty was making a name for herself and doing quite well indeed.

Marty's talent was apparent and her career well launched. So was her social life. "There were many friends and lots of parties where liquor flowed like water."[1] A writer who squired her to speakeasies and swank parties of the era recalls, "I can't remember a more beautiful and intelligent girl. And she could drink any man under the table. A hollow leg, that girl!"[2] It was further reported of Marty that she "drinks like a fish, you know, but very clever. She does her job better tight than others do sober."[3]

Of immediate importance to Marty's social life was Leopold Mannes, who had promptly resumed his career at the Mannes School of Music when Marty moved to New York. Suddenly he was no longer the superior mentor but an ardent swain. Marty tended to have this effect on her lovers. Long, impassioned letters flowed from Leopold's pen even though the two lovers were now in the same city. For three months the couple maintained a sizzling affair snatched in brief moments when they were both free. Marty was enchanted with his piano playing; he was enchanted with her. Then the love letters abruptly ceased, or at least Marty no longer kept them. The affair may or may not have continued until Marty left for London nearly two years later, but probably not thereafter.

Leopold Mannes was an example of Marty's ability to retain the friendship and fond regard of people who crossed her path, even in intimate encounters that cooled. Leopold remained a lifelong friend. He undoubtedly shared some of his technical knowledge of photography with Marty, always an eager student, and he may have been instrumental in her decision to establish a photojournalism business in London. A decade later, Leopold would be a crucial factor in Marty's recovery from alcoholism.

Perhaps the apparently sudden cessation of the affair with Leopold was because Marty was simultaneously discovering her lesbian orientation. The 1920s was a decade of considerable sexual permissiveness and experimentation. Marty certainly moved and worked in circles containing many homosexuals. There is a lively legend in the lesbian community, maybe true, of Marty, dressed in tuxedo and sporting a monocle, arriving by limousine at the stage door of musicals to pick up chorus girls.

While Marty was becoming established in New York, her father's financial problems were rapidly approaching the crisis stage in Chicago. He had been unable to promote backing for his investment schemes. In Pasadena, Lill and the three younger children were stranded without any income. She didn't even have money to get back to Chicago. Young Bill rode around Los Angeles with his mother in their chauffeured limousine while she visited pawnshops to hock her jewelry. Lill finally scraped together enough cash to flee Pasadena, leaving behind a number of unpaid bills.

Once back home in Chicago, the family was able to rent an apartment on Brier Place, closer to town than the former homes on Kenmore Avenue but still in a genteel, upper-class area. Creditors all over the city became more and more insistent. They called constantly on the phone to pressure Will for payment of his debts. Young Bill would have to answer and say, "Sorry, he's not here right now."

Seventeen days before the great stock market crash on October 24, 1929, Marty's father filed for bankruptcy.[4] The gambler had lost. It took him only three years—from 1926 when he left Marshall Field—to plummet from multimillionaire to pauper.

How the Manns were able to live in Chicago the next two years is a mystery. The New Mexico ranch was sold to a movie star, but that money wouldn't last long given the Manns' lifestyle. Very likely, Lill's still wealthy widowed mother was able to help out. In addition, Lill had some income from a trust fund established by her father in her name only. This was an unbreakable trust which Robert Christy had had the foresight to set up for his daughter before his death ten years earlier. He didn't want his drinking, gambling son-in-law to have access to it. And at the time the trust was established, Will Mann was already a rich man, anyway, and didn't need the extra income.

As the Depression deepened in 1930, and the Manns' finances grew more critical, Marty's father was utterly convinced he could find gold in Montana and save the family—and his reputation—forever. He was obsessed with the dream of striking it rich. No investor would, or could, stake him to a placer mine, however. He'd been trying for more than a year to find a backer. Will was desperate for an infusion of cash to buy equipment and get started. The only remaining possible resource to tap was his wife's trust fund. Will importuned her to mount a legal challenge to the trust and break it. She refused. He kept hammering away. Lill's aging mother was unable to counter her son-in-law's pressure on her daughter. Finally, Lill buckled under to the force of her husband's will. Together they challenged the trust and won. Robert Christy must have turned over in his grave.

At that point in 1931, Grandma Christy died. On one of her visits with Marty's family, she caught pneumonia and expired soon after in their home. Lill, grieving, could no longer claim her elderly mother as a reason to stay in Chicago. On the other hand, the Manns' cash flow would have improved with Lill's inheritance from her mother. That didn't mean Lill was ready to abandon Chicago for what seemed a harebrained scheme in the wilds of Montana. She dug in her heels and refused to budge. Will couldn't afford to maintain a household back home while he set up the Montana operation. He insisted that they all had to go with him—Lill, Chris (now almost fully recovered from polio), and the twins. Lill continued to stonewall. Finally, Marty's father threw down the gauntlet. Putting his arm around his twelve-year-old son, he said grandly, "Well, Bill and I will go out together then, won't we?"

Young Bill was appalled at his father's imperious impulse and at the threat that his father would separate him from the family. The emotional blackmail was too much for Lill. She caved in and agreed to move to Montana.

The site Will had scouted and selected was on Libby Creek near the tiny town of Libby in the northwest corner of the state, where gold had already been discovered. Ninety-five percent of the county was in federal lands, so a federal mining permit would probably have been required.

Why Will chose Libby, or how he even knew about it, can only be surmised. Newspaper and magazine stories about the Libby mines could have attracted his interest. The Chicago World's Exposition of 1893 may have included a display of mining and lumbering riches in the area around Libby. The 1933 World's Fair certainly did, but that was after the Manns had moved to Montana.

Although gold mining had actually declined by then, a famous deposit of vermiculite[5] had been discovered in what was originally an asbestos mine and was being developed by the Zonolite company. Philip Armour, of the Chicago meat-packing company, was a major investor, and B. D. White of Chicago was on the board of directors, so they may have been a source of information about Libby for Will. The opportunity to buy cheap penny stocks in Zonolite was over, however.

When the Manns arrived in Libby, Will's first task was to build two summer cabins in the woods. There was no insulation. Young Bill split wood for the heating and cooking stoves. Suddenly winter arrived with a vengeance. The thermometer plunged to fifty degrees below zero Fahrenheit. After a few days of freezing, Lill cried, "Enough!" and moved the family into Libby's small hotel to get warm. When they were finally able to return to the cabins, everything was ruined. The pipes had burst.

The next summer came and went without a gold strike. It didn't help matters that Will's drinking was worse. His legs broke out in sores. He developed a serious case of cirrhosis of the liver.

At the end of summer, Will rented a house in Libby for Lill, Chris, and the twins and went back to Chicago to try to raise more money for the mine. From Chicago he sent a few funds to the family. Will never returned to Libby.

In Chicago, his doctor, a German, gave him some medicine and told him to stop drinking. To everyone's surprise, he did. When Marty came into AA in 1939, her father had been sober for six years on his own.

Chris stuck it out in Libby for two more years. During that time she met a personable young man from New York City named Alan (Johnny) Johnstone, who served as an officer in the Civilian Conservation Corps (CCC), one of the federal government's means of creating jobs during the Depression. Chris was twenty-four years old and didn't see any future for herself in Libby. Johnny was her ticket out, so in 1934 she married him. They moved to New York, but the marriage didn't last long. Johnny and Chris separated, but she didn't divorce him until 1940. In the meantime, Chris was free to make her own life as best she could.

Lill and the twins stayed in the Libby area until Betty and Bill graduated from high school in 1936. Then Betty left for a federal job with the U.S. State Department Bureau of Inter-American Affairs in Washington, D.C. Her twin brother entered the University of Chicago. Lill, still separated from their father, returned to Chicago and moved into a hotel next to the Chicago Board of Trade.

Lill and Will were never divorced, but they never lived together again. Nor did Marty's father ever make a go of placer mining. Eventually, Lill's inheritance trickled out, and she was supported financially for the rest of her life by her children, mainly Marty and Bill. Chris was often able to provide personal care and companionship when she lived nearby. Betty was far away and didn't begin to have much income of her own until after her mother died.

An important fallout from Mr. Mann's rapid and catastrophic financial decline was the traumatic effect on Chris and the twins. They were suddenly cast into severe poverty, yanked from the security and surroundings they had always known, and denied the advantages their older sister, Marty, had enjoyed. Betty, in particular, long resented Marty's favored head start.

To be sure, they were not the only family experiencing abrupt deprivation during the 1930s. But there was a tragic dimension to the story of this family. External circumstances such as the disease of alcoholism and the Great Depression were beyond personal control, but they were not the sole factor in the Manns' downfall. There was also an inexorable human element of greatness brought low by hubris and flawed nature, especially Marty's father's.

Years later Lill was asked why she had ever agreed to the breaking of the trust. She replied, "Well, I had to give him that one last chance. I could never forgive myself if I didn't."

9

The Sleeping Lion Awakes

1930–35

DURING THESE YEARS OF HARDSHIP for the Manns, Marty could do little to help from New York. Her main job was at *International Studio Magazine,* but she also contributed a signed column, "Through the Galleries," to *Town and Country,* another upper-class magazine.

After two years in New York, Marty decided in 1930 to move to London. Her intention was to live on her savings while she produced the great American novel. Soon cocktails took precedence over the novel. "Give Marty another drink and let her tell you all about the book she's writing."[1] The money ran out in six months.

She then became a partner in a photojournalism studio with Barbara Clay. The two of them were highly successful, doing portraits, fashion assignments for London *Vogue, Harpers,* and *Tatler,* and advertising work at a time when, in England, the camera was fairly new in that field. Marty also arranged with *Town and Country* to write a London art column and to contribute freelance articles on England and the continent. For the next six years she lived abroad.

A year after Marty arrived in London, the death of her grandma Christy brought Marty a modest inheritance that lasted awhile.

Marty had opted to leave America for England partly because the Depression didn't seem to be hitting as hard there, partly because she craved greater freedom and excitement. That she was able to establish a new business and earn a very comfortable living despite the world economic situation says something about Marty's business flair, her drive, her natural selling talents, and her determination. Her life as a young divorcée in London was exciting, glamorous, filled with travel. She loved England and actually started proceedings to become a British citizen.

Marty fit right into the London social scene. She was bright, witty, and beautiful. One of London's attractions for Marty was its sophisticated laissez-faire attitude toward homosexuals. By this time Marty knew her sexual orientation as a lesbian. Many of the people whose talents she most admired—artists and writers—were gay and lesbian people. Popular and attractive, Marty was quickly welcomed into these fascinating, fast-moving circles, but she also continued and enlarged her straight friendships. All her friends, gay and straight, tended to be fashionable, intellectual, the stylesetters of the day. The gay and straight circles worked and partied together. Marty moved easily in and among the groups, as she did throughout her life. The general public would never have singled out this charming, cultured woman as a lesbian. She didn't fit the stereotype—whatever that was.

One of the circles that Marty associated with was the Bloomsbury Group, an influential upper-class literary and intellectual group that lasted from 1904 until about 1939.

> They were a group of rational and liberal individuals with an arduous work ethic and an aristocratic ideal. Each labored in his separate vineyard. They had a passion for art; they liked the fullness of life; they knew how to relax when their day's work was done. They wrote. They painted. They decorated. They achieved a large fame. With success came a certain amount of power. One of them became a peer. Another was knighted. Others refused honors. They were damnably critical. They criticized the Establishment but, unlike most critics, they worked to improve it. They hated war. Some refused to fight; others believed they had to see the 1914–18 conflict through to the end. All actively worked for peace. People who knew them were irritated, and some found them rude and abrasive. . . . They were the least boring people in the world, for they had intelligence and charm, though no doubt a certain high and gentry view of civilization.[2]

Here Marty knew Vita Sackville-West, Virginia Woolf, and others. Alex Strachey, a noted psychotherapist and the sister of Lytton Strachey, a renowned author, was one of Marty's friends, as was Elizabeth Cunard of the famous British shipping firm.

Marty regularly visited Paris, where she was delighted to find the local cafés filled with people at 7:00 A.M., drinking their morning coffee with brandy. In Paris she became friends with Janet Flanner, the *New Yorker's* Paris correspondent, and Natalie Barney, an American-born heiress, writer, and early feminist. There she also frequented Gertrude Stein's salon. Summers found Marty vacationing on the French Riviera with major literary, art, and intellectual figures of the day.

At some point she met a flamboyant, eccentric lesbian named Marion "Joe" Carstairs, possibly in doing a story on her. Joe was a debonair, not very sexy-looking, transvestite cross-dresser. She wore expensive, well-tailored, Savile Row men's clothes, shirts, and neckties. She had inherited a Standard Oil fortune, which she gleefully tapped for fast boats and cars, female lovers, and the purchase of a Caribbean island, Whale Cay in the Bahamas. In England, Joe raced motorboats built to her specifications and was famous as the "fastest woman on water."[3]

Marty and Joe became good friends. After Joe bought Whale Cay, Marty visited her there at least once during the London years with others of Joe's friends. When Marty got sober, and until Joe sold Whale Cay in 1975, Marty and others in her circle regularly used Whale Cay for much-needed rest and relaxation. Joe in her later years traveled to the mainland periodically, eventually living there, and would often visit Marty at her NCA office. She was very likely one of NCA's donors over the years.[4]

By the time Marty arrived in England, she had been drinking heavily for ten years without apparent problems. In fact, at first she drank less in London than she did during the prior two years in New York. She continued unknowingly to exhibit some important early signs of alcoholism, however, such as abnormal capacity and the need to drink to feel at ease socially, but she functioned responsibly and was having a wonderful time, protected by resilient youth and good health.

Then, without warning around 1932, the bottom dropped out of her world, and her drinking crossed the line into complete lack of control. Marty, the woman with the hollow leg, the one who never seemed to suffer any side effects, suddenly couldn't hold her liquor. Hangovers became monstrous, the morning drink an urgent necessity. Before long it took a pint of gin to ease the hangover pains. Later, she said normal nonalcoholics had no conception of the epic ferocity of an alcoholic's hangovers.

Marty had been a daily drinker for a long time before she learned about the "hair of the dog" to ease morning hangovers and withdrawal pains. She couldn't keep a morning drink down at first. She needed to throw up three drinks, one after the other, before her stomach settled and she could even begin to function. She'd prepare a bottle ahead of time to have ready by her bed for the morning, only to waken and find it gone. "And I didn't even remember drinking it!" So she began hiding the bottle from herself. "That was a hell of a note." Now, however, with mini-withdrawals occurring throughout the day and night, she began to drink steadily as long as she was conscious to stave off the shakes. She found that her photography darkroom was a great place to hang out and drink—and hide her bottles.

Blanks were more frequent. Marty seldom knew how she'd come home. Her first blackout actually occurred while sober. It followed a mild concussion when she tripped and fell headfirst down half a flight of stairs, hitting her head on the newel post. But the amnesiac episodes continued and became more frequent due to escalating drinking.

Marty once said that the precipitating factor in this abrupt downturn of her disease was the suicide of a dear friend. She began deliberately to drink heavily to ease her guilt and sorrow, feeling that somehow she should have been able to avert such a tragedy by giving her friend more time and understanding. When she recovered from alcoholism, she would learn that the disease of alcoholism progresses independently of any specific stress point and sooner or later would have caused her problems, regardless.

When alcohol turned against her, Marty worried but never talked to anyone about it. She was ashamed that she often couldn't apply her lipstick properly because her hand shook so much. In sobriety, Marty complained that "men can go to the barber when they're too shaky to shave themselves. Women can't go to a cosmetician to put on lipstick." Instead, as most women alcoholics do, she instinctively slipped underground, keeping her uncontrolled drinking deeply hidden as long as she could. After all, everyone she associated with drank, many of them to excess. Drinking was almost an occupational hazard in her general field of advertising and public relations. She used the common excuses that she had to drink in her business, that she did her best work over cocktails, that her business demanded she entertain.

"Later experience taught me that it may be essential to serve others drinks but that does not mean you have to drink with them, and it certainly doesn't mean you have to get drunk."

Yet her friends seemed to be more or less holding their own while she rapidly slid downhill past them. Her personality began to change. She was definitely a nuisance. Marty in her cups was the talkative type. She'd talk all night to anyone who would listen, never wanted to go home, was always eager to go on for just one more. She began to hear comments like, "Why can't you drink the way you used to?" "You're drinking too much!" "You're no fun anymore." "You're turning into a lush!" The awful term *drunk* was mentioned.

To Marty, as to most people, *drunk* meant "skid row bum from the other side of the tracks." It was a label of opprobrium, of hopelessness. Marty had never given much thought to skid row bums, but when she was called a drunk, that was a fighting word. In the first place, she'd never lived on skid row. In the second place, she wasn't a man, and women weren't drunkards. Marty literally could not identify with this picture. So she moved from one group to another as they objected to her drinking—public relations groups, journalists, photographers, artists, writers, society friends, drinking friends, gay and lesbian friends. In one year she went through some thirty groups "like a dose of salts." She loathed herself, her looks, her actions.

> I was in complete darkness as to what it was that was happening to me, and I spent five years trying to find out. Alcoholism is a progressive illness. During those five years I rode a chute-the-chute to hell. It was no fun. . . . And I suffered all the torments, although all this was while I was seeking help. I was desperately trying to find out what was wrong—what, if anything, could be done. No one could tell me. And no one could help me. I thought I had a severe mental illness, but I couldn't get such a diagnosis, and I couldn't get any name put to it. I merely knew that I was behaving as if I were insane and that I was going headlong toward death and destruction. This was in the 1930s. The stigma on alcoholism then, and even now, lay as heavy, and as destructively, as it had on tuberculosis fifteen or twenty years before.

Marty was no stranger to illness, yet she said, "I know of no more painful disease [alcoholism], and I have had a few others besides TB and

alcoholism." Indeed, her cumulative medical history became awesome.
Besides TB and alcoholism, it eventually included nine grave surgeries, five
of which were for cancer. There were emphysema, recurrent bouts of severe
clinical depression, a heart condition, and a variety of other serious ailments. After she sobered up, Marty spelled out why "alcoholism is the most
devastating disease loose on the globe."

Alcoholism hurts physically. We never feel well.
Alcoholism hurts mentally. Guilt and remorse consume us.
Alcoholism hurts emotionally. We lose friends, become isolated.
Alcoholism hurts socially. We are anathema to others, neither accept-
able nor wanted.
Alcoholism hurts financially. It is the world's most expensive disease.
Alcoholism hurts careers (including housewives). We cannot function.

But for now, Marty was terrified. Up to this point, she had always felt
in control of herself and of her destiny. Self-will and self-control were her
middle names.

"I had always gotten what I went out for. I had achieved quite a bit in
my life. I had never suffered from any lack of willpower or lack of character, either."

She believed she controlled alcohol, not the other way around. She
thought she must be going insane. Why had her father been able to stop
drinking on his own by applying willpower, and she couldn't? She knew her
will was at least as strong as his.

Baffled and desperate, Marty sought help from doctors. In those days,
people like Marty often consulted internists and chiropractors, but psychiatrists were preferred because alcoholics believed themselves to be insane.
Marty's psychiatrists assured her she wasn't crazy, yet they had no more
idea of what was her basic problem than did the general public. The best
they could come up with was an anxiety neurosis or a character disorder.
They tentatively proposed a mental hospital, leaving Marty aghast at the
prospect. Years later, a number of these British psychiatrists and subsequent
American ones ruefully told Marty, "We just didn't know what to do with
people like you."

Several doctors suggested she take a vacation—she was overworked
and burning her candle at both ends. They told her to get more sleep, eat

better, reduce the emotional stress in her life, get more exercise, slow down, cut down on her drinking for a while. Instead, she developed "rubber legs." That mortified her more than anything else. Many evenings she passed out[5] just as the fun was beginning and ended up under the coats. This was the woman who used to drive everyone home after the party.

Marty did follow one bit of advice from her doctors and took two "rest cures" in the country, where she found she could ease off the alcohol for very short periods (though not stop entirely). The difficulty was that she took herself wherever she went. Moreover, she was convinced her drinking was the result, not the root, of her problems. Surely psychiatrists should be able to help her untangle her complex emotions. Then she would be able to drink like she used to. She didn't know that was impossible. There simply wasn't any concept in those days of alcoholism as a primary disease existing independently of any other underlying disease. Nor was there the much later understanding that alcoholism could and often did coexist with one or more additional primary illnesses such as cancer, cardiovascular disease, or clinical depression.

Finally, Marty ran out of people in London who would tolerate her. Then the "geographics"[6] started. Concluding that the city and the hustle and bustle of the photography business were the problem, she sold her share of the studio and changed careers and location. Nearly a decade later she would observe that to the active alcoholic, "Work is the curse of the drinking classes."[7]

Two friends who owned an inn near Oxford, in the Cotswolds west of London, asked her to manage the property while they took an extended three-month vacation. With renewed hope for her future, Marty moved to the village of Broadway. It lay in the middle of the Avon hunting country. Most of the inn's guests were there for the hunting season. She anticipated a much-needed rest—just what the doctors had ordered. Since she was starting over, she decided to stop drinking for Lent.

A couple of days after arriving in Broadway, Marty became ill. She was nauseated, dizzy, with cold shakes and hot sweats, hardly able to get out of bed, yet she couldn't sleep. Alarmed, she sought out the local doctor. He was baffled by her symptoms. Since Marty had recently associated with world travelers, he concluded she must have picked up some strange tropical disease, and he prescribed a harmless medication. The doctor was elated when she miraculously recovered in three days. He thought he was a genius. He'd cured a tropical disease he couldn't even identify!

The truth, of course, was that Marty was detoxing from severe, prolonged drinking. However, this was the first time she had ever stopped cold. She had no idea about extreme withdrawal symptoms, nor did the doctor, who saw before him only a wellborn lady. And ladies didn't have problems with alcohol.

The shakes continued for a while. One day Marty had to cash a check at the bank. Her signature was nearly unrecognizable. The bank officer, suspicious of a stranger, thought she was a forger and asked her to repeat the signature in his presence. Marty tried fifteen times to write her name legibly, without success. Finally she excused herself, went out to the pub and slugged down several martinis, returned to the bank, and signed her name perfectly.

"That was the last time I tried to stop drinking on my own!"

Following this ill-omened beginning, Marty threw herself into managing the inn. Broadway was a beautiful picture-postcard town, the main street still sixteenth to seventeenth century. The mellow, honey-colored, old stone buildings had long lured tourists. Antiques were big business. Equally well known was the high-quality modern furniture produced in Broadway. Perhaps Marty counted on a renewal of her formerly strong interests in art and interior decoration to help her regain a degree of sanity and the prior lack of consequences from her drinking.

The sixteenth-century inn belonging to Marty's friends was a handsome old Jacobean building, white stucco with black trim, complete with English butler. Located at the foot of the main street, it had been modernized and added onto in the rear. A swimming pool had been installed out back. The inn had no alcohol license, but guests brought their own liquor and kept their bottles on the sideboard. In addition, there were two pubs in the immediate vicinity. One was across the street, the other through the orchard behind the inn.

Three weeks into Lent, Marty decided it would be all right to have some beer. She soon progressed to "old beer" (80 proof and "*very* smooth"), followed by gin from one of the pubs. Marty knew she couldn't trust herself to keep a bottle in her room, so daily she sent the butler to the pub across the street to pick up a trayful of individual pink gin drinks for her. He then stashed them in little hidden cubbyholes all over the inn. As part of her management job, Marty "inspected" the cupboards regularly every day and drank up their contents. Later the butler came around and cleared the empty glasses. In no time, Marty was also stealing from the guests' bottles on the sideboard. When they noticed their personal supplies were diminishing, she blamed it on "that new kitchen boy" and promptly fired him.

All the good chefs tended to be drunks, Marty learned. That was fine with her. She liked nothing better than sitting down every day to plan the menus with her head chef and a big bottle of sherry—until the day he began chasing the kitchen help with a carving knife. Then she fired him, too.

Marty discovered the attic was crammed to the rafters with a treasure trove of wine made by her friends, the proprietors. They had experimented with raspberry, dandelion, and elderberry wine. "Ghastly stuff!" Marty reported. But without a qualm she began drinking up this supply, carefully shifting the empties to the bottom to conceal the loss. Before long, Marty was incapable of doing anything at all, much less managing the inn. Her friends returned from their vacation and were dismayed by the shambles. They fired her on the spot.

Years after she got sober, Marty startled one of the inn's owners when she ran across him in New York. "I thought you'd be dead by now," he said. "Were you the one who drank all our terrible wine in the attic?"

"Yes," Marty admitted.

"Well," he laughed, "you deserved to die!"

After this ignominious failure, Marty returned to London. She pulled herself together enough to land a job managing publicity for the 1935 Covent Garden Jubilee opera season. After that, matters went from bad to worse. At last Marty "met all the people I wanted to meet; I saw all the people I wanted to see; I did all the things I wanted to do." That was what the observer would see on the surface.

"Inside," she said, "I was increasingly miserable. Headstrong and willful, I rushed from pleasure to pleasure, and found the returns diminishing to the vanishing point."

In the Fury of the Storm

1935–36

BY NOW MARTY WAS CONSUMING no less than a quart of Scotch a day, often up to two, and drinking anything she could lay her hands on. Twice she tried to commit suicide, and both times was nearly successful. First she imitated a friend who had died from an overdose of sleeping pills. Marty deliberately took the same kind and number of pills but survived intact. Her high drug tolerance may have saved her life.

The second time she was with many Americans at a Fourth of July weekend party in an English country house. She developed the blind staggers and had to be maneuvered upstairs to sleep it off while the rest of the guests were enjoying themselves on the terrace. Probably they were relieved at her absence. Drunk and in a blackout, Marty jumped or fell—she never knew which—out a second-story window onto the stone terrace below, landing on her face and one hip.[1] She fractured both hinges of her jaw, lost her lower teeth, broke a leg and hip, and bit off both sides of her tongue. For the rest of her life the hip would bother her, and she would need frequent dental attention. Marty's hosts evidently feared she would sue and told her in no uncertain terms she could never get away with it because everyone knew she was a drunk.

From the small village hospital, Marty was transported by ambulance to London. To endure the ride, she was pumped full of heroin as a painkiller. She loved it. "Don't try it," she told an AA audience in 1980. "It's beautiful!" Had Marty been born a couple of generations later than she was, she might easily have become addicted to street drugs as well as alcohol. Instead, like most alcoholics in her generation, she was addicted to two legal drugs for adults, alcohol and nicotine.

Marty spent the next six months in London's Royal National Orthopaedic Hospital recovering from her jump, "held together by plaster, wire, and liquor." Her hip was not set properly, so when she returned to the United States, the surgery eventually had to be repeated. By then the bones were too damaged to be completely repaired. She underwent a long process of wearing weights on both legs to straighten them out. The hip caused her increasing pain as she grew older, but Marty never let anything like physical discomfort slow her down.

A Scottish nurse, Eileen (nicknamed Sammy), took care of her in the hospital. Marty was on a liquid diet because her jaw was wired. Friends told the doctor that she needed liquor, so they were allowed to bring it in and store it in a small room. Marty was supposed to have two ounces of whiskey twice a day, once in the morning and once in the evening. Marty, however, was nothing if not charmingly persuasive. The student nurses decided what she needed was a chaser. They brought it in a porcelain pitcher, which contained whiskey, not water. As usual, Marty got what she wanted when she wanted it. Actually, a certain amount of alcohol was useful as a painkiller since the hospital had few drugs that could control her pain.

Marty was discharged between Christmas and New Year's, wearing a brace on her fractured hip. Her friends celebrated with a party where Marty got falling-down drunk. Afterward, she couldn't get out of bed. At that point Sammy, the orthopedic nurse, came to her and said, "I'm going home to Scotland. Come with me and I'll take care of you and see that you learn how to walk again. But you can't drink." So Marty went up to the tiny, isolated, northeastern Scottish village of Inver by Fearn, on the southern shore of Dornoch Firth, to continue her rehabilitation.

Sammy and her boyfriend lived out in the country. There was no toilet, only a bucket. It was a seven-mile bicycle ride into the village, where there was a bathtub. Marty biked the distance once a week and paid a small amount at the inn to soak in a tub.

Sammy had Marty knitting socks until she could move around better. Once Marty could ambulate, she helped earn her keep by getting up at 3:00 A.M. to aid Sammy's boyfriend in setting traps for wild rabbits—chief meat of the big-city poor. Marty thought the boyfriend's name was appropriate—

Skinner. He assuaged her conscience by assuring her that the rabbits were
vermin. Marty would ride home with the rabbits strung on the handlebars
of her bike. All the exercise helped restore her to better physical condition.
And the three young people ate well—rabbits, turnips, turnip tops, and produce from the garden in season.

While in Scotland, Marty persuaded Sammy to marry her sweetheart,
the rabbit hunter. The three of them pledged friendship forever. In gratitude
and affection for Marty, the newlyweds built a tiny extra room on their little
house and called it "Marty's room," telling her it would always be hers
whenever she wanted to stay there.

Marty wasn't supposed to drink during her rehabilitation. However,
the Scots had drinking parties, chasing Scotch with beer. She got to know
the locals, even learning a little Gaelic to talk with the older folks who
spoke nothing else. As Marty's health improved, she felt she not only had to
hold her own with the drinkers, but teach them a thing or two about real
drinking. She also taught them American country dances and cowboy yells,
learned from her days on the New Mexico ranch. By the time she returned
to London, she was spinning faster than ever before on the merry-go-round
of compulsive, uncontrolled drinking.

When Marty was vacationing on the Riviera in earlier years, a man
named William Seabrook was part of her crowd. She used to drink with
him. Willie was an alcoholic and a popular writer of sensational stories in
the 1920s and 1930s. The term *alcoholic* was still unknown by the general
public, but Marty recognized Willie as someone like her. Toward the end of
her time in England, Marty heard that Willie had overcome his problem
and written a book about it. The name of the book was *Asylum.*[2] In it he
described how he had found a treatment program that taught him how to
drink normally. In the public library of little Inver by Fearn, Marty found
Willie's book. Avidly, she read it over and over. She learned he had gone to
the Westchester Division of New York Hospital. *Asylum* fueled her determination to return to New York, find Willie, and follow his path to recovery.

"Maybe," she thought, "I've been in exile too many years. I need to get
home, back to where drinking wasn't a problem."

Several months passed before Marty was sufficiently restored physically
to leave her young friends in Scotland and go back to London. She had no
money and no job, and she'd resumed excessive drinking. How would she

ever manage passage to the United States to find Willie Seabrook? During the day, she rented a deck chair in a secluded section of Hyde Park for a shilling. There she sat huddled for hours, day after day, staring into space and sipping from a bottle. "I felt lost, homeless, friendless." Her former photography partner, Barbara, knew her hangout at the park and would come over and try to persuade her to stop. Finally, Marty was able to borrow enough money for passage on the *Queen Mary,* departing in early December 1936. After six years abroad, Marty would be home for Christmas with her family.

In retrospect, Marty's decision to leave England when she did was fortuitous. Hitler had come to power in Germany. Fifteen months after Marty sailed for home, he annexed Austria, and a year later Czechoslovakia and Poland. World War II had begun. Marty could easily have been stuck in London for the duration. With all her journalism contacts, she may have had some sense of impending catastrophe but probably was too besotted much of the time to be paying attention.

The *Queen Mary,* on which Marty sailed, was the national pride of England—a grand luxury liner barely half a year old. Already the ship was the height of the social scene at sea. The designers had utilized exotic and rare woods in the modern art deco style. Passengers both rich and famous booked passage, knowing the amenities aboard were as plentiful as one's pocketbook could afford. Excellent service was available to all, but many extras were offered to seasoned and sophisticated travelers.

First, however, there were all Marty's good-bye parties in London. She was determined to have one last fling, then sober up on the way home so she would be in condition to meet her family. They had no idea what had been happening to her with regard to alcohol. As far as they were concerned, Marty was the Manns' great success story—an accomplished professional career woman who moved in the highest social, art, and literary circles—returning in triumph to her native land.

Just in time for the night sailing of the *Queen Mary,* two young friends poured Marty on board the ship in Southampton along with a dog she'd acquired. Marty's intent to detox during the voyage never came to pass. Aboard ship, she decided to have just one beer to celebrate. That did it. She drank solidly the whole six days of the Atlantic crossing. She didn't know then that for an advanced alcoholic, it was the first drink that got you drunk (because uncontrolled compulsion was triggered). She went into a blackout and had no recollection of the trip except for hearing the announcement of King Edward V's abdication so he could marry Wallis Simpson. In fact, she squeezed in an extra day of drinking because the *Queen Mary* was delayed seven hours by trouble in the condensers. The elegant decor and service were wasted on Marty. The ship could have been weathering hurricane seas for all she knew.

As the *Queen Mary* sailed into New York harbor on December 15, 1936, Marty was tossing down drinks in the bar. An expatriate for six years, she'd longed for this homecoming so she could get well. But, locked in her relentless addiction, she never went on deck to view the Statue of Liberty or the city skyline.

The majestic liner slowly docked. All the passengers debarked, happy to be back on land, joyfully greeting families and friends who had come to welcome them. Marty's mother, sister Chris, and Chris's roommate eagerly scanned each person coming down the gangplank. The noisy crowd moved off inside the long shed to go through customs. Soon the three women were the only ones left on the pier. They waited and waited. Still no Marty. The temperature was in the low forties. The wind off the water chilled them. Impatient and anxious, they pulled their coat collars higher.

Then, slowly down the gangplank came a couple of stewards carrying a stretcher bearing the last passenger off the ship, one too drunk too walk.

Marty had come home. Merry Christmas.

The Lion Roars

1937–38

HENCEFORTH, NEW YORK CITY AND ITS SURROUNDINGS would be
Marty's home. She loved escaping to the desert and the countryside, especially the beach, but she was an urbanite through and through. Her energies
resonated with the dynamic rhythms of a big city. She relished the stimulus
of crowds and creative ideas. For the moment, however, she was in no
shape to respond to much of anything.

Marty's mother immediately hospitalized her. Lill stayed in Chris's New
York apartment a few days until Marty was discharged from the hospital.
Then she went back to Chicago. One can imagine Lill's shock in learning
that this gifted eldest child, so looked up to by the rest of the family, was
just like the father who had brought so much grief to his wife and children.
Marty may have tried to defuse her mother's anxiety and shame by invok-
ing mental illness as the real problem, but that couldn't have been comfort-
ing, either.

Chris was separated from Johnny Johnstone by this time and sharing a
two-room apartment with a girlfriend who was recently divorced and had a
small son. Neither of these young women had any money to speak of. The
Depression ground on. Jobs were very hard to find. The small apartment
was already crowded, but Marty and her dog were invited to bunk with
them until she found a job and could move to her own place. Little did
Chris know that in Marty she had a tiger by the tail. The year 1937 would
be Marty's year of sheer hell—what she called her "valley of the shadow."

Her brother, Bill, was having his own troubles. Before entering the
University of Chicago, Bill stayed briefly with his father, who was living in a

seedy hotel that smelled of urine. "It was terrible," Bill recalled. In 1937, he was in his second year at the University of Chicago. One noon at the beginning of the third quarter, he went into the dining hall for lunch as usual and presented his meal ticket. "I'm sorry," said the clerk, "your ticket is no longer valid. Your tuition hasn't been paid." Bill was in a state of shock. Dazed, he returned to his room, where his roommate found him in tears.

"My God, what happened?" the roommate asked.

"I've been kicked out of school. Dad didn't pay my tuition," Bill replied.

Bill's roommate was a wealthy young man. "Come on, we'll see about that."

The two of them got into the friend's car and they tore over to the bursar's office. The friend jumped out at the corner and told Bill, "Go park the car." And he hurried into the building.

Inside, he confronted the bursar, "How much do you need for Bill Mann's expenses?" The bursar told him, and Bill's roommate wrote out a check on the spot.

When Bill called his father to find out why the tuition hadn't come through, Will just shrugged and said, "That's the way it is. I had some bad luck investing in a silver mine and a pea plantation."

Marty, who in the past had been able to help the family out financially, no longer had any resources. Bill's grades weren't good enough for a scholarship, so he had to drop out. One summer he was an office boy for a brokerage firm that had handled many of his father's investments. His mother was nearby at a hotel, where she lived after separating from Will. Lill's son was now her only child still in the Chicago vicinity. For two summers, Bill worked in a Montana lumber mill. The physical labor was very hard, but the money was good. Blessed with the Mann energies, charm, and determination, Bill later spent most of his career as a successful businessman in Toronto, Canada.

Once out of the hospital and with her mother gone, Marty immediately returned to uncontrolled drinking. Her many friends in New York were as ignorant as Marty's family about her plunge into unmanageable drinking, so in the beginning they were delighted to welcome her back with free drinks, meals, and parties. Marty even took a train trip to Washington, D.C., to visit her youngest sister, Betty. Unfortunately, she got drunk on the way down and again on the way back. Betty was not pleased.

One New York friend was Grace Bangs, who would reconnect with Marty in an important way later. Grace was the head of the *New York Herald Tribune* Club Women's Service Bureau. She tried to help Marty find a job, but Marty couldn't stay sober.

Through a strange coincidence two weeks after arriving in New York, Marty ran into John Blakemore, her ex-husband. John was engaged to his third wife,[1] but he became Marty's drinking buddy over the next year. By that time, Marty could keep up with the man known as "the best drinker in New Orleans," an accolade not lightly bestowed.

After a good deal of searching, Marty was able to locate Willie Seabrook, the author of *Asylum*. He happened to be sober at the time. His recommmendation was that she seek treatment at a private psychiatric hospital where she could be a scholarship (charity) patient. He advised her that for tax reasons, hospitals were required to accept a certain number of charity cases. Seabrook's advice was sound. Unfortunately, he himself eventually relapsed into uncontrolled alcoholism and committed suicide—a victim of the prevailing belief that an alcoholic could change into a normal drinker.

Strangely, Marty never really liked the taste of liquor, just the effect. She recalled one noon at lunch in a hotel where three or four women at the next table were enjoying big, gooey desserts, which she normally loved. This time simply looking at the desserts made her sick. All she wanted was a drink. And another. And another.

> Oh, I made every kind of effort not to tip over, not to go too far, to take just enough to keep me feeling just the way everybody else feels all the time. God how I hated those people! I'd get on a bus, and I'd see all those healthy, comparatively happy faces, and I'd curse every one of them, because I had painfully arrived at where I could get on a bus [only] by virtue of a pint or two of liquor.

Every once in a while, Marty became so ill from drinking that she had to ease off for a few days. Even so, she "never drew a sober breath" that whole year. She used to say, "I've done my fieldwork in alcoholism both in the U.S. and abroad. I've been soused in the best salons and the worst saloons of Europe and America."

Desperate now for answers, she made the rounds of New York psychiatrists, but like the British physicians, they could only say there was nothing they could do for her. Marty saw more than half a dozen psychiatrists during the year after she returned from England. The medical approach of the day was that uncontrolled drinking was a symptom of an underlying psychiatric disorder. Correct the disorder, and the drinking would return to normal. For alcoholics, however, "return to normal" never meant "less," but instead that they could drink the same quantities again without suffering negative consequences or side effects.

None of the doctors Marty consulted, however, could identify an underlying psychiatric disorder in her, so they were baffled about why she drank so much. No one would take her as a patient because each told her honestly he didn't know what to do with "people like you." Marty hated the term *people like you*, partly because it felt pejorative, partly because it did not identify what was wrong with her and thus offer a way to address her affliction.

While Marty was abroad, the United States had passed the Social Security Act. In early 1937, Marty applied for a Social Security number, giving her current employer as Universal Travel Association, Inc. on Fifth Avenue, New York.[2] Because drinking interfered, she wasn't able to keep any job for long. Marty found another position selling photo murals on a commission basis. She looked terrible and always reeked of alcohol. Thirty-three years old, she was fat, bloated, and appeared to be in her fifties.

Work finally was out of the question. Marty wheedled some money from her father, then promptly went on a drunk. Dead broke except for an occasional quarter she sponged from Chris, Marty began bumming drinks in "cheap, tawdry Second Avenue dives. I had no money but that didn't matter. By then I had learned that a woman needs to finance only that first drink. The rest I cadged like an expert."

The bars usually had three shelves containing three grades of liquor, the best grades on the top shelf, the worst on the bottom. In Marty's affluent days, she naturally chose a brand from only the top shelf. Now destitute, she could scarcely afford the cheapest rotgut. At one bar down on the Bowery, the workingmen who patronized it would occasionally buy a round for Marty. And the sixty-year-old illiterate, drunken Irish bartender would stand treat when Marty was broke.

"One night he invited me to accompany him to a drinking party. An Irish bartender date a debutante? I told him I wouldn't fit in.

"'Shure, ye'll fit. Anyone can look at ye an see a drinkin' woman.'

"That hurt."

Marty broke five pairs of glasses from falling down areaways. Ten-day blackouts were common. She would find unknown names in her address book. People she had no recollection of were greeting her on the street. Worse, she would come out of blackouts in strange places with strange people.

What was I saying? . . . From far away, as if in a delirium, I heard my own voice—calling someone "Dorothy," talking of dress shops, of jobs . . . the words came clearer . . . this sound of my own voice frightened me as it came closer . . . and suddenly, there I was, talking of I knew not what, to someone I'd never seen before this very moment. Abruptly I stopped speaking. Where was I?[3]

By the fall of 1937, Marty had become a classic low-bottom drunk.[4] Chris kept threatening to throw her out. Marty was shamed to overhear her on the phone one day describing how disgusting Marty was.

"I don't understand how she can be like that! She's such a wonderful person, she's so intelligent, she's done all these things, been all these places—how can she *do* this?"

Before long Chris did demand that she leave. Marty then stayed with one friend after another, but no one would put up with her for long. All her relationships were superficial. Unable to work, she lay on her bed for days on end, suffering through the d.t.'s (delirium tremens) and the sweats. She "absolutely could not get up even to phone for liquor or food." She couldn't sleep, talk, or eat. When she looked in the mirror, she saw a face she didn't recognize—bloated, the eyes red.

"It was plain unadulterated hell. I used to wonder where the real me had got to. I hated what I was becoming and I didn't know what to do about it."

Scariest of all, Marty felt as if she were in a glass box, where she could see and be seen, but there was no communication with the outside world. It was an incredibly lonely, isolated sensation—the "most ghastly feeling" imaginable. "A slum of thinking, feeling, and fears." Marty knew she must be incurably insane. In despair, she finally decided she was either going to find out what was wrong with her or make a third suicide attempt that this time would succeed.

In the end, Marty was hospitalized for a week at Doctors Hospital in New York City, presumably for detoxing. The construction of this hospital had been financed largely by 180 of New York's richest families. Its elegant furnishings matched those of a Park Avenue hotel. Who paid the bill for Marty is unknown. Maybe she was a charity patient.

Following discharge, Marty returned to drinking, staying a few days with a friend who soon threw her out. Convinced that New York contributed to her drinking, Marty elected in desperation to take a geographic. She contacted old friends in Stockbridge, Massachusetts, Barclay and Janie Hudson. They had a young baby and not much money themselves, but Janie immediately drove down to New York and took Marty back to Stockbridge with her. It was a temporary solution for Marty at best, as the Hudsons were probably moving before long to take jobs out of state.

Marty tried very hard to stay sober at the Hudsons'. After a short time, however, she began drinking on the sly, hiding bottles behind books in the bookcases and under the bushes outside. Barclay, thoroughly exasperated, told her she was using her willpower *to* drink and suggested she use it to *not* drink. Marty would later describe alcoholics as "people who have lots of will power but use it in the wrong way for the wrong purpose."

During November of 1937, she considered her now-limited options. As she wrote in a heartbreakingly dignified but surprisingly lucid letter to her old friend Leopold Mannes, she had five choices. She'd investigated two private sanitaria where she could pursue admission as a charity patient. One, Austen Riggs Psychiatric hospital, was in Stockbridge. The other three choices were to enter the state insane asylum, attend New York's Payne Whitney Outpatient Clinic (for which she had no money, and the city itself was a major relapse risk for her, anyway), or continue to stay with her friends, the Hudsons, whose future plans did not include her.[5]

Leopold, who was in Europe, responded immediately with strong support and encouragement. He opposed the state insane asylum but offered to help out otherwise as far as he was able. Leopold's negative view of an insane asylum undoubtedly reassured Marty. She was terrified at the prospect of a state institution, for she was certain such a facility was truly a "snake pit" where she would be merely warehoused, not healed, and from which she would never emerge.

It so happened that living across the street in Stockbridge was a wealthy heiress to the Ryan steel fortune who was also an alcoholic, even worse than Marty. This woman sat in her house and drank all day, never getting out of her chair until she could no longer lift her glass. She and Marty became good friends, and she was impressed by Marty's valiant attempts to stay sober. Marty talked at some length with her neighbor about her predicament and fears. Many of this woman's large, extended family of alcoholics had been patients of Robert Foster Kennedy, M.D., in New York City.

One day the woman said, "Please don't be offended, but I would like to give you a Christmas present of a consultation with Foster Kennedy. He's had a lot of experience with the drinkers in my family and may be able to help you even though he's not a psychiatrist. Would you be willing to see him?" Marty gladly and gratefully accepted.

Kennedy was head of Bellevue Hospital's neurology department in New York City. He was also chair of the department of neuropsychiatry at Cornell University Medical School, known as one of the greatest medical schools in the world. At the time, neurologists were the "court of last resort" for alcoholics, and Kennedy was a leading diagnostician. However, he had found only one solution thus far—to lock up the alcoholic away from all access to liquor. It was a frustrating puzzle. After Kennedy became acquainted with AA through Marty, Bill Wilson, and other alcoholics, he had no problem accepting that alcoholism was a disease.

Kennedy, born in Ireland, was a major figure in New York society, a bon vivant on cordial terms with actors, writers, musicians, and politicians—thus a person after Marty's own heart. Indeed, Kennedy and Marty may already have been acquainted because of many mutual friends. "His aspiring young medical friends mingled at his dinner parties with many celebrities. Not uncommonly, following an evening out, the professor, wearing an opera cloak and Edwardian monocle and accompanied by one or more of his medical guests, would make a reappearance at the hospital to answer an emergency call. . . . Kennedy was also a mountaineer and tennis player."[6]

Marty's pre-Christmas appointment with Kennedy was exactly one year after her return from London. He was the eighth doctor she consulted that year. She had managed to stay sober for six unprecedented weeks. For two hours this prominent, busy physician talked with Marty. In her opinion, the meeting did not end favorably.

"Why," he said, "the trouble with you, Marty, is you need a job. You're idle. You have too much time on your hands."

Marty was outraged. She was too drunk all the time to get a job and couldn't even stay sober long enough to be interviewed. Didn't he understand?

"Look, Ken, I think I'm crazy," Marty implored him.

"Why [come to me then]?" he responded skeptically.

"Well, you sent a friend of mine to one of those nut crackers." Apparently, Marty wanted him merely to give her a referral to still another psychiatrist.

Kennedy replied, "You come in and let me give you a physical."

So Marty did. She said she had the best workup there was, and there wasn't anything physically wrong, "not seriously, not deeply." Nor did Kennedy believe she had a psychiatric disorder. However, he was impressed by the depth and sincerity of her desire to find out what was the matter.

Finally he said, "Well, in my experience people like you have one chance in a hundred of recovering from uncontrolled drinking. You may be that one person. But only you can make the decision to become whole." However, his medical orientation was that of the times—he believed that Marty could learn control and become a normal drinker.

Lacking any better solution for the time being, Kennedy agreed to admit her to the neurological ward of Bellevue Hospital. Why the neuro ward? Because he was a neurologist. Also, he was head of this unit and ran it as a fiefdom somewhat independent of the hospital management, choosing his own staff, for example. Marty, however, had to wait a couple of weeks until January 2, 1938. Although the delay was difficult for her, Marty was immensely relieved on two accounts. She would avoid the dreaded alcohol ward, and she would be in a safe place. Maybe Kennedy was right. If she could stay off booze long enough, her body would recover and she could return to drinking.

Contrary to prevailing medical belief, Kennedy insisted that mental illness had a physiological basis in the brain. He was also an authority on what is now called post-traumatic stress disorder (PTSD), specifically the form caused by war zone trauma. A renowned and popular teacher, he was often seen to slip a few dollars into the hands of a penniless patient from the Lower East Side by way of prescription for his ills.

Bellevue Hospital, where Foster Kennedy practiced and taught for thirty-four years, was, and is, New York's huge city hospital, serving the city's polyglot, largely poor population. It was also a mecca for top physicians because of the great variety of disorders and patients. Marty was an ignorant snob. All she knew about the place was "that was where they took people they picked up off the streets. It didn't sound very attractive," but if Kennedy thought she ought to go, she would. And in the process she discovered that people in her circle did go to Bellevue. "I found that plenty of blue blood ran in the test tubes there."[7] And she would gratefully acknowledge that Bellevue provided very good medical care.

The neuro ward, located in the old nineteenth-century part of the hospital, contained thirty-four beds. On this ward it was impossible to procure liquor. Marty's clothes were impounded, and there wasn't any way she could leave—so she was protected from her uncontrollable compulsion to drink.

Several of the women had incurable alcoholic neuritis, the term then used for polyneuritis, an alcohol-induced affliction that damages peripheral nerves in the body's extremities—feet, legs, arms, and hands—resulting, for example, in impaired senses of touch and temperature or permanently impaired balance and an unnatural spraddled gait. Two of the alcoholic women in wheelchairs were actually paralyzed from the waist down. Their plight frightened Marty, but she remained convinced that her problem was insanity. The remaining patients were typical neurological cases, some recovering from surgery, others being treated for various conditions.

Marty really didn't belong on the ward. For a patient to stay more than a short while was very unusual. She wasn't receiving any treatment except for brief visits from Kennedy once or twice a week. He was a busy man and there wasn't much he could do for her. On the other hand, he sent her to his own dentist and treated her well. The nurses and social workers knew she didn't fit and tried periodically to have her discharged, but Kennedy's clout overruled their objections.

Every so often Kennedy would ask Marty, "How about it? Are you ready to go yet?" Each time Marty would panic and say no, and plead once again for psychiatric help. She knew if they released her, she would revert to alcohol at the slightest provocation.

One day Kennedy said to Marty, "You know, Marty, you've not yet made a decision not to drink anymore. When you make that decision, you will become whole." He had hit the nail on the head, but Marty wouldn't budge.

For about six months, Marty stayed at Bellevue. She was dry but in a kind of suspended animation. All that time she remained in her terrible glass box. During the day, she sat at a window looking outside and yearned to be able to communicate with the people she saw. All she could think to herself was, "You're lost. You're lost. You're in a vacuum. You're nothing."

Finally, Kennedy arranged with a young psychiatrist who was doing some pro bono research at Bellevue to interview Marty and see what he thought. The researcher talked with her several times and concluded that she needed long-term inpatient care. Marty could have become his private patient, but his fee was more than she could pay. After he reported his rec-ommendation to Kennedy, Kennedy inquired around for a treatment facility that would accept a charity patient. (The good private institutions like Austen Riggs in Stockbridge generally charged $200 to $300 a week—$2,400 to $3,600 in year 2000 dollars.) Blythewood, an exclusive private psychiatric treatment center in Greenwich, Connecticut, had a few inebriate patients and seemed a possibility.

Harry Tiebout, M.D., a psychiatrist, was Blythewood's medical direc-tor. He visited Bellevue once a week to interview prospective Blythewood patients. Two or three times he consulted with Marty, then advised, "You know, people like you can't drink at all."

Marty's immediate reaction was, "Look, I don't *like* people who don't drink!"

Tiebout, nonetheless, was as impressed as Kennedy had been by Marty's sincerity and commitment to getting well. He accepted Marty as a pro bono patient, then checked with Blythewood's owner, Anna C. Wiley. She was an old lady with a big heart and agreed to admit Marty as a charity case.

Marty didn't know it, but her life was about to change forever. So was Tiebout's.

Part
TWO

"God does not call the qualified; God qualifies the called."

—REVEREND ROGER BARKLEY
Congregational Church of Northridge, California

Rebirth

1938–39

MARTY ARRIVED AT BLYTHEWOOD the end of June 1938. Thanks to the months in Bellevue, she walked in sober, under her own steam. Her entire worldly wealth was in one suitcase containing secondhand clothes. She had nothing left—no money, no job, no home, no prospects, no family to support her.

"Worst of all," she reported, "I had lost my self-respect, confidence, courage, and humanity. They were far more important losses than material goods. Material possessions could be regained relatively easily, but emotional and spiritual losses take time and hard work."

Perhaps fortunately for Marty's remaining shreds of pride, charity patients were never identified at Blythewood. As she rode through the big iron gates of the sanitarium, the contrast with Bellevue was "like going from hell to heaven."

Blythewood Sanitarium, once a private estate belonging to the notorious Boss Tweed, had opened in 1905 under the direction of Mrs. Anna C. Wiley, a nurse who had proved exceptionally successful with mentally disturbed patients. Situated on fifty acres[1] of rustic, wooded land bisected by a meandering stream, Blythewood at its peak had eight main buildings, eight cottages, a chapel, a building for occupational therapy, and even a little golf course. Handsome naturalistic landscaping and shrubbery graced the grounds.

Four separate buildings housed the seventy-five patients. Marty checked in at the main house next to the gate. This gracious mansion with white columns was the estate's original house. Blythewood's administrative center,

it contained the doctors' offices as well as the "graduate house" for patients
soon to be discharged. Each patient saw his or her psychiatrist for one hour
a day, five times a week. Dr. Tiebout was Marty's psychiatrist. However, he
would be away on vacation for the month of July. Until he returned, her
treatment would be supervised by one of the other doctors.

After being admitted, patients were sent to the "lockup house." There
they would be held a few hours or days for observation. Farthest from the
road was what was called the "violent house." Many of the patients in this
building arrived by ambulance. The violent house contained a padded cell.
Marty could hear occasional screams when she was walking back from pot-
tery class. Patients in the violent house were often restrained, with their
hands tied. Closer to the road was the "middle house." It had two floors, a
finished attic, common rooms, and a small central dining room. Patients
like Marty might start in the middle house, but this was also the residence
to which the recovering violent-house patients moved. Patients remained
carefully monitored in the middle house despite the greater freedom. There
was a nurse at the end of each corridor.

The graduate house was the final residence prior to discharge.

Marty watched very ill psychiatric patients arrive strapped to gurneys
and be directed to the violent house. As they improved, they moved to the
middle house, then the graduate house, and finally home. She, on the other
hand, stayed on and on in the middle house for months. Marty was confirmed in her belief that she must have a terrible, permanent disorder. Sometimes she wished her behavior could have been violent so that she would be
able to progress like the others. Most of all, Marty envied the violent-house
people whose psychiatric disorders could be named. Marty would later
often reflect, "It's terrible to have a disease and not know what it is, and just
be called 'people like you.'"

In an age when most hospitals for the mentally ill still had bars on their
windows, Blythewood was an outstanding example of no bars, believing instead in maximum freedom, permissiveness of expression, and opportunities for intellectual and creative development. Integrated into the treatment
program were reading clubs, libraries, concerts, musicales, and art of every
kind. Many famous performing artists included Blythewood on their tours.

Blythewood was also one of the first institutions where a destitute alcoholic could come for treatment.[2] When Marty arrived at Blythewood, most

of the patients had mental disorders. This suited her just fine since she believed her mind desperately needed fixing: "What had gone wrong was in my head." In addition to the psychiatric patients, however, she found in residence four "people like you"—that is, uncontrolled drinkers—a man and three women. From the medical point of view, however, Marty and her fellow inebriates had a nameless psychiatric condition that even their doctors didn't seem to know how to treat.

Though the sanitarium had been established as primarily a psychiatric facility, its location in Greenwich was ironic regarding services to alcoholics. The town, a moneyed, educated, urbane bedroom community of New York City, had a reputation for widespread inebriety. As late as 1979, the problem of alcoholism was so pronounced that a national study, reported in the *Greenwich Time* of July 30, 1979, called Greenwich the alcohol capital of America, second only perhaps to the San Fernando Valley of California.

Marty was assigned to the middle house. The dining room was small, with tables for four or six, requiring two sittings of the patients. Marty was in the second sitting. She was directed to a table where three other women were already seated. One, Martha, had been in the New York papers a week or two before, while Marty was still in Bellevue. Martha was a wealthy matron openly in trouble with drinking. She had escaped from a private hospital in the city and vanished for days before being found. Her story created a major scandal in the New York press. Marty loved the account of this bizarre adventure. She and Martha became instant friends.

A second female alcoholic patient, also a manic-depressive, was at Blythewood only a few weeks and remained shadowy in Marty's memory. The third woman, Nona Wyman, was a somewhat mysterious, nondisclosing woman who had some kind of ailment she didn't identify at that time. After a while she, too, was discharged to her home nearby in Greenwich. While Marty and Martha were still patients at Blythewood, Nona would invite them occasionally for lunch and a swim at her house, but she continued to be rather remote. Marty never figured her out until much later, when Nona would play an important part in her life.

At this first meal, Marty fancied she wasn't nearly as sick as the new patients at her table. After all, she had more than seven months of sobriety, and they were barely past detox. She told the three women a little of her story. When they all got up to leave, she was stunned to hear one woman tell her, "You know, you talk as if you're dead."

"What do you mean?" Marty stammered.

"Well, you talk about yourself, but it's as if you're over there—someone else," chimed in another woman.

Marty realized how isolated she had become in her glass box. In time, she understood that she had chosen isolation because she "was scared to death someone would get close to me and discover what I was really like." It was Marty's introduction to reality, a condition she came to cherish as an outcome of her recovery.

Marty was not entirely without funds. Leopold Mannes was providing financial support to some extent. He was in Europe when Marty entered Blythewood. She had wired him in June where she would be going, and he had responded that though he didn't know Blythewood, he was happy for her. From that point forward, Leopold was a steady cheering section in Marty's progress toward recovery. On July 3, 1938, he wrote, "I'm back of you to the limit—at least to my limit—and that goes a *lot* further than October—or than any definite date in sight." In September, Marty received a letter saying, "Sending you the enclosed in haste to tide you over the next two months." He continued to write regularly with affectionate words of encouragement.[3]

Tiebout was the only staff psychiatrist who believed that inebriates had to give up drinking permanently, but he didn't know why. His colleagues had no interest in following his lead, even though he was the medical director. Instead, the rest of the staff subscribed to the prevailing doctrine that inebriates could return to "normal" drinking once their underlying mental and emotional hang-ups were resolved. These doctors concentrated on teaching their patients how to drink, not on eliminating alcohol. Two of the inebriates were patients of one such doctor—one of the women, and a man nicknamed Grennie.

This psychiatrist (who later became prominent in his field and also a good friend of Marty's) was thinking of establishing his own treatment center in the Adirondacks and transferring his patients there. He wanted Grennie and the woman to drive up to the mountains with him one afternoon to see the place. Because Marty had already bonded with her new friends, they said they wouldn't go without her. The doctor agreed, so the three patients drove off with him. Up at the site, the psychiatrist met two other doctors and spent most of his time discussing plans with them. As the property was on a lake, the three patients amused themselves by taking a boat out.

"Then this man did something," laughed Marty, "that showed he didn't know a damn thing about alcoholics. He said he had to get down to Philadelphia in a hurry. He was going by train, and would we three patients drive his car back to Connecticut?"

Marty, Grennie, and the other woman immediately agreed. It took them days to make the afternoon return trip, stopping frequently for long drinking sessions at any convenient bar or hotel. They had a system. Every time they left a place, they'd call the sanitarium and say, "We're at so-and-so. We're just leaving!" Blythewood then had no way to contact them on the road. The staff never knew exactly where they were, and never could catch them. Somewhat the worse for wear, the three truants rolled into Blythewood on the Fourth of July. By this time, the psychiatrist had returned from Philadelphia and "he absolved Grennie and the woman right away." Dr. Tiebout, however, was still away, and Marty said, "I couldn't get absolved. It was a hell of a way to begin a stay in a new place."

Marty's sisters, Chris and Betty, had come to visit her over the holiday. Whatever high hopes they may have had for Marty were severely tested that day. Someone took pictures of the three sisters. Marty was drunk and being held up on either side by Betty and Chris. Nor was this to be the last time that Marty would try their patience and goodwill.

In accordance with Blythewood's liberal policy, Marty was often given a pass to go into New York to the theater or the dentist or to have lunch with friends. Sometimes she stayed overnight with Chris. Nine times out of ten Marty returned to Blythewood sober, not having had anything to drink, but the tenth time she'd experiment and invariably come back drunk without ever having intended to go overboard. She was utterly baffled as to why this happened. So was Dr. Tiebout. Neither of them could figure it out. Marty became very discouraged. She watched other patients move into the middle house, then the graduate house, and back home, while she stayed stuck in the middle house.

Looking back years later, Marty believed she understood the Blythewood relapses. Although she saw Tiebout every day and learned a lot,

steadily improving in discerning her emotions, her difficulty with relationships, her various fears and insecurities, and how to change herself for the
better, this renewed sense of self-esteem and self-confidence led her to believe that now she had the strength to control her drinking—ergo, the periodic tests. Unfortunately, whenever she picked up a drink, it always led to
drunken binges. She would learn in sobriety the hard basic truth for the true
alcoholic: It's the first drink that sooner or later gets you drunk.[4]

"The hardest thing for an alcoholic to learn," said Marty, "is that you
can't turn the clock back. Once you've crossed that line into a compulsive
drinker, you can never become a social drinker—never."

Tiebout was aware of the term *alcoholism* because it had been appearing in American medical and psychiatric literature for several decades. Apparently, he didn't use the term with alcoholic patients because it had not
yet come into common use in American psychiatry. However, he continued
to insist to Marty that she could never drink again. That was a prospect she
was unable to accept, so she discounted his opinion. To her, abstinence was
a sentence of "gray, gray, gray death." She argued vehemently with Tiebout.
With whom would she spend her time? What could she do? Where could
she go? She knew no other way of life. Furthermore, didn't his own colleagues think otherwise about the issue? None of their patients was being
advised to abstain. Why just her? Maybe she had the wrong doctor. One
day she questioned Tiebout closely about his own drinking. He said he had
a drink once in a while but didn't really care for alcohol.

"Aha!" retorted Marty. "No wonder you don't want me to drink. You're
just one of those sourpusses who wants everyone to be like you!"

Often Tiebout advised Marty she needed to find something bigger than
herself to think about, perhaps a cause. He suggested that religion might be
her path to sobriety and health. She totally disagreed. "I'm an intellectual!"
Despite Marty's touchiness about certain subjects, she trusted, respected,
and admired Tiebout. In a typical process of psychological transference, she
thought of him as a father, although he was only eight years her senior. At
the same time, he was near enough her age to relate well to her generation's
ideas and experiences.

Tiebout used to say that Marty "was the victim of his ignorance." Marty
replied that she hoped many others would be his victims, too. It is fairly
clear that in her single-minded search for wellness, she was a willing subject

in his search for knowledge about how to treat inebriates. Marty traded her nonpaying status, personal experience, and intelligence for his committed inquiry into what made "people like you" tick.

Harry Tiebout was a patient man. He kept trying with Marty, but finally, after a particularly bad drinking episode, Tiebout said, "This is the last. Look, I've done everything I know how to do, and you're certainly working hard. But if you go out and drink again, I'll have to give up. I'm not helping you. You'll be better off trying something else." He also told her that Blythewood could not afford to keep a charity patient who was continuing to relapse.

Marty was scared. She didn't know where else she could go or what she'd do. But instead of stopping the occasional binges, she just learned to hide them better from Tiebout. Patients, and even staff, were shameless enablers. They helped her sneak in the back way, got her hot coffee to sober up,[5] and steadied her in the shower so she could crawl into bed to sleep it off.

Marty knew from personal experience that no hospital or prison is truly safe for the alcoholic who wants to drink. For instance, a male patient who arrived after her at Blythewood would come to her room with bulging pockets containing a glass of booze for her and one for him. He told her he hid his liquor up the chimney in his room.

For weeks Marty continued to bait fate. One day in early 1939, she had a message to see Dr. Tiebout. He was home with a very bad cold. Being summoned to your psychiatrist's home was unusual, to say the least, and unheard of if he were ill. Marty's guilty conscience about her continued drinking flared into almost unbearable anxiety. Confronted with the consequences of her nameless condition and nearly overcome with fear and remorse, she went to Tiebout's house, sure she was getting her walking papers.

Tiebout was in bed, propped up with pillows, and obviously still sick. On the coverlet lay a thick 8½-by-11-inch multilith document with red cardboard covers held together with cord. To Marty's astonishment, the psychiatrist greeted her enthusiastically. Waving the document, he cried, "I've been reading something very interesting!" Marty began to breathe again.

Tiebout continued excitedly, "This is the prepublication manuscript of a book written by people like you. They seem to have found an answer. I think it may help you, and I want you to read it right away. Let me know what you think." He handed her the book.

The red cover was blank. Marty opened to the first page. There she read two words, *Alcoholics Anonymous*. Marty looked up and said, "What's that?"

Tiebout replied, "Well, it's a group of people like you. And in this book they tell about it, and what they did, and how they got well."

Subsequently, Marty discovered how Tiebout came to possess this near-final draft of *Alcoholics Anonymous*. When the manuscript was about to go to press, a New York AA member abruptly thought, "What if there's something offensive to doctors or clergy in the book?" These were the two professions from whom AA hoped to receive most of the referrals of alcoholics who needed help. Hurriedly, the little group made four hundred loan copies and distributed them nationally to every medical and clergy leader they could think of.

One of the first twenty men in New York to get sober had a sister-in-law who lived in Greenwich. He asked her if she knew any doctors who would review the manuscript. As it happened, she was serving on a town committee with another civic-minded person, Dr. Tiebout. She read the manuscript first, then knowing of Tiebout's interest in inebriates, she asked him to look at the book. Because he was sick in bed, he had the time to read it immediately instead of setting it aside, perhaps indefinitely. From such tenuous circumstances do earthshaking events occasionally arise. In time, Marty would consider this far more than a happy coincidence. To her, it became the blessed act of a loving God.

For now, Marty clutched the book closer and hurried back to her room to begin reading, slowly and skeptically at first, then with mounting excitement. The first part of the book contained the story of Bill W., an alcoholic New York City stockbroker. It described how he and Dr. Bob of Akron, Ohio, an alcoholic surgeon, had hit on an answer to their drinking when they happened to come together to help each other stay sober. In June 1935, Alcoholics Anonymous, probably the most famous grassroots, self-help health movement of all time, was launched on its shaky way.

Within four years Bill and Dr. Bob and a handful of other pioneers had attracted two small groups of men who had managed to achieve sobriety by helping one another. One group was in Akron (Dr. Bob's hometown), the other in New York City (Bill W.'s). The men decided to write down their experiences in the belief and hope that they could thereby broaden their outreach to other suffering alcoholics. Thus was born the book *Alcoholics Anonymous,* whose heart was the famous Twelve Steps, which have been adopted and adapted by literally hundreds of other kinds of self-help groups.[6]

As Marty read on, she was thrilled to learn that she truly wasn't crazy but instead had an illness called alcoholism. She was absolutely delighted to know that she was an alcoholic. At last there was a name for what ailed her and had been tearing her apart![7] A tremendous load lifted from her spirit. She was no longer a nonentity called "people like you." To the end of her life, Marty found it difficult to empathize and work with people who had trouble admitting they were alcoholics.

"People who dislike the terms 'alcoholic' and 'alcoholism' should consider the alternative of not knowing what was the matter with them, and could believe only that they were hopelessly insane." For Marty, the term *alcoholic* was sheer, joyful liberation.

"I love the word *alcoholic!*" she exulted.

She read that *alcoholism* was defined as "an allergy of the body coupled with an obsession of the mind." The manuscript said that the word *allergy* wasn't being used in its medical sense but rather to describe a physical inability to tolerate alcohol. Marty understood immediately. Based on her experience, she accepted that there was nothing anyone could do about this allergy of the body, which manifested itself in a physical compulsion. There was no scientific evidence that such a physically based compulsion existed, but Marty *knew* that AA had accurately intuited the basis for her heretofore incomprehensible loss of control over alcohol once she started drinking. Abstinence was the only answer, she read. Dr. Tiebout had been right.

The book said this group of alcoholics could not remove a person's physical allergy to alcohol. Alcoholics Anonymous did, however, promise to be of great help in reducing and even removing the obsession of the mind that kept alcoholics enslaved by thoughts and feelings that led to alcohol even when they didn't want to drink, for a relief that no longer worked. Marty would one day learn that during the long convalescent period from active alcoholism, an obsession for AA was a healthy substitute.

Then Marty suddenly hit a huge stumbling block. "On every page there were four or five capital Gs [God]!" Marty, a confirmed atheist, had long outgrown a belief in God and had no intention of returning to so childish a notion. The whole idea offended her. Then she found other shortcomings in the manuscript. The writing wasn't up to her standards. In addition, she began to realize the book was all about men. Actually, there was one brief story by a woman named Florence, but Marty couldn't relate to it. So the more she read, the unhappier she became. Disgusted, she hurled the manuscript out the window and flounced off the grounds of the sanitarium to tie on a big bender.

The next day Marty told Tiebout that she didn't think much of those alcoholics' reliance on God. What were they, weaklings? Furiously, she cried, "Here you've been telling me I'm ruled by my emotions, not my intellect at all. Now you want me to accept an emotional premise, God, which is nothing but self-hypnosis. I'm not about to accept this! I can't buy it."

Tiebout didn't agree with her assessment, but he didn't debate the issue. He just mildly but firmly said, "Oh, never mind about that. Go back and read some more, and we'll talk about it tomorrow."

Marty balked. Every day she'd read only a page or two, merely enough to give her ammunition to argue with Tiebout at their next session. He was very clever. He'd listen, then say, "All right. Now go read some more." Gritting her teeth, Marty would read another page and repeat the whole process. She knew without any doubt that what Alcoholics Anonymous had to offer wasn't for her.

The stalling went on for six weeks, and she still was only halfway through the manuscript. Somewhere in the book Marty had read that most alcoholics had to experience a crisis before they could surrender and accept the kind of help that AA offered. As far as she could see, her life had already been one crisis after another. But she was about to encounter a crisis of such mammoth proportions that it literally drove her to her knees. She would never be the same.

On a winter day in early 1939, Marty flew into a rage at the business manager of Blythewood. He was an English remittance man,[8] and the divorced son-in-law of Anna Wiley, the founder of Blythewood. According to Marty, this man was an SOB, and everybody knew it. He got involved somehow with her sister Chris. Grennie, who was already courting Chris, was also furious.

Possibly the business manager was leaning on Chris to start footing Marty's bill. The Depression still gripped the country. Chris was barely keeping her own head above water financially and would have been totally incapable of helping Marty out. Whatever happened, Marty said it wasn't Chris's fault. The man was simply a "no-good bum."

Worse, Marty felt it was her own fault. If she hadn't been where she was, the crisis couldn't have happened. Regardless of the nature of the argument with the business manager, Marty said she herself was completely helpless to do anything about it. She had hit a stone wall that she couldn't get over, around, or under, nor could she beat it down.[9]

A furious confrontation with the business manager failed to achieve satisfactory resolution. At first Marty was sad, then anger consumed her. She stormed upstairs to her room. By now Blythewood had advanced her to a tiny third-floor attic room under the eaves in the graduate house. "I was angry with a kind of anger I had never felt before, and thank God, never have since."

For the first time in her life, Marty literally saw red, a description she'd always thought was a literary figure of speech. The whole room was red. Little blood vessels were actually breaking in her eyes. "I was raging. I wanted to kill!"

Seething, Marty tore around the room, pounding her fists together, furiously plotting revenge. "I'll go out to the store and get two big bottles of whiskey and get good and drunk and come back here," she panted, "and I'll kill that guy and wreck the place! That'll show them!"

At this point in her story, Marty would pause and remark, "Isn't that just like an alcoholic! When we get really mad, we're so intelligent that we pick up a sledgehammer and bash in our own brains." Later, AA confirmed for her that "an alcoholic plus a resentment equals a drunk."

At the very moment she was about to fling herself out the door and race down the stairs, Marty glimpsed out of the corner of her eye "that damn book," *Alcoholics Anonymous,* lying open on her bed. "In the middle of the page was a line that stood out as if carved in raised block letters, black, high, sharp—'**We cannot live with anger.**'[10] That did it. Somehow those words were the battering ram that knocked down my resistance."

The next Marty remembered, she was on her knees beside the bed. The coverlet was wet with her tears. She'd been praying, though it had been so long since she'd prayed that she didn't think she remembered how. And she knew beyond the shadow of a doubt that a Presence she came to call God was in that room with her. The room was alive, and she was a different person.

"The walls crumpled and the light streamed in. I wasn't trapped. I wasn't helpless. I was free, totally and completely free! And I didn't have to drink to 'show them.' This wasn't religion, this was freedom! Freedom from anger and fear, freedom to know happiness and love."[11]

Marty lifted her head to a new world. She looked through her little window under the eaves, and everything was completely different. The sky was bluer, the grass was greener. Marty said she felt so free that she could have walked out of that third-story window into the open air and kept right on walking. The thought frightened her because years ago in London, while in the psychiatric ward following a suicide attempt, she had had an insane urge to do the same thing. It dawned on her that "now I *had* gone nuts."

In a panic, Marty flew down the stairs to Dr. Tiebout's office on the ground floor and pounded on his door. Opening the door, he took one look at her face, immediately dismissed the patient who was there, pulled Marty in and said, "Sit down. Tell me what happened."

Breathlessly, Marty told him, then concluded dejectedly, "I guess I really am insane."

"No," Tiebout replied, "I don't think you are. From what you tell me, I believe you've had an authentic spiritual experience. This is a wonderful thing. It's similar to what others reported in William James's *Varieties of Religious Experience*. You just hang on to it. And now you go back upstairs and finish reading that book."

So Marty went to her room and picked up the book she hated so. Somebody had switched books on her! This was the most wonderful book she'd ever read. Like "a sponge that soaks up water," she read it through "in one gulp." Then she started over at the beginning and read it through again. For weeks she was on a pink cloud, walking around with her feet off the ground. Everybody looked beautiful. People remarked on her radiance. They wanted to be near her.

Marty eagerly shared her experience and the book with the little handful of fellow alcoholics at Blythewood. Grennie had become her buddy and seemed especially interested. A good Roman Catholic, he, unlike Marty, had no resistance to AA's spiritual message and reliance on a Higher Power.

The only shadow on Marty's pink cloud was "that SOB," the business manager. Her furious resentment at him continued to burn. She made every effort to avoid the man. Whenever she walked into the common room and he was there, she stalked out. If she came across him outdoors on one of Blythewood's many paths, she would quickly veer down another path or duck behind a tree until he was past.

By January 1939, Leopold Mannes was back in New York and had visited Marty at Blythewood. He wrote, "I still can't get over you and am still excited over the way you looked and were. Really I've never been so proud of anyone's accomplishment for I know what it means. One way I can show you my admiration is to increase the piece of paper I'm going to send at the end of this month—so you'll have three instead of two hundred for February and March." [12]

After a week or so, Dr. Tiebout said, "Well, when are you going into New York and meet these people?" That, Marty did not want to do. She felt she already had what she needed. Besides, she didn't know what they'd be like, and she didn't want to find out. Marty had the same misconceptions as anyone else. She imagined the members of AA were either "praying mantises, mission stiffs, or Bowery bums, and they would sit around and pray over her." The prospect was revolting. Moreover, despite her outward poise and social skills, she was basically so ill at ease in new situations that she'd always relied on alcohol to ease her tension and anxiety. How could she possibly endure meeting all these strangers? So instead of attending an AA meeting, Marty wrote to Alcoholics Anonymous and began getting encouraging letters from them. They urged her to just take one day at a time and not think of quitting alcohol forever.

Tiebout let her procrastinate in this way for about a month. Then he quietly consulted by phone with Bill Wilson about what to do with Marty. On Tuesday, April 11, 1939, while she was in Tiebout's office, he picked up the phone, called New York, and said, "She will be in tonight at seven o'clock." Tiebout handed her a card with an address and told her, "You'll take the five o'clock train into New York. Catch a cab and go to this address. These people will take you to a meeting."

Marty glanced at the card. Sutton Place! A very distinguished address.

Well!—this might not be so bad. She knew that "derelicts don't live on Sutton Place."

First, Marty tried to talk Grennie into going with her. He didn't like strangers, either, and put her off, saying, "You go and see what it's like. If it's okay, I'll go with you next time." Marty was out of excuses. So off she went by herself, scared to death, but she went.

A Pioneer in the Making

1939

AT THIS TIME, FOUR YEARS AFTER AA'S BIRTH, there were still only two AA meetings in the whole country, one in Brooklyn, the other in Akron. Each little group met just once a week. Some members literally drove more than a hundred miles each way to attend the precious fellowship. It was a long time between Tuesdays. In the meantime, the AAs kept in touch by telephone and mail.

Marty's hosts, an older couple, were a big surprise. The man, Horace R. "Popsy" Maher, was the alcoholic, "a charming Virginia gentleman of the old sort," which she certainly hadn't expected. His wife, Sandy, had been a nurse and put Marty right at ease. Marty learned that it was Popsy's sister-in-law who had given Dr. Tiebout the manuscript of *Alcoholics Anonymous* to read.

The Mahers had also invited for dinner a gorgeous, curly black-haired, blue-eyed young AA Irishman named Brian as Marty's escort—the "handsomest man I'd ever seen." They all had an elegant dinner at the Mahers' fashionable home on exclusive Sutton Place in Manhattan. Soft drinks were served in cocktail glasses. Marty was relieved that the conversation was relaxed and pleasant.

After dinner, the four of them caught the subway to Brooklyn across the East River. Marty had dreaded this part. She was almost phobic about subways and heights in those days but didn't see how she could decline. With her panic barely under control, she followed along with the others. The subway route took less than half an hour. Marty's brave front was in danger of collapsing as several rather seedy men who were going to the same AA meeting got on at various stations. One man had a paper bag under his arm, and Popsy whispered to Marty that it contained all his worldly belongings, and he was living in a flophouse. This frightened her even more because now she believed she was walking into a skid row gathering after all. Later, her fellow AA travelers told Marty "she was the most wild-eyed dame they'd ever seen."

The motley group exited their subway stop and walked together over to 182 Clinton Street. It was cold, around thirty degrees, but clear. The fine old brownstone on a pleasant block shaded by mature trees was the home of Lois and Bill Wilson. Out on the sidewalk you could hear the voices and laughter of a crowd inside. What in the world had Marty let herself in for? As she walked up the steps and through the door, her heart pounding, she was already beside herself with apprehension. At the sight of some forty strangers packed into the living room, she panicked and ran upstairs, ostensibly to leave her coat. Gasping for breath, she burst into tears and threw herself down on the coats piled atop the bed.

Hypersensitive, self-centered in the extreme, all her nerve endings twitching, Marty would have stayed there but for Lois Wilson, who followed her when she didn't come down. Lois sat on the bed beside Marty and, putting her arm around Marty, said kindly, "We're waiting for you below, and we want you." Marty had never felt such love. Like a little lamb, she let Lois take her hand and lead her downstairs—tiny Lois shepherding tall Marty, who towered over her.

"Shaking and shivering," Marty entered the room. She was the immediate center of attention. One can imagine her impact. Here was a beautiful, vibrant, outwardly self-assured, articulate thirty-four-year-old woman—a real lady—wearing expensive, stylish clothes, albeit secondhand. The men were all considerably older, as were the few wives who accompanied them.

Five or six of the men began firing questions at her, like "When did you have your last drink?" To Marty's amazement, she told them the truth. She had never disclosed this variable fact to anyone before, not even her doctor. Without missing a beat, she found she was talking openly and freely to all these strangers, as if they were her closest, most intimate friends.

"I could finish their sentences! They could finish my sentences! We talked each other's language! It was not a room of strangers. These were my people. I had come home."

In her story in *Alcoholics Anonymous,* Marty said, "There is another meaning for the Hebrew word that in the King James version of the Bible is translated 'salvation.' It is: 'to come home.' I had found my salvation. I wasn't alone any more."[1]

To Marty's relief, no one asked her to sign a pledge. All they did was suggest that she promise herself she wouldn't drink for twenty-four hours, and when the twenty-four hours had passed to make the same promise again.

Yet, despite the warm welcome, there was an undercurrent of disbelief that Marty could be a real alcoholic. First of all, she was a woman. Besides, they thought she was too young to have gotten into much trouble. Moreover, she was "obviously from a 'good' background—well-brought-up, well-educated, and apparently meeting the specifications for that old-fashioned label, 'a lady.'"[2] As Marty shared some of her story, however, her fellow alcoholics recognized her as truly one of them. There was no question that she'd been a classic low-bottom drunk. Nevertheless, there remained for years among the men a residue of uncertainty and wariness about women alcoholics in general, and Marty in particular. There were serious unexpressed doubts about the ability of a woman to live the AA program successfully.

The major factor in Marty's acceptance by the men was Bill Wilson's attitude. He and Marty hit it off immediately. They were cut from the same piece of cloth, both of them visionary, charismatic, open-minded, entrepreneurial. Robert Thomsen described Marty as "[a]n attractive, intelligent young woman with tremendous charm, . . . [possessing] a drive which Bill immediately spotted as equal to his own."[3] Lois said Marty had a charismatic presence, "a force, a strength . . . that people could feel if she just came into the room."[4] Coupled with these attributes were a boundless enthusiasm and a logical mind that could express itself with great clarity.

The others took their lead from Bill, so Marty was probably integrated into the AA group faster than might otherwise have happened. He protected her against the men's skepticism. Eventually, she came to understand that skepticism. Bill became Marty's AA sponsor[5] and later heard her Fifth Step, for which Marty made a searching and fearless moral written inventory of herself.[6] Lois, too, though not an alcoholic, was a woman Marty could always talk some things over with. She and Marty became dear friends. Marty said, "Lois did as much for me as any alcoholic."

Gradually, that evening, Marty began to sort out the group at the Wilsons'. They seemed to be nice, middle-class folks, all of them dead broke. Among them were a high school principal, a founder of the *New Yorker* magazine, a man with a seat on the sugar exchange, another from Standard Oil of New Jersey, several writers, and a number of Wall Street types. Only two in the room were under the age of forty, Marty and her escort, Brian. (Unfortunately, Brian didn't manage to stay sober, but it was long enough to do Marty a lot of good.) Everyone was a white Anglo-Saxon Protestant (WASP). No Jews, no African Americans. No Catholics that evening, though a Catholic man named Morgan R. was a recent member, and Grennie started attending the following week. The members had come from all over the greater New York area—Westchester, New Jersey, and Long Island, as well as New York City. The group had no name. For the time being it was referred to as Bill's group.

About twenty-five of the people were alcoholics, all men. The rest were wives and some children. Marty asked, "Aren't there any AA women in this group?" An occasional alcoholic woman had tried AA. In New York, Marty once met Florence, the woman whose story she'd read in *Alcoholics Anonymous* at Blythewood. Florence, however, moved to Washington, D.C., resumed drinking, and died before Marty's first-year AA anniversary. Another woman, Mary Campbell, also preceded Marty. She actually visited Marty at Blythewood in 1939. Mary Campbell would have been the AA woman with the longest sobriety, except she relapsed in 1944. Thereafter, she stayed sober until her death in the 1990s.

The group that night was excited. Copies of the first printing of their new publication, *Alcoholics Anonymous*, were available at the meeting. Marty said, "I knew I was in, when I was asked to sign the book, along with the rest."[7]

The book acquired its nickname, the Big Book, because Bill Wilson and others, thinking it looked skimpy, purposely had it printed on extra-heavy stock, thereby increasing its size and heft. AA had a problem in distributing the book to the world outside, however. Then someone said that when a library had received ten requests for a particular volume, it was obliged to purchase it. So the AA members organized themselves to rotate through all the New York and suburban libraries until each library had received ten individual requests. The original price of the Big Book was $3.50 ($42 in year 2000 dollars).

In those early days of New York AA, there was no particular format or opening ritual to the meetings. Bill, tall and lanky, stood in front of the crowded room with an arm draped along the mantel, and started talking while everyone gathered round. Bill talked a long time. He had a homespun, laid-back, endearing, Gary Cooper style that immediately put people at ease. A charismatic man, he was very verbal, very persuasive. That night he described Dr. Bob, the Akron group, and anything else that came to mind. There was lots of laughter, yet also a pervasive sense that they were all engaged in a grim matter of life and death.

People would ask Bill questions. Someone wanted to know about hospital treatment. Towns Hospital, in the city, had the only program for alcoholics, but in 1939 Towns required as much as $100 up front ($1,200 in year 2000 dollars) prior to admission. Before a small gathering like this one, or person-to-person, Bill was highly effective. Unlike Marty, though, Bill was an indifferent speaker when the audience was large. Nevertheless, AAs loved listening to him wherever he spoke. His story and his unfolding journey of recovery were constant inspirations.

Marty was very taken with Bill. She saw how much he cared about helping another alcoholic, and she felt his concern and love. The meeting closed with the Lord's Prayer (though many groups subsequently dropped it because the specifically Christian connection implied that AA was a religious organization). Marty had been away from church for so long, she was embarrassed that she couldn't remember all of the prayer and got stuck in the middle of it.

Some of the early alcoholics had had a dramatic spiritual experience equivalent to Bill Wilson's.[8] AAs joked about Bill's "hot flash." They thought an experience like his was the preferred inauguration into recovery. Only later did the concept evolve into "spiritual awakening," to take account of the great majority of AAs, whose spiritual experience was a gradual unfolding of understanding over years rather than a sudden enlightenment like Bill's and Marty's.

People introduced themselves by their full names, not first name only, as was the later custom. For men to state just their given name is hard enough at first, but for women it is usually excruciatingly difficult even though they are in the company of fellow alcoholics. Marty was no exception. From her writings and speeches, it is clear that she was painfully conscious of the stigma of being a woman alcoholic. It is also a matter of record that AA men were themselves victims of their culture, having the same prejudices and misconceptions as did the general populace regarding women alcoholics. A drunk man might be pitied, he might be laughed at or scorned, but a drunk woman was totally unacceptable, beyond the pale of compassion or understanding. Some of the AA men objected to women joining the group because the women often appeared shabby and hungover. Marty retorted, "You've forgotten how *you* looked!"

Many women who have sought help through AA have been divorced or deserted by men who refused any longer to tolerate an alcoholic wife. A single woman in AA was vulnerable to inappropriate attention by AA men and also perceived as a threat by the wives of men in AA. Men entering AA, on the other hand, usually had intact families since their wives stayed in the relationship for "the sake of the children," for economic reasons, and because women have been socialized to be caregivers.

Many other women alcoholics, however, were hidden by their families' enabling their drinking and had thus not lost everything. The AA men didn't at first realize that "skid row" for such women could be a horrible place right in their own homes and minds.

It would be difficult to exaggerate Marty's anxiety at walking into a meeting room of AA men. She had two strikes against her from the start, and she knew it. She was a woman, and she was an alcoholic. Very few women could overcome this double stigma. To overstate the consequences of that courageous act would be even more difficult. She changed the future development of AA forever by her example. No longer would it remain exclusively masculine in either its membership or its outlook. Beyond AA itself, Marty was an authentic witness to the outside world that a woman alcoholic was no more loose or fallen than a man, and that it was permissible for women to come out of hiding and seek help for their disease.

After the meeting, several of the men—and Marty—retired with Bill to a smaller sitting room upstairs to continue the conversation. The wives who stayed went elsewhere in the house with Lois. Marty had already read the Big Book three or four times and had memorized chunks of it. She was so excited that she couldn't stop firing questions at Bill. The general topic, continued from the earlier meeting downstairs, was resentments.

"Resentments? I've never had a resentment," Marty claimed. The men guffawed.

"I don't know why you're laughing," Marty pouted. "What's so funny?"

Bill challenged her, "What do you do when you feel unfairly treated?"

"Oh, I get hurt!" Marty said.

The men chorused, "*That's* a resentment."

Bill went on to point out that by withdrawing into herself whenever she felt hurt, she was in truth only hurting herself. Despite Marty's years of psychiatric counseling, she began to learn at last the ancient Greek maxim "Know thyself."

"I had my first lesson with Bill as a teacher that night. He was a great teacher." [9]

It was the beginning of Marty's insight into how AA worked in people's lives. Finally, at three o'clock in the morning, the meeting ended when Bill laughingly said, "Marty, you don't have to get it all by Thursday."

That entire evening was Marty's introduction to the vital part of Alcoholics Anonymous that is its fellowship. Pragmatist that she was, she was instantly attracted to this pragmatic community that was likewise interested in what worked. She loved AA, saying, "I have never been bored in an AA meeting in my life." The fellowship, the sense of shared tragedy and shared triumph, of being like shipwrecked survivors in a lifeboat, is a powerful bonding experience that provides AAs the strength and courage to stay clean and sober. Over time, however, Marty, like most others who remain sober in AA, learned that fellowship alone is not AA, nor are individuals, clubs, rooms, or meetings, important though they are. Instead, she discovered the deeper meaning of AA as "a [spiritual] way of thinking and a way of living" built around the Twelve Steps.

Marty also came to appreciate the preventive value of AA meetings. One time she noted that "alkies have a built-in forgetter of pain. Forgetting pain is necessary for survival, and may have been put there primarily for women, or no one would have a second child. But alkies need to remember how this capacity [to forget pain] can work against them. This is why alkies need to remain active and involved in AA."

At the time, no one knew that AA had created the basic concept of group therapy. It was a concept that would later be adopted and adapted far and wide in the professional therapeutic setting.

That night, Marty stayed with Chris in New York. She fell into bed, exhausted by all the excitement, intending to sleep in late the next day. Grennie, unaware, phoned her first thing in the morning.

"How was it?" he asked eagerly.

Barely awake, Marty answered, "Grennie, there's just one thing I can say. We are not alone any more." At long last, Marty had "found her own people." It was the start of her rejoining the human race.

Nine months had passed since Marty entered Blythewood. Tiebout couldn't get over the drastic change in her because of AA. Suddenly she was far more responsive to psychiatric treatment than she'd ever been. So was Grennie, who had become Tiebout's patient and followed Marty into AA. Tiebout was "agreeably astonished."[10] His experience was an early confirmation of what is widely known today, that a degree of sobriety in AA prepares a person to be much more honest, stable, and receptive to professional counseling than before. Bill Wilson later described the impact on Tiebout:

> Harry was electrified. . . . Only a few weeks previously they [Marty and Grennie] had presented stone walls of obstinate resistance to his every approach. To Harry these were facts, brand new facts. Scientist and man of courage that he is, Harry faced them squarely. . . . As soon as he became fully convinced, he held up AA for his profession and for the public to see. . . . At very considerable risk to his professional standing, Harry Tiebout ever since has continued to endorse AA and its work to the psychiatric profession.[11]

Dr. Tiebout was certainly bucking the opinion of the American Medical Association (AMA) as expressed in its review of *Alcoholics Anonymous*.

> This book is a curious combination of organizing propaganda and religious exhortation. . . . The one valid thing in the book is the recognition of the seriousness of addiction to alcohol. Other than this, the book has no scientific merit or interest.[12]

Dr. Foster Kennedy strongly disagreed with the AMA's review. Subsequently, he wrote a letter to the editor, saying, "I believe medical men of good will should aid these decent people rather than loftily condemn them for not being scientific."[13] The editor declined to publish Kennedy's rebuttal. Nearly twenty years would pass before the AMA changed its mind about AA.

Tiebout was thoroughly intrigued by the healing possibilities in Alcoholics Anonymous. For the time being, however, he proceeded cautiously with Marty. There was no way of telling how lasting would be the changes wrought in her. So he arranged for her to remain an additional six months at Blythewood.

One crucial consequence of this extended stay was that whenever Lois and Bill Wilson were near Blythewood, they visited Marty. Bill and Harry Tiebout finally met face-to-face. The two men had a great deal in common and became fast friends. Bill educated the eager physician about AA. From that point on, Tiebout began to work closely with alcoholics and Alcoholics Anonymous. It proved to be a mutually enriching partnership. Bill and Tiebout labored together to bridge the gap between the lay membership of AA and the professional one of psychiatry. Tiebout was a central figure in educating his professional colleagues to the potential of AA's Twelve Step program. He sent all his alcoholic patients to AA and became an international authority in the medical treatment of alcoholics. Bill, for his part, was able to bring the insights of psychiatry into better focus for AA. Tiebout was also instrumental in understanding and addressing Bill's crippling depressions.

One day when Bill and Lois were visiting Marty, he asked her, "How are you doing with your resentments these days?"

"Well, I've got a beaut," Marty answered. "And I've got a right to *this* resentment!" She proceeded to tell Bill and Lois about the business manager.

"You're completely right, Marty," said Bill. "You do have a right to your resentment. I've met the guy and I agree he's an SOB. But you know, if he's that bad and that awful, *why* do you give him that power over you? If you can bring yourself to forgive him, you take away that power."

"My God," Marty exclaimed. "That's worth trying!"

In typical Marty fashion, she turned her attitude around immediately. Her resentment was gone—but she never did like the man.

Leopold Mannes was another visitor whenever he was in the area. Like Marty, he was an incorrigible flirt, but his letter on June 6, 1939, further indicates his loyal friendship.

Marty dear—You are a joy. If you knew how happy it made me even to have a finger in the magnificent pie you are making, you'd be even happier than you are. Not one person in ten thousand would have made as much of your situation as you are making. And I haven't a shred of doubt as to your ultimate success. Even if you "slip" twenty times between 1939 and 1999, I'll believe in you just as much and I'll be there ready to help all I can. There isn't a soul I know whom I respect more and I'd like to give you the biggest hug you ever had. (If that led to any other manifestations, so much the better!)[14]

During the fifteen months Marty was at Blythewood, Chris, Marty's sister, often visited her and met Marty's many friends among the patients. A perhaps unsurprising consequence of those visits was the flowering of a romance between Chris and Grennie, whose full name was Grenville Francis Curtis. Grennie, a graduate of Columbia University, was a very attractive, charming young man from a well-to-do New York family. Five years older than Chris, he had married twice but was now divorced. Early in his career, he was connected with New York's Rockefeller Institute, engaging in yellow fever research. The burgeoning romance may have been the source of Blythewood's argument with Marty that produced the crisis leading to her eventual recovery in AA.

After Grennie's discharge from Blythewood, he and Chris were married on May 18, 1940.[15] Chris's divorce from Johnny Johnstone had become final only a month before. Grennie joined the Civil Air Patrol (CAP), where he taught flying during World War II. Chris and Grennie moved to Long Island, then to Coconut Grove, Florida, where he had a wealthy cousin who backed New York plays. Lill Mann sometimes visited and stayed with Chris and Grennie for weeks at a time in Florida. The marriage, however, lasted only a few years. Then Chris was on her own again, returning to New York to live. Bill Mann believed she was the Mann sibling who had the hardest time in life and the worst luck of them all.

Grennie stayed sober from alcohol but became addicted to Benzedrine, prescribed by his physician to counteract a chronic lethargy. In those days, the addictive properties of amphetamines were not recognized. Eventually, Grennie remarried, settled on Nantucket Island in Massachusetts, and had several children. He became a well-known expert on antique watches and clocks, ending up as a watchmaker on Nantucket, where he lived until his death in 1976.

Marty's first year in AA was an education in more ways than one. She began to shed some of her narcissistic attitudes and to empathize with the difficulties of others. A month after Marty's initial AA meeting, the Wilsons' home was foreclosed, and they, like so many others, were homeless. For a year and a half, Bill and Lois lived around with friends in Connecticut, New York, and New Jersey, moving every couple of weeks until they were finally able to acquire through the help of friends a lovely permanent residence in Bedford Hills, New York. Stepping Stones, as the Wilsons' home came to be called, was a magnet for AA members while Lois and Bill were still alive and is now a beloved museum open by appointment.[16]

The loss of the Clinton Street house meant that the AA meeting had to find a new home, too. Marty and Grennie persuaded Anna Wiley, Blythewood's owner, to allow a meeting at the sanitarium. This was probably the third AA group, after Akron and New York City.

The New York group, in the meantime, met in a series of locations during the following year. One AA member, Bert Taylor, had a father who was a British tailor with elegant space on Fifth Avenue. In 1939, the store's suits sold for $300 ($3,600 in year 2000 dollars). Bert arranged for the group to meet in the loft of the shop after it closed for the day. During the very hot summer of 1939, people sat on high cutting tables in the roasting loft and dangled their legs. Marty brought Dr. Tiebout once to that meeting and also Dr. Kennedy.

The group moved next for a short while to an empty apartment lent by someone in real estate. Another location was the Aeolian Hall. There the AA door would be locked until there was enough cash to pay the rent. Sometimes the basket had to be passed two or three times. One member was famous among the New York AAs because he stayed sober when he went to his twenty-fifth Yale reunion.

During the Aeolian Hall phase, one of the men made contact with patients in the alcohol ward of the big mental hospital nearby in Nyack. The hospital administration was impressed with his beneficial effect on their alcoholics and agreed to send a busload of patients every Sunday afternoon to Aeolian Hall. Marty signed up to be a speaker for this group. She said it was where she learned how to speak simply and directly. The experience was excellent preparation for later speaking challenges.

After Aeolian Hall, the AA meeting moved to a house on West Twenty-fourth Street, in back of an apartment building. Marty was on the committee that chose it. The house had belonged to the Art Directors' Association and was beautifully remodeled. An advantage was that the Wilsons could sleep there. By this time the AA group had grown to fifty or sixty. There were other speakers besides Bill. Marty even spoke occasionally.

In the early 1940s, Grennie, now Marty's brother-in-law, suggested that the men start a closed meeting for alcoholics only. It was the first truly closed meeting. Until then, AA meetings were always open to attract as many newcomers as possible. When the United States entered World War II in 1941, the men's meeting disbanded because so many AA men enlisted or were drafted.

In between meetings, the early AA members hung out together. Within the AA fellowship there was no ostracism, no stigma. Work was scarce, so most of them didn't have jobs. They would visit in each other's homes, play records, and talk. Or they'd ride the double-decker buses, sitting up top in the open air if the weather was good, or go to the movies if they had a little money. They were keeping themselves sober and relearning how to relate to the human race.

Everyone in AA worked hard to attract active alcoholics to the AA program. AAs were utterly convinced that such outreach was essential to maintaining their own sobriety. In AA parlance, they would be fulfilling Step Twelve, ". . . we tried to carry this message to alcoholics . . ." Any new prospects were treated like diamonds in the rough, with everybody eager to help in the polishing. There were few treatment centers aside from detox, and most alcoholics detoxed on their own, anyway. Sober AAs would sit with the alcoholic who had asked for help, holding his hand and feeding him sugared milk, orange juice, and honeyed tea.

Marty bore a special burden because she was a woman who could contact other women—and she certainly knew lots of prospects among her very wide circles. In her first year, she tried unsuccessfully to help "at least 100 women." The AA men thought she was wasting her time, saying, "Women aren't alcoholics." Marty's lack of success led her to agree with the men that maybe she *was* a freak.

The next few years would prove excruciatingly slow in attracting women to AA. Later, Marty would write and speak about why she thought it was so difficult for women to accept the help AA offered. First, there was the double standard about women's drinking. Second, from force of circumstance, women had become used to concealing and sneaking their drinking. Suddenly to adopt an open and honest posture demanded more of them than it did of men, who were accustomed to drinking far more publicly. Third, women cared almost pathologically about what the neighbors would think. Not until they actually came to AA did these women appreciate how secure their anonymity would be. Fourth, women had themselves bought the cultural line that only degraded women drink. Therefore, their low self-esteem and guilt about their failures as wives, mothers, and women were unimaginably magnified despite any evidence to the contrary.

Up to the present, little has changed in how women feel about themselves and their drinking. Yet gradually they began to join AA regardless, until their membership passed some unidentifiable critical mass and they came into AA in such great numbers that today women comprise about half of AA's membership in many areas. Marty opened the door and steadfastly kept it open for women as well as men.

The Learning Curve Steepens

1939–42

As THE TIME FOR MARTY TO BE DISCHARGED from Blythewood drew near, she was filled with anticipation. Yet she couldn't help worrying about returning to the real world. She was reassured when she realized that the Twelve Steps were starting to change her. She was becoming more flexible, better able to roll with the punches. She could even accept criticism without reaching for a drink.

Marty was discharged in September 1939 with about seven months of sobriety. A changed woman, she found a world soon to be gripped by World War II. Adolf Hitler and the Nazis had marched into Czechoslovakia. The United States was barely beginning to pull out of the decade-long Great Depression, the worst in America's history. The job market was still terrible. Alcoholics Anonymous wasn't even a blip on the screen. The United States had far more important concerns than this handful of people who claimed they had the answer to something they had the nerve to call a sickness, not a moral issue.

Marty's first year of sobriety was the hardest, as she began the process of growing up. She was learning that convalescence from alcoholism is protracted. It took years for the buildup of the disease. While the body usually recovered within a few weeks or months, three to five years would pass as the mind and spirit stabilized. With no other women AAs nearby, Marty suffered a curious loneliness despite the wonderful love and support of most of the men.

Two days before she left Blythewood, however, things began to change. An ambulance pulled up and in a straitjacket on the stretcher was Nona

Wyman, whom Marty had met on arrival at the sanitarium and who had become a friend all those months ago. Nona was irrational, violent—and drunk. The mystery about what ailed her was finally revealed.

Marty returned to Blythewood each weekend during September. She tried to visit Nona, but Nona's psychiatrist refused because he disapproved of AA and feared that Marty would contaminate his patient. So Marty, living with Chris again, was subsequently startled to receive a wire from the psychiatrist, saying Nona had escaped and was holed up in a New York hotel. He asked Marty to see her and find out what could be done.

Nona was drunk again and acutely suicidal. Marty, out of her depth, called a doctor in AA for help. He gave Nona a shot to calm her, then arranged for a nurse to stay overnight. Marty was to take the following day shift. In the morning, Marty still didn't know what she could do, so she started reading *Alcoholics Anonymous* aloud to Nona. She read all morning long.

Nona was very receptive. She told Marty that the Big Book reminded her of a place where she and her husband, Walter (who had a lesser drinking problem), had been finding spiritual help for the last three or four years. It was a kind of farm in Kent, Connecticut, called High Watch Farm. For some reason, neither she nor Walt had any desire to drink when they were with Sister Francis at High Watch Farm.

Nona and Walter were separated at the time and in the process of divorce because her drinking had become intolerable. When Walter saw Nona a few days later, she had been to an AA noon meeting with Marty and the small new lunch group in Greenwich's Bristol Hotel. Nona was to be Marty's first successful female Twelfth Step call.[1] Walter was amazed at the change AA had already wrought. He and Nona reconciled, and Walter joined AA himself. They urged Marty, Bill and Lois Wilson, and some other AAs to spend a weekend at High Watch Farm.

The Wilsons, Marty, and two additional AA couples wasted no time in driving up to High Watch later that October. It was a brilliant New England fall day, the leaves in full color. High Watch proved to be a rustic retreat center owned and managed by a saintly old woman who had chosen the name Sister Francis in honor of her favorite saint. Nona and Walter hadn't exaggerated. The place had a special kind of spiritual atmosphere that you could feel the moment you arrived. As Bill Wilson stepped across the threshold of the main building, he turned to Marty and echoed what the others were thinking and feeling, "My God, you could cut it with a knife!"

Still awed years later by that first encounter, Marty groped for words. "The atmosphere, the feeling. There was something there, something that was really palpable that you could feel, and every one of us felt it. To say that we fell in love with it is not to use the right terminology at all. We were engulfed. . . . What is at the Farm was already at the Farm before we ever found it. It found us, in my opinion."

Sister Francis was a devoted follower of Emma Curtis Hopkins, whose teachings were similar to those of Mary Baker Eddy's Christian Science.[2] Sister Francis and the AA members took to one another immediately, recognizing they were soul sisters and brothers. At the end of the weekend, while they were sitting around a roaring fire, Sister Francis stunned the visitors by offering High Watch free to AA, lock, stock, and barrel. Bill immediately said AA couldn't do that because AA could not own any property. Eventually an arrangement was made whereby Sister Francis retained title, but AA ran the program.

From then on High Watch was essentially an AA retreat and detox center. Many newcomers and relapsers were brought there to detox. Marty was a constant visitor with the women she was trying to help. She was there so often that one small cabin became "hers" until it burned down. Other AAs came simply for spiritual refreshment and renewal in the unusual numinous ambience that enveloped High Watch. For many years, Marty served on the farm's board of directors and was instrumental in establishing and developing High Watch's policies.

High Watch Farm is still a functioning retreat primarily for AAs and an important part of AA history.[3] The name derives from biblical allusions to keep the "high, or upward watch . . . 'an elevated consciousness that looks up to [metaphorical] heaven to find God' . . . and the true reality. . . . Downward watchers are in 'matter's grip on the conditions of life and mind.'"[4]

When Marty left England on the *Queen Mary,* one of the friends who took her to the ship was a young woman named Mimi. Mimi had idolized Marty despite all the drinking problems. Not long after Marty connected with High Watch, she met Mimi's aunt, who was a main benefactor of the retreat center. From her, Marty was saddened to learn that Mimi had died of alcoholism. The news reinforced Marty's determination to help other people along the way, as Mimi had helped her.

The fall of 1939 continued to be a busy time for Marty and the AAs. Other meetings were springing up in various localities around New York. One evening two women appeared at Aeolian Hall. The older one was the staff escort for the younger one, who had been sent to the meeting from a private mental institution in Westchester. Marty took one look at the patient and decided she wouldn't spend any effort on her—"She didn't have one chance in a million." Marty was wrong. This woman did make it. Her name was Bobby Burger. Bobby eventually became the secretary of AA's General Service Office, and her name was known to AAs all over the world.

The experience convinced Marty that you couldn't predict who would recover and who wouldn't. The better approach was to assume the best for each newcomer and to welcome back those who happened to relapse.

One of Marty's many failures was a woman named Sibley D.

> Marty had found her in Bellevue Hospital and helped her into AA. An extremely talented violinist, Sibley had suffered a paralytic stroke and was most depressed. Her teacher, Leopold Auer, whose pupils also included Mischa Elman and Fritz Kreisler, is reported to have said she could become the top woman violinist of all time. . . . For several years she had long periods of sobriety. . . . But Sibley began to drink heavily again and was taken back to Bellevue and thence to an institution on Long Island. . . . Sibley was never heard from again.[5]

Not long after Bobby got sober, one of her Twelfth Step calls joined AA, Ila Phillips. Ila was a professional dancer in New York before she succumbed to alcoholism. Now New York AA had four women. Ila was followed fairly soon by Priscilla Peck, destined for a major role in Marty's story. Then women began slowly to join AA in small but increasing numbers. In retrospect, the process seems inevitable, but that was far from clear at the time. Months and months went by before one woman, then maybe another would be attracted to the healing that AA had to offer for their desperate alcoholic lives.

Meanwhile, in Cleveland, the twelve or so AA men wearied of making the long round-trip to Akron each week for a meeting and talked of starting their own group. In November 1939, the Cleveland *Plain Dealer* was persuaded to run a series of articles discussing the Twelve Steps and favorable to Alcoholics Anonymous. The response was tremendous. The mail poured in. But there was no AA office or meeting yet in Cleveland. Six of the AA Clevelanders were furious at the newspaper for printing anything about AA because their interpretation of anonymity was "*no* publicity." Period. They refused to help with the mail. An SOS went out to New York for assistance in responding to the mail and starting a group.

At 5:00 A.M., Bill and Lois Wilson, Jean and Jack Williams, and Marty piled into the one car among them that ran and drove straight through from New York to Cleveland. None of them could afford to stop overnight along the way. Once in Cleveland, of course, they could stay with AA families. This was Marty's first nonlocal trip since entering Bellevue nearly two years before.

More than one hundred persons attended a meeting where Bill, Jack, and Marty were the speakers. Marty commented, "Wouldn't it be wonderful if some day we could travel across the country and find an AA meeting in every town?" What grandiosity! Everybody roared with laughter. It was the biggest joke of the evening.

When the New York contingent arrived in Cleveland, Marty was very surprised to find two AA men there whom she'd known while growing up. One, Tyler Miller, was among the first two hundred members of Alcoholics Anonymous.[6] Ty was a rich socialite and an outstanding sportsman. Like Bill Wilson and a number of other early AAs, he was a stockbroker. Later, Marty lured Ty to New York to work for NCA for a while. He also served on NCA's board for eleven years. In New York, Marty introduced him to her sister Betty, who had been transferred to the New York office of the U.S. State Department Bureau of Inter-American Affairs, where she worked for Nelson Rockefeller. Tyler became Marty's brother-in-law, her second AA matchmaking on behalf of her two sisters.

Subsequently, Betty and Ty returned to Cleveland to live. Ty died in 1983. He and Betty had two sons, R. Tyler, a research physician, and Gregory M., an attorney in Seattle. Always deeply concerned with conservation issues, Betty initiated the development of the Shaker Lakes Regional Nature Center while raising her sons, and she also became a successful real-estate broker. When she died suddenly of heart failure at sunset in the middle of a lightning storm in 1997 at the age of seventy-nine, she was on safari in Tanzania, still exhibiting the energy and enthusiasm of the Mann siblings for new adventures.

While Marty was in Cleveland, she and the Wilsons drove down to Akron. Marty was asked to call on a woman who was drunk and in bed. The men had been frustrated in their efforts to help her get sober and thought a recovered alcoholic woman like Marty would have better luck. Marty was no more successful than they were.

Marty's trip to Cleveland and Akron may have been the first time she met AA's cofounder Dr. Bob Smith. As did many others, she saw that Bill Wilson and Dr. Bob were formed from the same Vermont granite of their home state. Marty later commented that, in her opinion, Bob never broke through the granite to become more personable, whereas Bill did. On the other hand, there was no question that Bill and Bob were an excellent balance for each other—Bob the cautious, steady conservative, Bill the risk-taking innovator. AA was the beneficiary of their complementary personalities and styles.

Marty felt that Bob communicated very well with men but perhaps more as a physician. Yet he was tolerant of women in AA. At any rate, Bob struck Marty as hard and something of a stuffed shirt. She sensed that his warmth was communicated through his wife, Anne.

It is a fact that women alcoholics found less of a welcome in the Akron-Cleveland area than they did around New York. This attitude had some basis in an unfortunate experience. An Akron woman who had joined AA proceeded to have sex with a male newcomer—on Dr. Bob's examining table, no less!—a behavior known as a form of "Thirteenth-stepping,"[7] and roundly discouraged even today. The midwestern reaction to women alcoholics also reflected prevailing cultural attitudes and thus set a pattern for subsequent AA groups in that area.

From Akron, the Wilsons and Marty went on to Chicago. There Marty was excited to find another woman AA, Sylvia Kaufman, who had a month of sobriety. Sylvia founded AA in Chicago. Her story, "The Keys of the Kingdom," may be found in *Alcoholics Anonymous.*[8]

A year or two later, Marty had occasion to visit Akron again and attended an AA meeting. AA was still small and composed entirely of men except for a stray woman now and then. One such woman, Elizabeth, was trying AA out at the time. The men were uncomfortable whenever a new

woman alcoholic came to one of their meetings. They feared sexual distractions—initiated by the women, of course.

Marty listened as the men concluded that Elizabeth should join their
wives, the nonalcoholics, in the next room. Women belonged with women.

Marty nearly exploded. "I wouldn't have given any of you guys the
time of day when I was drinking! Why do you think Elizabeth or I would
now?" As late as 1959, twenty-four years after the founding of AA, Marty
reported that in "a great midwestern city" several AA groups would not accept women.

Marty was fortunate to live in New York, a more sophisticated, tolerant city. She immersed herself in AA from the instant of her first meeting.
There were so many things to learn, so many people to meet! An important
early influence was a book called *Peace of Mind*. It was, in fact, very popular with all New York AAs, where it went through the fellowship "like a
dose of salts."

Marty learned there are no leaders or hierarchy in AA. She could not
throw her weight around and expect people to jump to her command. AA
functioned by consensus. Honesty, humility, tolerance, and love were the
four components of the fellowship.

Marty came to see that AAs need to be tolerant of everyone's different
ways of doing things. She said that during the first years, "Some people irri-
tated me. I began to notice that these faults were mine, too. Faults that
weren't mine didn't irritate me especially—only the ones that were mine.
These people became my mirror."

She observed that "probably there are as many interpretations of the
AA program as there are members. Despite surface variations in manners of
organization, underneath the fundamentals are identical. The Twelve Steps
are wonderful for their extreme flexibility. Each person interprets the Steps
according to individual needs at the time. And the meaning of each Step
evolves over time for the individual."

For months, Marty had no job, so she had the time to devote to this
early convalescent stage of AA. She became concerned about the intensity
of her involvement. She feared she was growing overly dependent. She went
back to Dr. Tiebout and said, "You know, I'm getting a little worried."

"Why?" he asked.

"Because," she replied, "I haven't seen anyone but AA people for the past six months, and don't want to."

"Never mind," Tiebout reassured her. "It won't hurt you. Gradually you'll begin to go out into the nonalcoholic world."

As much as she loved AA and believed that lifelong contact with the fellowship was essential for continuing sobriety and sanity, Marty also was convinced that recovery from alcoholism involved getting a life outside AA's doors. She was aware that some people in AA worried when members reduced their attendance as their sobriety lengthened, but she viewed learning to live life with others as a natural consequence of returning health.

The daily existence of these small bands of sober alcoholics in the year 1939 was tenuous. AA had four years of recovery experience, to be sure, and publication of the Big Book combined with some occasional publicity like that in the *Plain Dealer* was beginning to motivate people to join AA. Despite these hopeful developments, no one really knew whether people could stay sober over the long haul. Could AA last? Marty's pink cloud had carried her for eight months. On returning to New York from Cleveland, however, she crashed into a deep depression.

During the next year, between Christmas 1939 and Christmas 1940, Marty had three slips, or relapses, as they have come to be called. Two were mild and brief, but the first was a ten-day, nonstop binge. Chris had become engaged to Grennie, and Marty was a fifth wheel in the apartment she and Chris shared. Marty still had no job. There was probably a letdown after the excitement of Cleveland. In addition, she was experiencing a typical symptom of convalescence from alcoholism, namely that her emotional development had essentially ceased at the age she began drinking alcoholically. In Marty's case, that was seventeen, with all the mood swings, fears, and impulsivity of a teenager. Maturation would take time. Marty's sudden, black, clinical depression—a common disorder independent of alcoholism and one that would periodically afflict her the rest of her life—compounded her vulnerability. Just before Christmas 1939, she started drinking with a vengeance. For a week she hid out with drinking friends in Harlem. They finally had enough of her and sent her home in a cab.

Grennie and some other AA friends got her admitted to Bellevue again, but this time to the alcoholic ward to detox. Marty came out of her blackout the next day, Sunday. The ward was every bit as bad as she'd heard.

Patients were on mattresses in the hall. Someone was retching. Another patient was screaming with terrifying hallucinations (d.t.'s). Horrified, Marty managed to sneak out. No liquor stores were open, so she picked up a six-pack of beer at a deli and went to the apartment of an AA woman who she knew was not staying sober and would welcome a drinking buddy. The two of them continued drinking.

When Marty went out for more liquor, she passed her own apartment. A tall, thin, pathetic figure was stooped over, peering at the names on the mailboxes. His trousers were shabby. He had on a Navy pea jacket that was too small, the sleeves too short, the cuffs frayed. It was Bill Wilson.

"What are you doing here?" Marty demanded.

"I'm looking for you. Will you talk to me?"

"Well, I'm drinking."

"I know that. Can I come up?"

"Well, all right, if I can keep on drinking."

The real reason she let him in was that she felt sorry for him. He looked so sad. She had her drink; then Bill asked, "Do you want to go on drinking?"

"Of course not," Marty replied.

"I didn't think so." Then he told her to get cracking and sober up. There was work for her to do. "You know," he added gently, as he put his arms around her, "you and I have a long way to go together." He pulled a piece of paper from his pocket. "I have a note from Lois. We'd like you to come back with us if you'd like to."

Lois's note read, "We want you up here because we love you."

At the time, the Wilsons were homeless. It was winter, and they were staying in a summer cottage in the Pocono Mountains belonging to the mother of one of the AA members. "You know," Bill continued, "it's not too comfortable. If you'd rather go in a hospital, we've raised the money between us for you to go to Towns." And Bill started pulling rumpled ones and fives from his pocket.

Towns Hospital was expensive, about $100 guaranteed on admission ($1,200 in year 2000 dollars). Marty choked up at the thought that her little AA group in New York, none of whom had much money at all, had somehow put together enough cash at Christmastime to admit her to Towns.

"No," Marty said, shamed and turning away, "I can't take their money. I'll go with you and Lois."

So Marty went up to the Poconos. It was bitterly cold and the cabin was uninsulated. You could see daylight through the walls. She was very ill. Bill tapered her off. It took three days. Marty learned what other alcoholics who relapse do, that somehow the disease is silently progressive even in remission. If alcoholics return to drinking, they regress to a worse state than before they had stopped drinking.

Late at night, Marty was sleepless from alcohol withdrawal. About 3:00 A.M., Lois came to her room. Giving Marty a hug, Lois, with tears in her eyes, sighed, "Oh, Marty, I wish you could get a little love in your heart." And she left.

Marty puzzled over Lois's comment for days. What did Lois mean? Slowly, Marty came to understand that her own idea of love was, "You love *me* with everything you've got, then—maybe—I'll love you back." Furthermore, Marty saw that her modus operandi was to measure love out with an eyedropper. From then on, Marty began to change her ways and to practice unconditional love toward others. She stopped demanding love and started giving it instead. It took years and hard work to shift her attitude and actions, but she did it.

A year after this slip, Marty knew she was on the right track when AA had its first Christmas party. The party was organized because so many people had slips over Christmas.

"Many of us were single. We had a Christmas tree. I looked around that room and I was overwhelmed by a rush of love for all these people. And I realized that it didn't matter whether they loved me. What mattered was that I could, and did, love them."

Over and over, people who knew Marty remember how love for the individual poured out of her, even when they met briefly as strangers, and how they felt embraced and supported by it.

Just as alcohol withdrawal was ending for Marty while she was recovering at the Wilsons, she had what seemed to be a gallbladder attack. Jim W., a gifted con artist who had joined AA, happened to be staying nearby. He had everyone convinced that he was a medical doctor who'd lost his license from drinking. He borrowed an instrument from Rockland Hospital to remove Marty's stones. "After some trouble in persuading Marty that she could swallow the tube, he gently pushed it down her throat and apparently snaked up small, gravel-like stones. Marty soon recovered."[9]

Jim's conning abilities were far superior to his medical ones. LeClair
Bissell, M.D., says,

> To get to the gall bladder that way, you'd have to have a very thin in-
> strument to pass into the small intestine, then round a sharp corner
> and head north thru the bile duct (very tiny) and up into the gall blad-
> der. Such flexible tools were not in existence when Marty's alleged
> treatment took place and even now there's no such approach in use as
> far as I know. They do now break up stones with ultrasound and try to
> get some of them to pass by themselves but the usual approach is still
> surgery. Many stones do pass spontaneously so perhaps that's what
> happened.

Marty was lucky to have suffered no harm from this AA medical quack.

It took Marty a month to return to AA, not so much because of her
physical condition but because of her guilt and shame. She found it hard
to go back and face her friends. She felt she'd let them and all of AA
down. Fortunately, for herself and the many others who would find recovery through her example and leadership, she swallowed her pride and
returned.

When Marty analyzed her relapse further, she saw the importance of
what AA called the twenty-four-hour program. This was an attitude of taking one day at a time, very useful for alcoholics who often tend in early recovery to wallow in regret for the past and fear for the future and forget
their strength for today. Her second lesson was that she had been relying almost exclusively on the fellowship of AA to keep her sober and ignoring its
heart, the Twelve Steps. She secretly believed she was superior to the need
for the Twelve Steps, especially the inventory Steps (Four and Five), because
of her years of psychotherapy. She came to understand why sometimes AA
called itself a bountiful cafeteria, "strictly self-service." Yet people "could
starve to death if they didn't make an effort to get the food and eat."

Marty also noted the importance of repetition in learning new behaviors and attitudes, especially in the earlier years of recovery. The AA member needed to hear and practice over and over the teachings and concepts at
the core of recovery in AA: "Don't drink. Go to meetings. Help another
alcoholic. Live the Twelve Steps." In emphasizing the significance of repetition, Marty spoke from her lifelong knowledge of the publicity field, "Good-

ness knows, the advertising industry discovered the value of repetition years ago."

Marty said she was a slow learner, however. In the beginning she danced only the one- and two-step (Steps One and Twelve). Later on, she discovered that people tend to learn in a predictable pattern known as the learning curve. Assimilating new information may occur rapidly in a short, steep curve. Then there is a period of consolidation, a plateau, while the person digests the information. After that, the learning curve will be more gradual.

Around the middle of 1940, Marty had a second slip, mercifully mild and brief, from which she recovered immediately. A few weeks later she was maid of honor at the wedding of Dr. Foster Kennedy and Katherine Caragol de la Terga.[10]

Then in December, a third relapse started during the Christmas holidays. Before this one could really get going, Marty had the sense to call a friend right away, who drove her up to High Watch Farm on New Year's Eve day 1940. The snow was six feet deep. They had to hike in the last mile and a half. High Watch worked its magic for Marty, as it had for other alcoholics in the past year, and she recovered rapidly from the experience.

Later, Marty heard an experienced AA say that there is only one difference between a newcomer and an older member: "If you don't take that first drink, you'll be like me. If I do take that first drink, I'll be like you."

Marty's three slips didn't do her reputation much good among many of the AA men, despite the fact that a number of them were relapsing, too. A woman alcoholic simply had a very hard time being understood and accepted. Also, in those days almost nothing was known about relapses during the convalescent period. AA hadn't had enough experience yet to know that one or two relapses during the first year are more common than not. Then, as now, slips frightened other recovering alcoholics—for good reason. There were plenty of examples of alcoholics who relapsed and never made it back, their lives ruined, their minds permanently damaged—or they were dead. At the same time, a certain stigma adhered to the relapser. "You must be doing something wrong" was the often unspoken criticism. Many times that was true. Today, however, alcoholism is increasingly recognized as a disease particularly prone to relapse for a number of biochemical, psychosocial, and environmental reasons, each of which, however, can usually be overcome with time, effort, and commitment on the part of the alcoholic.

Most recovered alcoholics can tell you the exact date and time of their last drink and their first encounter with Alcoholics Anonymous. An exception is the person who has a history of relapses. Partly this is a matter of superstition. It might be bad luck to give the impression, even to oneself, that abstinence is now permanent. Because of her three early relapses, Marty preferred not to set a specific date for the beginning of her long-term sobriety. The closest she would say was the general time frame—Christmas 1940. In fact, though Marty openly described her three early relapses, she apparently much preferred to emphasize what she considered the date of her beginning recovery from alcoholism—April 11, 1939—the day of her first AA meeting.

Although Marty settled down after these three relapses, the compulsion to drink didn't really leave for another three or four years. The goal of a comfortable sobriety didn't come easily. Perhaps because of her slips, Marty again and again emphasized that she valued AA and sobriety above all else. "AA is life and hope," she would say. Throughout her long years of sobriety, Marty placed AA first.

Like most people who come to AA, Marty's sole purpose was to get sober—at least temporarily. Whether most people wanted to stay sober and were willing to do the footwork to achieve that goal was another matter. Marty's personal intention was permanent sobriety.

In New York City they called the Twelve Steps a design for living, tools with which to fashion a better self. These tools implied more than simply being dry. For Marty and others, they gave freedom from the preoccupation with alcohol even when not drinking. Marty noted, however, that for an alcoholic to work the Steps, the person must be sober. In other words, "Sobriety is the step before Step One. It is the door by which we enter the AA way of life."

Marty was learning how to apply her formidable willpower in a positive direction. And years later she would appreciatively appropriate an epigram from a man in early recovery: "You need *won't* power as well as *will* power."

Precious as was her hard-won sobriety, Marty could put sobriety in its global perspective. "You know, staying sober is not such a great thing. Most of the world does it all the time."

Gradually, her goal became quality of sobriety rather than just getting and staying sober. "What makes AA different is what we do with our sobriety. Sobriety is only the means to an end." She took to heart what she'd heard another AA woman say: "It's the quality of your sobriety that counts, not the length."

While all this recovery activity was going on during Marty's first year in AA, she was engaged in an intensive job search. Finding a job wasn't easy. She had begun to put out employment feelers well before she left Greenwich but was becoming disheartened. Leopold Mannes continued to encourage her from his solid experience as a successful businessman.

> In order *not* to be discouraged by reverses on the job-hunting front, all you have to do is to realize that, inasmuch as you are *not* under any time limit, the hunting process is the job itself for the time being and *there is no hurry.* Registering with the Red Cross is ok, but meanwhile, don't get hectic, and plan the campaign leisurely. Your past isn't so black—you simply haven't had a job in this country for an eternity and more experienced and younger people will get ahead of you *UNTIL* you make the right contact. That inevitably takes time and circulation which only now will you be in a position to do under conditions of assured income plus good health. So take it easy. Try WQXR [radio station] and stick to it without hounding them offensively. If you land a job by spring it will be damn quick work and you can be proud of yourself. And *do* be careful.[11]

Regardless, it took Marty a year to locate work as fashion publicity director at R. H. Macy's in New York City. She was there for two years, 1940 to 1942, at a salary of $40 a week ($480 in year 2000 dollars). Chris, too, began working at Macy's. During that time Marty met Priscilla Peck, who was Macy's chief copywriter. Priscilla may actually have helped Marty land the job at Macy's. Whatever the situation, Marty's life once more took a gigantic turn.

From 1943 on, Marty's story is intimately intertwined with Priscilla's.

Priscilla

1942—44

WHEN MARTY BEGAN WORKING AT MACY'S, she was so happy to be free of the compulsion to drink that, like many alcoholics in early recovery, she talked all the time about AA. Priscilla was very interested because she had an alcoholic sister.

Priscilla was also an active alcoholic herself until Marty "Twelfth-Stepped" her into AA around 1943. However, Priscilla didn't seem to have hit the extremely low bottom experienced by Marty and so many of the early members of AA, including the first women. In fact, Priscilla was an example of what AA was slowly learning—that there were degrees of disaster, and the earlier in the development of the disease of alcoholism an alcoholic sought help, the better the chances of recovery. Bill, Marty's brother, wondered sometimes if Priscilla really was an alcoholic, but that's a fairly common feeling when one meets an AA who's recovered. It seems impossible that an elegant, talented, successful person could ever have been in trouble with alcohol.

By 1943, Priscilla and Marty had fallen in love. In Priscilla, Marty had met her intellectual, spiritual, and creative match. They shared a passion for books and art and music, the theater and ballet. Physically, Marty was much taller, but both women had an outstanding sense of elegance, grace, and style. Feminine and glamorous, with dark brown hair and eyes, Priscilla was also lots of fun and full of life. The pair moved in together, partly to save rent. It was the beginning of a nearly forty-year devoted and committed partnership that ended only with their deaths. Gifted though they were as individuals, their loving union almost certainly provided the stimulus and nurture that enabled and enhanced their future great accomplishments. Nonetheless, like any couple in a long-term relationship, they had their ups and downs, some of them dramatic and heartrending.

Priscilla, three years younger than Marty, was born at home to Tracy and Ethel (Hill) Peck, in Brooklyn on December 2, 1907. She was named for her maternal grandmother, Priscilla Hill. The large frame house still stands in an attractive middle-class residential section of Brooklyn. Another child preceded Priscilla but had died in infancy.

Two years after Priscilla, Elizabeth (Liz) was born. Liz was named for her paternal Peck grandmother. Though Priscilla and Liz's parents were not superrich like the Manns, the Pecks were well off. The girls had many social and economic advantages as they grew up.

Priscilla was a talented artist and pianist as well as writer, born into a family with distinguished academic antecedents. Her grandfather, Tracy Peck, LL.D., a famous Latin scholar, was valedictorian of his class at Yale and a member of Phi Beta Kappa, the premier national honor society for academic achievement. Dr. Peck taught Latin language and literature for nearly thirty years at Yale. He was also an authority on Roman antiquities, archeology, architecture, and topography. As a professor (nicknamed "Pliny the Peck" by his Yale students), "He was intolerant of careless work but his own courtly and chivalrous character made him one of the best-loved and most respected of the scholars of a peculiarly rich period in American classical scholarship."[1] Following retirement, Dr. Peck lived in his beloved Rome most of the last thirteen years of his life, except for annual visits to the United States. He died in 1922 when Priscilla was fifteen, so she probably would have met him several times as well as heard a good deal about her distinguished grandfather.

Dr. Peck's wife, Elizabeth (Lillie), was mentally unbalanced and died before Priscilla was born. When Lillie failed to come home one February night in 1903, Yale suspended classes the next day so that more than a thousand students could join in the hunt for her. She was found dead at the foot of a cliff, just above the water's edge. It was believed that she wandered away while demented. The fall could also have been a successful suicide attempt.

The couple had two children, first Teresina, then Tracy Jr., who was Priscilla's father. Both children were highly intelligent. Teresina was identified as Teresina I by the Pecks. Fun-loving and witty, she graduated from

Smith College in 1894. In those days, it was rare that a woman even went to college. She married a Congregational minister from Yale, Wilfrid A. Rowell, and they moved to the Midwest. They had a daughter also named Teresina (nicknamed Terry and sometimes known in the family as Teresina II). In a reaction to her minister husband's unusually rigid temperament, Teresina I forbade little Terry to attend the church's Sunday school. Unfortunately, Teresina I, like her mother before her, had periods of some kind of mental disorder. She died in 1945.

The younger Teresina, Priscilla's cousin, was an intellectual power-house reminiscent of their Yale grandfather. In 1933 she earned a Ph.D. in comparative religions from Yale, thereafter teaching at several colleges including Smith. She was a lifetime practicing member of the Religious Society of Friends (Quakers) and met her husband, Joseph Havens, through a Quaker center at Pendle Hill, Pennsylvania. Before World War II, she lived in Japan for a year, where she became very attached to Buddhism. She remained an eclectic, however, open to many faiths and with a lifelong sense of mission to be a bridge-builder among the world's religious traditions. In 1971, Terry and Joseph founded a retreat center, Temenos, near Northampton, Massachusetts. Temenos was designed for basic living, meditation, and the fifth yoga—interpersonal relationships. Later the Havens retired to Oregon, where Terry died in 1992.

Apparently, there was little if any contact between Priscilla's family and her aunt Teresina's side of the Pecks, particularly after Priscilla's father died. Interestingly, however, Priscilla, also gifted with the Pecks' brilliant intellect, became a spiritual seeker like her cousin Terry.

Tracy Jr., Priscilla's father, carried on the family tradition by graduating from Yale in 1895. His field of concentration is unknown, but he received several Latin prizes. And like his father, Tracy Jr. was a member of Phi Beta Kappa. For eighteen years before he died, he managed the safety deposit vaults of the Lincoln Storage Warehouse Company in Brooklyn. Very little else is known about him. He died in 1913 at the age of thirty-eight—of a heart attack according to Peck family legend. However, his death certificate states that he succumbed to "nephritis and hemorrhage into the fourth ventricle of the brain."[2]

When their father, Tracy, died, Priscilla and Liz were little girls ages six and four, respectively. Priscilla, and probably Liz as well, felt abandoned—a natural reaction for children. A stabilizing factor for them and their mother, Ethel, was their grandmother Hill and aunt Lila, Ethel's unmarried sister. At least three years before Tracy's death, these two women came to live with them. Priscilla adored her aunt Lila and remained close to her until Lila's death in 1968.

Priscilla's mother, Ethel Hill, was a Brooklyn girl. Ethel and Tracy were married in 1899. Ethel's grandfather Hill was prominent in New York's music publishing business. Her father, Warren E. Hill, was vice president of Brooklyn's Continental Iron Works, the shipyard that built the famous Ericsson *Monitor* in 1862. This was America's first iron ship. While under construction, the *Monitor* was the butt of skeptics who could not imagine that a ship of metal would ever float. The *Monitor* not only floated beautifully, but it also bested the South's wooden *Merrimac* in a critical naval battle that determined the North's supremacy on the seas in the Civil War.

Priscilla's Hill forebears were very well-to-do, so even after Tracy died, neither Priscilla's mother, Ethel, nor *her* widowed mother ever had to earn a living. Ethel could afford a live-in servant. Apparently, Ethel was a careful administrator of her inheritance. When she died in 1931, her estate was divided almost evenly between Priscilla and Liz—approximately $23,500 to Priscilla and $23,800 to Liz—a lot of money in those days ($260,000 and $262,000 respectively, in year 2000 dollars). Priscilla also inherited a valuable painting by James Peale, a prominent nineteenth-century American painter.

Both Priscilla and Liz Peck were known as beauties. Priscilla's lovely looks can be seen in the Bouché sketch of her and Marty. Liz reportedly looked like Ingrid Bergman when she was a young woman.

The two sisters were markedly different in many ways, however. Priscilla, a rather quiet, introspective girl, was intellectually inclined from childhood. She loved reading, art, and music. Sometimes Liz thought her older sister was spoiled because Priscilla seemingly was allowed to evade chores in favor of reading or painting or playing the piano. Eventually, Priscilla graduated from Adelphi College on Long Island with a degree in English. Maturity would find her gifts flowering. Her interests expanded into philosophy and spirituality. People often commented on her brilliant mind and wicked sense of humor. She definitely seemed a worthy descendant of the illustrious Pecks.

Liz, on the other hand, was a sturdy, physical tomboy. Blond and blue-eyed, she was blessed with plenty of brains but preferred to concentrate on developing her body. An outstanding talent in sports led her to a master's degree in physical education, and she became an elementary school physical education teacher in Garden City on Long Island. Liz also had strong mechanical gifts. She loved boats, cars, and planes, worked on them herself, and earned a pilot's license. During World War II, she was reportedly a flying instructor for the Army, Navy, and Marines.

The basic personality differences between the sisters led to estrangement in adulthood. They would come together at holidays sometimes, but their interests were simply at odds. Priscilla, who moved in very high-style cultural, social, and intellectual circles, may have been ashamed of her earthier sister. Liz chose to be somewhat rough and unrefined and insisted on living in a low-class area on the West Side of Manhattan. At any rate, the general lack of communication between Priscilla and Liz appears to have been Priscilla's wish, with Liz looking on from a distance with some longing and much admiration.

Those were the differences. There were two prominent, life-shaping similarities. Both Priscilla and Liz developed alcoholism. Liz, however, never found permanent recovery as did Priscilla. She couldn't stay sober for long, though she tried AA off and on. Perhaps her continued drinking was the more important reason for Priscilla's distancing. After retiring from teaching, Liz moved to Florida.

And both sisters were lesbians. Since neither ever married or had children, their side of the Peck line died out with them.

Liz's sexual orientation was more obvious than Priscilla's, and her discretion regarding partners, questionable. Liz could never manage a permanent love relationship. In AA, she often got involved with young lesbians, years her junior, who were new to sobriety and vulnerable to unstable emotional entanglements. They usually left Liz when they learned of her continued drinking. Inappropriate crushes are also typical of straight men and women in early recovery.

Marty and Priscilla were active and known in New York's gay and lesbian communities, so it is possible they were acquainted before working at Macy's, especially since they had mutual interests in literature, art, theater, and related fields. In addition, their paths very likely would have crossed at

Cherry Grove on Fire Island, New York, at least after Marty got sober. Esther Newton, author of a definitive history, *Cherry Grove, Fire Island,* was told by a reliable source that both women were together there on a weekend as early as the summer of 1938.[3] That could have happened in the short period in June between Marty's discharge from Bellevue and her admission to Blythewood at the end of the month. Or Marty may have visited Cherry Grove briefly later in the summer when she was out on pass during her early weeks as a patient at Blythewood. Or both. There is no question, however, that Priscilla vacationed at Cherry Grove that summer of 1938. Esther Newton's documentation indicates that Marty and Priscilla knew one another from the time of Marty's Blythewood days, if not before.

Cherry Grove had started as a modest vacation spot, a nearby getaway for families in the Sayville, Long Island, area. A short ferry ride from Sayville on the southern Long Island shore, Cherry Grove later became America's first gay and lesbian town, attracting the professional, creative crowd from New York City's vibrant cultural center. Cherry Grove was a favorite retreat for these immensely talented people, who included the English poet W. H. Auden, Natalia Murray and Janet Flanner, singer Peter Pears and composer Benjamin Britten, set designer Oliver Smith, theater producer Cheryl Crawford, and writers Carson McCullers, Patricia Highsmith, Paul and Jane Bowles, Tennessee Williams, and Truman Capote.

When New York homosexuals first began to visit Cherry Grove in the mid-1930s, Marty was in Europe. After she returned to New York, she spent 1937 in a final alcoholic collapse. She said, however, that she'd partied in Cherry Grove during her drinking days while searching for other gays. Perhaps she was a guest of some of her well-heeled theater and literary friends. She herself was broke. Because of her drinking, Marty would have been a handful for any host, though.

When at first the New York gay community, and later the lesbian one, discovered Cherry Grove, there was a certain amount of tension between the homosexual newcomers and their straight predecessors. In time, this lessened as the original heterosexual vacationers came to know their new neighbors as human beings, and also as they saw the tourist value of the largely well-to-do visitors.

Fire Island is a long, narrow sand spit. At Cherry Grove it takes no more than ten minutes to walk the width of Fire Island from the ferry dock on the sound to the Atlantic Ocean on the south. As in Marty and Priscilla's day, all the paths are wooden boardwalks to protect the fragile environment. No cars are allowed. The only vehicles are electric golf cart types, including the volunteer fire department's small rigs. The shallow dunes are off limits, but the beautiful broad beaches are not. Development is strictly controlled, with the result that the area has a relaxed, uncrowded feel. Today, mature plantings provide surprising privacy for the rather small lots. Cottages can be rented or purchased.

After getting a job following discharge from Blythewood in September 1939, Marty probably visited Cherry Grove as often as she could.

In 1943, about the time they moved in together in New York City, Marty and Priscilla bought a summer home in Cherry Grove, on the Atlantic directly south of the ferry dock. Over the next two or three years, they purchased two adjacent lots. On Fire Island, Marty could let down her constant guard regarding her sexual orientation. She and Priscilla could relax publicly in a way impossible elsewhere. They could walk hand in hand on the beach and openly express their affection.

Both women were well known in Cherry Grove as lesbians, and equally important, as recovered alcoholics. Marty and Priscilla were often called on to help sober someone up. "Call Marty!" became a standard SOS among some of America's most famous art, literary, and theater names.

Marty started the first Cherry Grove AA group, which continues meeting to this day in the firehouse. Alcoholism was as rampant among homosexuals as among heterosexuals, and certainly among Cherry Grovers, so Marty and Priscilla's presence was a beacon of hope. The two women provided a bridge back to health and sanity. Marty's efforts helped make it possible for Cherry Grove AAs to carry that message of recovery to their home communities and thus enable the spread of healing for alcoholic gay and lesbian people.

Most people, even many who worked very closely with Marty, never knew she was a lesbian. Some of them suspected, but they either didn't really care, or they didn't want to know and be confronted with an issue that made them uneasy, to say the least. Her accomplishments and what she had to offer America, indeed the world, through her inspired leadership in the alcoholism movement were the important issues. As today, the attitude was generally live and let live, along with don't ask, don't tell. That Marty kept quiet about her sexual orientation is understandable, and consequently very few straight people had any idea of the extent of her active and continuing involvement and concern for gay and lesbian people in the United States and abroad.

The Third Tradition[4] of Alcoholics Anonymous ("The only requirement for A.A. membership is a desire to stop drinking.") came about because of controversy over a gay alcoholic. One of the very early groups in Ohio wrote to Bill Wilson, petitioning him to help them make a decision. A local man, whom they described as a sexual deviant, had applied to them for membership. The group was sharply divided. The man was clearly an alcoholic and much in need of help, so many in the group felt that they really needed to include him. But some believed that bringing in an openly gay member would harm the group or the movement. From that controversy came AA's Third Tradition. Today, one of the AA World Services Office's national advisory councils focuses on AA recovery for homosexual men and women, and AA publishes literature directed to alcoholic gay and lesbian people.

In New York, there were no special meetings at first for homosexuals. Instead, through word of mouth, gay and lesbian people found AA groups that were congenial. One's homosexual orientation was usually not mentioned when telling one's story before the group. Eventually, while mixed meetings continue to be the AA norm, specialized gay and lesbian meetings did arise, as they have for women, Spanish-speaking members, and so on.

Lois Wilson was reported as having held society's prevailing views of homosexuality in the early years of AA. However, her understanding and acceptance broadened and grew with the passage of time. Marty may have been the first lesbian or gay person she ever knew well. Lois loved Marty for herself and was one of her staunchest admirers and supporters.

Neither Marty nor Priscilla concealed the fact that they lived together. It was not uncommon, anyway, for single straight women to share a home. Marty and Priscilla always spoke of themselves as friends, the standard euphemism of the day among homosexuals for their partners. Marty's use of the title *Mrs.* served the purpose of blurring her real orientation. With respect to Marty's extensive travels, *Mrs.* also provided a degree of safety and protection that *Miss* did not. In addition, she often had male escorts for business-related occasions and times when Priscilla was unavailable. Marty obviously enjoyed the company of men as much as they enjoyed hers.

Among the gay and lesbian communities, however, Marty and Priscilla did not hide their sexual orientation. Nor did they go out of their way to advertise it. After working for Marty for some months, George Marcelle, an NCA staff member, accidentally discovered Marty might be a lesbian when he was thumbing through a photo file in the office and recognized familiar Cherry Grove landmarks and people in some of the pictures.

Priscilla was once challenged in a staff meeting at *Vogue* magazine about whether she was a lesbian. Waving her signature gold cigarette holder in a gracefully expansive gesture, she answered, "But of course, dahling, everyone knows that!"[5] End of conversation.

Priscilla was apparently an even heavier smoker than Marty, consuming four to five packs a day. Marty said Priscilla was never without her cigarette holder, either in her hand or between her lips, so she didn't believe Priscilla's claim that she never inhaled. Priscilla was also an absentminded smoker, forever removing a smoldering cigarette from its holder, setting it down somewhere, and forgetting about it. A friend told her she was the greatest fire hazard in America. Then, literally overnight, Priscilla stopped smoking. Marty, who continued to be addicted to cigarettes until the end of her life, was amazed that anyone could do this on her own. She decided that Priscilla must have been telling the truth about never inhaling!

Tennessee Williams, one of America's greatest twentieth-century dramatists and also a homosexual, conducted himself in a circumspect fashion similar to Marty's and Priscilla's. As his brother, Dakin, has noted, "[Tennessee] had never made a secret of this fact with his friends, and it had been known and accepted by them for many years. But in those days, before gay liberation, the concept of homosexuality was simply unspeakable to many ordinary citizens."[6]

With the possible exception of Marty's father, Marty's family all figured out she was a lesbian, and they continued to accept and love her and her friends unconditionally. It was not discussed among the Manns, however. And no one told the younger generation, Marty's nephews. They did not learn about this aspect of their famous aunt until after her death.

As Marty moved into the national arena of alcohol education, she was very wise to be discreet about her sexual orientation. She already had two huge stigmas to overcome in the public mind. She was a woman (and one in a highly visible leadership position of power) and an alcoholic. Homosexuality was a third stigma she didn't need. One of Marty's greatest gifts was a disciplined ability to keep her eye on the ball. So powerful was that sustained focus during her lifetime, more than one person has commented she was like a train barreling down the tracks. Jump on or get out of the way.

Marty's family loved Priscilla, and she loved them. She was vivacious, glamorous, and fun to be with, a gifted artist and pianist. Marty and others considered Priscilla's style of painting and drawing as "beautiful, extraordinary, and unique."[7]

Priscilla's knowledge of art was impressive, and her insatiable openness to avant-garde art and artists, infectious. She was an early collector of work by such artists as Jackson Pollock, one of whose paintings hung in the apartment. *Number 15, 1949* was a fine early example of Pollock's creative drip technique, for which he would become famous. Priscilla had acquired the painting from her close friend, the gallery owner Betty Parsons. In 1967, the painting was lent for a major retrospective of Pollock's works held at New York's Museum of Modern Art (MOMA).

Pollock was an alcoholic. Several psychiatrists attempted to help him, but their approach was the usual one of the day—unravel the underlying emotional disorder, and the drinking would cease to be a problem. Marty, and especially Priscilla, may have been among those who urged him to go to AA. He tried it briefly but claimed it was for "lonely hearts and mouth runner-offers." Gripped by denial, he boasted, "I only drink when I feel like it."[8]

For two years, he did manage to remain relatively sober. These were the years of his amazing breakthrough into abstract expressionism, culminating in the drip paintings of the late 1940s. Then the compulsion to drink returned with a vengeance. In 1951, he became a patient of Ruth Fox, M.D. A tough straight-talker, she told him he was an alcoholic. She insisted on abstinence and prescribed Antabuse[9] to help. He ignored abstinence even when hospitalized for detox and took the Antabuse only when he felt like it. Fox also sent him to AA, with equally poor compliance.

Finally, in 1956, Pollock died in a wild automobile accident while driving dead drunk. He was only forty-four years old. One of his two passengers was also killed.

At the moment he died, Pollock's paintings were bound to increase in value. By the time Marty sold *Number 15, 1949* in 1979, his reputation was secure as one of America's most important artists ever, and his paintings commanded very high prices.

Both Marty and Priscilla were crazy about animals and usually owned a couple of dogs, Welsh corgis as a rule. Two of the longest-lived were Taffy and Bunny. At one time, recounted Marty's brother, Bill, "Priscilla had this big sheepdog, spoiled to beat hell. Priscilla, eating at the table, would feed the dog right there." Off and on there were also cats. In the 1970s, Ting and Tang were in residence. Ting was a tortoiseshell, and Tang (short for Tangerine) an orange cat. Marty was always mixing up their names.

When Priscilla was away, she would sometimes scribble quick notes to Marty.

Darling—I love you up down in out now then forever—no sea, sky land bog flotsam jetsam or what-not can harm or separate us—All all all love—P. Love and kisses to Bunny (the hero) and Taffy![10]

Priscilla was a tease. Bill Mann recalled, "If I would go out the door, Priscilla would lock the door so I couldn't get back in! I loved Priscilla and she loved me." When he was in New York as a young single man, and Marty was off traveling, he and Priscilla would go out to dinner "many a time. She'd take me. She had more money than I did. As art editor of *Vogue*, she was making pretty damn good money, and she had her charge cards and so on."

Priscilla's greatest shortcoming was a huge blind spot about money. She spent money profligately, often on items like very high-quality art, to be sure, but sometimes beyond her and Marty's means. Bill Mann said, "She was a compulsive buyer. She picked things up anywhere. They had more junk. Priscilla would buy anything. She couldn't hold onto money."

The year 1943 brought a fascinating sixth woman into New York AA, Felicia Gizycka,[11] destined to play a central role in the lives of Marty and Priscilla. She had come from an even wealthier and more privileged background than Marty's, yet sunk to similar depths through alcoholism. When Felicia's New York therapist gave her the Big Book to read, she was offended by "all the God stuff" but dragged herself to the little AA office for help, anyway.

Bill Wilson talked with her and asked gently, "Do you think you are one of us?" She found herself nodding her head. He then phoned Marty, saying, "I've got a dame here with a name I can't pronounce" and sent Felicia to Marty and Priscilla's apartment.

Marty hadn't yet arrived, but Priscilla opened the door. Felicia wrote:

> The strange A.A. put me at ease. The apartment was charming; the shelves were full of books, many of which I myself owned. Marty came in, looking clean, neat, well-dressed and, like Bill, she was neither a bloated wreck nor a reformer. She was attractive; she was like the friends I had once had. Indeed, she had known my cousin in Chicago.[12]

Marty proceeded to tell Felicia her story. Felicia couldn't get a word in edgewise.

> Marty was smart. A load weighing a thousand pounds came off my back. I wasn't insane. Nor was I the "worst woman who ever lived." I was an alcoholic, with a recognizable behavior pattern.[13]

Marty and Priscilla escorted Felicia to her first AA meeting. Priscilla, quite new in AA herself, took Felicia under her wing. Felicia, who was not homosexual, and Priscilla became devoted lifelong friends. The two were what AA sometimes calls "littermates." Marty was their mutual sponsor.

Felicia's recovery the first year was fairly typical. When she couldn't stop drinking the first month, Priscilla decided she was a stubborn case. Another AA woman had just gone on a terrible bender. Priscilla told Felicia to take the woman to High Watch Farm and sober her up. Felicia reported:

> The farm, in those days, was primitive. There was no central heating, and this was the dead of winter. Anne and I went up in ski clothes and fur coats, and it was so cold we slept in them. . . . I completely forgot myself in trying vainly to help Anne, whose misery I understood.[14]

During the year, Felicia relapsed once more. Grieving the imminent death of a dear friend from drinking, she commenced a final drinking bout herself.

> I went to a bar and downed two double brandies in quick succession. I went to the phone booth and called Marty. I thought she'd say, "Where are you? Give me the address of that bar." Not at all. My smart and wise sponsor simply said, "Well, Honey, what can I do about it?"

That deflated me, but it didn't stop me. I drank all that night.
I don't know where I went or what I did. The next morning I called
John D, a wonderful old timer who had taken me to a lot of meetings.
He came right over to the apartment. I greeted him at the door and
said, "I just wanted to do the honesty bit. I'm telling you honestly: I'm
waiting for my stomach to settle. As soon as it does, I'm going right
out and tie on another one."

John said, "All right. Go ahead. But when *are* you going to stop?"

Marty hadn't let me dramatize myself, and John was scaring me. I
thought, "My God, maybe I can't stop."

Somewhere in my mind I must have reached for the brakes. Marty
has told me since that I kept calling her from various bars down in The
Village. Each time she'd say, "Call me when you're ready to stop," and
hang up. I don't remember any of this.

John nicknamed my slip, "Custer's Last Stand." I spent three days
and nights in the old familiar haunts, drunk as a doxy and hating every
minute of it. On the fourth morning I called Marty and said, "Help!"[15]

Marty immediately came over before going to work that morning and
nursed Felicia through several hours of acute detox. Felicia couldn't keep
anything down, so Marty used a common AA remedy—sweetened milk.
She dipped a teaspoon in the milk and had Felicia lick the spoon.

Marty had developed into a very good sponsor—one with patience and
wisdom. She nurtured her pigeons, as they were called, but she also practiced what became a core Al-Anon teaching, "detachment with love."[16]
Felicia was prone to mood swings and clinical depression. When she told
Marty she wanted to jump out of a window, Marty said, "You might hit a
pedestrian, you might cripple yourself."

Dramatically, Felicia replied, "I'll lie down on the railroad tracks."

"Just keep plodding along, put one foot in front of another," Marty
responded.

If Felicia talked about taking another drink, Marty answered, "Just
what is there about this situation that a drink is going to solve?"[17]

Within a couple of years, Felicia was able to return to her vocation,
writing. For many years, a basic part of her service to AA was contributing
articles to the *AA Grapevine* and serving on its editorial board. A few years

after she joined AA, Felicia became a pivotal influence in the spiritual lives of Marty and Priscilla. She outlived them both and in 1998 celebrated fifty-five years of sobriety in AA. Felicia died in February 1999 at the age of ninety-two.

These three women—Priscilla, Felicia, and Marty—and others used to "hold long discussions as to why it was so difficult to help women, why they couldn't stay sober, couldn't make the program work." Gradually, however, their efforts began to bear fruit. Without being involved in the feminist movement herself, Marty was the leader in freeing untold numbers of women from the bondage of a terrible and little-understood disease. In AA, women then found a personal liberation that acted as a leaven in their families and communities.

If Marty and Priscilla could have foreseen the future as 1943 drew to a close, they would have been uncharacteristically speechless. Their inner lives and their careers would undergo permanent, profound changes in the years between 1944 and 1948. In a way, the changes were predictable because far-reaching change for the better is what happens for people in recovery. But who could possibly have anticipated what actually happened?

$\mathcal{D}$awn of a $\mathcal{V}$ision

1944

AFTER TWO YEARS AT MACY'S, Marty landed a job in 1942 as radio scriptwriter and then as research director at the American Society of Composers, Authors, and Publishers (ASCAP). During her year-and-a-half tenure there, she continued to work diligently with alcoholics and to participate fully in AA. Yet she yearned to be more broadly useful.

She was inspired by the story of an AA man who, at the age of forty-five, remembered his youthful goals and ideals and began to work toward them. With sobriety, Marty found her own early ideals and goals were gradually awakened. At first the goals were simple. When she began to get near to one, she found another further on. The process brought growth and a sense of achievement. She believed that growth leads to being useful, and vice versa.

For Marty, an open-ended growth process and a sense of usefulness were two of the most important gifts of Alcoholics Anonymous. With increased sobriety, Marty realized that she would "never graduate from AA" because the struggle for personal change never stops. "The biggest room in the world is the room for improvement." Growth and usefulness in turn result in tremendous satisfaction and happiness. Again and again throughout her life, Marty taught that AA gives meaning and purpose to the individual and a way to be of service to others.

One day, while walking on Fifth Avenue, she looked up at all the upscale apartment buildings and wondered how many men and women like her were lost and suffering with alcoholism behind those windows. She yearned to reach them with the message of hope that had been unavailable for so long to her.

"Why people think alcoholics have fun with drinking," she said, "I'll never know. Alcoholism is a living hell. Alcoholics are living on borrowed time."

Marty became increasingly obsessed with finding a way to overcome the massive ignorance in the public mind regarding alcoholism. Her experience with TB and subsequent observation of the National Tuberculosis Association's (NTA) effective educational outreach set her to thinking how she could apply that model to AA. AA's growth seemed excruciatingly slow to her impatient nature.

Yet AA was steadily learning that while its members certainly needed to let the public know that help was available for alcoholics, this was best accomplished by AA members in a low-key, direct manner through word of mouth. AA's public relations policy evolved into one of "attraction rather than promotion."[1] Evangelism was out. Instead, AA relied on local and national media channels that occasionally publicized the existence of AA and provided a degree of education about alcoholism.

It was a difficult dilemma. Marty felt passionately that "we cannot sit on our hands and do nothing about letting the world know what we have," that there were help and hope. She knew that many alcoholics needed information before they would get help for themselves. Factual information would reduce the pervasive stigma.

In addition to NTA, Marty was greatly influenced by how AA was organized. She was committed to AA's insistence on avoiding all side issues and instead concentrating on the alcoholic alone. She decided to adopt the same single-focus policy in whatever educational endeavor she created. Like AA, she would not be sidetracked, for example, by temperance arguments, or later on by problems raised by the liquor industry, or by competition with other drugs. From the beginning, she set her sights firmly on the alcoholic and alcoholism and adhered to them.

Besides the powerful impulse to do something about the stigma of alcoholism, Marty was also experiencing a common phenomenon in the lives of recovered alcoholics in AA after the first few years of sobriety. They lift their heads from immersion in the protective, healing fellowship of AA, look around, and say, "What else is out there?" How Marty answered that question not only transformed the rest of her life but also set in motion forces that affected and continue to affect AA and all of American society.

Several external circumstances conspired to nudge Marty in the direction she needed to go. One was self-education. Bill Wilson and Marty were alike in their continual search for scientific information regarding alcoholism. In pursuit of knowledge, they attended in 1940 the third annual meeting of the Research Council on Problems of Alcohol (RCPA), an independent research organization founded in 1937.[2]

Marty and Bill also knew about, and Bill visited, Yale's new Center of Alcohol Studies, which was headed by a dynamic triumvirate of researchers subsequently renowned nationally for their contributions to the scientific understanding of alcoholism: Howard W. Haggard, M.D., a physiologist; Elvin M. (Bunky) Jellinek, Sc.D., a researcher in alcoholism; and Selden D. Bacon, Ph.D., a sociologist.

The Yale center emphasized a scientific model of addressing chronic inebriety. Haggard and Jellinek were committed to a scientific approach to research and treatment. In their influential book of the day, *Alcohol Explored,* they stated that "there is unanimity among physicians that the inebriate cannot become a moderate drinker."[3] In their opinion, the aim of treatment and recovery was complete abstinence. They rejected the idea that the problem drinker should be ostracized and condemned and were determined to find some answers to why alcoholics drank as they did. To this end, they sponsored two clinics for treatment (the Yale Plan Clinics, created by Giorgio Lolli, M.D., and educator Ray McCarthy) and established a Summer School of Alcohol Studies. Marty said that her first public non-AA talk was in 1944 at the new Yale Plan Clinic in Hartford.

In 1941, AA experienced the breathtaking impact of national publicity. Jack Alexander wrote an article on alcoholism and AA for the *Saturday Evening Post,* the country's widely read weekly magazine. Marty's story was briefly recounted at the end of the article, under the pseudonym Sarah Martin.[4] The requests for help poured in from everywhere, swamping AA's minimal resources. Marty was more convinced than ever that public education on a grand and continuing scale was necessary but wasn't sure how to go about it.

One important consequence of Alexander's article for Marty personally, as well as for her later work, was an introduction to a successful New York psychiatrist named Ruth Fox. Dr. Fox had read the *Post* article and consequently gone to an AA meeting to get help for her husband. Marty was the speaker. Ruth asked her out for coffee afterward. Marty and others tried unsuccessfully for two years to help Ruth's husband. In the process, Marty and Ruth grew into close, personal friends and later professional colleagues. Ruth Fox's husband died, but she became a pioneer in treating alcoholics. Her research and clinical practice using Antabuse and other techniques provided the medical field with the early knowledge it needed about this drug that is still sometimes prescribed.

At some point during her ASCAP career, Marty encountered an article by Dwight Anderson, public relations director of the New York State Medical Society (NYSMS). He was a recovered alcoholic who had found sobriety with the help of a psychiatrist before AA was even formed. In 1942, he was also chairman of the board of the National Association of Publicity Directors, a professional organization to which Marty likely belonged.[5] Anderson bridged and influenced an early important emerging network of researchers, clinicians, educators, and publicists in the field of alcoholism. In addition to his position with NYSMS, Anderson was a consultant to RCPA and directed its Committee on Public Relations. His 1942 article, "Alcohol and Public Opinion," appeared in RCPA's fairly new *Quarterly Journal of Studies on Alcohol.*[6]

Marty read Anderson's article and promptly adopted his fourfold thesis. Here were the concrete guidelines she had been seeking. At last, her education ideas had a practical focus. The public relations expert in Marty immediately recognized the public relations genius and potential of Anderson's four simple statements.

1. That the problem drinker is a sick man, exceptionally reactive to alcohol
2. That he can be helped
3. That he is worth helping
4. That the problem is therefore a responsibility of the healing professions, as well as of the established health authorities and the public generally[7]

Marty's rewording of Anderson's four principles is significant. First, she reduced them to three. Then she dropped any reference to gender. Finally, she plainly stated that alcoholism is a disease, a fact on which there was no scientific or medical agreement at the time. Her simple yet powerful mantra became, and still is, in the organization she founded:

1. Alcoholism is a disease and the alcoholic is a sick person.
2. The alcoholic can be helped and is worth helping.
3. This is a public health problem and therefore a public responsibility.

Marty began thinking seriously about how Anderson's ideas could be applied in a national educational endeavor akin to that provided by NTA. As was her fashion, she talked and talked—and talked—about the problem and its possible solutions. Bill Wilson was equally fervent about the need but believed AA should stick to its own proven method: one-to-one help. Priscilla Peck and the handful of early AA women were useful sounding boards for Marty.

Grace Bangs, still head of the *New York Herald Tribune* Club Women's Service Bureau, had come back into Marty's life. Grace's son was an alcoholic, and she kept prodding Marty to do something about her education obsession by applying it to community groups, not just individuals as in AA. Marty began to develop an idea for the mass production of grassroots outreach to the alcoholic, but she could not afford to leave her lucrative position at ASCAP.

Two years passed. World War II continued to rage in Europe and the Pacific. Marty's brother, Bill, was in the Army. While stationed at Fort Monmouth, New Jersey, he sometimes stayed overnight with her and Priscilla whenever he had leave. At the time, they lived on West Forty-eighth Street. The building had been a private club that was converted into apartments. Marty and Priscilla's unit was a little one-bedroom with a kitchenette. Bill would sleep on their sofa, his long legs hanging over the end. He never even thought of lesbianism. After all, Marty had been married. He assumed she was living with Priscilla until another husband came along. It wasn't until later in Bill's life, as he became wiser in the ways of the world, that he realized his sister was a lesbian. Two of his four sons would be gay, one of whom would tragically die of AIDS.

Marty saw Chris and Grennie regularly, although they lived on Long Island where Grennie was in the Civil Air Patrol. Her sister Betty was also very busy in New York City. Some of Betty's oversight responsibility with the U.S. State Department Bureau of Inter-American Affairs concerned the translation of representative American films into Spanish and Portuguese. As a consequence, she worked closely with Walt Disney Studios, especially Roy Disney, and with other famous film producers.

Meanwhile, part of Marty's job at ASCAP was to produce a series of ten-minute radio scripts for a War Information Office program called "Little Known Events in American History." When researching material, she came across a 1937 biography of Dorothea Dix. Marty was inspired by the account of Dix's crusade against the inhumane treatment of the mentally ill. The possibility of a similar national crusade on behalf of alcoholics came into still sharper focus. Marty would already have known about Chicago's famed reformer Jane Addams. (See chapter 2.)

Marty might have continued at ASCAP indefinitely, but her ideas and drive to reduce the stigma of alcoholism were coming to a head. In early 1944, she found herself irrevocably pushed by the many outer influences already recounted, and at the same time pulled by powerful inner forces into uncharted waters.

One cold February night in 1944, Marty was restive with insomnia. Around 2:00 A.M., she tried prayer to calm herself. "Give me something useful to do, something that's really needed, truly helpful." Then she added the Serenity Prayer, a favorite of AAs (who had adapted it from a newspaper obituary).

> God, grant me the serenity to accept the things I cannot change, courage to change the things I can, and wisdom to know the difference.[8]

Marty prayed especially to "change the things I can." She reflected that both earthly and heavenly help were necessary for recovery from alcoholism, and she ached to know how to dispel the ignorance and stigma, the sense of helplessness, that accompanied the disease. At 3:00 A.M., Marty finally got up and went to her typewriter. In what appeared to be almost automatic writing, she typed out in detail a lucid, full-blown plan of what would become her life's work.

Her goal was to teach people the facts about alcoholism and thereby remove the stigma of the disease. The vehicle was Education, with a capital *E*. She proposed to reach the general public, families, doctors, nurses, social workers, lawyers, ministers, industry, schools, colleges, politicians—everybody. Marty would never be accused of thinking too small.

Marty observed accurately that "for years we Americans have been viewing the problem from the corner of our eyes—obliquely—and we have formed a stereotype. We think of the alcoholic as a skid-row bum. . . . There will be no constructive action against the disease until we have a thoroughly informed public opinion. As long as the public refuses to take a straight look at the alcoholic there will be no results."

Marty outlined four avenues of action.

1. Organized local groups who would provide a constant stream of information and education at the grassroots level.
2. Alcoholism information centers.
3. Hospital beds for the acutely ill. [In those days hospitals were notoriously reluctant to accept alcoholics—they relapsed constantly and seldom had much money or paid their bills.]
4. Diagnostic and treatment clinics.

Marty then combined steps three and four so that her initial strategy had three parts. First would be a lecture program for medical professionals, social workers, and clergy. She and others believed these particular groups were essential in disseminating factual information and thus reducing stigma. Second was establishing at least one alcoholism information center in every state, preferably in every major city. Third was working with hospitals and clinics to provide treatment and beds for alcoholic patients.

It was a hugely ambitious plan, but Marty proposed to begin modestly. As Dwight Anderson later wrote, "It required very little money, just enough for an office, a secretary, and traveling expenses for a lecturer."[9]

Before any of the plan could be implemented, Marty saw that the first step was to organize a small working committee, then promote some seed money and obtain scientific backing. She was determined from the beginning to avoid the prohibition issue—the "wets" versus the "drys." Reliance on the facts from scientific research would be the means of neutralizing that whole messy controversy.

Bill Wilson's own public relations and entrepreneurial drives were in synch with Marty's. He thoroughly endorsed the need for broad public education and had himself sometimes chafed at the limitations of AA's one-to-one policy of spreading the word of hope about recovery. That, after all, was the impetus for publishing *Alcoholics Anonymous*—to reach a wider audience in a way acceptable to AA. Nevertheless, Bill doubted that Marty's ideas would appeal to either the general or professional publics. Because of AA's policy of not affiliating with outside causes or interests, he also threw cold water on any leadership or involvement by AA as an organization.

Moreover, he bluntly told Marty that her professional and educational credentials were insufficient for the task. She lacked scientific credibility. Although they both felt strongly that alcoholism was an irreversible physical condition and probably a disease, that was only an opinion supported by the experience of AA members and buttressed by prescient intuition. Valid scientific support was essential.

For several reasons, the decision to solicit scientific backing was crucial and far-reaching. It helped defuse the stigma surrounding alcoholism when people learned that reputable scientists were seriously involved in research and treatment of the condition. It provided Marty with the necessary status in delivering her message. And it permanently established in the organization that Marty was soon to found an attitude of eager openness to, and dissemination of, scientific discoveries and developments regarding alcoholism.

Marty plunged ahead and convened a planning group consisting of Grace Allen Bangs, from the *New York Herald Tribune;* Austin MacCormick, executive director of Osborne Association; Dwight Anderson, publicity director for the New York State Medical Society; Dr. Ruth Fox, a physician; and Priscilla Peck, Marty's partner. They recommended that Marty approach RCPA with her ideas.

The research council couldn't decide whether to adopt Marty's education proposal. After several weeks, they did communicate a degree of interest by suggesting they hire her to speak to medical groups. Marty declined, telling them they needed a physician for such a task.

Ruth Fox and Austin MacCormick then suggested that Marty discuss her plan with E. M. Jellinek and Howard Haggard at the Yale Center of Alcohol Studies. Dr. Fox was acquainted with these men because she'd taken her husband to the Yale center for help. She offered to write a letter of introduction to Jellinek to accompany Marty's threefold plan. Because she was a physician, Ruth's recommendations would carry weight.

Jellinek, a visionary medical researcher and administrator, was intrigued by Marty's communication and promptly arranged to meet with her and her planning group in New York City the next evening. Bill Wilson also attended. Jellinek immediately saw that Marty's educational ideas were compatible with those of the Yale Center of Alcohol Studies. He proposed that she join the center's staff and so recommended to his New Haven colleagues. Unlike RCPA, Jellinek moved fast. Only forty-eight hours had passed since he received Marty's proposal and Marty came officially on board the Yale Center of Alcohol Studies.

However, Marty needed first to catch up with the field of knowledge about alcoholism as it then existed. The solution was for her to move to New Haven during each workweek for the next six months and study intensively at the Yale center. Without regret, she resigned her prestigious position with ASCAP and never again worked in the traditional business world, nor earned the high salaries she could easily have commanded. She lived with the Jellineks while she underwent a crash course in alcoholism. In the process, Marty became a close personal friend of her mentor, "Bunky" Jellinek, and his family.

During this intensive educational period, Marty learned that the terms *alcoholic* and *alcoholism* were scientific terms coined by a Swedish physician, Magnus Huss, in 1848. The information confirmed for her that she had a legitimate medical condition that should not be stigmatized. In later years, Marty objected to practitioners and researchers substituting *ethanolism* and *substance abuse* for the perfectly good scientific labels *alcoholic* and *alcoholism*. She felt the newer practice betrayed continuing stigma toward the disease in the medical and scientific communities.

Marty learned, too, about a late-eighteenth-century, early-nineteenth-century contribution to the understanding of alcoholism that was made by Benjamin Rush, M.D. He was a signer of the Constitution and a prominent, influential physician with an enlightened outlook. Dr. Rush called chronic drunkenness a "vicious disease" that was treatable, and he recommended compassion, patience, and understanding by doctors. While some of his other ideas were erroneous in light of today's knowledge, he was on the right track in describing compulsive, uncontrolled alcohol abuse as a medical condition with a specific progression and a known corrective—abstinence. This information had been generally forgotten and was thus not available to the public by the time Marty's alcoholism was developing.

In the beginning of her association with Yale, Marty, who had the equivalent of only one year of college, was somewhat intimidated by the advanced academic degrees around her. This unease would undoubtedly contribute to what some persons experienced as snobbish, aggressive behavior. Edith Gomberg, for example, was then a young consulting psychologist and doctoral student at Yale (she later became a notable researcher and academician). She was uncomfortable around Marty because Edith felt Marty was contemptuous and condescending of nonalcoholics and lowly researchers. Marty, in spite of her openness to scientific discovery, may have been perceived by some as manifesting a belief held by many AA members—that alcoholism and recovery from it had to be experienced rather than researched to really appreciate the nature of the disease and its treatment. This belief often generated distrust and antiresearch attitudes among AAs. Later, Edith concluded that Marty's superior attitude could be accounted for, in part, by her advertising background and also that she had to be aggressive in a male-dominated research world.

In time, Marty's intelligence and drive compensated for any feelings of inferiority. She delved into the history of alcoholism, learning that it was not just a modern phenomenon, but an age-old scourge recognized and documented by ancient civilizations such as the Egyptians and Greeks. She studied the various education and treatment programs for inebriates that sprang up in this country during the late nineteenth and early twentieth centuries.

Jellinek and Marty collaborated on writing several educational pamphlets about alcoholism. The months of intensive scholarly concentration concluded with her attendance at Yale's second Summer School of Alcohol Studies in 1944. This would be her last experience as a formal student, though she would remain an avid learner the rest of her life. Thereafter, she was a recognized authority in her field and one of the most popular lecturers at the Yale Summer School of Alcohol Studies and in many other prestigious academic venues.

The summer school that year registered eighty-nine students, half of whom were clergy. There were a number of Methodists, some Baptists, no Roman Catholics, no Episcopalians. All the clergy attending came from denominations historically very antidrinking. Their churches had looked on alcoholism as a sin instead of a difficult and complex illness. In Marty's early years of recovery, she fiercely resented those who called the alcoholic a sinner. Later, however, she learned from a bishop whom she heard speak, that the classic biblical meaning of *sin* is "a separation from God and humankind."

She found this definition of sin fully acceptable and put it in her own words: "Sin means you've either been kicked out or walked out on the human race. You've resigned from it."

Every student at the Yale Summer School of Alcohol Studies was required to attend an AA meeting in New Haven. Marty overheard one clergyman say, "If I had my way, I'd put them all on a boat and sink it." One wonders how this particular minister happened to attend Yale's summer school in the first place and how much his mind was changed about alcoholism as a result. His attitude was in the minority, however.

Yale played a significant role in educating clergy about alcoholism as a treatable disease. These clergy in turn helped enlighten their denominations and congregations. Yale's outreach to the clergy is not surprising. While it has always offered comprehensive training in secular vocations, Yale College was founded in 1701 by Congregational ministers and has been a leader in clergy education ever since.

One clergyman whose inquiring mind was informed by what he learned at a subsequent Yale summer school (1949) and from Marty, Bill Wilson, and other AAs, was a young Methodist minister, Howard Clinebell. While he was doing his doctoral research at Columbia University and Union Theological Seminary, Marty and Bill Wilson were very supportive of the focus of his research on AA and other spiritual and religious approaches to counseling the alcoholic. So influenced was Clinebell by Marty that he asked her to write the introduction to the first revision of the book based on his research—a volume that became a classic in counseling alcoholics.[10] Dr. Clinebell has been a seminal influence in the lives of countless ministers who needed to learn how to respond to the cries for help from alcoholics and the families of alcoholics in their congregations. He is an excellent example of Marty's reach into an area for which she was personally not trained, but where she recognized and encouraged someone else to carry the message of hope.

Marty often spoke at clergy conferences. Like Bill Wilson, Dr. Bob Smith, and other early AAs, she believed that ministers were among the first to hear of someone's difficulties with alcohol. She urged pastors to remember that the alcoholic is a sick person. To preach to or lecture an alcoholic in the throes of his or her disease could close the door forever to any chance of rehabilitation. Clergy needed first to educate themselves about the nature of the disease of alcoholism and thereby assure the alcoholic of nonjudgmental support, while referring as necessary to community resources such as AA or a knowledgeable physician or health-care facility.

A somewhat surprising fellow student of Marty's at the 1944 summer school was Mrs. D. Leigh Calvin, president of the Women's Christian Temperance Union. The WCTU still existed, though with minimal influence following the final repeal of Prohibition in 1933. In the WCTU's view, alcohol per se was the problem and therefore its sale should be prohibited. Moreover, the WCTU existed to address the issue of excessive *male* drinking. For Marty, on the other hand, alcohol*ism*, the disease, was the problem. Since the disease appeared to affect only about 10 percent of the drinking population, Marty had no objection to the availability of liquor for the other 90 percent. Furthermore, if a woman could be an alcoholic, and if a woman could argue for tolerance toward the alcoholic as well as the sale of alcohol, as Marty did, then the temperance logic no longer made any sense.

Marty didn't flinch from trying to convince Mrs. Calvin that chronic inebriety was a disease, not a sinful absence of self-discipline and character. After several evenings of intense discussion, Mrs. Calvin changed her mind and was able to agree with Marty. From then on, Marty felt confident about tackling skeptical individuals and audiences.

Jellinek and Haggard recognized that Marty was uniquely suited for publicizing the work of the Yale Center of Alcohol Studies. Her speaking gifts were well known; she was highly intelligent, a formidable organizer and charismatic leader; her time was now her own; and she had impressive personal contacts in the journalism and public relations communities. In addition, she was a lady and a fast learner. Most important, she was in harmony with the Yale center's research and education mission. As her apprenticeship ended, she was asked to head up and expand the education part of that mission. Nothing could have thrilled her more.

The Entrepreneur

1944—46

YALE DECIDED TO ADOPT MARTY'S VISION of a National Committee for Education on Alcoholism (NCEA). NCEA would be part of the Yale center, subsidized fully by the university for the next two years, and then partially for a few years while Marty developed outside funding. Marty was named executive director. On October 2, 1944, NCEA opened a tiny office in New York City, at the New York Academy of Medicine building on East 103d Street. For the next four years the staff consisted of Marty and a secretary. The budget for the first year was $13,000 ($130,000 in year 2000 dollars).

The timing was excellent in at least one respect. AA, though still small and geographically scattered, was up and running as an organization. Therefore, Marty and NCEA had a functioning referral source for alcoholics. It would have been difficult to interest people in getting help if no help were available. Eventually, of course, clinics, hospitals, physicians and other health-care workers would join an expanded network of resources.

Marty immediately called a press conference. There was a large turnout of representatives from the many New York newspapers and the wire services. The response of an often cynical press was startling. Front-page stories and editorial comments appeared in newspapers all over the country. The tenor of most of the articles was that this new organization had taken a sensible approach to an important problem.

Marty's publicity and organizational skills went into overdrive. Her purpose from the beginning was to keep every possible media avenue provided with interesting, current information about the disease of alcoholism and what could be done about it. Within two months, NCEA was receiving mail from servicemen overseas who had read about the new venture in *Stars and Stripes.* (Marty had a personal interest in the military because her brother, Bill, was now in the Army, though stationed stateside.) Before the first year was out, NCEA sponsored the first National Alcoholism and Family Congress, prepared a detailed fact sheet on alcoholism and domestic violence, and initiated a blue ribbon commission on alcoholism and the aging. Marty was immediately on the cutting edge of public health by identifying these three major issues that would not be adequately grasped by either health professionals or the general public for decades.

A national monthly, the *NCEA Public Journal,* was started (later changed to *Alcoholism, the National Magazine*). Marty had set a pace that became the norm for NCEA and the astonishing productivity to follow.

The press loved Marty. She was lively copy and could be counted on for a telling quote. Nor did she ever hesitate to correct reporters. In a perhaps apocryphal story, one interviewer had described Marty as an "ex-lady lush." Her spirited response was, "I may be an ex-lush, young man, but I am definitely a lady!"

Marty immediately placed articles on NCEA in many journals and other media. A few months after the summer school session, she arranged for an interview by the Associated Press (AP) of herself and her fellow student at Yale, Mrs. Calvin of the WCTU. The AP's feature article, appearing in forty-two newspapers nationally, stressed the fact that Mrs. Calvin had endorsed the concept of alcoholism as a disease. The press accurately perceived a public victory over the temperance forces.

Nevertheless, the wets versus drys controversy continued to plague Marty. Her mantra was, "Drinking is a social pastime, and our organization is neither 'wet' nor 'dry'—we are interested in the alcoholic only." Despite this oft-repeated statement, NCEA was constantly challenged by both liquor interests and temperance societies—"The distillers say we are trying to get Prohibition returned; the temperance people claim we are just a front for the liquor trade."

Among Marty's early publicity venues was AA's new monthly, the *AA Grapevine.* Several AA members, most of them women who had journalism and publicity backgrounds, had been interested for some time in starting a publication that would help promote AA community and fellowship. Marty and Priscilla were two of the *Grapevine's* founders. They both continued to write for the monthly during the magazine's early history, and Priscilla was for many years on the editorial board.

One of Marty's inspired publicity ventures was arranging for New York's buses and subway trains to display public-service ads about alcoholism. Commuters could read the matter-of-fact, simple statement, "Alcoholism is a disease." Sheila Blume, who became an M.D. and later a medical director of NCA, recalls that she had no trouble with the disease concept of alcoholism because she had learned and absorbed that fact while riding New York's public transport.

On the organizational side, Marty spent hours consulting with the executive director of the National Tuberculosis Association, Kendall Emerson, M.D. Not surprisingly, NCEA strongly resembled NTA. Dr. Emerson cautioned Marty about the many pitfalls she would encounter and shared the details of his organization. He was a generous and very helpful mentor. Marty, in addition, had access to the experience and advice of Dwight Anderson, formerly NTA's public information officer. Now he held a similar position with the New York State Medical Society, worked across the hall from her, and was on NCEA's new board of directors.

Dr. Emerson and Dr. Jellinek cautioned Marty that revolutionary ideas like hers took about fifty years to percolate into public acceptance. She laughed and pooh-poohed such a conservative estimate. *She* would never take that long! "Of course the process could be shortened!" Thirty-five years later, she ruefully agreed, "They were right."

In addition to NTA, a strong resemblance to AA could also be seen in Marty's determination that NCEA focus on alcoholism and the alcoholic and not be distracted by outside concerns such as Prohibition, political elections, religious controversy, and other issues. Yet, although NCEA was designed to address communities and groups, Marty never lost sight of the individual alcoholic on whose behalf her organization labored.

E. M. Jellinek, Howard Haggard, and Selden Bacon were on NCEA's first board of directors, along with Dwight Anderson, Grace Bangs, Austin MacCormick, Edgar Lockwood, Edward G. Baird, and Marty herself. Haggard was NCEA's first president, and Jellinek the first chairman of the board.

An advisory board was also created. It boasted a number of nationally prominent men and women—Harry Emerson Fosdick, minister of Riverside Church in New York; Mrs. LaFell Dickinson, president of the National

Federation of Women's Clubs; movie legend Mary Pickford;[1] eminent psychiatrist Dr. Karl A. Menninger; writer Dorothy Parker; psychiatrist Dr. Harry Tiebout; Bill Wilson and Dr. Bob Smith, and several others.

Within six months of NCEA's founding, Marty had organized eleven local educational committees, including Boston, Minneapolis, and Washington, D.C. Attrition was great, however. By the end of the second year, only two of five committees remained: Pittsburgh and Boston. In a 1976 interview of Marty by Neil Scott, she was proud to report that those two cities were still NCA affiliates.

Santa Barbara accidentally became California's first affiliate. Franklin Huston, Marty's good friend, was energetically beginning to approach various California communities about establishing a local committee on alcoholism education. Marty pleaded with him to skip Santa Barbara, saying she had gone to school there and wanted one spot where she could relax among old friends. One such friend was Kit Tremaine, at whose first wedding twenty-five years before in New Orleans Marty had been a bridesmaid and met her ex-husband, John Blakemore.

While traveling for NCA in 1949, Marty took some time off to visit Kit, who threw a big dinner party for her. About twenty important, powerful citizens were invited. All the guests were curious about Marty—who she was and why she was in Santa Barbara. She tried to maintain her desire to avoid business but eventually found herself responding to the eager interest of Kit's friends about NCA. The discussion continued until past midnight. Right then and there, the hugely successful Santa Barbara Council on Alcoholism was founded.

Not long after, that same year, Franklin was in Pasadena to try establishing a local council there. His custom was to work through the Junior League if possible. He would call the program chair and arrange to speak about NCA. Katherine Pike was the current chair. "She took fire," Marty said, and Pasadena became the second NCA affiliate in California. (See the index for other references to this remarkable woman and her husband, Tom Pike.)

Despite these early successes and additional ones elsewhere in the country, Marty often commented on how difficult were those early years, particularly after the separation from Yale. Raising money and maintaining long-term local commitment were two constant challenges. It was very hard work.

"It was like pushing a boulder up a hill with your nose—three steps up and two back. When we received our first check for $5,000, I almost died of heart failure. It took us 10 years to really get going."

Marty's ultimate focus was always the individual alcoholic. Undergirding her vision, however, were her great strength and ability to think in terms of systems. Her conception was broad and inclusive. From the start, her intent was to impact entire systems, not solely individuals as in AA—medicine, school systems, the justice system, industry, the church, politics, the military, and so on. She saw clearly that if the stigma of alcoholism were to be mitigated so that individual alcoholics would seek help, whole systems would have to change their attitudes and actions regarding the disease. Community denial was as rampant as denial by the individual alcoholic. Marty's visionary and organizational genius lay in her sense of how to accomplish this goal of community education and sensitization.

Most persons would recoil before such a daunting task. Marty was no fool. She was aware she and her future organization couldn't spread themselves thin by tackling everything at once. She adopted two approaches. One was proactive. Here she worked directly to instigate systemic change at the community level. Communities themselves comprised a definable system. Through her speeches and writings, she proposed to identify, inspire, and enlist all the leaders and opinion-molders she could in her mission to educate their communities, then help them to get their communities involved. She firmly believed that a whole community was needed to counteract prejudice, hostility, and punitive attitudes. Her formidable networking and consensus-building skills were essential. The establishment of local groups to implement an ongoing educational program was the usual fruit of these proactive efforts.

Marty knew that many of the civic leaders in every community are women. Grace Bangs of the *New York Herald Tribune* convinced Marty that various kinds of women's groups would be ready-made audiences for her message. Unfortunately, what seemed like a good idea in principle didn't work in practice. Women's organizations were cool to inviting a speaker on alcoholism. And in the beginning, few women attended Marty's locally well-advertised lectures. So great was the stigma of inebriety, women felt their reputations and those of their families would be tarnished by appearing at such meetings. Therefore, Marty shifted her focus to mixed community groups and professional meetings.

Marty soon found that the nucleus of support in local communities tended to be recovered alcoholics in AA. Fellow AAs could also identify nonalcoholic community leaders in cities and towns where Marty had no other contacts. AA members themselves were inspired to pitch in and help organize NCEA affiliates, but NCEA was largely made up of nonalcoholic volunteers. Marty believed this was a healthy development if communities were going to own their public health responsibility toward the alcoholics in their midst.

Among the systems Marty identified as crucial were state legislatures. From the beginning, she worked hard to educate individual legislators and their committees about alcoholism. Her earliest appearance before a state legislature was when she addressed a joint session of South Carolina's legislature in 1946.

Considering future consequences, perhaps the most important of any target groups were the schools. Yet Marty and her supporters found it difficult to break into the formal educational system. It was a "slow, slow, slow" process. Teachers were a roadblock. They resented what they perceived as an infringement on their territory by an outside agency, so they didn't listen or respond well to NCEA's materials (or NCA's later on). A further complication was that, as Marty observed, "[t]here is a great deal more [alcoholic and heavy] drinking among teachers in this country than anyone realizes."

AA had also identified schools as significant objectives for education about alcoholism and was sending AA speakers into some classes to tell their stories of recovery. Although up to a point this could be helpful and inspiring to students and teachers, it was a single-shot approach with little or no factual, scientific information and no organized follow-up. Marty had a larger, more comprehensive educational vision that eventually was incorporated into many K–12 curricula.

In addition to proactive community action, Marty's second strategy might be described as watchful waiting for a strike. Each of the major systems remained on the front burner of Marty's consciousness, and she was always on the lookout for ways of implementation. When she encountered a capable individual or group that had an interest and expertise in a particular system, she promptly offered NCEA's support and training. She and NCEA functioned as a catalyst, nurturing people and setting them loose to educate and change a particular system. Huge as was her ego, she didn't need to feed it by micromanaging the change agents in any of these external systems. She would never have had the time, anyway. Her role was more that of a coach and mentor.

An early example of this second systems approach concerned the military. An Air Force sergeant, Bill Swegan, initiated an educational program on alcoholism in his squadron soon after he got sober in 1948. A born teacher and counselor, he began to have a positive effect on the men. Bill and his later supervisor, Dr. Louis J. West, then the psychiatrist in charge of psychiatric services at Lackland Air Force Base, Texas, submitted a paper on Lackland's comprehensive alcoholism program to the American Psychiatric Association (APA). The results were reported in the country's major newspapers.

Marty's antennae, ever sensitive, heard of Swegan's success. She obtained permission from APA to publish and distribute the paper under NCEA's logo, thus substantially increasing public awareness of the information. Subsequently, she used the persuasive argument of cost savings that helped induce the Department of Defense to adopt similar alcoholism treatment programs for the entire military service.[2] Bill Swegan later wrote:

> [Marty] had been attempting to change the negative attitude toward alcoholism in the military for some time. She had a keen awareness of the insensitivity toward the alcoholic and punishing those who become alcoholic rather than treating them as a sick person. The policy at that time was to deny pay to those who sought assistance for their alcoholism if they were hospitalized or unable to perform their prescribed duties. In addition, those who did not respond to treatment were discharged as undesirable. This caused a breach in those who wanted to recover but were afraid to seek help due to the administrative restrictions placed on their seeking assistance.
>
> Marty was a great crusader and recognized alcoholism as a disease rather than a character defect. She preached this concept worldwide including the military service. Having her as a staunch defender of my work in the field was the motivation needed to continue despite the resistance of some who were non-supportive.[3]

Marty promptly arranged for Swegan to attend the Yale Summer School of Alcohol Studies. He was its first military student. It was an unheard-of honor for an enlisted man to attend at all, and Marty had to pull strings with the top military brass at the Pentagon to obtain clearance

William H. Mann, Marty's
father, at the start of his career
as a Chicago businessman
(Tyler and Gregory Miller)

Lillian (Christy) Mann, Marty's
mother, the only child of a
prominent Chicago furrier
(Tyler and Gregory Miller)

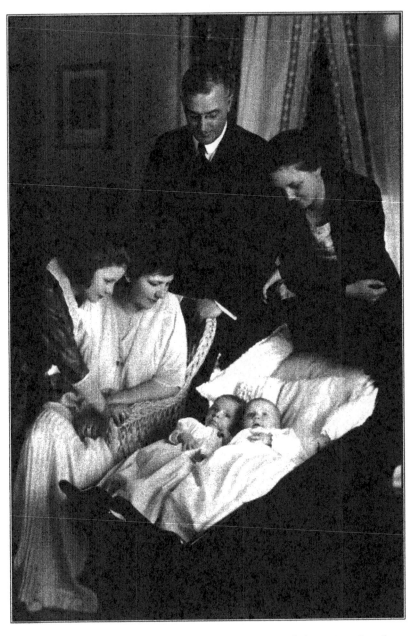

Chris, Lill, Will (wearing pince-nez), Marty, and the twins shortly after their birth in 1918 (Tyler and Gregory Miller)

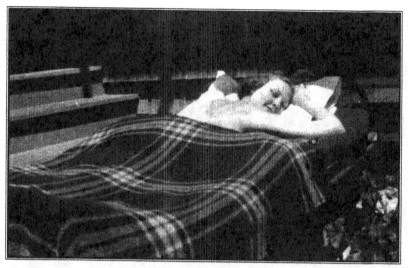

Marty Mann taking the sun cure while recovering from tuberculosis in Pasadena, California, 1919 (National Council on Alcoholism and Drug Dependence, Inc.)

Marty Mann at the time of her social debut in Chicago, 1925 (Tyler and Gregory Miller)

Chris, Marty, and Betty Mann at Blythewood Sanitarium. The picture was taken on July 4, 1938, after Marty returned from a drinking escapade with two other Blythewood patients. (National Council on Alcoholism and Drug Dependence, Inc.)

*Lieutenant John Blakemore, Marty's ex-husband, on board
the Patrol Craft PC-1198 on convoy patrol between the
East Coast and Trinidad, late 1942 or early 1943
(John Blakemore, son of Lt. John Blakemore)*

Dr. Frank J. Sladen, Marty Mann, and E. M. Jellinek (far right) *at the Detroit Economic Club, 1946 (National Council on Alcoholism and Drug Dependence, Inc.)*

Priscilla Peck in her office at Vogue *in 1947,*
soon after she started work there
(©1947 Condé Nast Publications Inc.)

Marty Mann and Priscilla Peck owned a cottage on
the beach at Cherry Grove, Fire Island
(©1948 by Irving Penn)

Alexander Liberman, Betty Parsons, and Priscilla Peck (far right) *viewing an exhibit of Priscilla's work (Nick De Morgoli)*

NCA publicity photo, Marty's favorite (National Council on Alcoholism and Drug Dependence, Inc.)

Marty Mann at home in New York City, working on her first book,
Primer on Alcoholism, *1950 (National Council on Alcoholism and
Drug Dependence, Inc.)*

Bill Wilson, cofounder of AA and Marty's AA sponsor, about 1950
(Searcy W.)

Lois Wilson, Bill's wife, about 1950 (Al-Anon Family Group Headquarters, Inc.)

Robert Foster Kennedy, the physician who started Marty on the road to recovery (Hessie Kennedy Rubin)

The Reverend Yvelin Gardner (National Council on Alcoholism and Drug Dependence, Inc.)

Bill Mann, Marty's younger brother, kept close to his sisters. (Patricia Mann)

Jane Bowles and Marty Mann at the home of Oliver Smith, Beverly Hills, California, 1952 (National Council on Alcoholism and Drug Dependence, Inc.)

In Marty and Priscilla's apartment (clockwise from lower left), *Lill Mann, Priscilla, LeClair Bissell, Marty, and two dogs, about 1954 (Dr. LeClair Bissell)*

*R. Brinkley Smithers and Marty Mann, at the NCA annual meeting
in Texas in 1969, soon after Marty retired as executive director and
became founder-consultant (National Council on Alcoholism and
Drug Dependence, Inc.)*

Felicia Gizycka, who became a close friend of Marty and Priscilla, aboard the RMS Queen Elizabeth *(Joseph Arnold)*

Marty Mann and Priscilla Peck at Felicia Gizycka's home in New Canaan, Connecticut, 1970 (Joseph Arnold)

Marty Mann at the 1980 International AA Convention in New Orleans
(National Council on Alcoholism and Drug Dependence, Inc.)

Priscilla Peck and Marty Mann, drawing by René Bouché, 1957. The artist was described in the New York Times *as "the most fashionable portraitist in the country." (Department of Special Collections, Syracuse University Library)*

for Swegan. Whenever necessary over the years, Marty continued to coach Swegan, in the best sense of the word—from the sidelines with support, encouragement, and educational resources. Gradually, Bill Swegan's groundbreaking example spread to the other armed forces. Marty continued to identify and nurture those programs as well. Today, the military as a whole provides good alcohol and drug intervention and treatment programs. Marty lived to see this system and others make mammoth changes in their attitudes and approaches to the disease of alcoholism.

All this was in addition to what Yale perceived as Marty's main task. Her principal assignment was to travel throughout the country, officially representing Yale University and speaking on alcoholism. Her message, based on Dwight Anderson's original proposal, was simple.

1. Alcoholism is a disease and the alcoholic is a sick person.
2. The alcoholic can be helped and is worth helping.
3. This is a public health problem and therefore a public responsibility.

A crucial difference between NCEA's threefold statement and Anderson's is that Marty deliberately identified alcoholism as a disease rather than a sickness. This may seem semantic quibbling, but the decision had momentous consequences, both positive and negative. William L. White, a historian of American addiction treatment and recovery, says, "I believe that this transition marks the beginning spark of the modern disease conceptualization of alcoholism. There are earlier allusions and use of 'disease' as a metaphor for understanding alcoholism, but Marty is the first of this period who will factually assert that alcoholism is a disease. I think she deserves credit for this."[4] (The difficulties and consequences of Marty's decision are discussed in the next chapter.)

The first order of business for the fledgling organization was to start informing people about alcoholism—what alcoholism was and how it could be addressed. That meant an educational campaign with printed materials of all kinds, plus a heavy schedule of public speeches. Marty and her little band quickly organized both.

Marty's first speaking date on behalf of NCEA was before the annual Congress of the Maine Parent Teachers Association, held in October 1944 in Waterville, Maine. It was the beginning of her incredible lecture schedule. She was an immensely popular, much sought-after speaker. In her first year she gave 106 talks, of which 14 were on the radio. She traveled 36,000 miles, speaking in 45 cities to more than 34,000 people. Within a year or two, she routinely spoke more than 200 times annually. And for many years later on, Marty's schedule peaked at more than 250 talks a year, often 4 or 5 a day.

Any politician who has run for office would immediately recognize this as extraordinary, especially when the schedule continued for decades, not just a single election season. Two things saved Marty from burnout. One, she was born with exceptionally high energy. Dr. Max Weisman, who lectured with her the last ten years of her life, marveled that "temperature changes didn't matter to her, climatic changes, jet lag didn't faze her at all." Marty especially loved flying east to west because that time change favored night owls.

Also, she rapidly learned to group her talks into two intensive annual national or international tours of about three months each. In between tours, however, she continued speaking in a wide area around the "local" Boston-New York-Washington, D.C., axis. In addition, she groomed speakers in many geographical areas to continue where she left off. Ila Phillips, a very early AA member, became one of NCEA's most effective speakers.

An important reason for grouping her talks was that neither Marty nor NCEA had enough money to finance completely the level of travel she embarked on. But that didn't stop her. By scheduling many visits within a specific geographic area, Marty could minimize air and train fare. The local AA community was often her host. She didn't need a car because there was always someone designated to meet her and be her chauffeur for however long she was there. Hotels were no problem. Either she stayed with friends, or friends paid for a hotel room. She rarely paid for a meal. Somebody would be hosting her and considering it a great privilege to pick up the tab.

Whenever her schedule permitted, Marty arranged to see her brother, sisters, other family members, or special friends. On a trip in March 1946 to the Southeast, for instance, she was scheduled to give a talk in Daytona Beach, Florida. Liz Peck, Priscilla's sister, had been working in Florida and was apparently trying AA and sobriety again. Marty, aware that Liz never had much money, wrote, inviting her to stay with her own hosts. "AAs are coming from all over the State and of course, I hope that you will be among them. . . . You'll never know how thrilled we were with your first AA letter."

In 1946, Marty was one of thirty thousand recovered alcoholics in some fifty cities. Through her public work on behalf of NCEA, she'd met most of them. Six weeks in the fall of 1947 are typical of Marty's speaking engagements.[5]

1947	PLACE	TYPE	SPONSOR	AUDIENCE
Sept. 19	Memphis, TN	Luncheon	Committee on Alcoholism of the Community Council	35
		Conference	AA Convention	450
Sept. 20		Public Meeting	Memphis Community Council	1,500
Oct. 20	San Francisco	Press Conference	San Francisco CEA,*	14
		Radio Talk	KYA, 15 minutes	
Oct. 21	Stockton, CA	Luncheon	San Joaquin County CEA Executive Committee	12
		Radio Talk	KWG, 15 minutes	
		Dinner	San Joaquin County CEA General Committee	56
		Public Meeting	San Joaquin County CEA College of the Pacific AA San Joaquin Mental Hygiene Society Adult Education Division, Stockton Schools (Entire speech broadcast on KWG)	800
Oct. 22	Oakland	Meeting	East Bay CEA for Public Health Officials, Health and Welfare Workers, etc.	55
		Radio Talk	15 minutes	
	San Francisco	Public Meeting	Univ. of Calif. San Francisco, Institute on Alcohol Studies (with Bacon)	900
Oct. 23		Luncheon	San Francisco CEA Executive Committee and some members of General Committee	32
Oct. 24	Los Angeles	Panel	Univ. of Calif. Los Angeles, Institute on Alcohol Studies	200
		Public Meeting	Univ. of Calif. Los Angeles, Institute on Alcohol Studies (with Bacon)	400
Oct. 25		Organization Meeting	To discuss starting a CEA	11

*CEA refers to "Committee for Education on Alcoholism."

And so it went that trip—continuing to four cities in Utah, back to San Diego and Los Angeles, then on to Dallas and Houston, Mexico City, and New Orleans—winding up 1947 back home in New York by the middle of December.

Nor was this all that was on Marty's plate in each of the cities she visited. On any given day, she maintained a full agenda of private meetings, airport meetings, dinner and coffee meetings, and so on. She scheduled rest and relaxation whenever she could, blocking out an afternoon or even just a couple of hours to sunbathe or swim, her favorite sport.

Most of Marty's days began around noon. Like many people with her circadian rhythms, it took her two or three hours to get going in the morning. Partly this was because Marty was a night owl. From the age of eight, she was an insomniac as defined by day people. She would sneak a flashlight to bed and read under the covers for hours. When she was an adult, her idea of relaxing was going out on the town until 3 A.M. and needing to sleep in the next day. Her engagement book often noted a 10:30 P.M. appointment that would usually end well after midnight. Marty was a jazz buff, dating back to her youth in Chicago, a jazz center. If there was a jazz group in town, off she'd go.

However, Marty was also plagued with bouts of clinical depression and found it difficult to wake up fully until the later morning. Her staff had standing orders never to schedule her before noon if they could help it.

Marty's audiences varied widely. In NCEA's first two or three years, she was often paired before major audiences with Haggard (himself an outstanding speaker), Jellinek, or Bacon of the Yale School of Alcohol Studies. Most often, she teamed with Bacon. Usually her lectures were connected with NCEA, where she was either inspiring a community to start an affiliate or cheering on one already established. Many times the audiences were AA groups, from local meetings to regional, national, and international conferences. A superb advocate and lobbyist, she testified before state legislatures and Congress on behalf of adequate treatment resources for alcoholics. As time went on, she was featured at meetings of professional societies such as the APA and as a lecturer in various university programs for alcohol and drug studies, such as Yale, Rutgers, and the University of Utah.

A topic that appeared frequently in Marty's talks from as early as 1944 was the appalling financial cost of incarceration of the alcoholic as compared with treatment. "Arrests of persons with this disease are about as effective for cure as arresting a cancer patient for the criminal act of having cancer." And she would quote irrefutable numbers provided by reliable researchers of the day to illustrate her claim. Yale University and others were also deeply concerned with the issue.

Again, in 1949 Marty pounded the rostrum before a group of concerned citizens in Santa Barbara, California.

> Here in these enlightened United States the prevailing attitude is one of "punish the criminal" rather than "treat the sick." In most of our cities and towns the only facilities for alcoholics in the delirium of their illness—acute intoxication—are the jails. We might as well put a malaria sufferer in jail and expect him to get well. His malady would recur just as intoxication recurs in the alcoholic, unless he were given proper treatment and taught to use a preventive.
>
> New York State annually spends $850,000 [$5,950,000 in year 2000 dollars] to keep alcoholics in penal institutions, from which they are released just as fundamentally sick as when they went in, often to become regular repeaters. For a fraction of the cost, vast numbers of these jail and prison inmates could be rehabilitated, becoming assets rather than liabilities to their State, and to their local community.[6]

Recent large-scale studies confirm that most people in jail and prison are there for alcohol- and drug-related problems and that incarceration continues to be the most expensive and ineffective possible solution to addressing the disease of alcoholism.[7] When Marty was asked why the laws weren't changed to reflect this fact, she answered, "Laws follow public opinion in this country." And changing public opinion was her basic job. Marty might also have said that laws follow public understanding of an issue.

An encouraging development of the 1990s that Marty would have cheered and championed is the grassroots growth of drug courts across the country. Since most inmates have been sentenced for nonviolent alcohol- and drug-related crimes, selected individuals are offered the option of intensive, closely supervised treatment instead of incarceration. Drug courts are thus a rational alternative to one-size-fits-all incarceration. They have proved to reduce recidivism in both relapse and rearrest for crime and are an effective method for breaking the cycle of drugs and crime. Employed, drug-free individuals are returned to the community.[8]

Whatever her topic, Marty was a powerful, charismatic speaker who mesmerized her audiences with her presence and her message. From the moment she walked onstage, even skeptical audiences were mysteriously disarmed. In NCEA's earliest days, she was recorded on reel-to-reel tapes, but these were supplanted by cassettes in the 1950s. A representative number of audiocassettes is available. The quality of some is poor, perhaps because they have been dubbed from old reel-to-reels. A few film segments also exist, such as one from *The March of Time,*[9] the popular one-reel news magazine shown in movie theaters all over the country between 1935 and 1951. TV and videotape didn't really come into their own until later. Marty was a natural for TV, appearing, for example, on the popular show *To Tell the Truth,* where she completely fooled the judges, who failed to identify her as the alcoholic.

To listen to the audiocassettes is to be awed by Marty's rhetorical gifts. Her personal power is unmistakable. Yet she said she usually had butterflies, sometimes severely, before speaking in public. She confessed that she took off her glasses before speaking so she wouldn't need to see the masses she addressed. Since she didn't speak from a manuscript, that worked fine. Walter Murphy, one of NCA's executive directors who later succeeded Marty, said he "was with her on many, many occasions when she spoke at AA meetings. We'd usually have dinner beforehand and most of the time she was too nervous to eat—in spite of the fact that she has spoken hundreds of times all over the world. She was always like an AA member making his or her first talk. She prayed that the words would come—and they always did."

An audience would never know Marty's fear because she was completely poised from the moment she stepped onstage. Almost invariably she spoke extemporaneously, rarely even using notes. Her thoughts were logical and focused, her delivery that of a flawless professional, her sense of drama and timing superb. More than one person has wondered what would have happened if Marty had ever been tempted to enter the political arena, the theater, or the formal ministry. Her eloquence reflected all three.

In 1946, following the release of the popular film *The Lost Weekend,* Marty consulted intensively on a movie script written by Dorothy Parker and Frank Cavett. Dorothy Parker was well known as one of this country's best writers (including many successful film scripts) and among its greatest wits. Her specialty was the rapier riposte.

The title of this particular film was *Smash Up—The Story of a Woman,* starring Susan Hayward. The story concerned the alcoholic wife of a successful radio singer. The script was autobiographical of Parker's life. Ironically, by the time Universal Pictures asked Dorothy Parker to work on the script of *Smash Up,* she was in serious trouble with her drinking yet hoped that writing her disguised story would help her overcome her drinking problems.

Though Marty's assigned task was to consult on the script and coach the star, it is reasonable to assume that she additionally consulted for the studio on Dorothy Parker and coached her, too—including about her drinking. Marty certainly made sure the script reflected the medical model of problem drinking. She also spent two weeks in Hollywood coaching Hayward in the leading role. Though *Smash Up* wasn't as successful as *Lost Weekend,* it enjoyed a moderately favorable public response. These two films showed for the first time that alcoholism is not the pursuit of pleasure but a terrible, destructive compulsion.

The set of *Smash Up* was not the first time that Marty met Dorothy Parker. Dorothy was a prestigious member of NCEA's early advisory board. She had also been a heavy drinker for many years, and the writer/humorist Robert Benchley suggested at one point that she "ought to have a chat with Alcoholics Anonymous. This she did, and brought back word to the drinkers at Tony's that she thought the organization was perfectly wonderful.

"'Are you going to join?' Mr. Benchley asked hopefully.

"'Certainly not,' she said, 'They want me to stop *now.*'" [10]

In those early days of AA, Marty was undoubtedly one of the handful of women detailed to try to help Dorothy Parker. Priscilla may have been another later on because of a connection through *Vogue.* Parker wrote many stories and articles for the magazine over the years. Also, Parker was always enchanted by the world of fashion, exemplified especially in Priscilla's career.

Dorothy Parker was never able to recover from her alcoholism. The disease progressed, and twenty years after *Smash Up,* her own life smashed up. She died alone in a drab hotel, blind, befuddled, ill, and drunk.

For too many alcoholics, this was the predictable end to their disease. Marty knew there was another outcome, another choice. All her energies were focused on getting that message of hope out to the public.

As exciting and productive as were these early years of the 1940s for Marty, however, the latter half of the decade would bring even greater challenges.

Rocking the Boat

1946

ACCOMPANYING NCEA'S SUCCESSES, several critical problems nevertheless arose as a consequence of Marty's activities. Four battles surrounding the issues of anonymity, professionalism, and fund-raising spilled over onto AA and threatened to tear it apart.

The first two battles concerned anonymity. Several aspects of anonymity were being developed by trial and error within AA. Originally, personal AA anonymity was based on anxiety and fear. With good reason, AA members believed that anonymity about their status as recovered alcoholics was the only way they could protect their reputations—and jobs if they had them. The outside world was still ignorant, biased, hostile, and punitive. It heard the word *alcoholic,* and that was enough to slam shut the doors of normal social intercourse and opportunity. The concept that an alcoholic could recover was unknown to the general public.

AA members also came to understand that they had a responsibility to protect each other's anonymity in addition to their own. This meant that an individual member should not identify his membership in AA in case others in the fellowship could be identified by association. In addition, Marty always observed the stricture never to reveal the identity of another recovered alcoholic in or out of AA unless that person had already gone public or had given explicit permission to share that information.

Marty also recommended discretion in revealing one's own recovery, saying, "A person should never reveal his sobriety to an inappropriate person in an inappropriate place at an inappropriate time."

Another piece of the anonymity issue was whether AA itself should remain anonymous as an organization to protect the anonymity of its members. But if AA were anonymous, then how would people know about it and learn that help was available? In the mid-1940s, just as NCEA was getting started, AA was still in the process of distinguishing between personal anonymity and anonymity about AA as an organization.

AA solved the issue of organizational anonymity at the meeting level by making some meetings open to the public and keeping most of them closed to protect alcoholic members.[1] Twenty years later, however, Marty was outraged to see in the AA meeting directory of a large city that at the bottom of each page was a line saying only families could visit any of the few open AA meetings listed. "How," Marty demanded, "are your meetings going to attract active alcoholics if they can't even [start by coming] to open meetings?"

Finally, as time passed and the stigma about alcoholism lessened, anonymity came to be appreciated as a potent ego-reducer and spiritual discipline for its own sake.

The first anonymity argument that Marty precipitated was due to her success in obtaining Yale's backing. This changed Bill Wilson's mind about her prospects, and he became an enthusiastic supporter of her NCEA project. He and Dr. Bob Smith were happy to lend their names to be printed on NCEA letterhead among the distinguished advisory board of the new organization. No one foresaw any problem since neither Bill nor Bob was identified as an alcoholic or a member of AA. Nevertheless, some AAs who received the advance publicity were upset at what they felt was a breach of Alcoholic Anonymous's most treasured asset—personal anonymity.

A worse storm immediately blew up. After much thought and discussion with her Yale colleagues and with Bill Wilson and others in AA, Marty, who was the first woman alcoholic to come to AA and stay, decided that whenever she spoke or wrote for NCEA, she would break her anonymity with regard to alcoholism and not fail to give AA the credit for her sobriety. Yale was strongly in favor. Bill Wilson urged Marty to go ahead for the greater good. For six months she resisted because she feared for her sobriety. Some AAs who went public had relapsed under the pressure of notoriety, thereby giving AA a bad name in some places. Marty was also acutely aware she would be violating AA's fundamental tradition of personal anonymity.

On the other hand, there was the example of Rollie Hemsley in Akron.

Rollie, a star catcher for the Cleveland Indians, announced in 1940 that he had gotten sober with the help of AA. As a result, he brought more people into AA than did the *Saturday Evening Post* article a year later. The professional publicist and journalist in Marty knew that her personal witness was the single most powerful weapon in her educational arsenal. People listened to someone who spoke from experience. And she knew the dramatic shock value of an upper-class, educated, dynamic *woman* opening her talk with the words, "I am an alcoholic."

Marty was also reassured because, as she said, "My mother is very proud and happy about me, and all my other relatives and friends, of course know my story, so I have no embarrassment in their presence."

Regardless, if admitting to one's alcoholism before men in the protected sanctuary of an AA meeting was an almost impossible hurdle, consider what this decision to go public must have cost Marty. Today the climate is far different—a Betty Ford, an Elizabeth Taylor, other women celebrities are free to seek treatment and speak out because Marty paved the way more than fifty years ago and kept it open.

All hell broke loose in AA, however. AA members feared Marty was off on a grandiose ego trip; even worse, she might drink again and so discredit AA itself. There is also reason to suspect that some of the men in AA had difficulty accepting the perceived effrontery of a woman challenging the status quo. Aside from the anonymity issue, the very act of establishing NCEA appeared to some as traitorous, self-aggrandizing competition with AA. In addition, it was unseemly for a woman to assume a man's traditional leadership role.

Marty distinctly had a mind of her own. Ernest Kurtz said her personality was that of a powerful chief executive officer (CEO) of a major corporation. Despite Marty's great personal charm, it took strong, secure men to accept and appreciate her, and alcoholics of either sex are not noted for tolerance in their first years of rehabilitation. Dr. Bob's son, Bob Jr., said the Akron-Cleveland AA groups were probably not as upset over the anonymity issue as were those in the New York area. Dr. Bob, however, withdrew from NCEA's board before Bill Wilson did.

Bill was not spared in the fallout over the anonymity issue. AA members held him responsible. He was not only in New York, he was Marty's sponsor. How come he couldn't control her? Letters and phone calls to him personally, and letters to the *AA Grapevine,* severely questioned his judgment and scathingly took him to task. He probably would have weathered the negative feedback without further dissension, however, since Marty was backing off from the decision to break her anonymity.

What saved Marty was partly her own discretion and common sense in not misusing her double-edged sword by flaunting and glorifying herself. Equally important in damping down the flames of resentment in AA was that every time she wrote or spoke, the AA group or groups in that area experienced a dramatic influx of new members directly attributable to her. The number of women surged upward for the first time in AA's history. Woman after woman tearfully thanked Marty, personally if possible, for having given them the courage to face their disease and seek help. As a model for recovery, she was made to order. Elegantly groomed, a marvelous speaker, she was a glamorous figure with whom women identified.

Men responded in like numbers even if they hadn't attended one of Marty's lectures. On one occasion, her talk was broadcast throughout Mississippi and Louisiana. A drunk man named Red was passed out in Louisiana's bayou country. He came to in a drunken stupor during the broadcast to hear Marty stating that alcoholics were sick people and that seeking help for alcoholism was not a sign of weakness but a sign of intelligence. He heard a reference to Alcoholics Anonymous. Groggy and confused, he nonetheless succeeded in locating an AA meeting ninety miles away in New Orleans. Several years later, when Marty was lecturing in New Orleans, Red greeted her at the conclusion with four men in tow.

"Mrs. Mann," he said, "you do not know it, but you are the sponsor of our little upstate group of Alcoholics Anonymous."[2]

For two years, Marty abided by her decision to acknowledge publicly not only her alcoholism, but also her connection with AA. Then she concluded the controversy was causing her and AA more anguish than it was worth. Besides, NCEA was well on its way and probably didn't need the extra publicity boost any longer. After 1946, Marty resolved her dilemma by keeping her AA life private and her NCEA one public and not mixing them. Consequently, she often good-naturedly described herself as schizophrenic. She continued to acknowledge her alcoholism publicly but refrained from mentioning her link to AA. Nevertheless, there continued to be discomfort and criticism by some AA members of Marty's work and her references to her own alcoholism. As a result, she was not welcome for a while in some AA communities as a speaker.

In her professional work, Marty would always use her full name, Mrs. Marty Mann, but at AA meetings and in all matters related to AA, she was simply Marty M. Whatever Marty's original reason for calling herself Mrs. after her 1928 divorce, retaining the title at this time of her life gave her a respectable cover and shield as a lesbian. She never publicly broke her anonymity on this issue. Most people assumed she was either married or divorced. They had no idea that Mann was her unmarried name. Marty already knew what it was like to cope with the double stigma of being a woman alcoholic. Society's censure would have been absolute had she revealed she was a lesbian. Her life's work would have been dead in the water before it was even launched. Those close enough to Marty to know about her orientation fiercely protected her privacy.

Reflecting later, Marty could well have been referring to what she learned from the hornet's nest she stirred up in AA over anonymity: "I believe that my once over-weening self-will has finally found its proper place, for I can say many times daily, 'Thy will be done, not mine' . . . and mean it."[3] She also came to understand that "I have the right to say I am an alcoholic and that I am here. I do not have the right to say you are an alcoholic and that you are here."

Marty is a prime example of a gray area of anonymity that exists in AA. How she eventually resolved it has stood the test of time. Her final pattern is the one followed today by other public figures who are also in AA—that is, publicly acknowledging their alcoholism and recovery but not stating their membership in AA. However, so many of AA's code words, such as *recovered, Twelve Step program,* and *Higher Power* are now recognized by the outside world that anonymity has become more pro forma in many instances than real.

It should be noted that there have always been persons who've recovered from alcoholism apart from AA. Included are several prominent alcoholics, underscoring the fact that AA's concern with anonymity is about AA participation only, not about one's having the disease of alcoholism nor is it about recovery.

All the foregoing turmoil was bad enough. The situation was further exacerbated within AA by the fact that Marty was hired to do work that, while it was certainly on behalf of the Yale Center of Alcohol Studies, was in another sense for the benefit of AA. Steering alcoholics to AA was Marty's ultimate goal, for she believed that was the only viable long-term answer to the chronic disease of alcoholism.

Marty noted that people come to AA very sick. Bill Wilson said they have a mortal illness. Marty cautioned, however, that AA doesn't do any medical work. Though Marty was a strong advocate of the medical model of treatment for alcoholism, she saw the medical setting mainly as providing a less-stigmatized entry point to treatment. If doctors, hospitals, and clinics were treating alcoholism, then alcoholism must be an acceptable and legitimate disease. Furthermore, she recognized that because of the chronic nature of alcoholism, the recovered alcoholic usually needed long-term, if not permanent, support for continued sobriety. AA and other support groups could provide this, whereas medical treatment was both unnecessary for the chronic phase, as a rule, and too expensive.

What muddied the waters for AA members was that AA was still trying to define and come to terms with what constituted legitimate employment in the alcoholism field. The question was whether AA members should *ever* be paid for entering fields that related to alcoholism, such as medicine, social work, state educational programs, and even secretaries in the AA office. Marty's high visibility brought the discussion to a loud pitch.

Bill Wilson led the way to a sensible resolution when he remarked in a 1948 talk at Yale:

> [When NCEA was formed], I was asked whether Marty's employment would make her a professional AA (and we all know that AA itself must not be professional). I answered, it would be the same as the employment of AAs as janitors, secretaries, etc. This job is an educational one, so could not be professional AA. (A professional AA is one who teaches AA, face to face with another alcoholic, for money.) . . .
>
> Too few of us are widening our responsibilities to the total picture and limiting our responsibility to only the small segment of the alcoholic picture in AA itself. How about the young people coming up, education of the general public and finally the courts?
>
> 15,000 are admitted yearly to Bellevue alone. AA only gets 200 to 300 of these a year. What are we going to do with the rest? Remember

the guys who can't get well and those who are not too sick to be helped. As individuals, don't let anybody deter you. You are paid, not for AA but for related work, which should be paid.

Money means the death of AA but is the life of the other movements. Don't be bashful about taking AA with you but don't use the AA name in money-raising or any like job. That might slow down the job of education.[4]

The fourth and final controversy was another explosive one. By 1946, Marty had essentially defused the issue of her anonymity. NCEA was now two years old. Its success dictated a need for expanded staff and facilities. However, 1946 was also the year in which Yale's financial subsidy was scheduled to start decreasing and NCEA was to begin standing on its own. In anticipation of this moment, Marty had already laid the groundwork for raising her own funds. NCEA launched a large-scale public appeal for funds. AA was referred to throughout, and Bill Wilson's and Bob Smith's names were still on NCEA's letterhead. Included in the mailing were some AA individuals and groups.

The letter confused AA members about who was doing the soliciting, AA or NCEA, and whether NCEA and AA funds were to be mingled. It was already AA's policy to be self-supporting and decline outside contributions, and to refrain from endorsing or otherwise affiliating with other groups. The response of the AA trustees and membership was swift and resoundingly negative. Bill and Bob promptly withdrew their names, and AA's Alcoholic Foundation issued the following unequivocal statement:

Alcoholics Anonymous looks with disfavor on the unauthorized use of its name in any fund-raising activity.[5]

This stern response led many AA members and others to the erroneous inference that Bill Wilson and the AA trustees disapproved of NCEA. Bill went to some pains then and later to set the record straight. In the same New Haven speech cited previously, for example, he concluded with, "I would like to make an end to all the talk about me being at loggerheads with Marty and Yale." Bill also wrote in an *AA Grapevine* article:

I cannot detail in this space the great accomplishments of Marty and her associates in the present-day National Council on Alcoholism. But

I can speak my conviction that no other single agency has done more
to educate the public, to open up hospitalization and to set in motion
all manner of constructive projects than this one.[6]

Today's AA members take for granted the AA policies that developed
into what were codified and adopted in 1950 at the first AA International
Convention as the Twelve Traditions. Yet in 1946, these policies were still
being hammered out on the hard anvil of experience. Marty and the afore-
mentioned events surrounding NCEA were significant influences on the
final form those AA policies assumed, specifically with regard to Traditions
Six, Seven, Eight, and Eleven.[7]

Clearly, Marty was a critical factor in the growth and development of
AA. NCEA was not her only accomplishment. Yet if she is remembered at
all in AA, it is usually as the first woman to achieve long-term sobriety—
unquestionably an outstanding personal event. However, her contribution
to resolution of the anonymity and employment issues of the organization,
a resolution essential to AA's survival as an organization, is largely unknown today. It is also fair to say that Marty had a more profound and irreversible effect on the numbers and membership composition of AA than
did its founders, Bill W. and Dr. Bob. Without Marty's efforts, today's AA
might have looked very, very different—if it even existed. In a keynote
speech at NCA's 1956 annual meeting, Bill Wilson acknowledged AA's debt
to NCA, as he did repeatedly over the years:

> We [AA] are realizing again, afresh, that without our friends, not only
> could we not have existed in the first place but we could not have
> grown. . . . I think that I can say without any reservation . . . that this
> Committee [NCA] has been responsible for making more friends for
> Alcoholics Anonymous and of doing a wider service in educating the
> world on the gravity of this malady and what can be done about it
> than any other single agency.[8]

Sowing the Future

1946–48

ALONGSIDE THIS INTENSE AA-RELATED ACTIVITY, NCEA devoted its primary efforts to four major tasks, serving as

1. an information center on new research developments, clinics, and treatments
2. a consultation bureau for professional groups
3. a speakers' bureau
4. the guide of the local committees

Local NCEA affiliates and committees were organizing as a result of Marty's speeches and unremitting outreach. Between 1947 and 1949, the number of local committees and affiliates grew from twenty-five to fifty. In addition, Marty continued to lead NCEA in the direction of effecting change in those systems she always had on her mind. Her efforts directly contributed to the following actions and their consequences (in authors' italics):

- Medical Care: St. Francis Hospital in Hartford, Connecticut, and Knickerbocker Hospital in New York City opened their doors to treatment of alcoholics. *(Before Marty ended her career, thousands of hospitals would follow suit.)*
- Religion: The New York Conference of the Methodist Church adopted a report recommending that alcoholism be viewed as a disease and that alcoholics be treated as sick people. *(Other denominations and the National Council of Churches eventually adopted similar recommendations.)*

- Education: The University of California conducted an Institute on Alcoholism featuring Haggard, Jellinek, Bacon, and Marty. *(The Universities of Utah, Texas, and Arizona helped lead other universities to establish similar institutes.)*
- Industry: In 1949, with NCEA's help, the Consolidated Edison Company of New York, DuPont de Nemours & Company, and companies in Wisconsin developed employee alcoholism programs. *(The modern employee assistance programs grew out of these early efforts supported by NCEA.)*
- Legislation: NCEA published a special bulletin on legislation, together with a digest of existing legislation. *(Landmark state and federal legislation followed in succeeding decades.)*

While all this was happening, Marty continued to reach out to individual suffering alcoholics. One of the first persons who may have been affected by Marty's efforts to achieve sobriety was John Blakemore, her ex-husband. In 1944, she told a reporter, "He has reformed and is now commander of a PT-boat in the Pacific. He stopped drinking when I tried to stop. He was one of the rare people who can stop by their own efforts. I was not."[1]

Blakemore's first WWII command was a submarine chaser, assigned duty escorting convoys in the West Indies, especially ships laden with petroleum from Argentina and Curaçao. During sea trials, his skillful devil-may-care abilities demonstrated one of the qualities that attracted and charmed people. In bringing his ship, PC-1198, to berth, he ran "full bore for the pier with the admiral and other brass to greet them. Will he slow down soon? Will he slow down? He's not slowing down; the bastard is not slowing down—get out of here! To which John threw the ship hard right rudder and all astern and came to a gentle stop alongside the dock with nary a scratch. Certain brass were brassed off, but he was awarded commendations for the efficiency of the shakedown period in his reviews."[2]

John's daughter, Bruce Blakemore, recalls that her father also served as commander of a patrol-craft escort (PCE-891) in the Aleutians off Alaska. This may have followed his service on the PT boat, or Marty may have been deliberately misleading to avoid disclosing war secrets.

Later, Blakemore was executive officer of the USS *Vixen* (PG-53), a gunboat that was the flagship of the U.S. Atlantic Fleet at the end of the war. A supremely efficient administrator, Blakemore was awarded a citation at the time of his retirement from the Navy for his contribution toward the efficient operation of the flagship. The commander-in-chief of the U.S. Atlantic Fleet, Admiral Jonas H. Ingram, and John apparently had a good relationship, as the admiral once lent him his plane to fly home.

Blakemore's two children believe their father may have remained generally sober during his Navy years. However, at some point following his retirement around 1945 from the naval reserves as a lieutenant commander, he resumed binge drinking. Bruce wrote, "He would be on the wagon for several months and then would crash off it. He could stop by his own effort, but when he started again, it was no holds barred."[3]

Despite the family problems John caused, his daughter also recalls, "Whatever his faults, I do think of him as an honourable man, a southern gentleman, and someone who could charm the birds out of the trees."[4]

In 1963, John died of lung cancer. By then his estate was insolvent, though he still owned two recent cars and a 17.5-foot skiff.

Increasing publicity about Marty's role with NCEA brought people in need of help to her doorstep. One of these was a particularly interesting woman, in view of her historical antecedents and her own subsequent accomplishments. Susan B. Anthony was the grandniece of *the* Susan B. Anthony of nineteenth-century suffragist and temperance fame. The younger Susan had a fine, well-deserved reputation as a New York radio interview host when alcoholism caught up with her. She sobered up in Marty's NCEA office in 1946, immensely grateful that Marty provided a witness that an upper-class lady can turn into a low-class drunk and then climb back up again.

Susan went on to earn a Ph.D., become a theologian and therapist, found a treatment center, and carry the message of recovery to women's groups all over the country, exactly as Marty had envisioned. Nonalcoholic women were slow to listen, even though their lives were often seriously demeaned by alcoholism in their families. The process has taken decades. Women like Susan were pivotal in delivering to women information that originated in the crucible of Marty's passion. How ironic—that alcoholic Susan should be the namesake and female descendant of the first Susan, a teetotaler who was America's peerless advocate for women. And that the

AA Susan would also become a passionate advocate for women, but from the nontemperance side.

Another woman, Ruth O., got sober in 1948. Ruth was an AA volunteer at Dr. William D. Silkworth's Towns Hospital. One time Ruth took a newcomer to an AA meeting, saying, "You're in luck. We're going to hear a great woman, Marty Mann."

After the talk, the newcomer marched up to Marty and boldly asked, "If I stay sober one year, will you speak at my anniversary?" The newcomer did stay sober, and Marty did come and speak at her anniversary.

Marty also spoke at Ruth O.'s second AA anniversary. Ruth asked her because Marty was the only woman at the time who would say she was an alcoholic. And finding a female AA sponsor was difficult. Marty was "sort of on a different plane from most women in AA—like a goddess to the rest of us."[5]

In those days, AA looked down on fancy gifts for AA anniversaries. Bill Wilson said, "Why do you need a gift for sobriety?" Marty gave Ruth a gift, nonetheless—a card with the Twelve Steps printed on it.

In the midst of all this activity, Marty grew more and more concerned about her mother. Lill had been living in straitened circumstances in Chicago and was not in good health. The Mann children sent her money when they were able, but Marty, as the eldest, felt the most responsibility. Bill gave his father an allowance "practically every week, in fact I often had to draw some of my pay in advance to give him enough so that Mother [would not give him money]." After Bill was discharged from the Army, he tried to help as much as he could but was hard put for several years to support himself. An ill-advised, brief marriage drained him of any extra funds for a period.

Finally, in the late 1940s, Marty and her sisters persuaded Lill to leave Chicago, where she'd lived all her life, and come to New York. At first Lill moved in with Betty, but that didn't work out well for independent Betty. So Marty found an apartment for her mother near hers and Priscilla's in Manhattan. Somehow the Mann children were able to support Lill financially. For quite a while, Marty was the main source; then she and Bill shared the major contribution. That Marty managed to help her mother when she herself sometimes went without a salary in NCEA's early years must have been very difficult. To ease the burden at one point, Marty suggested to High Watch Farm that Lill be hired as manager. This Lill did for one year.

Lill had no professional skills, and her age and poor health militated against further employment, so she never worked after High Watch. However, she volunteered at the Red Cross, rolling bandages and so on.

Marty, Chris, and Betty, who all lived in New York City, remained close to their mother and included her in their lives. Bill would visit from Toronto whenever he had the chance. Priscilla and Marty often had Lill over for dinner, and Marty would regularly take her out to a restaurant and the theater. Lill was a tender mother who loved to cook and do for her children. Bill, being the only son and now living in Canada, was special to her.

Marty's father was also in New York City by this time. Usually he had little money and would occasionally try to weasel some from his children. Under Marty's strict tutelage, they all learned firmly to say no. One time he pressured Betty to cosign a note. She asked Marty what she should do. Marty answered, "No way."

Even Lill had learned her lesson. Several years before, Will proposed to Lill that he put the family on his tax return as dependents. Lill retorted, "Absolutely not. You haven't been supporting any of us." Although Marty kept her financial distance from her father, she did stay in loose touch with him.

Since Yale expected NCEA to help in fund-raising, Marty explored every avenue available to her. Mrs. Julius Ochs Adler, wife of one of the owners of the *New York Times,* was an NCEA board member. She had the idea that she and Marty should call on bank presidents to raise money. Marty and Mrs. Adler also wanted to interest one of these men to accept the position of treasurer on the board.

The two women made appointments with eight bank presidents. A maximum of fifteen minutes was scheduled for each visit with these busy executives. Mrs. Adler's chauffeur would drop her and Marty off, expecting to double-park on New York's jammed streets only a short time. Instead, the sessions lasted up to an hour and a half. Every single one of the presidents started picking Marty's brains for advice about what to do with an alcoholic family member—but no money was raised, nor did NCEA find a treasurer among the bank presidents.

On the way home, Mrs. Adler said, "You know what, Marty? I'm beginning to believe that an alcoholic is standard equipment in the American family!"

Marty would later comment, "One thing we'll never run out of is alcoholics. There's no end to the supply. And it's being added to all the time."

The Yale Center of Alcohol Studies, in the meantime, was engaged in an innovative consultation with Connecticut that resulted in America's first state-sponsored alcoholism education and treatment program since the years preceding Prohibition. Thanks to Yale's leadership, Connecticut's enlightened approach incorporated a modern nonmoralistic interpretation of problem drinking. New Hampshire soon followed suit. Eventually, nearly every state in the Union enacted comparable enabling legislation. Although Marty was not directly concerned with these early developments, she observed them closely. They were valuable lessons for her future involvement in state and federal legislation regarding alcoholism education and treatment.

Both Yale and Marty intended that she be a bridge between the scientific community and the public at large. Yet, as Ron Roizen, a prominent sociologist and researcher of the alcoholism movement, and others have pointed out, the scientific understanding of alcoholism was in its infancy.[6] Questions outnumbered answers. Was alcoholism really a disease? What caused it? Was it genetic, environmental, cultural, psychological, spiritual, characterological? All of the above? Could it be cured? How?

Science always addresses the "what," "why," and "how" of a problem. The scientific approach is rooted in experiment that provides results both replicable and predictable.

By the 1940s, quite a lot was known about the "what" of alcoholism. The condition had specific, identifiable symptoms, progression, and consequences. That had been understood in America for at least 150 years. The larger problems were "why" it happened and "how" to treat it. Hypotheses were plentiful about the "why." By and large, the hypotheses posited a sinful, immoral, weak character as the cause of inebriety. Society thus believed that ethics and religion should be able to cure drunkards.

A hypothesis of emotional problems was also gaining popularity as the primary cause. This hypothesis offered fertile ground for the emerging field of psychiatry. Although no one realized it, very little could actually be known until recent times about the "why." Scientific advances on a broad front were required. Researchers kept trying, but the answers to "why" would have to wait forty years after NCEA's founding for developments to occur in neuroscience and biochemistry.

The more fruitful approaches concerned the "how" of treatment. Many individuals and institutions have been involved in this aspect. For a complete history, please see William L. White's *Slaying the Dragon.*[7]

AA's contribution was from the "how" side. Through painful trial and error, its members had found a method of arresting their problem that worked for large numbers of them. Most had already tried other solutions in vain, so they tended to believe their way was the only one. Total abstinence, the Twelve Steps, and the fellowship of AA were their basic empirical tools. Marty, always a pragmatist, believed AA was the best long-term treatment for this chronic disease, but she acknowledged that AA might not work for some—and that was all right (though Marty remained skeptical about the extended efficacy and benefits of alternative methods). The important thing was to find a solution the individual sufferer could live with.

Yale was also working on the "how" of alcoholism. The Yale Plan Clinics emphasized experimental treatment approaches. The bulk of these approaches were psychological but also included investigations into physiology and nutrition. Yale considered four avenues of psychological treatment—lay therapy, psychiatry, conditioned reflex (aversion therapy), and AA.

One of Marty's most important contributions to public understanding was the introduction of the terms *alcoholic* and *alcoholism* into familiar usage. Before she set out to educate the United States and numerous other countries, these words were largely unheard-of among the general public although known to physicians and the few researchers and treatment providers in the field. Today it seems impossible that *alcoholic* and *alcoholism* haven't always been part of the standard English lexicon, but fifty years ago they were not in the public vocabulary at all, or adequately grasped if they were. Thanks to Marty and the great educational grassroots network she created, *alcoholic* and *alcoholism* are now widely known, understood, and most important, accepted and destigmatized to a large extent. For Marty, their big advantage was that they were scientifically neutral and relatively free of the moralistic, demeaning freight of prior terms such as *inebriate* and *drunk.*

Marty came to prefer saying, "Jim has alcoholism," rather than "Jim is an alcoholic." The former emphasized the disease aspect with an immediate connection to the hope of treatment and recovery. Marty also felt strongly that AAs should refer to themselves as *recovered,* not *recovering.* Bill Wilson firmly advocated the use of *recovered,* too. For these two pioneers, *recovered* meant "I'm well today"—*recovering* meant "I'm still sick."

As Marty was fulfilling her mandate to lecture about alcoholism and what could be done about inebriety, she emphasized the scientific validity of her presentations. The general public needed facts about inebriety and needed to know that prominent, reputable scientists were engaged in a serious inquiry about it. Otherwise, people would remain mired in old ideas about sin and immorality. To the extent that accurate information was known, it could sweep away the cobwebs of ignorance, stigma, and fear. Marty always kept herself and her organization up to date on current scientific discoveries and advances related to alcoholism.

Although scientific research into alcoholism was just beginning, Marty asserted as factual what she and other AA members believed, based on their experience and intuition—that alcoholism was a complex condition involving one's body, mind, emotions, soul, and personal relations. AAs were convinced it had a physiological, irreversible component. The Big Book used the term *illness* to describe this perplexing yet very real malady. Marty's unscientific extrapolation in identifying alcoholism as a disease in the absence of explicit supportive data, questionable at the time, was eventually proved to be largely correct.

Marty said that the disease concept of alcoholism was valuable for two reasons. One, she believed it explained "why" both to the alcoholic and to the general public. Two, it removed guilt as an issue. A person needn't feel guilty for having a legitimate disease and could instead direct energies toward recovery.

Marty's personal conviction was that "alcoholics are born that way." Research to date indicates some sort of genetic vulnerability to alcoholism for 40 to 60 percent of alcoholics. This suggests that the remaining alcoholics arrive by another route. Over time, the most consistent predictor for alcoholism is a pattern of continued heavy drinking. In other words, you can be born to it, or you can drink your way into it.[8]

The scientific community, including Marty's sponsors at Yale, became increasingly uncomfortable with her calling alcoholism a disease. When people think of *disease,* they usually have in mind germs—bacteria and viruses. But there are many conditions commonly called diseases, such as diabetes, that are not caused by germs but by malfunction of some part of the body. In the case of diabetes, the pancreas malfunctions. AA intuited that alcoholism also had its roots in a malfunction of the body.[9]

Some diseases have genetic causes, such as sickle-cell anemia. Alcoholism, too, seemed to have a familial or genetic basis. Still other diseases can be traced to the environment, such as lead poisoning. Another group of diseases seems to exhibit combined genetic, environmental, and sociocultural components. AA members observed that in the individual with this constellation of vulnerabilities, the potential for alcoholism was greater.

Marty's personal observation was that alcoholism was spread, not by germs, but by culture. "Tell me any other instance of a disease," she said, "that is dependent on accepted social custom for its existence. Maybe diabetes—but sugar does not have the emotional content of alcohol."

Marty died before research showed that alcohol is but one of a class of addictive psychoactive drugs that includes nicotine and street drugs as well as some prescription drugs. In addictive disease, how the drug is ingested doesn't matter, whether by drinking, smoking, in a pill, via a needle, or whatever. However, this disease will not be activated unless the individual ingests a psychoactive drug.

Labeling a known affliction as a disease before either its cause ("why") or cure ("how") were known had good historical precedent. Such has been the case with all the great scourges of humankind—typhoid, malaria, cholera, syphilis, cancer, tuberculosis, pneumonia. For centuries, the courses of these diseases ("what") could be clearly described and often predicted. However, until scientific knowledge and tools matured, the explanations for disease, born of ignorance, tended to be an act of God and punishment for individual or societal sins. Treatment, based on trial and error, myth, and folkways, occasionally seemed to help, mostly did nothing, and sometimes actively contributed to the patient's death.

What complicated defining alcoholism as a disease was the apparent willfulness of alcoholics in pursuing their affliction despite knowledge of the consequences and contrary to medical advice. How could alcoholism be a true disease if the patient persisted in behavior that worsened the situation? Which came first, the alcoholic behavior or some mysterious cause?

Marty once said somewhat wistfully that she wished she could be around when the cause or causes of alcoholism were determined by science. She was convinced that the answers would be found in three areas: biochemistry, psychology (in particular with regard to vulnerability to stress), and social or environmental issues. These are indeed the areas that have proved most fruitful. Marty would find thrilling the late-twentieth-century discoveries in biochemistry and neurochemistry that have identified the addictive pathways and mechanisms of the brain.

Jellinek and the others at the Yale Center of Alcohol Studies went along at first with Marty's presentation to the public of alcoholism as a disease and therefore a scientific fact, but they were uncomfortable with the terminology because of the patent absence of an identifiable cause—the "why." Haggard, Bacon, and even Jellinek eventually also differed with Marty over whether AA was the only, or even the best, framework for long-term recovery. After a few years, they all distanced themselves from Marty's single-minded emphasis on the disease concept and AA as the solution.

Bacon, in particular, became less than enthusiastic about the disease concept of alcoholism. He also disagreed with NCEA's emphasis on Alcoholics Anonymous as *the* answer for the long haul. When he succeeded Haggard as director of the Yale center in 1948, that program took a direction that was increasingly incompatible with Marty's vision and her leadership of NCEA.

Life Happens

1948

WITHOUT QUESTION, MARTY WAS KNOWN for her public face and public contributions to society. However, she also led a rich personal life, some of it within AA, some not. At this particular time, fascinating changes were occurring for Priscilla that would affect Marty, too. Priscilla's star was about to rise in spectacular tandem with Marty's.

Priscilla had had several jobs prior to Macy's, where she met Marty. For a time, she was engaged in making experimental films for the Mrs. Willard Straight Foundation. That was followed by assistant art director at *Harper's Bazaar*. After Macy's, Priscilla became chief copywriter at Saks Fifth Avenue, then art director there.

By 1947, Priscilla had been Saks's art director for some time. Her drawings in *Town and Country* magazine, especially the witty cartoon "Professor Tarragon," attracted the interest of Alexander Liberman, the longtime influential art director of *Vogue* magazine. He hired her as art editor of *Vogue*. She remained with *Vogue* from January 1947 until she retired in 1972. The last ten of those years, she succeeded Alex as *Vogue's* art director.

Liberman described his first interview of Priscilla.

A very interesting young woman named Priscilla Peck appeared in my office. She was neat and dark-haired, very chic in an American way, very sophisticated, very intelligent, a chain smoker. She showed me more of her drawings, and I just thought, with her personal style and dash and ability to draw, let's bring her in. . . . I thought she would be a marvelous art editor for *Vogue*. . . . It was a gamble that paid off.[1]

For the next twenty-five years, Priscilla was in charge of layout at *Vogue*. Liberman said that her devil-may-care attitude "did away with much of the stodginess that had overtaken Edna Chase's magazine." Twice a week, he and Priscilla lunched together at Jansen's, where she always ordered steak tartare.

> They would have long, deep, philosophical discussions. "She had read enormously—Ouspensky, Gurdjieff, and all that mystical business, and also Kandinsky's *Concerning the Spiritual in Art* and Laszlo Moholy-Nagy's *Vision in Motion,* books that influenced modern artists. I was very impressed by her absolute dismissal of things that I revered. I remember telling her that Cezanne was one of my gods, and her saying, 'My dear, Cezanne is not that great.' She had tremendous self-assurance and self-confidence."
>
> An artist herself, Priscilla was a close friend of Betty Parsons, whose gallery had inherited Jackson Pollock, Mark Rothko, Clyfford Still, and most of the other first-generation Abstract Expressionists in 1947. . . . She introduced Alex to Betty and to the avant-garde milieu—in those days a tiny and embattled band that included, along with the artists, a handful of dealers, two or three collectors, and the critics Clement Greenberg, Harold Rosenberg, and Thomas B. Hess. Without Priscilla Peck to stimulate and encourage Alex's thinking, it might have taken a lot longer to make his own breakthrough as an abstract artist. . . .[2]
>
> In October 1951, *Vogue* ran an article by Aline B. Louchheim (the future Aline Saarinen) on Betty Parsons and her artists. Alex admired Betty Parsons enormously. He had met her through Priscilla Peck, who was a close friend of the dealer—they were both charter members of the lesbian underground in New York—and to celebrate the *Vogue* article, which he had commissioned, he gave a lunch party for Parsons and her artists at Chambord, the most elegant and expensive French restaurant in New York. Betty sat at one end of the long table and Alex sat at the other end, flanked by Jackson Pollock on his right and Mark Rothko on his left. Clyfford Still was there, and Barnett Newman, and Ad Reinhardt. (This was before their quarrels split the New York School into warring factions.) In Alex's recollection the lunch was a

quiet and mannerly affair. Newman and Rothko talked about the large-scale paintings they wanted to do—"Give us billboards," Alex remembers one of them saying. . . . Pollock, who had come into the city from eastern Long Island for the occasion, stayed relatively sober. The party and the *Vogue* article "helped put over the gallery," according to Betty Parsons, who was still having a very hard time selling the work of the Abstract Expressionists at that point. "It helped me get the word to people. It helped the artists."[3]

Under Liberman, *Vogue* became an important showcase and forum for modern art and he himself an influential tastemaker. The magazine often featured articles by leading artists and art critics. The March 1951 issue of *Vogue,* for example, showed two Pollock paintings, *Lavender Mist* and *Autumn Rhythm,* as backdrops for full-page pictures by Cecil Beaton of models wearing "The New Soft Look." In addition, Alex, who was already a recognized artist with a rather traditional representational style, was inspired to break into new experimental modes. His paintings and especially sculptures have been acquired by a number of major museums around the world.

Priscilla's responsibilities entailed extensive contact with the world of art, style, and money. Marty's already considerable acquaintance with that world was enhanced and enlarged by Priscilla. Priscilla didn't travel nationally nearly as much as Marty, but she did visit the European fashion shows periodically. In fact, Priscilla preferred to stay close to home, whereas Marty loved the stimulus of travel.

There were many perks for someone in Priscilla's position at *Vogue*— tickets to first nights, discounts on designer clothing, invitations to parties and social events featuring the beautiful people, and so on. Marty and Priscilla themselves entertained often, especially after they moved in 1948 to a spacious apartment at 10 West Ninth Street, in the northern part of Greenwich Village. Guests who didn't know the two women were lesbian partners might have figured it out when using the bathroom. There the towels were embroidered with *Mann-Peck* instead of the standard *his* and *hers.*

The apartment, which they kept for thirty-two years until Marty's death, was a fourth-floor walk-up, the topmost unit. In 1980, the landlord must have been ecstatic to once again have a vacancy since the rent on this spacious rent-controlled unit in a prime Manhattan location was only $350 a month when Marty died—many times below market rate, which today probably approaches $8,000 to $10,000 per month.

When Priscilla and Marty initially viewed the apartment prior to signing the lease, Priscilla entered first, then immediately exited, saying to Marty, "You can't go in. This place needs to be exorcised!"

Marty stepped across the threshold anyway, but backed right out, exclaiming, "There *is* an evil presence here!"

The two women consulted a Jamaican priest they knew. He was familiar with exorcisms and agreed to perform one for their new home. Telling them to wait outside, he was in the apartment for nearly an hour. When he came out, he looked drained. Marty said that walking into the apartment then was "like a beautiful meadow." The atmosphere was completely different.

Once guests negotiated the three flights of stairs leading to the apartment, they entered a small foyer, which led into a large living room with a fireplace. Bookshelves flanked the windows. To the rear, French doors opened onto steps down to a good-sized rooftop patio. To the right of the living room were a dinette and kitchen. Upstairs, over the living room and kitchen, were two rooms and a bath. The smaller room was used as a study and guest room. The large one, which had ample cupboard and closet space, was Priscilla and Marty's bedroom.

The apartment's most striking feature was a very large two-story studio to the left of the living room. Flooded with natural lighting, this wonderful space had a second fireplace and was comfortably furnished with sofas and easy chairs. There was a piano, which the talented Priscilla especially enjoyed. For many years a Jackson Pollock drip painting, *Number 15, 1949,* was the highlight of the room.

Marty always believed in having liquor available for nonalcoholics who enjoyed a drink, so she kept a fully equipped and stocked bar. She herself drank a "horse's neck"—ginger ale with a slice of lemon. Her attitude toward liquor was consistent—abstinence for alcoholics, usage for everyone else who wanted it. In a *New York Herald Tribune* interview, she "laughed at the notion that she would prefer tea in a non-alcoholic restaurant rather than at the Artist and Writers Restaurant at 215 West Fortieth Street, where cocktails flow in the late afternoon."

I go everywhere my friends go, and I serve liquor in my own home. I feel that my condition is like that of a diabetic. I cannot take alcohol any more than a diabetic can take sugar, but the diabetic does not refuse to go to restaurants or to serve sugar to his friends at home. Similarly, we do not speak of the alcoholic as being cured, any more than the diabetic is cured. It is simply that we are happy when we remain abstinent and continue the routine under which we have been taught the right way of life—for us. It may be psychiatry, group therapy, hospitalization or Alcoholics Anonymous—as in my own case.[4]

Like many well-to-do working couples, Marty and Priscilla had a regular maid. She was devoted to her employers and came in for years until Marty died. Priscilla didn't cook, but Marty was a fine cook who loved good food. At times, she had to watch her weight. She was very knowledgeable about foreign cuisines and enjoyed all kinds of dishes.

In March of 1948, Marty's sister Chris married for the third and last time. Jesse Doyle (Jess), a Boston stockbroker, was a limited partner in his firm. Marty and Chris had always been close, so Chris's moving away to Boston must have had its sad side for Marty even though she would have been happy for her sister. After Jess's firm went belly-up in the mid-1950s, he and Chris relocated permanently to their summer place in Dublin, New Hampshire, where they owned an old farmhouse that they winterized and restored.

When Jess died in 1979, Chris sold the house and rented an apartment in the nearby town of Peterborough. As time went on, some secondary effects of polio returned for Chris, but she continued to live a full life. Her hands became more and more crippled. Muscle weakness returned, and she used a cane constantly. Then she fell and cracked a vertebra. A spunky, independent woman to the end, Chris was in and out of the hospital a couple of times but finally died there in 1985.

Just as Priscilla was settling in at *Vogue*, an exciting opportunity arose for Marty in 1948 to travel to Great Britain and Europe. The occasion was the International Conference on Alcoholism, held that July in Lucerne, Switzerland. Marty was an official member of the U.S. delegation led by Dr. A. V. Vestermark. Vestermark, based in Washington, D.C., was in charge of administering the funds appropriated by Congress under the National

Mental Health Act. Marty began her three-week trip with a weekend respite on Whale Cay at Joe Carstairs's estate, then continued to London, Paris, and Lucerne.

Twelve years had passed since Marty left England, penniless and more or less in disgrace. In many ways, this return was a triumphant homecoming for her. To be named to the U.S. delegation was a great honor, but equally important, the trip gave her a chance to renew friendships and to support the expansion of British committees on education modeled on those Marty was forming in America. Before she left, she contacted a number of good friends. One was Natalia Murray at Cherry Grove on Fire Island, asking if Janet Flanner (Genet), the *New Yorker*'s Paris columnist and Natalia's lesbian partner, would be in Paris when Marty was there.

The publicity Marty arranged for her visit was formidable. Her appointment book was packed solid with engagements. Among the people she saw was Ingrid Bergman, who later wrote a gracious note thanking her for taking the time to meet. One reconnection with an old friend, Forbes Cheston, was particularly touching. He later sent her a copy of his introductory remarks at an AA meeting where she spoke to an enthusiastic audience of 136, signing it "To Marty, with love—Chesty."

Ladies and Gentlemen.

I have already, this evening, had the pleasure of seeing and hearing Marty Mann in the celluloid. You now have the opportunity, and I hope the pleasure, of seeing her in the flesh.

I asked for, and very generously received of the committee, the priviledge [*sic*] of introducing Mrs Mann tonight, because she is an old friend of mine from our unregenerate days.

Mrs Mann flew to Europe from America about ten days ago as one of the three official United States delegates to the International Congress [*sic*] on Alcoholism held in Lucerne. She arrived in London on Sunday, after a long absence, and we met for the first time in many years, and moreover, for the first time ever when both of us were sober, or, at any rate, when neither of us had a hangover. We hardly recognized one another.

You are not here to listen to me, but I would like to add one thing. Some two years or more ago, I ran into a mutual friend of ours and asked what had become of Marty. I was told that she had given up drinking and was speaking all over America for something called Alcoholics Anonymous. I laughed like anything—but—some months ago, when I myself had to admit that alcohol had me licked, when I was desperate, I saw a little paragraph in the *Evening Standard*. It was headed Alcoholics Anonymous. And I should have passed it by, but that I remembered my old friend Marty Mann. I got in touch with AA and though she was 3000 miles away and didn't know it herself till much later, I have always thought of Marty as the person who got me into AA.

So I am here tonight and she is here tonight and that is why it gives me such particular pleasure to introduce to you, Ladies and Gentlemen, The First Woman Member of AA—Marty Mann.[5]

Following the European trip, Marty was in Mexico City, speaking before the American Society of Mexico, which resulted in the formation of a committee on alcoholism education there. Then back to the United States and more talks and networking.

The year 1948 was also notable for Marty and NCEA because it marked the advent of Yvelin Gardner as her associate executive director. Yev, a recovered alcoholic who had found sobriety through AA, was active in New York real estate. A modest inheritance allowed him to volunteer his services to Marty. (NCEA was later able to place him on the payroll.) An excellent administrator, he was crucial to the daily operations of a fast-growing organization, especially since Marty was gone so much. His calm style balanced Marty's energetic one. For the next twenty-five years, he became what Marty called her alter ego. He and especially Betty Gold, Marty's longtime secretary, were protective of Marty.

Fortunately for Marty, Priscilla's position at *Vogue* was very well paid. Marty was about to enter a period of high stress and low income. The exceptionally productive year of 1948 concluded with an extremely serious health problem for Marty. She was unexpectedly diagnosed with cancer requiring immediate surgery. The NCEA staff and her friends were in a state of shock. One can imagine the torrent of emotions she must have felt, knowing that her mother had had breast cancer when Marty was fourteen, and wondering if she carried yet another possible negative genetic marker in addition to alcoholism.

Like many women anticipating hospitalization, Marty visited the hair-dresser a couple of days before entering Doctors Hospital for major surgery in early January 1949. Her physicians, Mortimer D. Speiser and William Studdiford (consulting), recommended she recuperate in the hospital for at least two months, followed by three or four months at home before she returned to work. To everyone's relief, the malignancy was reported as completely removed.

In accordance with the customs of the time and her own sense of modesty, Marty didn't specify the nature of the cancer beyond a small circle of friends and family. Letters from her friends indicated they understood she'd had skin cancer. It was undoubtedly a severe form considering the impact of the surgery and the length of her convalescence and was probably located in the genitoreproductive area. When Marty's brother, Bill, visited her in the hospital and asked point-blank what was the problem, she airily answered, "Oh, just some little female thing" and changed the subject. On this particular visit, Bill had brought Marty a small bucket with a goldfish in it—a novel change from flowers. When he opened the bucket's lid to show her his gift, the fish jumped out and down her cleavage!

Bill, like his siblings, often turned to Marty for advice. He told Marty that he was having trouble in his first, brief marriage. He wanted a divorce, and his wife wouldn't give it to him. In the meantime, he'd become reacquainted with a former girlfriend and wanted to marry her.

Bill walked in to see Marty, sank dejectedly into a chair, his shoulders slumped, and said, "I'm really down."

"Stand up!" she ordered.

"Look," Bill answered, "I'm married and I'm not happy. I can't get a divorce. My wife won't give it to me. I want to marry Betts. What should I do?"

"Stand up!" Marty repeated. "Put your shoulders back. Look like a man. Put your head back. Go ahead and do something about it. Quit your moaning."[6]

Bill did take his big sister's advice. He divorced his first wife, married Betts, and they had four sons. (One was Betts's son by a former marriage. Bill adopted him.) The three still living are William J. C. (Bill), a Toronto businessman; Edward K. (Ted), an attorney in Ottawa; and J. Stephen (Steve), a businessman in Australia. Betts died in 1980. Later that year, Bill married Pat Sewall, a widow his sister Chris introduced him to.

While Marty was still in the hospital, she received a warm letter from Foster Kennedy, the Bellevue neurologist who had started her on the road to recovery more than a decade earlier. After telling her he hoped she was making a successful and happy recovery, he commented, "Convalescence is one of the most delightful experiences in the world. One has no responsibility and one gains day by day a sense of power—an unbeatable combination!" Then he continued, "I want your opinion on a grave matter." The twenty-four-year-old daughter of a medical colleague was in trouble with drinking. What should Dr. Kennedy advise?

"It is indecent to put this problem before you on the bed of your recovery," he said, "but I know that you have a great heart and a wise mind. Of such is the Kingdom of Heaven and they get all the bad jobs!"[7]

Marty's response is unknown. What a difference in their relationship, though, from eleven years before! Dr. Kennedy must have felt great satisfaction at the part he played in starting Marty on the road to recovery. She in turn had educated him about AA, including introducing him to Bill Wilson. Kennedy was a strong supporter of AA. His eminent national and international position in the medical community undoubtedly helped persuade physicians, at least in the New York area, to reserve judgment if they could not outright support AA. And in his prominent teaching role at Bellevue and Cornell, he would have been a powerful educational force for AA among medical students. In the early history of Alcoholics Anonymous, Foster Kennedy should be included in that select handful of appreciative and influential doctors: W. D. Silkworth, Harry Tiebout, and Ruth Fox.

So valued was Kennedy's support for AA that the official history, *Alcoholics Anonymous Comes of Age,* contains his stirring response to a pivotal paper Bill Wilson had just presented in 1944 before the New York State Medical Society. Dr. Kennedy said in part:

> We have heard a truly moving and eloquent address, moving in its form and in its facts. I have no doubt that a man who has cured himself of the lust for alcohol has a far greater power for curing alcoholism than has a doctor who has never been afflicted by the same curse.

No matter how sympathetic and patient the doctor may be in the approach to his patient, the patient is sure to either feel, or imagine, condescension to himself or get the notion that he is being hectored by one of the minor prophets.

This organization of Alcoholics Anonymous calls on two of the greatest reservoirs of power known to man, religion, and that instinct for association with one's fellows which Trotter has called the "herd instinct.". . . This movement furnishes an objective of high emotional driving power in making every cured drunkard a missionary to the sick.

We physicians, I think, have always had difficulty in finding an occupation for our convalescent patients of sufficient emotional driving power by which to replace the psychical results of the alcohol that has been withdrawn. . . .

I think our profession must take appreciative cognizance of this great therapeutic weapon. If we do not do so we shall stand convicted of emotional sterility and of having lost the faith that moves mountains, without which medicine can do little.[8]

Yale Files for Divorce

1948–50

MARTY HEALED UNUSUALLY FAST FROM HER SURGERY and was discharged from the hospital a month early, providing, said her doctors, that she continue her convalescence at home. Predictably, she ignored their orders and insisted on returning to work before her body was really ready. There was simply too much to do. An urgent major crisis that had been festering for some time was coming to a head. NCEA and Yale were about to split. The impetus for severing the association was Yale's. From early in 1949 until the end of the year, Marty and her NCEA board of directors would be involved in increasingly heated discussions with Yale.

The timing couldn't have been worse, considering the state of Marty's health. Inevitably, she was pulled back into active participation, thus delaying by several months her complete recovery from cancer.

From Marty's point of view, NCEA's primary goal had always been to reduce stigma through education and thus attract alcoholics into recovery. For Yale, the primary goals were to teach, to conduct research, and to raise money for the center through public awareness and education. Within four years, these two understandings of NCEA's mission diverged. Complicating the differences in organizational goals were personality and philosophical differences between Marty and Selden Bacon, now the executive director of the Yale Center of Alcohol Studies.

While Marty was still convalescing, Yale decided that it was no longer appropriate for the university to sponsor its offspring NCEA. For one thing, NCEA had become a national organization, and Yale felt it "was

207

illogical for such an organization to be so strictly tied to one department of one university."[1]

Second, Yale was primarily an educational institution, and the staff of the Yale Plan on Alcoholism had "become increasingly uncomfortable to find themselves involved as the responsible directors of a national health program."[2]

Third, money-raising was a core issue, perhaps the most important issue of all. NCEA's rapid growth had caused it to siphon off a larger portion than anticipated of the funds available to the Yale center, thereby becoming to some extent the tail that wagged the dog. There was also confusion in the minds of donors about whether they were giving to the university, to the center, or to NCEA. (And in AA, some members continued to object that NCEA used the name of Alcoholics Anonymous to raise funds for NCEA.) An amusing, seemingly trivial incident, deadly serious at the time, proved to be the proverbial last straw.

> A little leaflet called "My Daddy Didn't Do It" was circulated nationally. This little promotional piece was a story told by a child concerning her father and his progressive drinking. The name "Harry Brown" was used in the pamphlet and he was noted as a banker. It seems there were quite a few Harry Browns who had graduated from Yale and who had entered the banking business.
>
> A number of irate letters from such people came to the Dean's office at Yale University since these men had been teased, and even gossiped about, by friends who had received the appeal for funds and the leaflet enclosed. This, combined with the fact that a number of people had already questioned the use of Yale University's official seal on the stationery and letterheads of appeal letters for such a controversial subject as alcoholism began to influence the University officials and board members. Such was the power of the still existent stigma surrounding alcoholism![3]

Finally, Yale insisted that NCEA maintain offices in New Haven as well as New York. Since this was too expensive, and since Marty refused to close the New York office and consolidate her activities in New Haven, away from America's main communications center, two irresistible forces had each met an immovable object.

Marty, still convalescing from cancer surgery, sought frantically for funding to keep NCEA afloat. In May of 1949, NCEA launched "a campaign to place coin boxes in the city's bars for contributions from drinkers for the treatment and cure of alcoholics." The campaign started May 20 and aimed to raise $100,000 ($700,000 in year 2000 dollars). On boxes or containers appeared the legend:

> You Can Drink.
> Help the Alcoholic Who Can't.
> Alcoholism Is a Disease.

People were asked to contribute the price of a drink. Eleanor Roosevelt, widow of the president, had accepted membership on NCEA's permanent advisory board, and she heartily supported the coin box drive.

Once this strenuous campaign concluded at the end of May, Marty's convalescence had been so seriously compromised that her doctors insisted she take a three-month leave of absence over the summer. Thereafter, she was able to return to work only part-time until early February 1950, when her doctors again advised her to stop entirely. At that point, Marty escaped to the Bahamas for a couple of months, presumably to Joe Carstairs's Whale Cay retreat, returning to NCEA full-time in mid-April 1950.

Before Marty left for the summer, she sent a desperate memo on June 30 to her NCEA advisory board, appealing for $5,000 ($35,000 in year 2000 dollars) to keep the organization going. "This is a matter of life or death!" And on a copy she forwarded to Bill Wilson, she added a note, "So this is it, Bill. Too bad. Too bad."[4]

On hearing the devastating news that NCEA might not survive, Bill Wilson immediately wrote Marty.

Marty dear,

At first reading, that memorandum which you dated June 30 was terribly dispiriting to me. Yes, and more. It was devastating, because I think I understand, better than some, how much of your blood and courage has gone into the Committee. As one who has made an expenditure of this kind himself, I find it quite impossible to picture such a disappointment.

Then I read your footnote and there, between the lines, I could see you at your best even though enduring the worst. Somehow I could see you rising, Phoenix-like, from the ashes of the great flame you kindled; a flame whose warmth will be felt by many a generation of our brothers and sisters.

God bless you and keep you, my dear girl. See me at any time you can.

> Affectionately,
> Bill

Lois added her own note of encouragement.

Marty dear,

Your work in the National Committee has been so outstanding and so beneficial to the alcoholic that I hope you won't have any sense of failure now because there's the chance of not having the money to go on. Many AAs don't understand how much you've helped the public to understand. Bill and I are proud of you, dear, and love you very much.[5]

While Marty recuperated, the divorce continued to be negotiated between Yale and NCEA during the summer and into the fall. Considerable ill feeling erupted between NCEA's board and Selden Bacon. In the fall, Marty waded back into this quagmire.

At the November board meeting, it was obvious that a phased withdrawal by Yale was not an option—if it had ever been. Hostile feelings between the Yale and non-Yale members of the board exploded. As Marty commented in a long letter to Franklin Huston, her close friend and NCEA's representative in the western states, "The minutes of that meeting, which are being sent to you today, give only the pallid and thoroughly cleaned-up version of what was actually a knock-down-drag-out fight."

Marty's description of the meeting follows.

All hell broke loose at our Nov. 18 Board meeting, when the Board finally got its chance to reply to the long peroration Selden had drowned them in at the previous meeting. Led by Austin MacCormick and Dwight Anderson, seconded by Tiebout, Powdermaker, Lois Knowlson and even the usually silent Col. Dougherty, they questioned everything, starting at the budget itself, and going from there to the repayment of old debts and the schedule for that, up to and at great

length about the true functions of the NCEA, the lack of necessity for
two offices and the question of where the one should be, New Haven
or New York. Unanimously the Board went on record that the Committee work as conducted out of the NY office was of paramount importance, and that shutting that office would in their opinion be
tantamount to killing the NCEA. There was considerable discussion as
to the "two underlying philosophies" (Selden's phrase) regarding the
proper function of the NCEA—quite honestly he made out a pretty
poor case for his (or Haggard's or Yale's or whosoever it really is) and
was told so by each and every member of the Board. . . .

I never spoke, and thank God left the room during the discussion—ostensibly of Austin's resolution to pay me half-salary during my
sick leave, which I knew was going to end by being a discussion, at
least on Selden's part, of why I was no longer useful to this work. I
heard afterwards he didn't get very far with that angle, but from far
away outside the meeting room I heard loud and angry voices raised so
high I carefully moved still further away. I wasn't called back for a
good half-hour, so it must have been hot and heavy. The resolution finally adopted was to pay me half-salary beginning Nov. 1, and add the
amount of my half-salary from July 1 to the debts. At the same time
the discussion of those back debts was taken up, and the Board (always excepting Selden) unanimously agreed that *human* debts came
first: in other words, they intended to pay all the people who were
owed back salary before considering the payment of the so-called Yale
debt. Selden's schedule of priorities as outlined at the meeting you attended, with the entire amount owed Yale, $7400 [$51,800 in year
2000 dollars], to be paid before paying back salaries from July 1st to
Nov. (mainly yours) made the Board verbally angry. . . . Incidentally,
Yev and I had drawn up a new budget which was considered more re-
alistic than the one presented by Selden, and this was adopted in place
of his. It should be attached to your copy of the Minutes. . . .

Selden was thoroughly ruffled—in fact good and sore—by the end
of the meeting, and I wasn't surprised at finding messages to call the
New Haven operator when I got home the next evening. Too late to do
so. At 9 the following morning he got me, and announced that
Haggard wished to withdraw from the NCEA, and he also wished to

resign as Treasurer. A solid hour of verbalization boiled down to an ul-
timatum: either go along with their original plan, which actually meant
an early closing of the NY office, preferably by Dec. 15, or cut free of
Yale and let those "irresponsible big-talking Board members" really
take over. And get those who had talked the most—Anderson, MacC,
Knowlson, Tiebout and Powdermaker—to meet with him in the next
few days to discuss which it should be if they really meant what they
had said. This was on a Friday morning, and I got them all, excepting
Tiebout and Powdermaker, who had medical meetings, to meet the following Tuesday night.

Anderson said he would not attend such a meeting without legal
representation there, and asked me to go down and see his own lawyer,
one Henry Mulcahy, and give him the background. Mulcahy was present [at the Tuesday meeting] and knocked the props out of any tough
talk from Yale by announcing that under our present Articles of
Incorporation and By-Laws, *every* member of the Board of Directors
was automatically a member of the [Yale] Corporation, thus giving the
Board the real power by possessing a majority vote in any important
decision as to the future of the NCEA.

After that, the meeting progressed very amicably with no more
mention of ultimatums, and the Board members present getting legal
answers as to how to go about reorganizing without the Yale contingent. It even became so friendly that I was able to say I hoped very
much Selden would remain as a Board member, to which he replied
that under the circumstances he would have to resign with Haggard
and Jellinek,[6] but he would welcome an invitation to rejoin the Board as
an individual a month or so later. The same invitation will be extended
to Jellinek. . . .

As the Board stated, they would rather see us go down on our own
and for reasons we couldn't help, than be throttled to death by Yale—
or perhaps smothered is a better word. Naturally only a little of our
problem has been solved—most of it remains ahead. But for the first
time I feel we have a real Board of Directors who care and are willing
to work for the NCEA as we of the staff have done. And that is a good
feeling.[7]

Yale's obvious determination to cancel the affiliation nevertheless came as a shock to Marty and the NCEA board. The timing and the utter totality of Yale's intentions were apparently unexpected. No wonder Marty feared desperately for the future. After all her hard work, she must have felt the Yale center's action as a painful personal rejection. NCEA would be losing the Yale center's financial support, the center's scientific credentials, and the university's prestigious name. How could NCEA possibly survive on its own? The organization was barely past the toddler stage.

The formal cutting of the strings occurred on December 31, 1949, but it took several months for the actual transition to be implemented. NCEA changed its name to the National Committee on Alcoholism (NCA) (and in 1957 to the National Council on Alcoholism [still NCA]). The next few years would be touch and go as NCA sought to become financially viable, independent of the Yale umbrella. Marty was now free to sink or swim while she labored exhaustively to fulfill her vision.

In retrospect, Yale did Marty a big favor. As executive director of NCA for the next eighteen years, she could stamp her own dynamic mark on the organization that became America's most eloquent and influential voice on behalf of alcoholics and on the understanding of alcoholism as a disease that could be permanently arrested through appropriate treatment.

Part THREE

*"I will pour water on the thirsty land,
and streams on the dry ground;
I will pour out my Spirit on your offspring,
and my blessing on your descendants.
They will spring up like grass in a meadow,
like poplar trees by flowing streams."*

—Isaiah 44:3–4

Unsettled Weather

1950–54

THE 1950S DID NOT START as an auspicious decade for NCA. America had settled down to recoup from World War II. In a natural reaction to the stress of war, people didn't want to hear about anything disagreeable if they could help it—and that included alcoholism with its historic baggage of stigma and hopelessness. Instead, the fifties was a generally optimistic era with a maximum of attention to economic prosperity. People were busy having babies and raising families. This was the decade of the silent generation, preoccupied with consumerism and getting ahead. Yet below the country's benign surface, alcoholism festered as virulently as ever—a growing health and social issue.

The 1950s was also the decade of McCarthyism, that vicious witch-hunt to eradicate Communists and other imputed subversives, including homosexuals. Homosexuals were identified as perverts and sinners, dangerous to their country. Harassment grew into state and federally sanctioned persecution. Lesbian and gay people were forced even further underground. Many homosexuals wedded to acquire the protection of marriage. Even after Senator Joseph McCarthy was censured by the Senate, and after the extreme Cold War mentality he promoted had subsided somewhat, suspicion and oppression of homosexuals persisted.

McCarthyism was certainly not Marty's first experience of homophobia. The Leopold-Loeb case in Chicago a quarter century before was an early stern lesson in the perils faced by homosexuals (see chapter 5). Even though Marty surely would not agree with the logic that equated homosexuality with criminal behavior, as happened in the public mind during the Leopold-

Loeb trial, she would have understood long before the McCarthy era the personal disaster for her reputation as a public figure if she publicly revealed her sexual orientation to the straight world.

In this ugly climate of McCarthyism, Marty's foresighted adoption of the title Mrs. twenty years before may have saved not only her own reputation and future, but also NCA itself. One can imagine the savage attacks if her sexual orientation had become a matter of public record. Being a lesbian, no matter how much Marty may have accepted her own sexuality, must have made her life very hard. A complicating factor would have been AA's insistence on honesty. Fortunately, the AA philosophy did not extend to injuring oneself or others. Considering the serious personal risks involved, Marty's courage in continuing to lead the alcoholism movement into the light of understanding and acceptance becomes all the more remarkable.

The 1950s was also a decade of personal loss for Marty. Within a span of six years, three persons central to her life would die: Dr. Foster Kennedy, Marty's father, and her mother. In addition, all AA would grieve the loss of Dr. Bob Smith, AA's cofounder.

For AA, the decade opened in sadness with the death from cancer of Dr. Bob, on November 16, 1950. In just fifteen brief years, he and Bill Wilson had birthed and nurtured an organization that changed the world and continues to do so. Marty was but one of the millions who would benefit. For the next twenty years, Bill, increasingly with Marty, would carry forward the improbable work launched in Akron in 1935—Bill tending the AA side, Marty the NCA side. It is fair to say that Marty had as great an impact on the evolution and expansion of AA as did Bill Wilson and Bob Smith. Both Bill and Lois Wilson recognized and acknowledged AA's debt to Marty and NCA.

In an odd mirroring of the period, however, Marty experienced a kind of disjointedness between her personal and professional lives during the early years of the decade. Sometimes her two selves were in harmony, other times dissonant. Marty, always a direct person, would learn at a very basic level what AA told her, "Your insides have to match your outsides. Walk the talk."

At the public level, Marty ignited civic concern wherever she went, but the local communities she educated and inspired had yet to coalesce into a truly national movement. As the difficult months of the early 1950s went by, the flame of Marty's vision was in danger of extinction by circumstances beyond her control. The demand for NCA's services was exploding, but financial contributions were meager, no matter how hard Marty, Yev, and the increasing number of volunteers tried. Seventeen of the local affiliates collapsed, including Houston in 1948, which had been a major center of activity. (Five years later, the Houston NCA reorganized itself and has been a strong affiliate ever since.)

Marty enlisted her sister Chris to help lick stamps and get out the mailings. Different volunteers were sometimes able to provide short-term financing to pay the staff and the landlord. Marty and Yev went for periods without any salary. Marty, who had no independent income like Yev's, often relied on handouts from friends. Mary Pickford, the brilliant star of silent films, was a friend who became a supporter of NCA. She often tided Marty over with personal gifts.[1] And undoubtedly Priscilla's income was helping to support Marty during these dark days at NCA.

By 1950, Priscilla was a star at *Vogue*. A superb art editor, she was idolized by younger staff. Her mentor and boss, art director Alex Liberman, admired and championed her. (In contrast to Priscilla, Liz Peck continued to live by choice in a poor area of Chinatown on the Lower East Side—an unfashionable residential district in those days. She was unable to stay sober.)

There was a grave danger that Marty's travels would have to stop or at least be severely curtailed. Yev Gardner later wrote, "Fortunately, she was appreciated by the groups of Alcoholics Anonymous as an outstanding and dynamic speaker and was often asked to come to their meetings with expenses paid. Frequently, while visiting in such communities, she would [arrange to] speak to nonalcoholic community leaders and as a result stimulate interest for the formulation of a local committee on alcoholism."[2]

One important long-term modest source of income did materialize. By the end of the 1940s, Marty had enough material to write a book that would reach a far wider audience than she could ever hope to meet through individual speeches and articles. Priscilla urged her on. Simon and Schuster turned the book down, but Rinehart and Company published *Marty Mann's Primer on Alcoholism* in 1950, just in time to save Marty and NCA from possible financial disaster. The book was dedicated to "Priscilla, who made me write it all down." In the next eight years, *Primer* sold about eighty thousand copies.

When *Primer on Alcoholism* first came out, Marty told her brother, "You have four boys. You have those boys read my book. You don't inherit alcoholism, but you may inherit the trait for alcoholism. So you have them all read it." Bill did. Luckily, none of his sons became an alcoholic.

Primer on Alcoholism was included in the October 1950 *Book of the Month Club News*. Marty was in good company. Other books reviewed that month were *The Disenchanted,* by John P. Marquand; *Fifth Chinese Daughter,* by Jade Snow Wong; *Chimp on My Shoulder,* by Bill Westley; and *War and Civilization,* by Arnold J. Toynbee. Eight years later, so much new information was available, Marty revised the book, retitling it *New Primer on Alcoholism.* A third edition came out in 1978. It has been translated into Spanish, Japanese, Finnish, and Afrikaans.

All this was fine and good—except that many AA members once again became agitated over the issue of anonymity. How dare Marty put her full name on a book that talked about alcoholism and recommended AA at great length? The fact that the book was a classic of factual information and advocacy and that Marty didn't reveal her own membership in AA, or that she was an alcoholic, didn't matter to the objectors. It would be a long time before the arguments over publication of *Primer* and *New Primer* died down. In AA, the controversy would leave among some a continued residue of resentment and distrust of Marty and NCA.

Primer and *New Primer* were pioneering publications. However, if Marty were alive today, she would undoubtedly revise the book again, adding data about the recent scientific discoveries in neurology, genetics, and the biochemistry of addiction. She would also need to include current material regarding prevention, relapse, treatment (especially for women, adolescents, older adults, and ethnic or racial minorities), addictive disease, legislation, insurance, and corrections, to name some major contemporary concerns that have continued to evolve since her day. NCA (now NCADD—National Council on Alcoholism and Drug Dependence) is completely up to date, of course, in its many publications available to the general public, revising them constantly as new information becomes available about the disease of alcoholism.

Sales of *New Primer on Alcoholism* and its companion volume, *Marty Mann Answers Your Questions about Drinking and Alcoholism* (1970), were steady over the years until they went out of print after Marty's death, but Marty once joked that the royalties were only enough to keep her in cigarettes.

Marty intended to write another book directed to the layperson, *The World and Alcoholism,* and in 1951 submitted a long proposal to her publishers, Rinehart and Company. Either she couldn't find the time to write after all, or else a publisher was never found. It would have been an interesting book, presenting "an accurate, unbiased, factual account of what is being done about alcoholism, both by private organizations and by government, in all of the countries represented on the WHO [World Health Organization] Committee."[3]

In addition to the constant worry about NCA's future, Marty was also concerned about her mother's living arrangements. Lill was in an old Manhattan building that had been converted to apartments. One time she was stuck between floors in the elevator. Then the owners of Lill's apartment building decided to convert it to offices and evict the tenants. Marty got hold of the owner and said, "Find another apartment for my mother. Move her out of there. *You* get the apartment for her." Marty prevailed, and Lill was reestablished in a nicer unit on Fifth Avenue at the corner of West Tenth, a block from Priscilla and Marty, who lived just off Fifth Avenue on West Ninth.

Lill often felt depressed. Her life certainly hadn't turned out the way she thought it would. Nothing Marty or her sisters did or said seemed to help much. By the early 1950s, Al-Anon Family Groups had formed in New York. Marty took her mother to an Al-Anon meeting, and Lill began to find some comfort and relief there.

Marty herself gained from Al-Anon, saying, "I qualify for Al-Anon because of an alcoholic husband." She could have added, "and because of my father and to keep my sanity around all the alcoholics I associate with every day."

From NCA's earliest days, Marty had recognized the needs of families. Two-thirds of the people who contacted NCA for information and help were family members. She was very grateful that Al-Anon existed as a referral resource. Sometimes NCA started an Al-Anon group where there was none. Marty firmly advised treatment professionals to say to families, "We can help you handle the situation," instead of the condescending "You're as sick as the alcoholic."

Marty also encouraged both the many alcoholics in recovery who had alcoholism in their families and their relatives to attend Al-Anon meetings. She completely endorsed the purpose of Al-Anon members—to understand themselves, not to get the alcoholic sober. She knew from personal experience that "[i]t's harder to live with an alcoholic than to be one—the alcoholic at least has his 'medicine' to screen out reality." And she cautioned recovering alcoholics that family members usually continued worrying for a year or two that sobriety would not last.

As if all the foregoing weren't enough during this tense period for NCA, with the small staff treading water as fast as they could, Marty temporarily lost her bearings in her personal life. Two notable alcoholics significantly disturbed her relationship with Priscilla. Both were women and well-known authors and playwrights. Both were emotionally immature. Both were already married. Both were thirteen years younger than Marty. And both fell madly in love with her.

Marty and Priscilla had probably already been acquainted with the women for several years during the 1940s, because they had many mutual friends in the New York and international literary, theater, and gay and lesbian worlds. One of the women was Carson McCullers, perhaps best known to the general public as author of *The Member of the Wedding*.[4] A talented pianist as well as a gifted writer, she was as tall as Marty, lanky, her hair in bangs and a thick, shoulder-length bob.

Carson was married to Reeves McCullers, a severely ill alcoholic whom Marty and Priscilla tried several times to help. In 1950, Marty, though perhaps initially attracted to Carson, was able to sidestep a serious involvement. Indeed, the conviction that Marty was in love with Carson may have been wishful thinking on Carson's part. Over the next year or two, Carson continued to write passionate love letters to Marty despite Marty's insistence that she stop.[5] It wasn't easy, however, to turn off someone like Carson.

Marty told Virginia Spencer Carr, Carson's biographer,[6] that "she [Marty] had to insist that Carson not call her at home, that she write nothing else to her that would suggest either a fling or a generous outcropping of declarations of love on Carson's part."[7]

Marty and Priscilla couldn't help feeling sorry for Carson, however, after she had a stroke and became a semi-invalid. They "welcomed Carson in their home whenever she felt the need to get away from Nyack [New York] or simply wanted a place to stay in the city, where they also had an apartment. Carson kept most of her music there after Miss Peck began encouraging her to play the piano and exercise her left arm and finger joints. . . . In the home of Marty Mann and Priscilla Peck, Carson also began to write poetry again."[8]

The second woman was the author and playwright Jane Bowles, who was married to Paul Bowles, himself a prominent writer and composer. Tennessee Williams considered Jane to be America's most original writer despite her small *oeuvre*.[9]

Marty probably would have felt an immediate kinship with her because Jane had had tuberculosis of a knee bone when a teenager and was confined in a Swiss sanitarium for two years. They both knew how difficult it was to lose their normal adolescent years.

Jane and Paul lived in Tangier, Morocco, but they were in and around New York City a good deal during the early 1950s while they were involved in various writing projects. Marty succumbed to a serious love affair with Jane that severely strained her relationship with Priscilla. Bill Mann believed Marty may even have left Priscilla for a while.

Jane (like Priscilla) was a small, slight woman. Truman Capote described her vividly.

> Jane, with her dahlia-head of cropped, curly hair, her tilted nose and mischief-shiny, just a trifle mad eyes, her very original voice (a husky soprano), her boyish clothes and schoolgirl's figure and slightly limping walk . . . the eternal urchin, appealing as the most appealing of nonadults, yet with some substance cooler than blood invading her veins and with a wit, an eccentric wisdom no child, not the strangest *Wunderkind*, ever possessed . . . her personality's startling blend of playful-puppy candor and feline sophistication, remained an imposing, stage-front presence.[10]

> Jane Bowles is an authoritative linguist; she speaks, with the greatest precision, French and Spanish and Arabic [all self-taught]. . . . Cooking is but one of her extracurricular gifts; she is also a spooky accurate mimic. . . .[11]

> And yet, though the tragic view is central to her vision, Jane Bowles is a very funny writer, a humorist of sorts. . . . Her subtle comprehension of eccentricity and human apartness as revealed in her work require us to accord Jane Bowles high esteem as an artist.[12]

Jane, despite these attributes, was jealous of Priscilla and intimidated by competing with Priscilla's intelligence, glamour, and beauty.[13]

In the middle of Marty and Jane's affair, one occasion that provided relief from personal, family, and NCA worries for Marty was South Africa's invitation in 1951 to speak at its first national conference on alcoholism, all expenses paid. Marty spent six weeks in South Africa and visited thirteen cities as she helped local groups plan how to address the issue of alcoholism and start NCA-type organizations.

AA was already established in South Africa when Marty arrived, with a ready pool of interested and willing citizens. It had been started in that country by a relapsing alcoholic, "Johnny Appleseed." He was a gifted businessman and highly successful proponent of AA, but he could not stay sober. Regardless, wherever he traveled and got drunk and sobered up, he left literature about AA.

On this trip, Marty arranged to visit Jane and Paul Bowles in Tangier. Paul was unaware of any affair and said that "Mrs. Mann was quiet and reserved."[14] Nevertheless, the visit may have been what fueled Jane's expectation that Marty would open a European branch of NCA in Lucerne, Switzerland, and move there part of the year to be closer to Jane's permanent home in Tangier.

Jane Bowles wrote to Libby Holman on February 12, 1951:

> Marty is wonderful. It all works out she will be a resident—next year in Switzerland—near enough to Paris for weekends. But it is a dead secret so tear this letter up.[15]

A week later (February 18, 1951), Jane again wrote Libby:

> Marty has given me a little Hermes Rocket typewriter for my birthday and I am very happy about it. She is wonderful to me and I think really loves me devotedly. I know it. It is extraordinary that I should have found at last someone so sweet and trusting and gay and brave and beautiful. She has moments of being extraordinarily beautiful. Particularly in black evening dresses cut low and with long sleeves. She looks not only beautiful but distinguished and as if she could not even possibly have ever met me. . . . As I have told you there is a great amount of pain in this situation, mostly because of Paul, but it is not insoluble and something will work out eventually. . . .

If Marty gets away next year because of her work she will be centered in Switzerland, which will be near enough to Italy and France but not terribly near Africa. However I shall certainly get down there to spend some time with Paul. I look forward to a day when Marty would have some part-time work which would allow her to spend half her time in Morocco. I think this work she may do in Europe (the only hope I have of ever living with her) is very likely to be only for part of the year. I hope so. It is silly of course to plan anything. Some days I am in misery because I seem to feel two equally strong destinies and one of them is to be with Paul. I miss him of course terribly. My life would have been simpler if I had never returned here but having known Marty I will not die still searching and feeling cheated.[16]

Who knows whether Marty seriously intended to establish a European base, or whether the immature, imaginative Jane Bowles simply wanted to believe it? On the other hand, the visit may actually have helped Marty realize there was no practical future in a relationship with Jane. In any event, Marty clearly was romantically involved with Jane for a year or more. It was Marty who broke off the relationship. By mid-1954 the affair was all over, apparently having ended sometime before on a less-than-harmonious note.[17]

Both Jane and Carson appear to have been addicted to drugs and alcohol. This could well have been a major reason Marty ended the affairs. Alcoholics in recovery often find that actively addicted partners or spouses are a serious risk to their own hard-won sobriety. Also, relationships can simply be unsatisfying for the sober person. More than one sober AA member has commented, "I never know whom I'm talking to. And I hate the taste of alcohol on someone's lips, and the smell of alcohol fumes!"

Neither Carson nor Jane joined AA, although Carson's sister, Rita (Margarita) Smith, who was an AA member and literary editor of *Mademoiselle*, tried hard to interest her. Carson, in fact, was not above taking sly pokes at AA. Marty and Priscilla's commitment to one another survived these affairs and was perhaps strengthened. Marty, at least, was learning what AA meant when a recovered alcoholic was expected to "practice these principles in all our affairs" (Step Twelve).[18] And by *affairs*, AA was not referring to romantic dalliances, either, but to the lifelong task of honor, trust, and fidelity in the secular ethical sense of the Golden Rule. ("Do unto others as you would have them do unto you.")

At some point in the early 1950s, Felicia Gizycka and Marty had a temporary falling-out, perhaps related to the affair with Jane. Marty was not setting a good example as Felicia's AA sponsor. Felicia was certainly distressed about her AA buddy, Priscilla, and could well have blamed Marty.

A further destabilizer for Marty occurred in January 1952, with the death of her dear friend Dr. Foster Kennedy. After being stricken at his New York home, he was taken to Bellevue Hospital, the poignant locus of his long, distinguished clinical practice and teaching, where he expired a week later. Kennedy's death was a loss not only to his students, colleagues, and patients. AA would also miss his exceptional understanding and advocacy. And Marty was forever grateful to Kennedy for starting her on the road to recovery from alcoholism.

The house at Cherry Grove provided a welcome respite during these difficult times. Priscilla and Marty spent their weekends on Fire Island as often as possible. Yet Cherry Grove had an undeniable hothouse atmosphere. And it was at Cherry Grove that Carson's crush on Marty erupted. Also, Jane and Paul Bowles were frequent visitors, and that was even more of a problem. A final negative factor was probably that Cherry Grove was becoming known as a gay and lesbian town. Marty could ill afford to have her name associated publicly with the homosexual community.

At any rate, for whatever reasons, Marty and Priscilla decided after eleven years of ownership to sell the Cherry Grove property in favor of a weekend home elsewhere—one where Marty's mother and other family and friends could visit, and one more suitable for retirement. This they did in 1954, buying a lovely home and acreage in Easton, Connecticut.

For the next fifteen years, while Marty and Priscilla were working full-time, the Easton house was mainly a weekend retreat. They continued to live in the New York apartment Monday to Friday. When they retired, the Easton house became the main residence, with the New York apartment used only one or two nights a week.

After the permanent move to Easton, many of Marty's friends and relatives were delighted to take advantage of standing invitations to stay at the empty apartment whenever they were visiting from out of town. Her sister Betty's college-age sons, Greg and Tyler Miller, recalled how sophisticated they felt whenever they came down to New York from Harvard University for a weekend and had the use of such a pad.

Easton was and is a charming, small New England town west of New Haven, about an hour from New York City. Easton had no commercial center, so Marty and Priscilla did their weekly shopping on Saturdays in the larger neighboring town of Westport. Felicia lived nearby in New Canaan.

Marty and Priscilla's house at 475 Westport Road was on a low rise, set back from a two-lane winding road. Fairly near the uncommercialized center of Easton, the property was in the country, surrounded by more than six acres of woods and fields. A magnificent old maple towered in the center of the spacious parking circle at the top of the drive. A mature Concord grape arbor produced an abundant crop from which Marty, Priscilla, Felicia, and anyone else who happened to be around made quantities of superior jelly in season.

In the fields behind the house was a swimming pool. Marty and Priscilla and their close women friends usually swam nude if no other guests were around. If unexpected visitors dropped in, whoever was in the house would urgently ring a big bell by the door. Out by the pool there would be a mad scramble for robes. A drawback of the Easton house was the short, curving driveway that wound down to intersect the road at a blind curve. Both Priscilla and Marty had minor accidents over the years as they pulled out onto Westport Road.

Many times, Felicia joined Priscilla for dinner when Marty was away on her travels. During the week they would meet in town after Priscilla was through work. On weekends, Felicia took great pleasure in cooking for an appreciative Priscilla. They enjoyed walking and birdwatching together and snowshoeing in winter. Priscilla often worked in the garden or painted.

Marty's affairs with Carson and especially Jane must have been very painful for Priscilla. Felicia recounted in her journals that Priscilla's unhappiness was exacerbated by a "cynical, brilliant, and bitter mind." Always an avid reader, Priscilla had been concentrating on the morbid and occult. She had become suspicious and analytical of everyone. Felicia described her as the "dark suspector of the worst."[19]

During this same period, Felicia, possibly influenced by Nona Wyman, discovered a new spiritual life for herself in the Church of Religious Science. Founded by Dr. Ernest Holmes, Religious Science's intent is to unite religion and science. A metaphysical healing ministry, it is related to Christian Science and Science of Mind, but does not forgo medicine and physicians.

Prayer and positive self-affirmations are taught as central to the healing process. Felicia found this denomination congenial with AA's Twelve Steps. The minister of New York's First Church of Religious Science was a dynamic man named Raymond C. Barker.

One day Priscilla, deeply troubled, came to Felicia for help. Felicia, still new in the church but concerned for her dear friend, somewhat tentatively invited her to attend a church service and meet the minister. Felicia felt as if she were walking on eggshells by making this proposal. She feared a backlash from arrogant, agnostic, angry Priscilla. Instead, Priscilla gratefully accepted the invitation. She was spellbound by the preaching and by the healing, loving atmosphere and people.

Within a few weeks, Felicia observed dramatic changes for the better in Priscilla. The two friends decided to take the church's prescribed course to better help themselves and others. From this time on, Priscilla and Felicia were active students and practitioners of Religious Science. They became members of the church. Eventually, they interested Marty, and she, too, adopted the teachings and joined the church. Barker supported NCA's program, contributing $50 annually to NCA ($300 in year 2000 dollars).

Ray Barker was an important spiritual adviser and source of encouragement for Marty. She said her two greatest teachers were Bill Wilson and Ray Barker. One time, Barker dashed off a note to her when she was apparently feeling low:

> Your good note came this morning and "there's not a word of Truth in it." You are under a Law of growth and expansion. Troward says the Infinite Spirit is always producing something better than that which has gone before. This is the only Truth of the Council.
>
> With Joy do I know it. It is easy to treat you [pray for you] because I love you so much.
>
> Be happy,
> Make others happy,
> And let the Action of God take place,
>
> Raymond[20]

Felicia was Liz Peck's AA sponsor and introduced her to Religious Science. The four women—Marty, Priscilla, Felicia, and Liz—all practiced and believed in the healing power of prayer. Liz stayed involved for a while, mostly to please Marty and Priscilla, then dropped away.

By 1952, NCA was managing to keep one step ahead in the funding battle. For the next three years, the New York headquarters held its own. Salaries and expenses were in line with other nonprofits. Marty made her payments on the Easton mortgage. Yev earned enough to support his family on Long Island. Lila Rosenblum, first a secretary, then Marty's executive assistant from 1952 to 1954, said the only setback was failure to grant the usual Christmas bonus in 1954. For some reason, neither Marty nor Yev announced this decision to the staff, who sat around waiting for bonus checks that were never handed out. No explanation was offered the staff.

Marty's work was increasingly recognized as an important contribution to the field of public health. Accordingly, in 1952 she was made a fellow of the American Public Health Association. Like the great historical leaders in that field, she understood that change on a community-wide scale was necessary. Marty was an heir of the pragmatic, optimistic social gospel that led to the establishment of such life-enhancing community health efforts as safe public water supplies, public sewage systems, and vaccination against hitherto deadly epidemic diseases like smallpox. She subscribed to the reliance of public health on science and scientific discovery.

Meanwhile, Marty's private life continued on a parallel track to her public one. Priscilla was regaining her balance. Then in the spring of 1953, Marty's father was admitted as an indigent patient to a public welfare hospital on Staten Island. He had pneumonia. Marty was notified. She visited him at least once before he died on April 4. Identified as the next of kin, Marty called her sisters and brother and made funeral arrangements. They decided that Lill, who was not in good health herself and who felt understandably bitter about Will, need not be told just then or included in the service. Bill and Priscilla represented the family at the crematorium. Marty and Priscilla selected the Church of Religious Science for the private service that was conducted by Raymond Barker.

Although Marty had kept her distance from her father, she was the family member who did stay in touch and who seemed to bear him no resentment. While saddened at how his life turned out, she was the one in her family who would have understood best the inexorable consequences of untreated alcoholism and compulsive gambling. His death, although perhaps

a relief, may also have brought her a time of reflection and regret. Yet the
work at NCA had to continue. Marty couldn't afford to be distracted for
long. A month after her father's death, she was in Bermuda to help their
provisional committee on alcoholism establish a program based on the
American NCA.

Once back in New York, Marty resumed her growing attachment to the
Church of Religious Science. One of the many persons attracted to Barker's
church was Alger Hiss. By 1957, Hiss had been released from prison after
serving his sentence for passing secret information to the Soviets. He was attending Barker's worship services and discussion groups. One discussion
was about the devil, whom Hiss called "Arthur." Hiss claimed it was convenient to have a devil. Some in the group could see how "Alger could have
handed the papers to Chambers in the days when it seemed all-important to
combat Fascism and the Communists seemed our friends." Others felt that
"Alger drew those who believed in him into trouble."[21]

Felicia commented that "Alger is absolutely brilliant, learned, informed—one does not meet a mind like this more than once or twice. At
least I haven't. But he is also considerate and sensitive and knowing what
you are thinking, and very gentle. And Priscilla is wonderful."[22] Priscilla
was one of the very few who could match Hiss's brilliant intellect.

Marty was much taken by the positive thinking of Religious Science's
teachings, including "Money is God in action." The healing power of inten-
tional prayer, called "treatment," and of positive self-affirmations were central to Religious Scientists' belief and practice. They believed strongly in the
efficacy of intercessory prayer, or praying for someone else.

Another advantage of the Church of Religious Science for Marty was
that it reintroduced her to the Bible. She seemed especially attracted to the
Gospels in the New Testament. As time went on, these biblical teachings became more and more apparent in her talks, both explicitly and implicitly.
One of her favorite observations was, "We are a perfect example of the biblical injunction that you have to give it away in order to keep it."

In 1954, a year after her father's death, Marty, Priscilla, Felicia, and
others in AA took the masters' course at the church. From time to time,
Marty and Priscilla's enthusiasm for Raymond Barker and Religious Science
would result in their insistently inviting reluctant friends to church with
them.

Later that same year, Marty injured her foot. X rays reportedly showed a break. In two days, she was perfectly well and walking on the foot. According to Felicia, "Priscilla, of course, did the healing—hence her modest silence. Our dear Marty is not yet able to give other people credit."[23]

In the summer of 1954, Felicia and Marty renewed their friendship as the result of a chance meeting in the theater where *Carousel* was playing. Felicia believed that much of the estrangement had been due to their egos. She had felt intellectually competitive with Marty—as if each of them was continually trying to one-up the other. Now Felicia was willing to live and let live.

Life was more than one problem after another, however. Recovered alcoholics know how to have fun. One day, Felicia and Priscilla lunched together at an exclusive New York café. Though Priscilla didn't cook, she loved gourmet food as much as did Felicia and Marty, who were both excellent cooks. This day, Felicia and Priscilla indulged themselves with chicken liver omelettes, raspberries, and pots of coffee. During lunch, the conversation turned to fashions. Felicia was quizzing Priscilla about the latest designer collections. The new Dior clothes were rumored to have belts around the hips, no bust, and so on.

"Wearable?" asked Felicia eagerly.

"Maybe no," answered Priscilla, "but lovely."

"How about Chanel? Where is she?"

"Perhaps she thinks she's launched a fashion and is resting."

Afterward, Priscilla dragged Felicia next door to an exciting bookstore, where they spent a giddy half hour racing through the aisles looking at titles. Before returning to work, Priscilla confessed that she had rashly opened an account at the bookstore. Everyone knew about Priscilla's extravagances, especially her penchant for books.

"Fatal," commented Felicia. "You must go only at lunchtime."[24] Priscilla made a face, then escaped further censure by claiming she had to rush back to *Vogue*.

For Marty, the financial problems at NCA precluded some of such lighthearted diversion. During the summer of 1954, even Yev was feeling uncharacteristically discouraged. At one point, NCA owed everyone—staff, landlord, suppliers, telephone company, etc. There was no way out that he could see. It was Marty's turn to play the optimist and cheer *him* up. With mordant humor, she declared, "Yev, there is a rich drunk out there somewhere who will get sober and help us."[25]

"Pack it in," a rational businessman might have said. "You've had ten years and can't make a go of it. Quit daydreaming about being rescued!"

But there is a saying in AA that God takes care of poor drunks, even ex-drunks. Marty's joking remark to Yev was solidly based on the faith she was slowly forging, a faith grounded in experience, her own and that of the thousands of other recovered alcoholics she constantly met on her travels.

Little did Marty know how soon her prediction would come to pass.

The Sun Breaks Through

1954

SHORTLY AFTER MARTY'S HEARTFELT HOPE, Yev received a routine Twelve Step request to visit a forty-seven-year-old patient detoxing at Towns Hospital. This man had been a patient more than fifty times in many hospitals but had always returned to uncontrolled drinking. Now he thought he'd look into Alcoholics Anonymous. Yev told the man he had a disease called alcoholism, then talked about his own experiences and recovery. The patient was responsive and said he wanted to get sober.

As the man listened to Yev and heard about NCA's history and its mission to educate America about alcoholism, he grew enthusiastic and said, "That's wonderful, but why haven't you made more progress in ten years?"

Yev explained, "We're trying, but we've never had enough money to do the job."

"Now you do," the patient replied. "I want to solve NCA's money problems."

Yev privately thought, "Sure, you'll solve our money problems"—he'd heard that many times before. Out loud he said, "The important thing is for you to stay sober one day at a time and then you can give us all that money." The man's name was R. Brinkley Smithers.

"Brink" Smithers was not exaggerating when he told Yev that he could help bankroll NCA. He was the son of Christopher D. Smithers, a multimillionaire cofounder of International Business Machines (IBM). Brink himself had wanted to become a physician but majored instead in drinking and parties. So his father hauled him out of school and demanded he enter business, where there was thought to be greater discipline and productive effort.

Brink actually had an excellent aptitude for business as long as he was reasonably sober. He joined IBM's sales force and in four years became a star. In 1936, he landed the biggest order in the history of the company, a sale of IBM machines to the newly formed federal Social Security Board. Then he quit IBM, saying it "interfered with his drinking." Seventeen years later he discovered AA.

Brinkley Smithers became the single largest benefactor in the field of alcoholism. He ranks among the greatest influences in the advancement of the cause of alcoholism. "A million dollar man, with a heart of gold."[1]

Brink, advised by his cousin C. Francis Smithers, who managed Brink's investments, reportedly never sold a single one of the half million shares of original IBM stock he inherited. That investment (said to have multiplied many times over) provided a munificent income. NCA and the whole field of alcoholism were fortunate indeed that Brink Smithers chose to apply his wealth on their behalf. He inspired many other wealthy donors to follow his example, but none exceeded his philanthropic reach. It would be fifteen years before significant government support of alcoholism education, prevention, and treatment developed.

While still drinking, Brink had by 1952 established the Christopher D. Smithers Foundation (named for his father). The foundation became the financial cornerstone of the professional alcoholism movement after he recovered from alcoholism. The foundation's practice was to provide seed money for a variety of projects and community groups. The initial grant in the alcoholism field was to NCA for $10,000 ($60,000 in year 2000 dollars). While Brink's first love remained NCA, his alcoholism interests extended to industry, the criminal justice system, education, research, prevention, and legislation. For the rest of his long life, he dedicated himself to the cause of alcoholism rehabilitation and recovery, giving generously of his time, his expertise, and his concern, as well as his great wealth.

Soon after they met, Yev introduced Brink to various NCA board members and to Marty. Smithers had served on the boards of numerous charitable organizations and was a strong exponent of voluntarism. Marty invited him to join her board, where he shortly became treasurer. His advent on NCA's board in 1954 was the catalyst for the development of that agency from a struggling organization with a tentative future at best to one of stature and national recognition.

Marty and Brink became fast friends, for many years lunching together twice a week when they were both in town. The elegant, exclusive restaurant in the Stanhope Hotel was their frequent choice. After Marty died, Brink continued to work diligently on behalf of NCA until his own death in January 1994. To this day, the Smithers Foundation has endured as an important philanthropic resource for both NCA and a wide variety of other alcoholism causes.

An important consequence of Brink's association with NCA was his meeting a young woman who had come to work there from 1960 to 1964. When Brink's first wife died in 1983, he and Adele Croci were married. Adele Smithers remained an admirer of Marty's and supporter of NCA. Since Brink's death in 1994, she has been president of the Smithers Foundation and continues to serve on NCA's board (now NCADD). In 1999, she remarried and became Adele Smithers-Fornaci.

When Brink became involved in the alcoholism movement, few people in the field had business experience. Brink's business and financial acumen proved invaluable. Many times he felt he had to say no, but many other times he provided funds, both personal and foundation, to individuals and organizations he was not completely in tune with as long as they benefited alcoholics.

To further his education about alcoholism, Brink attended the 1956 Yale Summer School on Alcoholism. There his interest was captured by the needs of industry for education about alcoholism and adequate intervention and treatment of the disease for employees. "Occupational alcoholism programs were the direct application of NCEA's core ideas in the workplace," notes Bill White.[2] Brink is yet another example of Marty's encouragement of an interested party to work on improving attitudes and services within a particular system. At Rutgers and Cornell Universities, the Smithers Foundation subsequently endowed an Institute for Alcoholism Prevention and Workplace Problems.

Brink made unusually large bequests to fund two significant institutions in the alcoholism field. One endowment came about when the Yale Center of Alcohol Studies relocated with his help in 1964 to Rutgers University in Piscataway, New Jersey. Subsequently, he personally gave a grant to what was renamed the Center of Alcohol Studies in Adele and R. Brinkley Smithers Hall at Rutgers.

The second institution, the Smithers Alcoholism Treatment and Training Center, was created in the late 1960s. Brink and others had been interested for some time in providing more hospital beds for alcoholics. One of the persons he discussed his ideas with was a fairly new, young physician at Roosevelt Hospital in New York City, LeClair Bissell. Dr. Bissell, a recovered alcoholic, had made a study of ward patients at Roosevelt and discovered that a large percentage of admissions were for alcoholism and alcohol-related problems.

With this information, Brink felt justified in creating a pilot alcoholism treatment program at Roosevelt with an initial gift of $225,000 spread over three years ($1,125,000 in year 2000 dollars). LeClair was appointed the first director of the new unit. The grant allowed her to get started with a couple of counselors, a part-time social worker, and a secretary.

The Smithers center developed into a forty-four-bed rehabilitation unit with a comprehensive twenty-eight-day recovery program tied to AA philosophy. It was the only such facility in New York City. Under Dr. Bissell, the Smithers center became an important model for treatment, research, and professional training.

Marty, of course, already knew the exciting news about Roosevelt Hospital's new treatment center. She promptly contacted LeClair and announced, "I'm going to be your sponsor. You need me to help you negotiate working with Brink successfully." Marty proved to be a valuable adviser.

In 1971, three years after the Smithers center was founded, Brink invited LeClair to lunch one day and to her astonishment told her that he was endowing the center with a block of IBM stock worth ten million dollars (fifty million dollars in year 2000 dollars). It was the largest single grant ever made in the alcoholism field, public or private, up to that time. Brink immediately released five million dollars of the grant, with a promise of the remaining half to follow later.

Almost from the opening of the Smithers center, however, there was friction between the donor and the doctors. Brink disagreed with the staff about who should be admitted. They advocated an open-admission policy, with the center serving people from all walks of life. Brink, on the other hand, preferred patients from his own social and economic level, namely, the rich and well-to-do. In addition, Brink insisted that detailed project plans and staff appointments must have his approval, an interference in management that both Roosevelt Hospital and Dr. Bissell regarded as objectionable.

Eight years later, the other half of Smithers's original ten-million-dollar grant had yet to be awarded. Although the above conflicts with Brink had been largely resolved, continuing pressures contributed to LeClair's decision to leave the Smithers center in 1979 and become the founding director of a new for-profit alcoholism treatment facility, Edgehill-Newport in Newport, Rhode Island. Dr. Bissell subsequently said, however, "There is no question in my mind that Brink has been the single most generous philanthropist that ever existed in the field of alcoholism. . . . I don't think to this day that people have any awareness of all that he did or tried to do."[3]

When LeClair was named director of the Smithers program, Marty's and her paths crossed for the second time after many years. Their initial encounter occurred in 1953. LeClair, a newly recovered alcoholic, was a librarian, not yet having entered medical school. She had met another lesbian, Liz Peck, Priscilla's sister. Liz was sober at the time. An immature, temporary romance blossomed between Liz and LeClair. They moved in together and for a year or more were partners. Liz introduced LeClair to Marty and Priscilla, and the foursome would get together socially. Then LeClair and Liz broke up. LeClair moved on to medical school and lost touch with Marty for the next fifteen years except for running across her occasionally.

Marty knew what she was doing when she approached LeClair those fifteen years later. She was battle-hardened from that same number of years' working with her friend Brink.

Marty had an ego and a will to match Brink's. Fortunately, she'd had a lifetime of experience with a similar man, her father. That Marty had a king-size ego of her own—"the size of Mt. Everest," remarked Cora Louise B., an early AA—was evident to anyone around her. Marty knew what she wanted, and she expected to get it. "How else," commented Walter Murphy (a later executive director of NCA), "could she have accomplished the task of starting NCA during a period in our history when alcoholism was not yet recognized as a disease and the typical alcoholic was viewed as a so-called skid-row bum, and a woman alcoholic even worse." He went on to say, "But Marty's ego was without arrogance. She would drop everything to lend a hand to any alcoholic seeking her help."[4]

As Brink's health returned with sobriety, his own powerful ego was increasingly evident. He and Marty could have clashed with disastrous consequences for NCA. Instead, they joined forces in the common cause to which they were both devoted. Adele Smithers-Fornaci, Brink's widow, reported that sometimes Marty and Brink had "very strong differences of opinion as to how to achieve certain objectives," but "both were extremely intelligent and very focused regarding the need for removing the stigma on alcoholism, getting education to the public about it and having it accepted as a respectable and treatable disease. They both knew first-hand about the unnecessary suffering and ridicule alcoholics endured. . . . [Brink] firmly believed in and loved NCA and he loved Marty as a partner and colleague."[5]

Adele added, "Marty never played games. You always knew where she stood. Sometimes Marty won on an issue, sometimes Brink."

Since Brink was NCA's major donor and on its board of directors for most of his sober life, and for long periods was the treasurer, president, or chairman, he was well situated to exert his power and desire to control. Marty, however, wasn't about to yield control of her organization to anyone. Brink acknowledged her right but described their relationship this way: "She's the queen, and I'm the king. So I won half the time."[6]

In discussing with others the difference between AA and NCA, he depicted AA as the retail side (one by one) and NCA as the wholesale side (system or community by system or community).

The Clouds Lift

1954—60

MARTY CERTAINLY WASN'T BASHFUL. She was well aware of her power and consciously used it. At one level, she knew she was one of the great women of her time. As Walter Murphy affectionately said, "I know that to be a fact because Marty told me so—again, and again, and again." Yet she could be genuinely shocked when paid generous public homage as the years of her accomplishments accumulated.

Marty and Bill Wilson rarely attended each other's meetings or functions. Marty said, "I'll steal his thunder if I go to his party, and vice versa." Years after Bill had died and Marty had retired, an AA friend asked her whether people flocked to her the way they did Bill.

"Do they bow and salaam when you walk down the hall?"

"Hell, no," Marty replied with a twinkle in her eye. "They don't even know who I am. No, thank God, they don't do that."[1]

Both Marty and Bill loved the limelight, but Marty, in particular, had a fine sense of theater. Nancy Olson, a close friend and legislative colleague in the late 1960s and early 1970s, described arriving at a conference on crutches because of a bad ankle sprain. Marty was in a wheelchair, recovering from a broken hip. Even in a wheelchair she radiated regal power.

"My dear Nancy, what happened?"

"I was just jealous. I wanted some of all that attention you're getting in your wheelchair."

"Did you get it?"

"No."

"My dear, you need a wheelchair!"

As Marty was wheeled onstage, her escort was no layperson but an attractive R.N., conspicuously in uniform with a swirling navy cape and white cap.

When Marty wanted something, she went after it full tilt. Even in the mundane task of hailing a taxi, she exuded authority and power. Not for her an attitude of politely standing on the street corner and waving in lady-like fashion. Out into the middle of the street she would stride, plant her tall commanding self, and compel an empty cab to stop, take her aboard, and make a U-turn in the direction she wanted to go.

Marty's irrepressible sense of humor served to counterbalance her ego. One time, she agreed to speak at the first annual meeting of an AA group. Posters advertising her appearance were widely distributed. The group engaged a large hall to accommodate the expected crowds. When Marty arrived, police had been called out to handle the traffic.

"Marty, we've never had such a turnout," said her host.

"Certainly not," she laughed. "I've never spoken here before."

Strong though she was, Marty also wanted and attracted strong people around her at NCA. Yev Gardner wrote, "She had the ability to command attention and develop loyalty and affection among her followers. Staff members would say, 'You can always tell when MM is back from a field trip—there is a feeling of electricity around the office.' Yet the atmosphere of loyal devotion was always apparent."[2]

The staff was composed of nonalcoholics as well as alcoholics in all stages of recovery. Some were paid; many were volunteers. Most of the staff, as at AA national headquarters (General Service Office), were female. Marty was an exacting boss, insisting on accuracy but granting her staff a lot of freedom.

"She was a very discreet lady, though powerful, principled and sometimes very demanding. She set standards and was an example to all. She was a brilliant, hard, tireless worker and because of her *leadership*, she was respected and usually revered. When I think of her in this regard, it brings to mind what Albert Schweitzer said. 'Example is not the main thing in influencing others. It is the *only* thing.'"[3]

When Marjorie Reid Pope, a young, outspoken friend of Brink's, was hired at NCA, another close friend of Marjorie's advised her not to give Marty the idea that she was a follower. While Marty was interviewing her,

Marjorie couldn't get her cigarette lighter to work. Marty tossed her own across the desk. Marjorie couldn't get that one going, either.

Marty teased, "A little bit helpless, are we?"

Marjorie leaned forward, put her elbows on the desk, and replied, looking Marty in the eyes, "Marty, I'm about as helpless as a tigress with her cubs."

Marty was startled, then threw back her head and roared with laughter.

Yet Marjorie was always petrified of Marty, who simply exuded power. Marty tended to have that effect on people, especially in her earlier days of running NCA. Marjorie took to calling Marty "the Dragon Lady" behind her back.

One day Marty summoned Marjorie to her office and coolly said, "I know the name you have for me—Dragon Lady. Why?"

Marjorie gulped, then said firmly, "You're ruthless. You don't let anyone stand in your way. You run over people like a Mack truck—and you're beautiful!"

Marjorie thought Marty would explode. Then suddenly the Dragon Lady burst out laughing. No hard feelings.

One time Marty was fuming about some board members, and Marjorie reminded her, "Have you forgotten that sugar catches more flies than vinegar?" Marty, on the other hand, could remind strong-willed Marjorie on a different occasion to "let go and let God."

Mary Clark Ross was an early NCA program assistant and fieldworker. She described Marty's management style as "fair, dominant, positive. Marty liked to manage and be in command." After five years, Mary left the New York office because of a policy proposal to Marty. Marty had asked the staff to submit ideas, but Mary's were too different from Marty's. Mary said that Marty "fired her with 'velvet gloves' because I appeared to be a power threat." That didn't discourage Mary Ross from continuing to work diligently on behalf of NCA in the Delaware Valley, Pennsylvania, and Monterey, California, affiliates.

Another side of Marty's ego was vanity—the vanity of a woman who knew she was a knockout, and as a public figure needed to maintain a polished image at all times. She could spend ages on her makeup and grooming. She used makeup lightly but with a sense of perfection. Her clothing and accessories had to be just so. She carried a stylish, expensive purse that she replaced in the same style as soon as it started to wear out. Tucked into an outside pocket of the purse was a pair of spotless white gloves.

During her adult life, a tendency to be overweight constantly threatened Marty's self-image. A love of good food and rich desserts didn't help the situation. She would gain, then have to concentrate on taking it off. Luckily, her height and build could accommodate a certain amount of extra weight, but she said she'd gained and lost the same twenty-five pounds "thousands of times." Later in life, she preferred natural and organic foods prepared with gourmet attention.

Despite a healthy appetite when she sat down to eat, Marty said she had trouble recognizing she was hungry during the day when she was preoccupied with work. She'd skip meals, then would suddenly be ravenous and tend to overeat. Her solution was to have light snacks available to munch on.

Brink understood the importance of image and of Marty's being well dressed, so he arranged a generous clothing allowance separate from her modest salary. Once a year, she went on a shopping spree for her wardrobe. From childhood, she'd loved expensive furs and would sometimes wear them for effect even when the weather was warm.

Once, Marty was a guest of Kaye Fillmore in New Jersey. Kaye, a noted sociologist and early protégée of Selden Bacon at Yale, is now on the faculty of the University of California, San Francisco, where she directs an international longitudinal study of alcoholism in seventeen developed countries. Kaye's two little boys were enthralled with Marty and would do anything for her, but Kaye was piqued when on the way to a big New Jersey meeting, Marty insisted on holding everybody up while she dried her underarm deodorant before the hall mirror. On that occasion, Marty wore a beautiful silk dress—topped with a gray fur stole although it was the middle of summer and very hot.

The same year that Brink was appointed to NCA's board, he was joined by a remarkable woman, Katherine K. Pike of Pasadena, California. Katherine was the nonalcoholic wife of Tom Pike, whose family wealth derived from profitable oil wells. In 1946, Tom had found sobriety through AA. Both Katherine and Tom were activists—politically, socially, and in their Roman Catholic church—though Katherine was known as the more diplomatic and appealing half.

In 1949, the Pikes met Marty when they helped found the Pasadena NCA affiliate, the third in California, after Santa Barbara and Monterey. From then on, Katherine and Tom were devoted to Marty's mission of educating the country to remove the stigma of alcoholism. They gave generously of their time, their contacts, and their wealth. Each of them played critical roles in NCA.

Regardless of what else was going on, Marty never let up in her focus on reaching as many people as she could in the shortest time possible with the message that there was help for alcoholics. Women alcoholics were always a special concern. Stigma toward women alcoholics blinded and immobilized them. And then, women who did find their way into AA often had no other recovering woman in their area. It was as if they lived in the remote reaches of Africa. Marty became their sole contact. One such woman wrote from Bennington, Vermont, that she was the only female AA in that mill town group of men. She was very discouraged. She'd tried to help another woman but never heard from her again. These tales touched Marty's heart. She would respond and keep in touch as long as she was needed.

In her drive to use every available avenue, Marty wasted no time exploring the potential of America's newest medium, television, for getting her message across. In 1954, she presented a detailed proposal for a TV series on alcoholism. Had she so chosen, Marty could have made a name for herself in the field of television alone. Her creativity and innate understanding of that medium are impressive. TV and radio spots about alcoholism would eventually catch up to her vision.

Marty and NCA could take legitimate credit and satisfaction for the changes that were occurring in public opinion regarding the major public health problem of alcoholism. By 1954, there was growing awareness of the disease concept of alcoholism. Alcoholism was regularly covered in the press. Governmental, professional, and lay groups of all sorts were interested in the issue. Marty reported that more than three thousand general hospitals accepted acute cases of alcoholism, compared with only ninety-six nationally ten years before. Industry and state governments had become involved. NCA had created forty-eight local committees on alcoholism in twenty-three states, one territory, and three other countries. Twenty-nine alcoholism information centers had been formed.

Health professionals, however, were slow to join the modern alcoholism movement. For many years, it was the kiss of death if a doctor chose to work in a clinical or research setting concerned with alcoholism. Marty wasn't the only individual active in changing this attitude—Yale was an important early influence, as were a few dedicated physicians across the land who provided leadership among their medical colleagues. But Marty's unrelenting support of the need for health professionals to become informed about alcoholism helped reduce the stigma for doctors who entered the field.

NCA was also instrumental in encouraging the medical profession to organize a medical society composed of physicians with a specialized knowledge of alcoholism. Slowly, medicine and psychiatry developed specialties in addiction treatment. The seeds for the creation of the first such group, the New York City Medical Society on Alcoholism, were nurtured when NCEA began its existence by sharing the offices of the New York Academy of Medicine back in the 1940s. There was an inevitable cross-fertilization of ideas about addiction.

In 1954, the New York City Medical Society on Alcoholism was formed by six physicians meeting in Marty's office, the first of many medical societies on alcoholism to follow.[4] A key person in the founding of the New York City Medical Society on Alcoholism, and its first president, was Dr. Ruth Fox, Marty's close friend and colleague. This group was the forerunner of today's national professional medical association—American Society of Addiction Medicine (ASAM).[5]

An essential element in the development of addiction specialties was the need to define alcoholism. Marty and NCA stated that alcoholism was a disease. (See chapter 19 for a discussion of this issue.) NCA also had a simple definition of an alcoholic—"someone whose drinking causes a continuing problem in any department of his life." That included a problem that the alcoholic might deny but that others recognized, such as by the family or at work. NCA clearly stated that it was not concerned with the social or normal drinker. Let them enjoy the grape and the grain, God bless them. This policy supported Marty and those who wanted NCA to avoid addressing alcohol problems in general (such as sale and distribution) and instead focus on the -*ism* or disease aspect—a continuing conflict within NCA.

In 1950, the World Health Organization (WHO), largely through the efforts of Dr. Jellinek, was the first modern medical organization to propound that alcoholism was a disease. Such international advocacy strengthened Marty's position.

By 1956, New York's example had influenced the whole American Medical Association (AMA) to pass a landmark resolution declaring that the alcoholic should be viewed as a sick person and therefore not be barred from admission to a hospital. The AMA was not yet ready, however, to state outright that alcoholism was a disease. Nevertheless, a central principle of Marty and NCA's educational efforts was finally being recognized and accepted at least in part by the powerful AMA.

The AMA's action did not mean that individual physicians immediately implemented the resolution in their practices, but gradually the tide began to turn. Eleven years later, there was sufficient consensus within the AMA for it to state formally that alcoholism is a disease.[6]

Marty laughed as she commented, "Alcoholism was the first disease they ever had to vote was a disease!"

In 1990, NCA and ASAM jointly adopted a definition of alcoholism.

Alcoholism is a primary, chronic disease with genetic, psychosocial, and environmental factors influencing its development and manifestations. The disease is often progressive and fatal. It is characterized by continuous or periodic: impaired control over drinking, preoccupation with the drug alcohol, use of alcohol despite adverse consequences, and distortions in thinking, most notably denial.[7]

Marty had long ago recognized the genetic, psychosocial, and environmental factors of alcoholism when she said, "Alcoholism is like fame. Some are born to it. Some acquire it. And others have it thrust upon them."

She would have been pleased that in 1998, the AMA adopted a resolution that supported the value of self-help programs and urged managed-care programs not to deny authorization for payment of medical treatment when patients and their families also attended Alcoholics Anonymous and similar self-help groups.[8]

Among physicians, Marty's conviction that alcoholism is a disease has been vindicated. The disease model of addiction is no longer a questionable oddity but has been mainstreamed into the medical profession. Every medical school in the United States includes education in chemical dependency, though some schools admittedly do a better job than others.

Through a series of letters discussing the nature of alcoholism during these mid-1950 years, Marty became ever better acquainted with Dr. Karl Menninger, the cofounder of the Menninger Clinic and a charter member of NCEA's advisory board. Marty was clearly communicating with the renowned psychiatrist not only as an equal, but as his mentor in several respects. Such had become her reputation in the field of alcoholism that even medical authorities like Menninger sought and respected what she had to say.[9]

These monumental shifts in the medical community are taken for granted today. Yet not so very long ago, the alcoholic was as much a medical pariah as the leper in biblical times.

In its efforts to reduce the stigma of alcoholism, NCA had concentrated on changing society's perception of alcoholics from that of exclusively homeless indigents to the reality that the vast majority of alcoholics were ordinary "people like you and me." This shift was essential if society were to become interested in doing something constructive about alcoholism. Other civic groups besides NCA, however, were paying attention to the small percentage of alcoholics who were poor, homeless, and often in jail because there was no other place for them or understanding of alcoholism as a treatable disease.

By the mid-1950s, NCA decided to undertake the development of the National Committee for the Homeless and Institutional Alcoholic, and to join forces with those who were already active in the field. NCA provided an important role in bringing the different groups together through an annual institute addressing the issue. The institute began to serve as a forum to discuss the legal aspects of alcoholism and the rights of the alcoholic. In addition, NCA was invaluable in providing factual education to communities so they would see the need for more enlightened responses.

Marty's work was making such a national impact that Edward R. Murrow, then the United States' leading international news correspondent and TV anchor, listed her in 1954 among his choices for the ten greatest living Americans.

In the meantime, life outside NCA went on. On April 7, 1956, Marty was undoubtedly among Yev Gardner's many AA friends to attend his ordination as deacon in the Episcopal Church. The solemn ceremony and subsequent celebration took place at the imposing Cathedral of the Incarnation in Garden City, New York. In addition to his excellent administrative skills at NCA, Yev by temperament and inclination already functioned as an informal, quiet spiritual resource in both NCA and AA, so his ordination merely formalized his existing pastoral value to those organizations.

Later that same year, Marty was a delegate to the third conference of the International Union for Health Education of the Public, held in Rome, Italy. Of the more than one thousand in attendance, forty were Americans. Marty gave two talks that aroused intense interest. As a consequence, all of the conference's twenty-six working groups included alcoholism as a major problem in their final reports. This was the first time alcoholism had been considered by this worldwide group of health educators, doctors, nurses, social workers, and other public health workers.

While in Rome, Marty was privileged to have a special private audience with the pope. In her report to the NCA board and others, she wrote:

> This was preceded by a 3-hour conference with Bishop O'Connor, Rector of the North American College in Rome, who emphasized that His Holiness had been thoroughly briefed on Mrs. Mann and expressed his own deep interest in this work. The Holy Father blessed the work of the National Committee, commented that it was "of the first importance," and further blessed Mrs. Mann and all who worked with her. A further conference with Bishop O'Connor indicated that this event would have far-reaching consequences in the cooperation of the Catholic Church with the modern approaches to alcoholism symbolized by NCA, and by Mrs. Mann as its representative.[10]

Marty also arranged to have a medal personally blessed by the pope for a devout Roman Catholic friend in California, Ethel Mary de Limur.

The conference was followed by jam-packed visits to Geneva, Paris, London, and Dublin to meet and confer with the leaders in alcoholism education, treatment, and research in those countries. Five days were spent with her old friend Dr. Jellinek, then the secretary-general of the International Institute for Research on Problems of Alcohol. She was at WHO headquarters for a day and in addition met the head of the Yugoslav Red Cross, which was starting work on alcoholism in that country.

In Paris, Marty learned that "alcoholism in France does not usually manifest itself in behaviour symptoms, but rather in continuous saturation, almost from infancy, resulting in loss of productivity and in physical and mental deterioration and/or breakdown."[11] The French authorities estimated that alcoholics in that country were possibly as high as 15 percent of the population.

Both Croydon, England, and Dublin provided fine examples of functioning treatment programs for alcoholism. Marty discovered that AA was growing faster in Ireland than in England, partly due, she felt, to the absence of reluctance among early Irish members to talk about it.

On her return to America, Marty plunged immediately into activities awaiting her. Among many other responsibilities, Marty continued to work with state legislators around the country, so that they would have accurate information for writing and enacting legislation to help alcoholics get treatment. In 1952, she addressed a joint session of the Michigan legislature, and in 1957, Utah's. As noted by William L. White in *Slaying the Dragon*, "[Marty's] political savvy and spellbinding oratory—like those of Dorthea [sic] Dix before her—coaxed many a legislature into formulating a public-health response to the problem of alcoholism."[12]

These were exciting years for Marty—starting new programs and consolidating advancements. In 1957, NCA changed its name from National Committee to National *Council* on Alcoholism—still NCA—to reflect a more permanent, professional status.

In the midst of these rosier times for NCA, however, Marty had to confront the imminent loss of her mother. Lill's health was failing. As Marty's sisters moved away from New York, and with her brother still living in Toronto, Marty became the one most responsible for the care and oversight of her elderly mother. After Marty returned from Italy, she grew more and more concerned about Lill's accelerating decline. Marty asked an NCA physician friend (possibly Harold W. Lovell, at that time president of NCA's board) to pay a social call on Lill and see what he thought about her appearance. Lill looked ill to him, so he recommended she come to his office for a physical. He discovered she had a fibrillating heart, and he immediately hospitalized her for further tests. Lill was also found to have a "great big open sore [on her chest]." It was cancerous. She'd had it for two years but never told anyone.

"Why didn't you say something?" Marty asked her.

"I didn't want to bother you. I thought I'd be dead before I had to bother you." It was what Lill said, but Marty believed it was a case of that old devil, denial. Marty was lucky that she didn't follow in her mother's footsteps and instead was willing to seek help for her own cancers.

By late 1957, Lill Mann knew that she was in the latter stages of metastatic cancer. Her decline was irreversible. The spread of the disease might have been averted if she had followed doctors' orders and maintained periodic checkups after her 1918 mastectomy. Instead, she concealed the return of her cancer as long as possible.

Then Lill fell and broke her arm getting out of bed while visiting Priscilla and Marty in Easton. Marty took her mother to a local doctor, and he confirmed she was loaded with cancer. Sometimes Lill was very much worse, sometimes better. Marty maintained her usual busy schedule, but she never went away "without leaving telephone numbers for every hour of the day, and being prepared to come back on short notice." The last six months of her life, Lill was bedridden in her New York apartment—her arm in a cast from the fall at Easton. Marty spent a lot of time looking after her. Marty's friend in California, Ethel Mary, consoled her, "There is no greater sorrow than to see someone you love deeply in pain and not be able to help in any way."[13]

During this period of the later 1950s, Marty's own internist, Dr. Stanley Gitlow, happened to have his office in the same Fifth Avenue building as Lill's apartment. He, too, kept an informal eye on Lill for Marty, but there wasn't much anyone could do. Finally, on Saturday, January 11, 1958, Lill died in her apartment of natural causes related to her cancer.[14] She was seventy-eight. A memorial service was held at the Funeral Church, then located on Madison near the Metropolitan Museum.

Expected though it was, Lill's death must have hit Marty hard. For years, they had been very close. Marty, especially, but also her siblings, had reversed roles with their mother, they assuming that of her parent in many ways. On the other hand, there would have been relief from the long emotional and economic drain.

Dr. Stanley Gitlow played a central role in Marty's life, both as her doctor and through his service to NCA. He was a New York physician who became interested very early in alcoholics and specialized in their care. With Ruth Fox and a few other physicians, he was one of the founders of the New York City Medical Society on Alcoholism. Gitlow and Fox were important spokespersons in the alcoholism field, educating a whole generation of physicians. One time Walter Murphy, first a public information director at NCA and later one of its executive directors, asked Gitlow, "What's a normal drinker?"

> That's someone who thinks about alcohol the way you do about broccoli. You can take broccoli or leave it. You like broccoli but you don't have to have it every meal or between meals. You don't have to eat it before going out to a dinner party. You don't bring home the broccoli you don't finish at dinner.[15]

During the 1950s and well into the 1960s, hospitals generally didn't admit drunk patients, even for detox. Twice Marty had the horrifying experience of individuals dying in taxicabs with her because hospitals refused admission, saying they cared only for sick people. Furious, Marty cried, "They weren't sick enough to get into a hospital, but sick enough to die in a cab!"[16]

In New York, only Bellevue and Towns Hospitals would officially consider admission for treatment after detox. A third hospital, Regent, accepted alcoholics for detox only. If an AA member made a Twelfth Step call on an alcoholic who needed medical attention, AA had learned to take the person to one of those three emergency rooms. At Towns and Bellevue, the AA Twelfth Stepper would tell the ER doctor this was a suicide case and he should contact either Dr. Gitlow, Dr. Fox, or Dr. Tiebout for treatment instructions.

Once Marty was past the weeks and months of grieving her mother's death, she would normally have been able to give her full attention to NCA and AA without her energies being sapped by worry and responsibility for Lill. Six months after Lill died, however, Marty's skin cancer returned. Surgery was once again performed. The surgery was not as serious as ten years before, but Marty's aunt Edith (a family friend of the Manns) wrote, "I can imagine it is difficult to get comfortable with the trouble located where it is—and not good for a trip to the country yet."[17]

Aunt Edith also enclosed a clipping announcing the death of Jessie Simpson, the widow of Jim Simpson, who was Will Mann's old boss at Marshall Field. Jim Simpson had died thirty years before. It seemed as if all the important adults in Marty's Chicago childhood were now gone.

Marty was worn out and badly in need of rest. In addition to the responsibility during her mother's long decline, grieving her death, and having to maintain a demanding work schedule, all followed by her own surgery, Marty's energies had been exhausted in attending to a power play among some of NCA's leading board members. She believed one group's actions dangerously threatened the focus and future of NCA. Her countermove was to support Brink Smithers for nomination as president of the board. Fortunately for Marty, Brink was elected to the first of several terms in that office.

The year 1958 was also notable for Ruth Fox's appointment as NCA's first medical director. By the end of 1959, Marty could breathe a sigh of relief. NCA had become an organization stabilized through the largesse of Brinkley Smithers and others. In addition to its extensive public education activities, NCA was energetically moving ahead with expanded activities by several major committees: the scientific advisory committee, a department of professional education, a committee on research, and a maritime committee.

The next decade promised to be even better. The only cloud on the horizon, and it was a small one, was a kind of neurodermatitis that nagged at Marty. Her major health problems appeared over, however, and she looked forward eagerly to implementing new plans and opening up new areas for NCA in the United States and abroad.

25

Leo Redux

1960–64

THE 1960S WAS A HEADY DECADE, noted for its sometimes painful ups and downs. John F. Kennedy, a youthful symbol of hope, was elected—only to be assassinated three years later. Lyndon B. Johnson succeeded him with strong backing from the country to enact social legislation—then floundered in the morass of the Vietnam War. Martin Luther King Jr. was assassinated—and the Civil Rights Act was passed. Street drugs spread into the middle and upper classes—and the birth-control pill revolutionized sexual mores. Civic activism contrasted with personal hedonism. Environmental, consumer, and women's movements coexisted with the violence of the antiwar and black-power movements.

Against this backdrop, Marty and NCA were poised for an expansion and implementation of their mission. By the end of the decade, they would be able to take pride in what they had helped bring to pass. But in the years between, Marty would know a personal roller coaster as dizzying in its heights and depths as in the 1930s, when she hit bottom with her drinking and sought recovery.

Sometime during 1960, Marty was given a book by one of her NCA staff members. *The Inebriate,* published in 1898, "could have been written today," said Marty. "It had great understanding of alcoholism, but no solution." And a solution was what Marty was about.

In 1961, Marty's international travels resumed with a trip to Australia and New Zealand to help start local councils modeled on NCA. While she was in New Zealand, Marty began to have trouble with her voice. As she grew older, her voice had deepened normally, but now it was sounding

hoarse. Perhaps the strain of so many talks plus plain weariness was beginning to tell—and all those cigarettes didn't help. In writing to thank Marty
for her assistance in New Zealand, a new friend forcefully told her, "I am
concerned for your health and I am sure it is meant to be so much better
when you accept full responsibility for all you are still meant to give. Firstly,
it is just crazy for you to continue to smoke as you do."[1]

Upon her return to the United States, a polyp was found on Marty's
vocal chords. In May 1962, an operation removed what proved to be cancer. Cobalt therapy was started. The treatment was successful. A few
months later there was no trace of huskiness. Marty's voice was as essential
an instrument for her ends as is a fine cello for Yo-Yo Ma. Had the use of
her speaking voice been diminished or lost, NCA might have suffered.

The year after Marty returned, Priscilla was riding the crest of major
changes at *Vogue*. Diana Vreeland was appointed editor-in-chief in 1962,
and Alex Liberman moved up to be editorial director. Priscilla took over
Alex's position as art director. In the world of fashion and publishing,
Priscilla had now achieved well-deserved status and scope for her immense
talents. She was as famous in that special international world as Marty was
in hers.

Under Vreeland, *Vogue* underwent some significant changes. Dee-Anne,
as she was known, was theatrical and extravagant in her approach to life
and to fashion. Into flower children and orange hair, she understood the
burgeoning sexual license of the time and promoted fashions that expressed
it, like miniskirts and bikinis—standard women's wear today. The photography grew increasingly suggestive and erotic. Some of the Seventh Avenue designers were up in arms. Most of the *Vogue* editors, however, succumbed to
Vreeland's spell without a struggle because she was so much fun to be
around. Priscilla "quite literally fell in love with Vreeland."[2]

> Although never a beauty, Vreeland had a personal style that was as se-
> ductive as Alex's, and a great deal more vivid. Truman Capote, who
> became one of her great pals, said she was like "an extraordinary par-
> rot—a wild thing that's flung itself out of the jungle and talks in some
> amazing language."[3]

Priscilla, Alex's former protégée and confidante, turned against him
when he refused to sanction Vreeland's excesses. In her championship of

and devotion to Vreeland, Priscilla became "obsessed with hatred for Alex, like a love affair in reverse."[4] Such an extreme attitude was strange for Priscilla, whose spiritual life in AA and Religious Science had been on another plane entirely. It seemed as if her very personality was changing.

At the same time, Priscilla dashed off one of her notes to Marty, who was returning from yet another protracted trip: "Beloved—to have you back is to live again—instead of just marking time. All, all, all LOVE—P."[5]

In the early 1960s, a new face appeared at NCA—Walter Murphy. At the time, he was public information director at the National Tuberculosis Association (NTA). Through a series of fortuitous circumstances and a subsequent long conversation with Marty in her office, he achieved sobriety in 1960. For a while he did some volunteer work at NCA but couldn't stand the way public relations (PR) was being run there. He kept telling Marty (the expert!) what she was doing wrong. Finally, she retorted, "OK, wise guy, why don't you come over here and do it right?" So Walter resigned from NTA and was employed as NCA's PR director.

Walter was devoted to Marty but soon found he couldn't work for her. She would send him memos detailing his faults and mistakes. He would snap them right back. Finally, Walter left to set up his own PR company, and NCA became one of his clients. He and his wife, Debbie, remained fast friends with Marty, and Walter continued to work *with* Marty until her death. Marty loved the Murphys' son, Jamie, and considered the three of them an important part of her extended family.

The 1960s saw the beginning of many distinguished professional memberships, awards, and honors for Marty. In the United States, she was a fellow of the Society of Public Health Educators, a fellow of the American Public Health Association, and a member of the American Association for the Advancement of Science. Abroad she was a fellow of the Royal Society of Health in London and an honorary science member of the Society for the Study of Addiction to Alcohol and Other Drugs, also in London.

In 1963, Hobart and William Smith Colleges of Geneva, New York, honored Marty's accomplishments with the prestigious Elizabeth Blackwell Award. Elizabeth Blackwell was the first woman in the Western Hemisphere to receive a medical degree (1849).[6] The award is presented periodically to a woman who has demonstrated "outstanding service to mankind." Recipients have included Congresswoman Barbara Jordan, Senator Margaret Chase Smith, and Supreme Court Justice Sandra Day O'Connor.

Marty was the sixth person in the world entitled to wear the gold medal of the award. She also received a large, stunning Steuben glass vase inscribed with the phrase "Outstanding Service to Mankind." In presenting the award, Merle A. Gulick, chairman of the board, said, "In this our era of scientific and technological enlightenment, a dynamic woman came forth in 1944 to lead this nation out of an area that had remained in darkness and ignorance. . . . Marty Mann has been described as one of the great women of our time. Indeed, she is."[7]

A year later, Marty was made an honorary fellow of the American Psychiatric Association (APA). She was one of only a few laypeople ever to be so honored, and the fourth woman. APA granted her this recognition because she "has almost single-handedly changed the concept of an alcoholic derelict or drunkard to that of the alcoholic as a sick person, and alcoholism as a disease."[8]

Dr. Jellinek published an important book in 1960, *The Disease Concept of Alcoholism*. (He had actually come to prefer the term *illness* rather than *disease*.) He credited AA and the AMA's Committee on Alcoholism with playing decisive roles in supporting the disease concept of alcoholism. But his greatest praise was for NCA: "NCA and its local affiliates achieved the widest spread of the idea that 'alcoholism' is an illness."[9]

As public awareness of NCA's message continued to grow, Marty and her staff stepped up their activities even more. NCA pioneered in developing themes for TV dramatic shows. Tom Swafford, an NCA board member and also a vice president at CBS, worked with Norman Lear, then a leading producer of TV shows like *Maude*. Swafford made possible much of NCA's input into TV shows. To highlight alcoholism information week, NCA initiated the first celebrity public-service TV spots, featuring Art Carney, Robert Young, Dana Andrews, Jane Wyatt, and Jonathan Winters—famous TV stars of the day.

The TV spots were made possible by Robert Young, a TV superstar (*Father Knows Best* and *Marcus Welby, M.D.*). When Marty went to Hollywood in connection with the project, Bob Young and his wife, Betty, gave a dinner party in Marty's honor at their Beverly Hills home. Many celebrities were present, and they made a big fuss over Marty. When she and Walter Murphy drove back to their hotel, Marty asked, "What was that all about?"

Walter marveled, "She had no idea she deserved such attention. She simply didn't think she was important enough or famous enough to warrant it."

NCA's patient educational efforts with federal and state legislators and agencies began to pay off in concrete actions. At the state level, Marty addressed a joint session of Tennessee's legislature in 1965. Developments at the federal level were also exciting. A committee on alcoholism was established within the Department of Health, Education, and Welfare (HEW). In 1963, the federal government granted nearly two and one-half million dollars to individuals and agencies for research on alcoholism. NCA itself received several grants to examine the impact of alcoholism, such as one from the National Institute of Mental Health (NIMH) to study "The Prevalence of Alcoholism in the Urban Community."

Legal issues surrounding alcoholism were coming to the fore. NCA's Washington, D.C., affiliate vigorously supported one of two landmark cases that determined that public drunkenness was not a crime and that alcoholics could not be arrested for being drunk in public.[10] The stage was set for the decriminalization of intoxication. Marty was wholeheartedly in favor of this outcome. However, she firmly believed that neither the NCA national office nor the affiliates should be involved directly in noneducational issues, however important for the alcoholism movement those issues might be. A rift consequently occurred between the powerful Washington affiliate and the New York national office. Differences of opinion between some affiliates and the New York headquarters continue today concerning the proper role of the affiliates and their independence to address alcohol and drug problems as they see them in their immediate communities. Friction can also occur over the degree of financial support of the national office by the affiliates.

During all these intense events, Marty maintained her strenuous speaking schedule. No part of the country escaped her attention. One of Marty's memorable talks came about by accident. President Kennedy had accepted the invitation of the National Tuberculosis Association (NTA), now the American Lung Association, to be the keynote speaker at its annual convention in the fall of 1961. The convention theme was voluntarism. Kennedy was an obvious choice because of his leadership in inspiring Americans to roll up their sleeves and "Ask not what your country can do for you, but what you can do for your country." The Peace Corps was a going concern.

At the last minute, Kennedy had to cancel his NTA speaking commitment. The program committee turned to Marty. This was not as odd as it might seem. Although Marty's energies had for years been directed toward alcoholism, NTA was well aware that she had had TB and recovered. Her speaking gifts were already established. In fact, Marty was occasionally a volunteer speaker on behalf of TB societies, having been in Oregon for that reason shortly before she was asked to substitute for President Kennedy.

Marty was deeply honored to pinch-hit for the president of the United States. It was also the first time in the history of NTA that a woman had been asked to deliver the keynote address. Two difficult obstacles had to be overcome, however. First, her audience would be supremely disappointed that the president of the United States could not appear. Marty was second best, no matter how excellent her reputation as a dynamite speaker.

Second, despite her seventeen years as an accomplished speaker, Marty was uncharacteristically flustered in preparing for this talk. She said it was partly the word *keynote*, which sounded very august. The other reason was that she had "deep feelings about the Voluntary Health Movement, what it is and what it has done for us as a Nation, and what it has done for people— people in trouble, people in need, people in pain and sickness and sorrow." She felt a responsibility to do justice to the topic.

Though her style was heretofore extemporaneous, Marty spent hours writing down ideas, "waking up in the middle of the night and scrawling things." For the first time in her rather long career as a lecturer or speaker, she carried a yellow pad around with her "as if it were one of my fingers." She wrote "about 12 [speeches] for tonight. They are all upstairs in the wastebasket." Extemporaneous the speech would be.

In this keynote talk, Marty would express her mature philosophy and pragmatic beliefs born of experience. This speech is such a seminal expression of her whole life and work that her words are extensively quoted in the following paragraphs.[11]

Marty opened by emphasizing the importance of the volunteer movement. She praised NTA for its great success since its founding in 1904 in gradually eliminating the stigma on tuberculosis. She reminded her audience that back in the early days, it wasn't easy to get people of standing to associate themselves with tuberculosis. "It was not a popular subject."

Moreover, in those days, NTA didn't have the broad medical support that it developed over the years. That support "didn't come about by Government fiat. It didn't come about by a decree handed down from a dictator, however benevolent. It came about in this country of ours because a few citizens, some of who were doctors, some of who were non-medical citizens of various kinds, were determined that something had to be done—and they organized themselves to try and get it done. This is the heart of the Voluntary Movement—a free and spontaneous and determined desire to take action on a matter of their choice—on a problem that they feel needs tackling."

Today the voluntary health movement has expanded beyond its early specialty subgroups in TB, cancer, heart disease, and alcoholism, to include many more, such as Alzheimer's, Parkinson's, and mental retardation. Family members and patients past and present form the backbone of these organizations, but numerous others also care. Pounding the lectern with her fist in a characteristic passionate gesture, Marty noted that "the Voluntary Health Movement is made up of people who care deeply. Volunteers don't have to do this. They do it because they want to. They do it because they have a feeling about it. They do it because they *care*."[12]

To Marty, the voluntary health movement was "something that springs out of the heart. It speaks the language of the heart." It was also "the bridge between medical and scientific knowledge that we have, of which we are always trying to get more, and all those people out there who need to use and apply this knowledge."

For Marty, the people who "work in this field are working on spiritual principles. We're trying to gain more knowledge so we can give it away. We're also trying to make other people understand the need for caring about other people. It's not just the Christian religion that suggests that we are our brother's keepers, that there may one day be such a thing as the brotherhood of man, that we who care for others and try to give to others are the ones who will receive the most. These are ancient principles. They're all over the world. They crop up in other religions besides Christianity. They are basic spiritual principles."

One of the most important spiritual principles, Marty believed, was the capacity to give. She related this to the experience of fund-raising by telling the story of a Buddhist monk and his master.

> It is said that a Novice asked a Master of Zen Buddhism why it was that the Monks who were Novitiates had to go out for three years with just a robe and a staff and a bowl, and beg. The student asked if this was intended to produce humility in them, and the Zen Master said, "No. This is our sacrifice, this is the great gift that we give the world."
>
> The student asked his meaning, and he said, "The greatest thing that a human being can do is give. Someone has to ask, and our Monks serve their Novitiate by giving people that opportunity—by asking—and therefore by allowing others to give."

Prevention and early intervention in illness were major concerns of Marty's. "I know that one of our jobs, in addition to eliminating the stigma through every kind of educational and public informational device that we can use, or that will accept our voice, or our message, is to reach people at earlier and earlier stages of their illness where they have not lost so much, or done so much damage to themselves or others, and where their chance of recovery is greater. This is life-saving work. This is a direct means of saving lives."

Marty noted the "hidden tuberculars out there . . . And there are hidden cancer cases, and hidden heart cases—and hidden cases of every killing disease we have. How are we going to reach these people? The medical profession alone can't do it, you know. They don't go out with butterfly nets and catch every fifth man on the streets and haul him in and test him for all the diseases. It can't be done that way. *We* have to reach these people and persuade them to go to the doctor. *We* have to urge them to have the kind of checkups that are needed. *We* have to show them what earlier and earlier symptoms are so that they may be able to recognize them in themselves or someone else."

For Marty the means of accomplishing the task was "that much maligned word *education*." Here she recognized a necessary and legitimate role for government at all levels. The various subgroups of the voluntary health movement could never do everything. They needed the help and resources of government, for instance, in developing treatment facilities. What good was the most wonderful educational outreach if there were no affordable, accessible community public health resources available? She pointed out that government programs on tuberculosis did not exist when NTA started, despite the fact that TB was a pandemic public health problem that knew no state or geographic boundaries. NTA was responsible for creating the climate that corrected the shortage of treatment resources.

Marty concluded by forthrightly addressing two thorny issues constantly confronting the voluntary health movement. The first concerned fund-raising and in-house management of those funds. She was obviously disappointed that the business community did not as a rule contribute financially to the voluntary health movement. Businessmen believed volunteer organizations were inept at handling money. Marty commented somewhat bitingly that she "came to this work out of business, and I have worked in big business—in two of the biggest in the country—and I know exactly how efficient they are—on the inside." Then she went on to point out several examples of inefficiency in big business, private as well as public. She didn't really blame business for having inefficiencies. A certain amount of inefficiency was just part of being human. "Human beings aren't that efficient. And as far as I know there isn't much on this earth doesn't have to be run by human beings."

The second issue was what she considered a canard against the voluntary health movement—namely, that "the American people don't trust you [volunteers], the American people are challenging you, the American people don't believe you. This is nonsense. I travel 45,000 to 50,000 miles a year. I visit in that time 40 or 50 different cities, am there for a few days and meet all kinds of people. I sit down with them. I probably meet more people in a year than anyone you know, and to my knowledge the American people aren't distrusting us, or challenging us, or complaining about us at all—not the American *people.* I think there are groups here and there that are, but I don't think the American people are doing any such thing. Why? Because, we *are* the American people. It's the American people that we're helping, it's the American people that we are reaching, it's the American people that we care about—and they know it."

Marty closed with the observation that "the Voluntary Health Movement in the United States is one of the greatest things about America. I receive many visitors from all over the world in my office, coming to see what we're doing about alcoholism, because in some areas we're way ahead in that. And time and again they say, 'The most wonderful thing about America is your Voluntary Health Movement. We didn't know there was anything like this.' They have been moved. They have been struck by a Nation that does that kind of thing. So we can be proud—and I think we should act proud and talk proud. And I think we should walk taller because we are a part of a very great thing."

The speech was a blockbuster, delivered by a consummate artist of the spoken word. The packed audience sat stunned for a moment, then erupted in an unprecedented eight-minute standing ovation. President Kennedy had more than met his match. Marty's keynote speech is still a classic in the voluntary health movement.

In addition to her public speaking gifts, Marty was a born educator. She saw education as indispensable for reducing stigma in the public's mind, thereby motivating people to seek treatment. Every talk she gave, regardless of the audience, contained explicit as well as implicit factual information about alcoholism. For example, in telling her AA story, she always wove into the account a statement that her hollow leg was an indicator of an abnormal biochemical reaction to alcohol and an important early sign of alcoholism. In the same fashion, she would mention two other early signs she experienced—the need for alcohol to reduce her shyness and the need for several drinks before she felt the sought-after relief.

Marty was explicit that alcohol is a drug but that it does not cause alcoholism. "If that were the case, the other 90 percent of those who drink would also be alcoholics." Today it is further known that not all drugs are equally addictive to all users. Depending on her audience, Marty might also include comments on the history of alcoholism, or the development of treatment, or the status of legislation.

A popular lecturer, Marty taught many times at all the major academic centers that housed or hosted alcoholism education programs—Yale, the Menninger Foundation, Columbia Teachers College, and the Universities of Utah, Washington, Texas, Colorado, Georgia, Louisiana, and Arizona.

In July 1961, Marty spoke in Houston at the Institute of Alcohol Studies of the University of Texas. Either then or earlier on one of her many visits to Texas, she would have heard the stories about Sam Houston, the revered liberator of Texas, and especially about his alcoholism. Probably she learned that for the last twenty-three years of his life, this hero of Texas history said he controlled his excesses by sipping only Angostura Bitters.[13]

By at least the 1960s, many New York City AA members knew that bitters contain 45 percent alcohol, approximately the same as 90-proof whiskey. AAs who thought that bitters were not alcohol and could thus spike their club sodas were firmly warned.

Despite this background, Marty, now an AA old-timer and hopefully beyond temptation, relapsed briefly on alcohol sometime between 1959 and 1964,[14] probably closer to 1960 than later. It began with her drinking bitters. Marty, of all well-informed alcoholics, conned herself into thinking she could get away with a small amount of alcohol without having it constitute that dangerous first drink. Instead, one drink led to another—and it may not have taken very much alcohol to intoxicate her. After so many years of abstinence, Marty's body was probably very sensitive to the reintroduction of a toxin.

At that time, a young AA woman with about a year of sobriety lived in Bronxville, an exclusive suburb of New York City. She had heard a great deal about Marty and longed to meet her idol. The other AA members in her home group finally said, "Why don't you just go down to New York and see her?"

When she arrived unannounced at Marty and Priscilla's apartment, she was shocked to find Marty drunk, the place a mess, the dogs needing attention. Not knowing what else to do, the AA visitor cleaned up the apartment as best she could, loaded Marty and the dogs into her station wagon, and took them all back home with her.

Confused and upset, the young woman phoned Bonnie R., a Bronxville AA friend with nearly ten years of sobriety, and tearfully asked her advice. Bonnie assured her she'd done the right thing and advised her to keep Marty there until she'd detoxed. So Marty and the dogs stayed with their rescuer for several days. Marty refused to go to an AA meeting, pleading a need for confidentiality, and finally was able to return to the New York apartment.

Marty was very fortunate that her slip was cut short by the visit of the Bronxville woman.[15] What precipitated the drinking is unknown, but the accumulating stressors of her work, her health, her guilt about Jane Bowles in particular, the long illness of her mother, and the deaths of her parents would be danger signals for the ordinary recovering alcoholic. The where-abouts of Priscilla during this time are also unknown. By October 13, 1964, Dr. Ruth Fox had written Marty a prescription for Antabuse, a recognized deterrent to drinking.[16]

This relapse of Marty's has remained a closely held secret among AAs who were aware of it at the time. Some of them didn't even know that others knew. One woman knew—Lila Rosenblum, a recovered alcoholic in AA who worked for Marty in the early 1950s, but Lila had told no one until interviewed by the authors.[17] They will never forget Lila's look of stunned relief when asked if by any chance she was aware of a late relapse of Marty's. Her instant response was a startled, "Yes." Lila marveled that such an undirected conspiracy of silence could have existed. Nearly forty years later, she still felt much pain in having covered up for Marty—a decision she never discussed with Marty or anyone else—but "there was something about Marty that made you keep her secrets."

Another person who knew was Ernest Kurtz, noted historian of Alcoholics Anonymous. In doing research for his definitive account of AA, *Not-God*, he learned of Marty's relapse.[18] When he asked Marty directly about it, she became flustered, immediately changed the subject, and strongly signaled that she did not wish to return to the topic of her last relapse.

In one sense, the secrecy expressed AA's tradition of anonymity and not gossiping about one another. A similar cloak was drawn over Bill Wilson's alleged womanizing. However, *within* AA, a member's slip, while not an occasion for casual gossip, *was* usually known. The relapser generally talked about it in AA meetings. Anyone's relapse was an important learning experience for all. A slip was viewed as the lapse of a fallible human being. "There but for the grace of God go I!" AAs would say. They were grateful that the relapser was able to return to the fellowship. In fact, Marty had years before counseled as follows a woman named Pauline who'd relapsed:

> You certainly asked the $64 question about your slip. Frankly, I think that your own welfare is the most important to you, and that, therefore, you had perhaps better follow the usual procedure of getting it off your chest when you feel able to do so. It is a heavy burden for you to bear I am sure. I quite understand the reasons for both the priest and the minister advising against it, but I am not sure that they carry sufficient

weight as reasons. I frankly do not believe in my heart that any one person's behavior, attitude, or anything else can "hurt the whole movement" as you put it. AA is far bigger than any one of us and that the fact that we have failed in no way reflects on AA.[19]

So the secrecy about Marty's slip was not customary, neither her own silence, nor even more remarkably, the silence of those who knew. To be sure, advertising the failings widely in AA and beyond could bring great harm to the reputation of NCA, which Marty personified. Her name was virtually synonymous with NCA. This fear seems to have been a primary impetus for the silence. In retrospect, it may be fortunate that those who knew about Marty's relapse did choose to remain silent. Her contributions before and after her relapse to public understanding and acceptance of alcoholism as a disease and the alcoholic as a sick person worthy of help far outweigh the fact that after some twenty years of sobriety, she relapsed briefly.

Marty's personal silence must also be considered from the perspective that women alcoholics still bore a heavy portion of society's stigma. For someone as well known as she, a relapse could have been a serious deterrent to other women seeking recovery, as well as discouraging those already in AA. AA women could have been subjected to unfair backlash. Her painful reasoning to remain silent may be deduced from a conversation with an AA woman a few years later.

This woman held an important position. She'd been sober ten years when she relapsed briefly with a drink on the Metroliner between New York and Washington, D.C. Unfortunately, the single drink led to a binge that lasted months. The woman learned that once an alcoholic, always an alcoholic. And for some reason the disease seems to progress even during abstinence. The physical body doesn't cure itself of alcoholism. A relapse soon leads right back to the point—or beyond—where the drinking last stopped. Recovered alcoholics often describe the disease as a down escalator. The individual can get off at any point and be healed. But if the person starts drinking again, he or she steps back onto the escalator at a lower level. The drinking is worse, the consequences (or "yets") are greater.

Marty had become this woman's good friend. Though Marty wasn't her sponsor, the woman often turned to her for advice about AA, work, and life in general. So she confided in Marty about the slip, too—confused and torn about what she should do—tell her AA group, resign from her position, what?

Marty was both understanding and wise. She responded, "Given your public position as a role model, you can't afford to do any of those things. We all have built-in forgetters. The way we remember is working with others. What are you doing to help other alcoholics?" Not much, it turned out. The woman had been too swamped with her work responsibilities.

For many months, Marty's friend was able to stay sober, but eventually she relapsed again and ended up at the Smithers center in New York. There Dr. LeClair Bissell counseled her, "You can't keep this secret to yourself. You need someone to whom you can be accountable. Tell one person you trust." That's what the woman did. She selected an AA friend with whom she could be completely honest and never relapsed again. After she retired, she felt free to talk, in and out of AA meetings, about her relapse.

Whom in AA did Marty choose to confide in? Her sponsor, Bill Wilson? Ruth Fox probably knew the whole story. So would Priscilla.

About the same time as she counseled her friend, Marty made a sudden digression in a San Francisco speech.

> The more I learn about alcoholism, the more frightening it becomes, let me tell you. This is a fearful disease that we've got. . . . You and I know that we haven't eliminated it out of ourselves. It's still there. We don't get up here and say, 'I was an alcoholic,' do we? I am an alcoholic. . . .
>
> One drink—that's all we need to start down that spiral into that lonely glass box again. And it *is* cunning, baffling, powerful. It *does* come back. And when you have a lot of problems over a period of time—a lot of stress and strain, a lot of crisis in your life—and all of us do one way or another—what is going to sustain you from taking that first drink, with the instant relief (but temporary relief) that we remember so well?
>
> The thing that is going to sustain us is what we have here. The thing that is going to sustain us is having very, very clear in our minds that *that* [a drink] is not the answer. One of my favorite little statements: 'There's nothing so bad that a drink won't make it worse.' And there have been days when I've had to say that to myself many times.

A factor in relapse, better understood in the years since Marty died, is that alcoholism is now often characterized as a disease in which relapse, particularly in the first year, is common. Alcoholic relapse is dangerous, of course, because the outcome is unpredictable, and the person risks death or permanent disability to self or others. But relapse need not be a moral issue. Relapse is typical in other chronic conditions, such as heart disease, where the patient may revert to less dramatic but still life-threatening behaviors like smoking, not exercising, or eating high-cholesterol foods.

Marty's observation from her travels was that all the old-timers who had gotten drunk again were, almost without exception, AA dropouts. Though Marty believed this, it is too simplistic an explanation today for relapse. Contemporary and continuing research into the phenomenon of relapse shows it to be a multifactored, individualized occurrence.[20]

In October 1963, Marty learned that her old friend and mentor in the alcoholism field, Dr. Jellinek, had died. A few months later she was laid low with yet another health problem, this time a genuine gallbladder attack necessitating real surgery—unlike the 1939 quack doctor's intervention. In February 1964, her gallbladder was removed, and she went to Whale Cay for a month to recuperate.

By mid-November of 1964, Marty was back in full circulation. She returned to England for several strenuous weeks, and this time Scotland and Ireland as well, to help kick off a British campaign to raise £750,000 for establishing information and research programs to address alcoholism.

Six months later, Marty presented to NCA's board her vision for the next decade—"A 10-Year Plan for NCA."[21] In essence, she proposed that NCA continue and expand its thrust toward becoming a consulting group. She wasn't interested in "bigness for bigness' sake or an organization for an organization's sake." Instead she proposed ten task forces of consultants who were experts in their particular specialty in the field of alcoholism. These consultants would go out and "show other people how to do it." She wanted NCA to be a "don't-do-it-yourself organization." The ten consultant areas she outlined were communications, funding, community consultants, industrial consultants, medical consultants, church and denominational consultants, education consultants, law consultants, rehabilitation consultants, and a research fund.

That same June of 1965, Marty was honored to be chosen to address

AA's thirtieth International Convention in Toronto with Bill and Lois Wilson. The theme of this convention made a deep impression on her. She referred to the theme in many speeches over subsequent years. It was clearly a turning point in her thinking and obviously resonated with something in her own life. Conceivably that something was her relapse and what she was learning from it. The theme was created by an anonymous AA member specifically for the 1965 convention and has since been adopted by and disseminated throughout AA.

> I am responsible when anyone anywhere reaches out for help.
> I want the hand of AA always to be there.
> And for that, I am responsible.

Marty said it took her many years to understand that she bore a rock-bottom, indivisible, personal responsibility for AA's great gift of life so freely given—to realize that how she conducted herself mattered to the future of AA, not just to her own welfare and NCA's. One can almost hear the gong sounding in her mind with this obvious yet hard-won revelation.

In addition to responsibility, the second aftereffect of Marty's relapse may have been the increasing spirituality in her talks and in her relationships with others. She mellowed noticeably from 1965 on. Partly this could be due to the aging process, but the shift seems fairly abrupt. Her association with Religious Science probably influenced her changing attitudes, but she'd been involved with those teachings for at least ten years without noticeable spillover into her speeches. At any rate, Marty, first the flaming atheist, then the agnostic, finally the intellectual believer, returned to her Christian roots in a very basic, healing way for her. Three New Testament teachings became pillars of her newly felt faith.

> It is more blessed to give than to receive. (Acts 20:35)

> For whoever wants to save his life will lose it, but whoever loses his life for me will find it. What good will it be for a man if he gains the whole world, yet forfeits his soul? (Matthew 16:25–26)

> AA is the bridge whereby the lost become found. All of us were lost. That is what alcoholism does to you. It's been called the loneliest disease. (See Parable of the Prodigal Son, Luke 15:11–32)

Marty interpreted these biblical teachings and those of AA to mean that the souls of human beings were intended by God to grow and flourish. Again and again in her talks after 1964, she dwelt on spiritual growth. As far as alcoholics were concerned, she interpreted spiritual growth to mean a responsible life of grateful service to others. Passionate as Marty was about education and the self-knowledge it brought, she came to realize that education and self-knowledge were not sufficient in themselves. A person needed a spiritual core. Spiritual growth was Marty's personal cornerstone from at least 1964 until she died.

Once, speaking at an AA meeting, Marty held up a piece of paper folded into a triangle. She said, "One corner of the triangle is your sponsor. Your sponsor might get drunk or move away. The base of the triangle is your meetings and other AAs. But *you* might move away. The top of the triangle is God—and God is always there, ready to bring new things into your life. Ready to do all the good in the world through and for you—sobriety, growth on the program."[22]

Along with her renewed faith, Marty continued to explore other traditions. She and Priscilla studied Eastern mysticism. Marty was interested in Zen Buddhism and tai chi. Transcendental meditation (TM) became popular in the United States during the 1960s. TM was also an effective relaxation technique. And relaxation had never come easily or naturally to Marty. Marty loved TM. She described how kind the young men at the TM center were to her and "the beautiful little ceremony with flowers and fruit" when she was initiated. Her enthusiasm influenced others to take the TM course.

Marty scheduled her meditations for early morning and late afternoon. They were a regular daily routine. After rising, she would have a cup of tea and a cigarette, followed by the meditation period. At 5:00 P.M., when everyone had vacated the NCA offices, she closed the door to her office and relaxed with her second meditation. If she was traveling, she had no trouble meditating for fifteen minutes in a taxi, an airplane, or a hotel.

As the years went on, however, she found that every time she stretched out for a fifteen-minute meditation, she fell asleep. Her doctor's response was, "At your age, Marty, it's not a bad idea to have a fifteen-minute nap twice a day."[23]

In analyzing why people relapsed, Marty frequently emphasized that

slips were related to not going to AA meetings. She renewed her own attendance and also vowed to be quiet and listen for a change. Comments from
those who met or knew Marty only from the mid-1960s on tended to include her kindness, whereas that particular virtue was seldom mentioned
before then, except as warmth. It was as if her ego had been taken down a
peg or two, perhaps by being scorched in a relapse. She was now free to be
an equal among equals, not just an icon.

26

$\mathcal{L}etting\ \mathcal{G}o$

1964–70

PARALLELING MARTY'S INTERNAL CHANGES were significant shifts on
the political front. In November 1964, Lyndon B. Johnson of Texas was
elected president of the United States by a huge majority. He was the first
president to recognize the importance of alcoholism *and* to do something
about it. One of Johnson's actions on taking office was to appoint a national advisory committee in 1966 to advise John W. Gardner, the secretary
of Health, Education, and Welfare (HEW), on priorities and programs concerning alcoholism. Johnson's intention was for the federal government to
cooperate with voluntary organizations like NCA in waging a "decisive
campaign against the human and economic threat of alcohol addiction."[1]

This unprecedented action by Johnson didn't come out of nowhere.
Lyndon Johnson had a long-standing interest in the issue of alcoholism. He
was the son of an alcoholic father. His teetotaling mother was devoted to
the Women's Christian Temperance Union. In addition, the state of Texas
had for twenty years been a major center of NCA activity.[2] From 1948,
Johnson was for many years a board member of the Texas NCA.

Marty, from her end meanwhile, had been working for several months
with Secretary Gardner to consider what role the federal government might
take. The tragedy of Kennedy's death created an opening for the first significant federal activity in addressing the monumental public health problem
of alcoholism.

Amid all this excitement, Marty was deeply saddened by the death of
Dr. Harry Tiebout in 1966. For twenty-eight years he had been her psychiatrist, her colleague, and her friend. She adored him and never failed to single

out his immense contributions to the field of alcoholism. AA, too, lost a valued champion whose lasting effect on that organization was unique. Tiebout's impact on psychiatry was equally powerful, as he helped lead his field into a modern understanding of alcoholism.

Clinical depression, a recurring problem for Marty, was difficult to manage. Priscilla sympathized with her but had trouble understanding Marty's condition because she herself was not prone to depression. Marty, perhaps influenced years before by Dr. Foster Kennedy's conviction, believed that clinical depression could have a physical basis. Sometimes Marty "felt like Job," but she was also certain that "God didn't save us in order to throw us into the jaws of Hell." Bill Wilson also endured extreme clinical depression for many years. He and Marty had learned from experience that "the depression will end. It always does." In the meantime, Marty said she was like Dorothy's aunt Em's family in the *Wizard of Oz*. When the tornado hits, go down in the cellar and wait it out.

Marty knew that alcohol directly caused at least one-third of suicides. She knew also that clinical depression is a principal cause of suicide. Since alcohol is a major depressant, she couldn't help wondering how many people who were clinically depressed were hidden alcoholics.

Around 1961, Bill Wilson heard that niacin, or vitamin B₃ (also called nicotinic acid), could be helpful in correcting hypoglycemia (low blood sugar) and was thus useful in addressing depression and its not infrequent outcome, relapse. His enthusiasm for the vitamin spread rapidly through AA. Marty, Felicia, Priscilla, and Liz were among the many who began taking niacin—nico, as they called it. The vitamin was administered in periodic shots. Marty said nico never did anything for her. Perhaps niacin was helpful for some people, but the effect often appeared to be the power of suggestion. Later on, when over-the-counter tablets supplanted the injections, it was learned that in the frequently self-prescribed doses of 500 mg or more a day, the vitamin could be toxic to the liver.

Bill Wilson was also enthusiastic about lysergic acid diethylamide (LSD) as a spiritual catalyst that would help alcoholics achieve sobriety. In those days, the potential dangers of LSD, especially for alcoholics, were at first unrecognized. Whether Marty tried this drug is unknown.

In 1967, Marty succumbed to a particularly bad siege of depression, where she could hardly move or pray. She said, however, that she *could* count her blessings and drag herself to AA meetings. At an AA Kansas conference, she went to meetings morning, noon, and night, and slowly the depression lifted. The Lord's Prayer helped. Most of all, she relied on AA's Third Step: "Made a decision to turn our will and our lives over to the care of God *as we understood Him.*" A stoic, Marty seldom mentioned her depressions in public and just kept putting one foot in front of another.

Suitable antidepressants were beginning to come onto the market. By the end of the 1960s, Marty's doctor, Stan Gitlow, found that Elavil was effective with Marty.[3] The use of antidepressants has been a controversial issue in AA. Sometimes a blanket judgment against all drugs of any kind, at any time, is apparent in the recovery communities. This can cause extra conflict and distress for the alcoholic, even leading to relapse. Some AAs are uninformed or misunderstand that there is a legitimate use for medication, provided the need is medically demonstrable, the physician is truly knowledgeable, and the client is a responsible partner.

Regardless of depression, Marty kept forging ahead. In 1967, she repeated her trip to England and Ireland to speak on behalf of the British and Irish National Councils on Alcoholism.

Carson McCullers died that fall. The brief affair with Marty was long in the past, but Carson had remained part of her and Priscilla's lives. Priscilla was upset when anyone she knew died, and she took Carson's death especially hard. Felicia tried to comfort her. They shared some stories about Carson. "Priscilla recalled that Elizabeth Bowen and Virginia Woolf came to the U.S. to worship at the shrine of Carson. Carson invited them to tea in Nyack. She had a special blouse to wear but spilled something on it. The entire interview between Carson, Bowen, Woolf, and Priscilla was conversation about blouses!"[4]

Priscilla's memory was faulty, but it makes a good story. McCullers did not achieve wide public notice as an author until June 1940. Virginia Woolf died in 1941. There is no reference in biographies or edited diaries of Woolf to a visit to the United States in 1940 or 1941. In the case of Elizabeth Bowen, it was Carson, "a star-struck devotee of Miss Bowen,"[5] who went to see *her* in Ireland in 1950. Bowen, in fact, though she admired McCullers's writing, did not care for the flighty, childish, hard-drinking Carson and would not likely have gone to worship at her shrine. Around

1960, however, Bowen did visit Carson, who by then was an invalid living in Nyack. Possibly, Priscilla joined them for tea.

Felicia described her idea of death to Priscilla: "Wherever you are, it's always here. It can always be great. When you love someone and they go, it's only for awhile. They've gone to Australia. They have no phone." Felicia privately thought, "I suppose we think of Marty and how Marty might go first."[6]

During the 1960s, Marty focused increasingly on two issues, one that dated from her early days with NCEA, the other a product of this particular decade. The first concern was intervention. The earlier it occurred in the disease process, the better. Early intervention was the difference between fishing someone out of the river way downstream, when they were half-drowned, and being upstream to prevent the person from falling in the river in the first place or being swept away by the current. In a 1968 address before the NCA affiliate in Cincinnati, Ohio, Marty laid out the nuts and bolts of intervention. It was a teaching session by a master teacher.

> Professional people don't ask that persons with other diseases "be ready" before they will treat them. Professional people, especially in medicine, can be effective interveners by providing accurate information. A Dallas social worker actually wrote an article that alcoholism was due to a domineering wife. Wrong! Before you try to help an alcoholic, learn as much as you can about the disease.
>
> How do you intervene? Tell them! Many, perhaps most, alcoholics have no idea what is wrong with them. The world often assumes the alcoholic knows already what is wrong.
>
> How do you actually tell a person? Start by tactful, nonthreatening questions. Say, "[Do you know] you have alcoholism," *not* "You are an alcoholic."
>
> Consider, What kind of treatment does an alcoholism center recommend? What else besides AA and Al-Anon? Use other resources, e.g. doctors, psychiatrists, etc. I believe AA is the only long-term resource for comfortable sobriety, but many people start in other ways. We need many more [long-term] halfway houses. People deserve this kind of help.

Why do some people fail to achieve sobriety? Personal reserva-
tions, accompanying conditions for which they need additional help
[dual diagnosis], they know someone who stopped on their own, or
they're unable to accept help.

There is no such thing as an instant cure.[7]

Marty forcefully repudiated the commonly accepted notion: "No one
can help an alcoholic until he's willing to stop drinking." Her experience
and observation of others was that few alcoholics were willing in the beginning to stop drinking. To wait for that level of acceptance could be a death
sentence for the alcoholic. But if an alcoholic had a modicum of willingness
to accept help for whatever reason on even a temporary basis, then there
was a chance that the drinking could be arrested. Today, specific intervention techniques have been developed that work successfully with a majority
of alcoholics.[8]

The new issue that Marty focused on was society's obsession with the
spread of street drugs. People who used street drugs were called *addicts*.
That term began to replace *alcoholic* as the greater stigma. Pressure by a
frightened, uninformed middle class led to the major local, state, and federal funds and attention being directed to street drugs and primarily emphasizing punitive control. Marty was incensed that people could be so diverted
by a relatively minor problem compared with alcoholism, which was endemic and had far greater negative consequences. All the street drugs put together didn't equal a fraction of the problems caused by the disease of
alcoholism. Alcohol, however, was a familiar—and legal—drug and didn't
engender the public terror produced by America's emerging drug culture.
The public mistakenly believed the manifestations of street drug abuse to be
more violent, disruptive, and unpredictable than the abuse of alcohol.

Similar societal denial and misapprehensions exist today, though they
have been reduced. Marty partly blamed the media for skewed public per-
ceptions and a lack of accurate information. "After all," she said, "it took
the *New York Times* 20 years to run a page-one story on alcoholism."

Marty saw clearly that whole systems of society were in denial. Her response was to work even harder at getting NCA's message to the people and
places that mattered. She also insisted that NCA, like AA, work only in the

field of alcoholism. She believed that NCA could not afford to spread into the area of illegal street drugs.

Marty herself was so focused on the major problem of alcoholism that she, like most other professionals in the alcoholism field of the day, failed to see there might be an underlying physical connection between addiction to street drugs, certain prescription drugs, nicotine, and alcohol. Research that occurred after Marty's death has confirmed the connection. Pure alcoholics are relatively rare today. Most addicted persons are polyaddicted to two or more psychoactive drugs, one of which, however, is usually alcohol. The comprehensive term is now *addictive disease*. In recognition of this development, NCA officially changed its name in 1990 to National Council on Alcoholism and Drug Dependence (NCADD).

Despite the street-drug distraction, NCA had grown sufficiently stable that Marty could begin giving serious attention to the future of the organization beyond her lifetime. For one thing, she was nearing normal retirement age. Almost twenty years before, Bill Wilson had persuaded AA to adopt a structure that would outlast his leadership and continue to flourish. His situation in AA was different from Marty's in NCA, however. AA from the beginning had had shared leadership between its two founders, Bob Smith and Bill Wilson, whereas Marty was the single founder of NCA. In addition, though both Marty and Bill were unusually charismatic leaders, Bill's leadership style was more collegial than Marty's. It was easier in a way for him to let others gradually take over and to remain somewhat aloof from management issues.

Marty, on the other hand, loved to manage. She was a very strong woman who relished being in charge. Despite the spread of decentralized NCA affiliates across the land, despite NCA's success in educating the country about alcoholism, and despite Yev Gardner's administrative skills, NCA remained largely a one-woman show. Marty knew she had to start backing off at NCA—and she better have something in place, or there could be a dangerous power vacuum.

NCA was changing, too. Like many start-ups, it had grown beyond its revolutionary beginnings into a larger corporate phase. By the late 1960s, the NCA board was reaching the point where several members felt the need for a different sort of person as executive director and wanted Marty to step down. Marty wasn't yet ready to relinquish the reins, however. The struggle within her and among the staff and board members was painful.

As important as NCA's reorganizational needs was the fact that Marty's health was slowly deteriorating. Brink Smithers was especially concerned about her physical condition. She was sixty-four years old, and two decades of a punishing travel and speaking schedule, punctuated by life-threatening illnesses, strenuous surgeries, and debilitating depressions, had taken their toll. Friends joked that no matter what dire ailments they had, Marty had had them—and worse. Now she was falling occasionally. One fall put her in the hospital, but fortunately no bones were broken. Her energies weren't what they used to be. However, you wouldn't know it if you saw just her public face. Like an old war-horse, she was recharged by an audience, even an audience of one.

One time, a friend ran into her at an airport baggage counter. "I didn't know you were on the plane!" the friend exclaimed.

"Well, yes," responded Marty in some embarrassment. "I was flying first-class this trip. Sometimes I just get so tired."

Yet people remember Marty in these later years as the picture of health. The incredible force of her personality obscured her failing physical capacities. Even when she needed to use a cane or wheelchair, people were more conscious of her energy field than they were of any disability.

Most troubling of all for Marty as the decade progressed was Priscilla's odd behavior. When Marty and Priscilla were by themselves, Marty noted that Priscilla didn't seem herself. Her previously excellent short-term memory came and went. She could turn mean, even nasty and paranoid, for no good reason. She became more irresponsible, spending large sums for beautiful art books she didn't need. One time, she came home with a huge sheepdog they also didn't need. Then when they had guests, Priscilla appeared normal. So people thought Marty was imagining everything. Felicia finally noticed the personality change, too, and thought it was due to hardening of the arteries.

At *Vogue*, Priscilla's emotions were patently erratic. Her long, distinguished tenure would draw to a close before long. She had developed a form of dementia that was eventually diagnosed as Alzheimer's disease.

With all of these considerations on her mind, Marty finally began coming to terms with the future. In January 1967, she started to explore semi-retirement options with NCA's new president, Tom Carpenter. Apart from Marty's natural reluctance to hand over the control of her creation to someone else, the main problem was financial. NCA's retirement fund was inadequate, especially if Priscilla was going to require extra help. Carpenter proved to be an effective arbitrator between Marty and what had become the Brink-led board faction. Marty put her thoughts in writing so that Tom could present them to the whole board.

My major concern, quite naturally, is for the future of NCA, just as it has always been since I founded the organization in 1944. . . .

Like all voluntary agencies, NCA's organizational structure has of necessity been formed and has grown, according to our financial abilities. Because of these limitations the number of staff has increased slowly, and it has been a constant strain to keep pace with the demands of an expanding field. This has imposed undue burdens on all NCA staff but most particularly on me as executive director. For many years I have performed two distinct functions: my public role as spokesman for NCA and for the cause of alcoholism, as advisor and consultant to groups and individuals, as lecturer and writer; and my office role in day-to-day administration of the organization.

Of course the Board will have to make the decision, but it is my considered opinion that in the best interests of NCA these functions should be divided at the earliest opportunity. I believe the Board must consider the appointment of a topflight administrator qualified to direct the day-to-day operations and expansion of the organization, and responsible directly to the Board. I believe that my own most valuable contribution to NCA lies in my public role which now takes so much of my time and energy. I also believe that my long experience and knowledge could best be utilized at the Board level in shaping policy and giving direction to program. . . .

It should not be necessary to point out that I will not be available indefinitely. Planning should begin now to assure NCA's future. . . .

I'm sure I don't have to tell you that I would never want to be entirely detached from NCA and its affairs. But I do feel that now is the right time to transfer the administrative responsibilities from my

shoulders and to start the kind of future planning that will assure the
future of NCA.[9]

Carpenter responded with understanding, support, and affection, and
agreed to present Marty's proposal to the NCA board. His optimistic opinion was that Marty would be able to relinquish control even though she
continued to maintain an office on NCA's premises. He also believed that
Brink would help out financially, as he'd so often done in the past.[10]

Brink and Marty had a long discussion, during which he generously
pledged a lifetime annual salary of $25,000 ($125,000 in year 2000 dollars).
Brink guaranteed this pledge would be paid by him, the Smithers Foundation,
or both, "despite any disabilities which may occur to her."[11] The salary
would commence when a new executive director was hired. In the meantime,
Marty would continue with her regular duties as executive director.

In April 1967, the board formally approved the proposed contract for
Marty.[12] When the time came for her to relinquish her executive director-
ship, she was to be named founder-consultant. Marty and the new executive
director would each report directly to the board but would be expected to
coordinate their daily plans and activities. In addition to the $25,000 salary
pledged by Brink, various benefits were discussed and informally approved
by the board. NCA for its part would provide office space for Marty, the
sharing of a secretary, and travel expenses. NCA would also continue the
usual payments to FICA and the Blue Cross and Blue Shield hospitalization
and medical plans until she reached retirement age. Assuming a new executive director was in place by November 1, 1969, contributions to the retirement fund would cease on that date.

The search for an executive director was immediately launched.

In May 1967, a month after the board's action, Brink had second
thoughts about the proposed benefits portion of Marty's package. He confi-
dentially recommended that the board rescind its intent to provide Marty
with office space, secretarial help, and a travel allowance. Brink was concerned that NCA was committing itself to expenses it might be unable to
meet in future years. In addition, he foresaw management problems if
Marty was on the premises while a new executive director was breaking
into her old position.[13]

Brink's suggestions did not prevail. However, the intent to provide a full benefits package was left open for the time being, and Marty's future contract as founder-consultant was affirmed with no mention of the benefits described above.[14]

In April of the following year (1968), William "Bill" W. Moore Jr., head of the American Heart Association (AHA), formally took over his new duties as Marty's successor. The question of logistical support for Marty (office, secretary, and travel expenses) immediately arose and was quickly resolved in her favor.[15]

Marty now assumed her new official title, founder-consultant. She moved into another office and promptly carpeted it in red.

More than a year went by. Marty was out of the office a great deal, not only because of her travel schedule, but also because she was needed in Washington, D.C., as passage of critical new federal alcoholism legislation approached a climax in the Senate. Whenever she returned to NCA, there was a certain amount of predictable friction between her and Bill Moore. At times they were bitterly antagonistic. Moore's style was radically different from Marty's. He was a professional public health administrator, unfamiliar with alcoholism. He resented Marty's maintaining an office on-site. She came to believe he threatened the entire structure of NCA. In fact, much conflict did develop between him and the affiliates. Factionalization increased. As a result, Marty's charisma was diffused. She was no longer a potent organizing force.

A dynamic, long-established leader is a difficult act to follow, even with the best intentions in the world and the most compatible of personalities and management styles. Business knows it, churches know it, school districts know it, all major systems know it. Marty and Bill Moore were in a near-impossible situation with Marty's continuing to maintain an office on the premises. Regardless of her absences, she was still a Presence—as Brink had predicted.

A further loss besides her leadership position at NCA would befall Marty shortly after Bill Moore took over. Bunny, one of her and Priscilla's two corgis, died. All who have owned and loved a pet for many years will understand the grief this can bring. To Marty and Priscilla, their dogs were like their children. At least Taffy was still there. Several years appear to have gone by before Marty acquired a replacement for Bunny. The new pet was named Robin, but it is unclear whether Robin was a kitten or a puppy.

By the end of 1968, Marty was past the acute stage of career and home changes. She went into seclusion at Felicia's the last half of December 1968 to start her second book, *Marty Mann Answers Your Questions about Drinking and Alcoholism,* and to write a proposal to her publishers, Holt, Rinehart and Winston. In January 1969, she received $1,350 ($6,750 in year 2000 dollars) from the publishers, the first half of an advance. During the year, she completed the manuscript in time for publication early in 1970.

When asked who had influenced or helped her most in her writing throughout her life, Marty replied, "Priscilla Peck, a friend who is Art Director of *Vogue.*"

Once this new book was out, the anonymity issue arose again. AA members asked why Marty was using her name as part of the title. Moreover, in the preface, she identifies herself as a recovered alcoholic. However, though she describes AA, Al-Anon, and Alateen and emphasizes AA as a treatment of choice for alcoholics, she does not mention her own affiliation with AA. She does stress her role in NCA and especially what NCA does to help alcoholics and their families. Marty would have known she would again become a lightning rod but must have felt secure in her interpretation and application of AA's Tradition Eleven, the anonymity guideline.

By October of 1969, Bill Moore had been executive director for sixteen months. Marty would turn sixty-five that month. Again the proposal to cancel her benefits package surfaced, even though she would be continuing to provide NCA with the speaking and consulting services for which she had contracted as founder-consultant.

Tom Pike, of Pasadena, was on the board and got wind of what was happening. He immediately rode to the rescue, alerting others to the situation, including Marty. Pike was indignant that so valuable a representative of NCA as Marty would be deprived of basic logistical support like an office and part-time secretarial help. He reminded Bill Moore of her sheer virtuosity in striking a "telling blow for NCA and alcoholism" in her testimony before the Senate.

> Public information is the main name of our game and Marty plays it with consummate skill for us.[16]

The conflict over benefits was resolved, though relations between Marty and Bill Moore remained strained. With time and circumstance, Marty was able to back off more and more from detailed involvement with NCA issues and devote much of her attention elsewhere. It is interesting to note that since Marty's long tenure as executive director, all of the ensuing directors were men until Stacia Murphy was appointed in August 1999. The title was also changed to president.

While Marty and NCA were undergoing all these retirement challenges, she was preoccupied with exciting developments in the nation's Capitol. Harold Hughes, a three-term governor of Iowa, was elected to the Senate in 1968. An openly recovered alcoholic, he was determined to improve treatment resources for alcoholics. Hughes, much like Marty, was a charismatic leader. A tall, well-built, ruggedly handsome, large man, he also suffered from bouts of clinical depression. Marty, apparently used to these episodes, knew there was nothing anyone could do about them—just leave him alone for the duration.

As chair of the Senate's Subcommittee on Alcoholism and Narcotics, Hughes plunged into public hearings that generated political momentum for federal support of alcoholism treatment as a public health problem. He solicited broad input from alcoholism treatment advocates, including Marty and Bill Wilson.

Nancy Olson was Hughes's professional staff aide for alcoholism legislation. She met Marty at an early hearing in 1969. At the break, the young aide followed Marty into the ladies' room and introduced herself. Decades later, Nancy still remembered how Marty took both her hands, saying, "I'm so happy to meet you, Nancy."

"She was so warm, so gracious, so giving. She acted as though I was the one person in the world she wanted to meet," Nancy recalled.

The hearings began in 1969, and the legislative process lasted into 1970. When Marty testified before the Hughes subcommittee, she had their total attention. People said you could have heard a pin drop. Marty was thoroughly prepared whenever she appeared. She'd done her homework and knew her audience, having studied in detail the political interests of each senator on the subcommittee and how to appeal to those interests. Her political skills were enviable.

The dramatic hearings were televised. The whole country found itself being educated about alcoholism. Marty must have been thrilled at this grand opportunity to carry NCA's message. Alcoholics, in particular, were riveted by Marty and Hughes, as well as by Bill Wilson.

> Marty [however,] played a key role in the genesis of the federal alcoholism effort and was a major figure in the public policy arena at the national level until the time of her death. Until she died, she was the person the Senate Subcommittee on Alcoholism and Drug Abuse called on most for advice. She testified over the years before many Congressional committees and state legislatures.[17]

The result of Senator Hughes's superb leadership was passage of the Comprehensive Alcoholism Prevention and Treatment Act of 1970, known as the Hughes Act, which created NIAAA (National Institute on Alcohol Abuse and Alcoholism).

The bill then went to President Nixon, where it hit a dangerous snag. Two influential cabinet members had advised against signing the bill—Charles Schultz, director of the Office of Management and Budget (OMB), and Elliot Richardson, secretary of HEW. Time was running out. If Nixon didn't approve the bill by December 31, it would fail because of a "pocket veto."

Into the breach jumped two powerful NCA men, both of them prominent Republicans, Brinkley Smithers and Tom Pike. They personally lobbied Nixon, their fellow Republican. Brink also enlisted the support of Don Kendall, CEO of Pepsi, to call Nixon. Pike had special clout as a long-time Republican leader and financial supporter in Nixon's home state, California. In the evening of that last day, Nixon was finally persuaded to sign the bill into action.

> The creation of NIAAA marked the growing political power of the alcoholism constituencies that had rebelled against the placement of alcoholism within the bureaucratic umbrella of mental health. Their efforts pushed alcoholism into a category of its own. The political recognition of alcoholism as a disease and public-health problem in its own right had arrived.[18]

Marty and Tom Pike were appointed to NIAAA's advisory council. After her NIAAA term was up, Marty was named a special consultant to the new

NIAAA director, Dr. Morris Chafetz, a position she still held at the time of her death.

In 1974, the bill was amended to require all hospitals that received federal funds from any source to stop discrimination against alcoholics. Another amendment stated explicitly that alcoholism is a disease, an important addition to justify large federal appropriations.[19] Thirty years after NCA was founded, Marty's insistence that alcoholism is a disease was bearing fruit in concrete public health action that reflected an understanding and consensus by communities and individuals throughout the land.

Bill White has cogently described the power and breadth of Marty's impact on the institutional response to alcoholism.

> Marty Mann and Harold Hughes almost single-handedly created the national network of alcoholism treatment programs that exist today, and there couldn't have been a Harold Hughes without a Marty Mann. When Marty started NCEA in 1944, there were almost no hospitals that treated alcoholism and little treatment outside of hospitals. When she died in 1980, hospitals across the country were getting into the business of alcoholism treatment and there was an evergrowing network of free-standing alcoholism treatment programs throughout the country. The hundreds of thousands of alcoholics who initiated their recovery within the walls of a treatment program owe a debt of gratitude to Marty because those programs would not have been there without her. It is the reach of her influence both on the institutional response to alcoholism as well as her influence on hundreds of thousands of alcoholics and their families that makes me suggest that she was one of the most successful public health reformers in American History.[20]

Marty and NCA could justifiably take credit for having created the social climate that produced Hughes's landmark legislation. The next ten years would see a proliferation of recovery facilities for the first time in America's history. It was a fitting hosanna to Marty's twenty-six years of effort to educate the country about alcoholism so that alcoholics would move past stigma and denial into recovery.

A New Path

1970

THE EARLY 1970S WAS ANOTHER UNSETTLED TIME. It marked the end of the Vietnam War, an experience that left bitter feelings among Americans, lasting into the 1980s and even 1990s. Among other Vietnam consequences, many GIs returned with addiction to drugs illegal in the United States. The Beatles were at the top of their form, then broke up, thereby saddening large numbers of younger citizens. The TV program *Saturday Night Live* hit it big. The country was traumatized by the Watergate affair and President Nixon's resignation in 1974. An OPEC-created oil shortage led to long lines at the gas pumps. Severe double-digit inflation and a deepening recession threatened the country's economy as well as individual incomes.

Marty and NCA had two difficult dilemmas—how to keep the country focused on alcoholism when illegal drugs were grabbing headlines, and where to find enough money when inflation was drying up sources. On the plus side, the future looked bright for the development of treatment centers under the new Hughes Act.

Although Marty recognized that hard drugs were currently more glamorous than alcohol, she also understood that much of the country was in denial about the far greater prevalence and consequences of alcoholism. She insisted that NCA keep its eye on the ball and not be distracted from the issue of alcoholism. However, since the United Fund, which helped support many NCA affiliates at the local level, was pressuring those affiliates to include street-drug education, prevention, and treatment in their programs, she agreed the affiliates should comply with United Fund requests—but demand support for extra staff.

Marty knew she was entering a different phase of her life and had every reason to anticipate the well-earned satisfaction of seeing so many of her dreams start to come true. She had no intention, however, of relaxing her efforts on behalf of alcoholics. As she frequently noted, "This is not a one-shot deal. We have to push, push, push, and keep on pushing, to reduce the stigma, to give people the facts about alcoholism, and how to do something about it through prevention, intervention, and treatment."

She was also fully aware by this time that information alone was not enough. Just hearing did not lead to action. The only way to move attitudes into action was to reach people emotionally at a gut level.

Probably no one, however, could have predicted how personally traumatic these years of the 1970s would be for Marty.

The decade opened on a celebratory note with the publication of her new book, *Marty Mann Answers Your Questions about Drinking and Alcoholism.* Intended as a quick-reference companion to *New Primer on Alcoholism,* it was a response to the many repetitive queries she continually received. Like Marty's first book, this next one was practical, to the point, and even easier to refer to. She dedicated it to her three siblings, "Chris, Betty, and Bill Mann, with love." Now that the big legislative push was past in Washington, and she was semi-retired, Marty was looking forward to promoting the new book and thereby enhancing her educational efforts on behalf of alcoholics at the same time.

Marty's publishers, Holt, Rinehart and Winston, organized a three-month publicity and personal appearance tour, beginning in January 1970. Marty would integrate this schedule with her NCA speaking and consulting dates. On February 26, she was slated to be interviewed on the *Phil Donahue* TV show, at that time originating in Dayton, Ohio. She was also to appear on the *Allan Douglas* show and to autograph copies of *Marty Mann Answers Your Questions about Drinking and Alcoholism* at a book signing. As she usually did whenever possible, Marty arranged a brief visit with a family member, this time by stopping in Cleveland on the way to Dayton to see her sister Betty and husband, Tyler Miller.

The plane landed at Cleveland airport. Passengers deplaned by portable stairs to the tarmac, then walked to the terminal building. As Marty came down the steps, she caught her heel, fell—and fractured her left hip. Fortunately, the Millers were there to meet her and so took charge of the situation.

Marty was transported immediately to University Hospitals in Cleveland, where four pins were implanted in the hip. For the next three weeks, Marty was a patient there until she could be moved to New York City's Institute of Rehabilitation Medicine.

Marty later commented that if she'd been drunk, she wouldn't have hurt herself. "I would have been too relaxed!"

Meanwhile, back home in Easton, Priscilla had one of her car accidents as she pulled out from the house's driveway into the blind curve on Westport Road. Felicia was sure it was Priscilla's fault. Though Priscilla was physically unhurt, the Alzheimer's symptoms apparently became noticeably worse from then on. Nevertheless, Priscilla was able to make a quick trip to Cleveland to see Marty for a few days.

Marty's hospital roommate in Cleveland was a thirteen-year-old girl from Port Clinton, Ohio—Linda Fastzkie. Port Clinton was a small town on Lake Erie, about halfway between Toledo and Cleveland. Linda had been referred to Cleveland University Hospitals for major foot surgery.

Marty had a way of relating to people immediately, regardless of age or background, although she sometimes intimidated young people who didn't know her. In the late 1960s, for example, one of her then twelve-year-old nephews, Ted Mann (Bill's son), upon meeting her for the first time, found her "quite a forbidding figure." He didn't have any warm, fuzzy feelings toward his aunt. Another nephew, Tyler Miller (Betty's son), felt somewhat the same way when he first met Marty at the age of seven or so. Later, when he and his brother, Greg, were students at Harvard, they often visited her in both Easton and New York and found her a wonderfully worldly and wise woman, with a sense of humor about herself and everything else. As an adult, Tyler realized she probably wasn't used to seven-year-old nephews.

Young Tyler related to his aunt Priscilla more immediately, even though she lived in a rarefied world, to him, of art and literature. However, they shared an interest in popular music, a genre Marty didn't particularly appreciate. Also, Priscilla, who had a strong childlike streak in her sophisticated nature, was very indulgent around young children, related well to them, and was genuinely interested.

A third youngster was one of Felicia's grandsons, Joe Arnold. He saw a good deal of his grandmother as he was growing up and as a young man, and that meant he was around Marty and Priscilla occasionally, too. Joe is a well-known artist living in Laramie, Wyoming. Even as a child, the artist in him resonated with Priscilla. She would invite him out to the barn, which was her studio, and enthusiastically share whatever she was currently working on. One time it was a long calligraphic scroll she unrolled dramatically on the floor of the barn.

Linda, Marty's hospital roommate, was instantly charmed by Marty. In addition, they were united by their painful conditions. The teenager and Marty, fifty years her senior, obviously hit it off. The Fastzkies had probably never been around anyone like Marty—a cultured, funny, up-front, zestful woman whose personality would have lit up her surroundings despite pain and immobility.

Marty autographed Linda's cast, and so did Marty's visiting "cousin [Priscilla], . . . the art director of *Vogue* magazine."[1] Linda was impressed by meeting the many TV personalities who were frequent visitors to the hospital room. As always, Marty's concern was education to remove the stigma of alcoholism. She presented an autographed copy of her new book to the Fastzkies. It's a safe bet that Linda and the Fastzkies heard her story of "what it was like [before she got into trouble with drinking], what happened, and what it was like now." Marty, the consummate advocate, would never pass up even an informal chance to share with others what she knew about alcoholism.

Linda was discharged on crutches before Marty returned to New York. They corresponded for several months. Marty's warmth comes through clearly when she writes, "I envy your skill at using crutches. I am still struggling with them although I'm getting better. You're probably right—they are an awful nuisance, but I guess I'm stuck with them for several months at least, so I'd better get good on them."[2]

In the same letter, she wrote, "I'm very glad that you all liked the book and I hope your father has finished it by now." Marty didn't miss a trick!

Marty was discharged from Cleveland University Hospitals and returned to New York on March 18, where she was admitted to Dr. Howard Rusk's Institute of Rehabilitation Medicine. Marty had known Dr. Rusk for many years. He was on the NCA board from 1959 to 1966. There was no chance of returning home to her and Priscilla's fourth-floor walk-up apartment for the next few months. Marty's New York rehab physician, Dr. Chester A. Swinyard, arranged for a private room—essential because of

Marty's continuous stream of visitors and her need for a temporary office in which to conduct her ongoing work.

Dr. Swinyard added, "Dr. Rusk asked me to send you his best wishes and to assure you that you will be a very special patient here and be provided the very best that we have. Today's mail brought an invitation to attend the gala event in your honor on April first. It appears that every time I go out of town some important event is scheduled that I cannot attend. I think you will look very good on that dais in a wheelchair."[3]

The event to which Dr. Swinyard referred was NCA's annual meeting, at which Marty was to be honored as the sixth recipient of NCA's Gold Key Award. Marty had initiated this award to recognize outstanding persons in the field of alcoholism. Bill Wilson was the first recipient, in 1959. The annual meeting was only a little over two weeks away. Secretly, Marty was determined not only to attend, but to stand for the presentation and her acceptance speech, even if she had to be in a wheelchair the rest of the time.

Marty's most pressing immediate problem, however, was not rehab, but hair. Before leaving Cleveland, she sent an urgent note to her hairdressers, Enzo and Anne. How was Marty to get her hair done while she was undergoing rehab?

"Please give this some thought because I will be telephoning you as soon as I am settled in New York. Thank God I had that permanent before I left! It still looks bearable, but it badly needs doing by now. Please give my regards to everyone at the shop."

Once Marty was in residence at Rusk, the anticipated stream of visitors materialized. Bill Wilson was one who couldn't make it, however. He was debilitated with emphysema and had gone to Vermont for treatments by his brother-in-law, Leonard Strong, a well-known osteopath. Lois, in the meantime, visited Marty but couldn't come again after Bill returned home because he needed so much help. Marty, knowing she'd be well on the road to recovery by July, agreed to substitute as speaker for Bill at AA's thirty-fifth International Convention in Miami.

Another person who was unable to visit until several weeks later was Felicia. She was on an extended auto vacation that found her in Florida when Marty broke her hip. To Felicia's amazement, she happened to see Liz Peck one day when Felicia pulled into a parking lot in downtown Naples and parked next to Liz's VW bus. Liz had dropped out of sight before this.

Neither Marty nor Priscilla knew where she was. It turned out that Liz was retired and had been living with four cats and a dog named Skip in a little trailer at a mobile-home court in Bonita Springs since 1964. Like her sister, Priscilla, she cared passionately for animals. To supplement her small teacher's retirement income, Liz had a newspaper route that paid fairly well, but she certainly was far from well-off. On the other hand, she looked quite healthy.

Felicia was staying with a friend. They asked Liz to coffee, then to dinner. "Liz ate like she'd never seen food before. She said, 'I haven't been in a house for so long.'"[4]

Felicia had been Liz's AA sponsor when Liz was still in New York and had thus come to know her very well. Liz was never able to stay sober for long. She said she wasn't an alcoholic yet kept getting into trouble because of her drinking. Felicia felt for both her and Priscilla.

"Liz's had one hell of a time and worries Priscilla to death."

Some years before, Marty and Felicia had persuaded Liz to join them in taking nicotinamide. When Felicia asked Liz about nicotinamide this time, Liz "went into one of her violent speeches, so I dropped it."

Felicia concluded that Liz "certainly has a couple of buttons missing, and is unable to come clean and really *talk* and admit her drinking. The buttons she has are very bright ones, and she's wonderful company when we're out doing things. But her thinking is full of bad holes, anger, resentments, etc. Also, she's full of vitality—and at night when she comes for supper and *has* to best us at Scrabble or bust, it is wearing. She's a compulsive talker, but she can listen. . . . Liz, the small boy, with the soul of a small boy."[5]

As a good sponsor, albeit an ex, Felicia took Liz to an open AA meeting. Liz enjoyed it and even offered to help on a mission to help an alcoholic. Later they tried to phone both Marty and Priscilla but were unable to make contact.

Although Felicia loved the outdoors, she was definitely not the athletic type. Walking, bird-watching, and gardening were more her style. Liz, however, persuaded her to rent a bicycle, and the two of them spent days biking, bowling, swimming, and eating like horses. Over the next week or more, Felicia got a wonderful workout from a "great former athletics teacher." At the end of her stay, Felicia did the unthinkable—bought a bike and carted it home to New York. Liz had talked her into it.

Felicia reflected on the visit, saying, "Liz was wonderful and did me immeasurable good. With all that bicycling, I'm in great shape. . . . I *hope* I helped Liz. Dunno. Maybe our meeting was only to teach me to be patient. Liz can be extremely trying. Also likeable and charming. About 50–50. Very black and white."[6]

In talking with a New York friend, Felicia was surprised to hear that Marty was already using a walker. When the Rusk doctors learned of Marty's insistence that she stand unaided to receive the Gold Key Award and give her acceptance speech, they almost threw up their hands. They knew her broken hip couldn't possibly heal in time to permit her injured leg to be weight-bearing. But Marty wouldn't take no for an answer. She was like that train coming down the track. What the rehab staff agreed they would try to do was strengthen the other leg so that it could take all the stress and permit her to stand for a limited time.

Most people assumed Marty would be unable to attend the dinner and ceremony at all. Instead, she stunned and delighted everyone by appearing as scheduled. When she arrived, they all sang, "Hello, Marty" (written by Debbie Murphy) to the tune of "Hello, Dolly," and she cried. Edward L. Johnson, Firestone's employee assistance professional (EAP) manager, was at a table with Bill and Lois Wilson and others and later wrote down his recollections.

> The conversation was light and joyful as we were waiting for the doors to open for the banquet, when down the hall came Marty Mann in a wheelchair, and her entourage.
>
> The entourage stopped briefly at the our table. Amenities were exchanged, the look of mutual respect, the warmth of friendship that passed between these great ones was electric. Bill was already in very poor health—breathing was difficult, but for the moment color returned to his cheeks and the sparkle in his eye was more than evident.
>
> The doors to the banquet hall opened, Marty was wheeled to the dais and ate, while still in her wheelchair. In the rush I became separated from Bill and Lois by two tables.
>
> Dr. Luther Cloud, . . . president of NCA, acted as Master of Ceremonies that night. Finally, the moment came for the "Marty" bit. She was wheeled to the podium to receive her award—and she stood up.

Leading the ovation was Bill Wilson—first to stand, last to sit, giving credit.[7]

After dinner, Bill Wilson presented Marty with the Gold Key Award. She then delivered her acceptance speech, standing on her good leg for twenty minutes. It was the kind of dramatic tour de force typical of a very gutsy lady.

Two giants of the recovery movement were on stage that night—Marty and Bill. Especially in earlier days, both had been periodically resented for their public visibility, which went against the grain of anonymity as it was interpreted at the time. Marty once observed that "when you raise your head a little above the crowd, you're an irresistible target." Yet she and Bill had survived the criticism with dignity and persistence and between them turned a whole country around in its attitude toward alcoholism.

The occasion was a bittersweet one for all. People could see the frailty and sense the imminent loss of these two great leaders. Marty felt it, too. That evening she realized that her NCA baby had become more like a big business, not so much a cause. She knew there was no turning back, but the evolution felt a bit alien.

After all the excitement, it was back to Rusk for Marty. Weeks of further rehabilitation awaited. Every day she received therapy in the swimming pool. She would be strapped in a harness and lowered into the pool with a crane. Marty, still somewhat acrophobic, found the suspension frightening.

Lila Rosenblum, Marty's executive assistant in the early 1950s, was completing an internship in rehabilitation counseling at Rusk. (She later became a psychotherapist and a fellow of the American Institute of Psychotherapy and Psychoanalysis.) Lila visited Marty several times and found her touchingly more vulnerable and easier to talk to than in the past. Priscilla was around, and Lila saw her, too. Lila hadn't known Priscilla before but thought she was "very intelligent, stylish, devoted to Marty—and strange." Lila was somewhat puzzled by Priscilla's behavior, which was remote though friendly enough. She spoke rapidly in a rather affected way that seemed pressured and somehow almost hysterical. Lila had no clue about the developing Alzheimer's but later wondered if the odd speech pattern was a harbinger.

Priscilla worried obsessively about Marty's dying. When Felicia returned to New York from her extended vacation, she spent a fair amount of time reassuring Priscilla and calming her down. Felicia distracted her with funny stories about Liz instead and brought Marty and Priscilla up to date about her.

By July, Marty was pronounced ready to leave Rusk. Four months had passed since the accident. She had another four months of recuperation, which would be spent in Tucson. On her way there, she would swing through Miami to fulfill her promise to substitute for Bill Wilson as speaker at the AA International Conference. Bill made it to the meeting, but he was in a wheelchair most of the time and periodically on oxygen. It was his last major appearance. Six months later he would be gone.

Probably there wasn't an important spot in the country that Marty hadn't visited on her extensive travels over the years. Tucson was no exception. She had friends there already, and she'd loved the Southwest, dating from youthful days on the Manns' ranch in New Mexico. Four months of a scorching summer in Tucson wouldn't be everyone's cup of tea, but Marty fit right in with the Arizonans. She swam every day, went to an AA meeting every night, and made hordes of new friends. A special delight was experiencing the western style of AA meetings, where, when a person says, "My name is Marty and I'm an alcoholic," everybody hollers back, "Hi, Marty!" She liked it so much, she took the custom back to New York with her. She came home with a beautiful tan and feeling on top of the world.

Tom Carpenter, NCA president when Marty retired in 1968 and became founder-consultant, was correct when he predicted that Marty would be able to back off and stay out of the new executive director's way. But if Marty hadn't been incapacitated for these eight months in 1970, that healthy process may have taken a good deal longer. As it was, she was now able to cut her ties pretty well. People in AA would say that God was doing for her what she couldn't do for herself.

Sorrow and Serenity

1970—79

WHEN MARTY RETURNED TO NEW YORK, she eased back into her role as founder-consultant, coming into the city from Easton no more than a few hours once a week. Gradually, she was able to resume a travel schedule, though one more limited than in the past. Then, on January 24, 1971, came the inevitable news that Bill Wilson had finally died. All AA was in grief. Marty, who had been so close to Bill both as his pigeon and through their decades of mutual endeavors on behalf of AA, must have felt a special loss.

Felicia, Marty, and Priscilla were among the five hundred mourners at Bill's memorial service, conducted by Yev Gardner at St. John the Divine in New York City. Marty was one of the speakers, saying of Bill, "He was my inspiration, and not mine alone. He was one of the most gifted human beings who ever lived on this earth."[1] One AA man, a little loner whose life was AA, died at the service. "So appropriate," people said. Afterward, Marty and Priscilla had steak at Felicia's house; then they went to an AA meeting where Felicia was the speaker. It, too, was a memorial for Bill.

Bill's death was a harbinger of further stresses for Marty in 1971. At *Vogue,* heads would roll. The magazine was losing money. Diana Vreeland was abruptly fired. Alex Liberman, who was her adversary, and by extension, Priscilla's, returned to power with the hiring of a new editor with whom he could work well. Lacking Vreeland's protection, Priscilla's increasingly odd behavior and emotions could no longer be tolerated, no matter how much talent she had as art director. By December 1972, Priscilla had served *Vogue* with distinction for nearly twenty-five years. That month she turned sixty-five and could legitimately be terminated for retirement reasons.

Now that Priscilla was at home most of the time, Marty became acutely aware of the seriousness of Priscilla's condition. Ever the realist, Marty didn't blink at the facts. Priscilla's mental deterioration was obviously irreversible. Down the line they would need live-in help when Marty was away. Between them, however, the two women didn't have the resources to finance this extra expense.

The solution was fortuitous. Since 1969, Marty had been on the board of directors of Silver Hill Hospital, an exclusive private treatment center founded in 1931 in New Canaan, Connecticut, near Easton. Marty's interest in Silver Hill went back a long way. The hospital's founder, John A. P. Millet, M.D., had been on the staff of the Austen Riggs Foundation for the Study and Treatment of Neuroses, in Stockbridge, Massachusetts. In late 1937, Marty spent her last few weeks of drinking, or rather trying not to drink, with friends in Stockbridge. Austen Riggs was one of her treatment options, except she couldn't afford it.

In addition, Silver Hill resembled Blythewood, Marty's old treatment center, which no longer existed. They both started as psychiatric facilities, then expanded into treatment for alcoholism. Their informal yet upper-class country settings were similar. Their programs sought to be comprehensive, even to providing an on-site chapel to address spiritual needs.

Silver Hill's history had one further connection for Marty. Dr. Millet's original training was in TB clinics. Silver Hill was deliberately laid out to imitate the best of the open-air, cottage-style design in the housing and treatment of TB patients. Silver Hill would have felt much like Barlow Sanatorium from Marty's adolescent years as a TB patient.

In 1971, Marty became a part-time paid consultant at Silver Hill. Her duties included ongoing education of the staff, a one-hour weekly lecture on alcoholism for the patients, acting as liaison between Silver Hill and AA, and relating to selected patients on an informal basis. With increasing national competition among treatment centers that were coming on line during the 1970s thanks to the Hughes Act, Marty's presence on staff could help influence a patient's choice. Famous persons were attracted to such high-quality, comprehensive programs as those offered at Silver Hill. Marty personally knew many of these prominent potential patients, or they knew of her, so she was a magnet for selecting Silver Hill as their treatment center.

Marty's reputation for protecting the anonymity of such patients was flawless. She was no name-dropper. Regardless of background, all the patients loved Marty. She was a living example of recovery. If Marty could do it, there was hope for them, too.

Marty was in the right place at the right time for Silver Hill. Dr. James Katis was appointed clinical director in 1971. Until then, the hospital employed an old-fashioned medical model of treatment. Katis initiated a modern alcohol and drug treatment program. Some of the staff resisted. One of his innovations was immediately to hire an ex-patient as a counselor—a well-tried and successful approach for many years elsewhere. Marty backed Katis completely.

Katis said, "Marty had a wonderful open mind. She was just full of wisdom. She openly talked about psych medications at patients' meetings. She was very tactful in working with the staff and with difficult patients."

Marty and Katis lunched regularly. One day he was bemoaning a patient who kept relapsing. Silver Hill was failing the patient, etc., etc. Marty looked Katis straight in the eye and said sternly, "Jim, who do you think you are? Seven out of eight alcoholics never make it to sobriety." Marty's bracing reminder restored his perspective.

Marty's lectures at Silver Hill were taped, but many have been lost. They are an interesting adjunct to her more formal speeches. The Silver Hill talks are no less lucid or organized, but they have a degree of informality and camaraderie not possible when speaking before a public audience. Marty obviously knew the patients well, having sat in on many of their group sessions. It is in these tapes that we hear her skillfully guiding, teaching, and supporting men and women new to recovery, much as she had learned to do with countless alcoholics over the decades. And it is in these tapes that we often hear Marty's spontaneous sense of humor—and her wonderful, deep, infectious laugh and contagious giggle.[2]

One of the Silver Hill patients whom Marty would never have mentioned was the celebrated author Truman Capote, an old friend who had suffered from alcoholism all his adult life. Three of Capote's best-known books are *In Cold Blood, Breakfast at Tiffany's,* and *The Grass Harp.* Truman adapted the last successful novella into a play that soon folded. On the night that *The Grass Harp* expired in 1952, Marty and Jane Bowles (then in the middle of their love affair) joined Truman and a few of his stoic friends to commiserate "in the mortuary silence of the Ritz bar."[3]

Twenty-five years later, following a drunk-driving accident in 1976, Capote entered Silver Hill to dry out. The "cure" would not last. He was in and out of AA, and the following year, after yet another blackout, "decided to kick, once and for all, his dependence on drugs and alcohol"[4] by arranging to spend a month at the Smithers clinic in Manhattan. "The Devil's Island of alcoholism clinics, Truman termed it, and he seemed genuinely afraid that he might not survive the course."[5]

Dr. LeClair Bissell, the founding medical director of Smithers, was still in charge. Despite the fact that the Smithers regimen worked for Capote as long as he was an inpatient, he relapsed immediately on vodka when discharged. He was also very public about having been at Smithers, an announcement that annoyed LeClair because she wished her center to be known as successful in treating alcoholics. Ironically, Capote's celebrity status proved to be potent favorable publicity, attracting many alcoholics to Smithers in the same way patients would be drawn to the Betty Ford Center years later.

Today it is known that some people need months and months of inpatient care, especially if they have been addicted to other drugs in addition to alcohol. This extended care increases the odds of permanent recovery. Even so, there are always those for whom the disease proves virulently fatal.

The next year, 1978, Truman admitted himself to a treatment program in Minnesota, but again he drank as soon as he left. Addictive disease finally killed him six years later.

In addition to providing education and consultation for the staff and patients, Marty continued to be an eager student of new developments in the alcoholism and psychiatric fields. For example, her initial attitude at Silver Hill toward psychological testing was one of lifelong contempt, because she had seen these tests broadly misused in big corporations. What she observed at Silver Hill changed her mind about the validity of such testing when it was conducted by responsible professionals for a legitimate therapeutic purpose.

The results of Silver Hill's psychological testing and the personality-profile outcomes being reported in many scientific studies across the country confirmed Marty's belief that "there is no such thing as an alcoholic personality." Alcoholism could certainly affect personality adversely with irresponsible, dishonest, emotionally disruptive, neurotic, even temporarily psychotic behaviors, but once the alcohol was removed and recovery progressed, the individual personality of the alcoholic was usually indistin-guishable from the normal range of personality. There were exceptions, of course, in the case of alcoholics who were independently afflicted with some form of mental or emotional disorder, but their personality problems were related to the psychiatric issue, not the alcoholism.

A major psychiatric focus of alcoholism treatment centers like Silver Hill was to introduce their patients to the importance of behavioral change as essential for relapse prevention and a comfortable sobriety. Although AA is often singled out for its spiritual aspects, that organization has always strongly emphasized behavior modification. Marty explicitly taught that "many times, changed behavior leads to changed thoughts and feelings." Or as AA would say, "Bring the body, and the mind will follow." Or "Just act as if."

One of Marty's pet gripes was the term *flawed personality*. Instead, she recommended the less derogatory and more accurate statement, "People have flaws."

As of 2000, Silver Hill continues to flourish. Based on her years of visit-ing and observing treatment centers across the country and abroad and meeting with their staffs and patients, Marty strongly believed that those treatment centers with close ties to Alcoholics Anonymous, like Silver Hill, were most apt to survive.

The extra income from Silver Hill meant that Marty could hire daytime caregivers to keep an eye on Priscilla. At night, Marty took over. Physically, Priscilla was fine. But she was more and more forgetful, and she would wan-der. And when she wandered on her own, she spent money rashly. Another advantage to working at Silver Hill was that whenever Marty needed some psychiatric and counseling support for herself, it was available from the professional staff.

Upon the permanent move to Easton following her 1968–70 NCA retirement, Marty established residence in Connecticut and began to put down deeper community roots. She now had the time and the opportunity to rediscover AA by attending all the local meetings she wished. She loved starting over, as she called it. The AA fellowship grew even more precious to her. A Friday night meeting became her home group. From 1970 until she died in 1980, Marty was nearly always able to arrange her reduced travel schedule to be home in time for that meeting.

Around 1971, Marty had a startling encounter at an AA convention in Seattle. The local papers carried extensive publicity featuring her as a speaker. A young man active in Seattle theater recognized her name. During a break in rehearsals, he wandered over to the Colosseum and inquired of her whereabouts. He was directed to a group of people standing around a woman. He joined the group, listening to things being said that meant nothing to him at the time. After a while he introduced himself to Marty.

"I'm John Blakemore's son. My name is also John."

One can imagine Marty's shock. For once she didn't know what to say. Neither did John. Later he reflected that for him "it was like a need to touch into some mystery." Marty quickly recovered her wits and asked John to call her when she finished her commitments at the convention, but he never got around to it.

"So it was an unfulfilled opportunity and that was the first and last I saw of her."[6]

During the rest of the 1970s, John floundered around as an ACA (adult child of an alcoholic) "with no knowledge of how or why I behaved the way I did."[7] Then in the 1980s, he found himself on a spiritual path. Since 1989, he has worked as a drug and alcohol counselor in the United States and Australia.

Throughout Marty's life, interesting new people continually entered her orbit. Dr. Maxwell N. Weisman, a nonalcoholic psychiatrist, met Marty when he was invited to speak at an NCA national convention in Flint, Michigan. Max fell in love with her, in the sense of one soul meeting another. Her energy, charisma, and political smarts were magnets to him, as they were to so many others. He admired "the elegance, beautiful grooming, and utterly stylish clothes this tall, well-built woman always presented." That meeting was the beginning of a fruitful collaboration between Max and Marty that lasted ten years until her death.

Throughout the 1970s, Max joined Marty on her speaking circuit. On these lecture tours, he was the distinguished, credible voice of medicine describing the medical aspects of alcoholism, while Marty would make her NCA education pitch. So influenced was Weisman by the power of the Twelve Steps, he personally adopted their practice in his own life, saying they'd done more for him than years of intensive psychoanalysis.[8]

In 1968, Maryland passed an enlightened, comprehensive approach to treatment of addictive disease, the first in the nation. Max was named director of the new public health division. The law mandated a shift from the police and jails to public health. A public drunk picked up by the police was taken first to a designated hospital for evaluation. Brief hospitalization might follow. The next step for all was a halfway house for treatment. The length of stay depended on the needs of the patient, or client.

Long-term inpatient treatment for alcoholics scarcely existed in those days. Maryland desperately needed halfway houses. Kay Tanzola, a registered nurse, administered Maryland's new law in Harford County and thus worked for Max. Max and Kay founded a halfway house for men in Bel Air, Maryland. They christened it Mann House in honor of Marty.

Marty was very pleased but said with a chuckle, "I could understand asking to use my name if it were a halfway house for women. But I was surprised that they wanted to use my name in a halfway house for all men. I finally decided it was because my name is Mann."

Whenever Kay was in New York for the evening, she would stay the night at Marty and Priscilla's apartment. Other times, Kay attended parties or receptions with Marty. Once Kay asked Marty how she ever managed to stay so fresh in a reception line when she was greeting people. Marty answered that she focused on one person at a time "to save my sanity."

On occasion, Kay would be Marty's daytime chauffeur. At 3:00 in the afternoon, they stopped promptly for ice-cream sundaes to satisfy Marty's sweet tooth. (Others, like Riley Regan, a New Jersey pioneer in the alcoholism movement, were also familiar with Marty's passion for ice cream.)

As did Max, Kay admired Marty's finesse. Nor did Marty bear grudges. What you saw was what you got. "When you met Marty," said Kay, "you knew this was a person with great strength of character, interested in other people, and wanting to help people. She was a leader and you wanted to follow."

A third project that Max and Marty engaged in was starting the School of Alcohol Studies in Tucson. The two of them designed a one-week curriculum appropriate for the region. Native American spirituality and sweat lodges were included. Marty and Max lectured there the first three years. The police department, the schools, and the general public were so fired up that many Arizona communities began their own local programs and opened halfway houses.

Another influential person who came into Marty's life in the early 1970s was Paul Sherman. He was an example of many persons whom NCA supported who introduced alcoholism education and intervention into industry through employee assistance programs. A personnel executive at International Telephone and Telegraph (ITT), Paul was inspired by Marty's book *New Primer on Alcoholism* to find recovery. After a year's relapse, he stayed sober. At his urging, ITT initiated in 1972 a corporate assessment program for alcoholism. At that point, he contacted Marty for help.

From her earliest days, Marty had positioned NCA to promote alcohol education in business and industry, because that was where the greatest reservoir of alcoholics was located. Marty's rallying cry for industry was, "Save the man, save the investment!" At first, much of industry was upset by letters from NCA offering to help. However, persistent efforts by NCA, Yale, and a handful of physicians and personnel directors in industry slowly turned the tide. By 1959, NCA had funds to establish the agency's first Office of Industrial Services, headed by Lewis F. Presnall. NCA's most successful programs became their industrial ones, because those employees were highly motivated to recover in order to keep their jobs. (Marty quoted a 75 percent recovery rate.)

Brink Smithers was additionally involved in industrial responses to employee alcoholism. He independently supported a wide variety of management initiatives. His focus differed from NCA's in being more indirect, but his approach and Marty's were not in conflict. The Smithers Foundation sponsored a number of publications for use in industrial alcoholism education. Brink's influence and affluence also gave him entrée to many executives who could set policy in their organizations about alcoholism education. Presnall and NCA, on the other hand, specialized in direct on-site, hands-on training and consulting with supervisors, managers, and personnel staff.

So when Sherman appeared, Marty and NCA were ready for him. Even though Marty was a semiretired founder-consultant, she was still a powerful figure at NCA. She supported Sherman's efforts and mentored him as he built one of the most prominent programs in the United States to assist alcoholic employees. Ross Von Wiegand of NCA and Paul Sherman worked closely together.

Subsequently, Paul was active in ALMACA, the first professional organization for alcoholism counselors in business and industry. It is now called

Employee Assistance Professionals Association (EAPA), and its certified counselors are known as EAPs. In 1976, Paul became ALMACA's third president.

NCA's policy was to address only the issue of alcoholism among industrial employees, whereas the EAPA field believed a whole range of employee issues was grist for their mill—for instance, financial and marital or family problems, as well as alcohol and drugs. In the general alcoholism field, as distinct from EAPA, there was considerable concern during the early 1970s that alcoholism would be overlooked by the more inclusive EAPA approach. However, if EAP counselors did their job, they identified alcoholism in an employee years earlier than would most alcoholism programs, which tended to encounter middle- to later-stage alcoholics. On the other hand, by addressing all the employee's other problems, EAPs ran the risk of never reaching an alcoholism issue. Sherman pioneered a number of EAP approaches to ensure prompt identification of the alcoholic.

Marty was a person of vision who understood the value of an EAP. Nevertheless, while she supported the broader approach that worked for industry, she continued to recommend NCA's focus on alcoholism. When she spoke at the EAPA annual meeting in 1975, she endorsed EAPs but urged them not to overlook the alcoholic.

Toward the end of the decade, Paul Sherman left ITT and went into business for himself as an EAP consultant. Silver Hill became one of his clients.

By 1972, Marty's retirement, transition, and physical problems had settled down. She attended the thirtieth International Congress on Alcoholism and Drug Dependence, held in Amsterdam, the Netherlands, September 4 to 9. Marty presented a paper recounting the history of the alcoholism movement in the United States.[9] In this paper, she expressed her conviction that "the active partnership of the scientists and the alcoholics" was necessary for the advancement of knowledge on the one hand and the growth of recovery programs, specifically AA, on the other. She was proud that the catalyst in this inspired partnership of scientists and alcoholics was NCA.

Intensive efforts were made to change public attitudes—not only toward alcoholism, now described as a disease rather than a moral delinquency, but also toward alcoholics themselves. . . . The public began to see that alcoholics were useful and valuable people who had much to contribute to their society and their fellowman.

Over the next few years, Marty continued her national consulting and lecture tours but on a somewhat reduced schedule. George C. Dimas became executive director of NCA in 1972. This relieved a good deal of the tension surrounding Marty and her first successor, Bill Moore. Marty had known and worked with Dimas from the early 1950s, when he was first involved with the alcoholism movement in Oregon. Dimas understood that Marty needed to continue a relationship with NCA and was more hospitable toward her involvement. Marty told one friend that "George Dimas has been very good to me."

Until 1972, NCA's policy had been to promote funding from private sources solely, supplemented by occasional limited grants for seed money to start a variety of educational and consulting programs. Marty felt strongly about voluntarism and avoiding government bureaucracies in NCA's affairs. NCA was a private, not-for-profit educational agency. She distinguished NCA's educational mission, however, from society's need for treatment programs.

"What good is it," she continued to ask, "to educate the public to the need for treatment if there are no treatment facilities?" In her view, however, treatment programs were not the direct responsibility of NCA. That responsibility was a public one, because alcoholism was a public health issue. Therefore, Marty lobbied all her life for government support of treatment programs.

When Dimas took over, private financing of organizations such as NCA was drying up, partly because of double-digit inflation. However, the Hughes Act, for the first time in history, provided large sums of federal and matching state funds so that agencies and communities could begin providing treatment for the vast numbers of alcoholics. And not only treatment but also a comprehensive array of services—education, prevention, intervention, and so on. The NCA board was convinced that it needed to take advantage of this largesse. Although somewhat reluctant, Marty went along with the board's plans to apply for these moneys, in part because she had always been concerned about relying so heavily on one person, Brink Smithers, for financial support. Dimas was specifically engaged to secure federal funding, which he did with great success.

By 1975, NCA was managing several large federal contracts. Suddenly the agency had an enormous payroll and a huge office. Unfortunately, the congressional appropriations didn't last forever. By the end of the decade, government policy changed, and programs had to retrench. NCA fell on hard times. So did the hundreds of independent treatment facilities that had opened across the country. NCA cut its staff and moved to much smaller quarters. Burned by the experience of relying so heavily on government funding, the NCA board reaffirmed its original policy of accepting only private donations. However, as many community programs lost their funding, some of the local NCA affiliates started providing limited outpatient services of different kinds to continue alcoholism programs their communities found valuable.

George Marcelle joined NCA's staff in 1975, serving for fifteen years until 1990, first as a volunteer, then in a number of positions. His last several years were as public information officer, which included arranging the annual conference and overseeing NCA's publications operations. He asked Marty once what she did with all her anger.

"That's how I do this work," she answered. "That's how I get the energy for this."

George believed she was being quite literal, that she had found the means to divert a lot of anger that she had about her own experience as an alcoholic, about the treatment of all alcoholics, perhaps about her status as a woman and a lesbian, into doing the work she had chosen. He observed that it was a concrete example of what people in recovery can learn to do. Character defects don't disappear, but they can be constructively rechanneled. Marty was a master at that. Now that she was in her later years and suffering a series of physical, financial, and personal problems, she nonetheless managed to sublimate her frustrations by maintaining a rigorous outreach schedule that others would find daunting.

At the decade's midpoint, three events highlighted these tumultuous years for Marty. One was an honorary degree, doctor of humane letters, awarded to her on May 25, 1975, by Adelphi University (formerly Adelphi College) on Long Island. Adelphi was Priscilla's alma mater. Sadly, Priscilla was unable by this time to share in or appreciate fully the honor being accorded Marty.

The second significant event was the establishment of NCA's first official Office on Women. Jan Du Plain was named director. The slogan of the new office was "Alcoholism is a women's issue."

Marty, of course, had advocated for alcoholic women from the day she encountered AA through the manuscript of *Alcoholics Anonymous*. Early on, she acknowledged the special difficulties of women in overcoming stigma and seeking help for their disease. However, she was a good strategist and understood that focusing on women alone could easily undermine the total effort of educating the public and reducing stigma for everyone.

Influenced by the younger Susan B. Anthony, Jan Du Plain was a live wire in Marty's mold. With Dimas's enthusiastic backing and Marty's occasional coaching, Jan was off and running on several fronts. In 1975, all the literature coming out of the National Clearinghouse for Alcohol and Drug Information in Washington was devoted to the male alcoholic. All the federal and private research was on the male alcoholic. Jan and NCA advocated vigorously to include women in these arenas.

Jan immediately launched a program of outreach to Congress. Her initiatives produced the first national Congressional task force on women and alcoholism. This led to a reception for the alcoholism establishment, held in the U.S. Senate Caucus Room in honor of Susan B. Anthony's thirtieth sober anniversary and hosted jointly by NCA and the Senate Subcommittee on Alcoholism and Drug Abuse. The following month saw the first Congressional hearing on women and alcoholism.

As a result of massive press coverage of these Senate activities, Susan B. Anthony began an extensive, four-year lecture tour on behalf of women alcoholics that would carry her to forty-seven states and Africa. Many of the talks were before the great mainline women's organizations, finally fulfilling Marty's early dream that these women would grasp the importance of education about the disease concept of alcoholism, especially in relation to girls and women.

Jan started the first course at Rutgers on women and alcoholism and named it in honor of Marty Mann. As an active member of the National Organization of Women (NOW), Jan initiated a task force on women and addiction there.

Within a year, NCA's Office on Women sponsored the first Leadership Training Institute on Women and Alcoholism, held at American University in Washington, D.C. Thirty-five states were represented.

Jan turned her attention to AA itself. That membership was still dominated by older, conservative, white males. Jan set out to encourage more gender inclusiveness. She began the District of Columbia's first women's AA meeting so that women there would have a place to share their recovery with greater honesty and sense of safety than in the male-dominated AA meetings.[10] Some women's AA groups had formed during AA's earlier years, and many more sprang up across the country and are now a permanent fixture in the fellowship. Most women also attend mixed meetings.

At NCA's annual meeting in 1976 (held in Washington, D.C.), Jan unveiled her Office on Women with a series of workshops and prominent speakers. The agenda was to be comprehensive, including other drug addictions, for instance. However, Katherine Pike, a powerful, conservative board member and a member of Jan's planning committee, told Jan, "We don't want any feminists on the Women's program."

Jan, a feminist to her core, responded, "These women are leaders of women's organizations!" She had no intention of screening out any speakers who happened to be feminist.

The keynote speaker selected was Adela Rogers St. John, a best-selling author. Jan had never met her. The evening before the conference opened, Jan went to St. John's hotel room to greet her and finalize any last-minute details. To Jan's horror, St. John spent an hour berating alcoholics and alcoholism. Jan learned for the first time that the gist of St. John's keynote message was, "Nothing is worse than an alcoholic woman. Women should be at home taking care of their children."

This wasn't supposed to be the message of the conference! Frantic, Jan ran to Marty's room and cried, "What can I do?"

"Well, Jan," Marty calmly answered. "I could have told you about Adela's point of view. But this conference is bigger than just one person. It's fine. Relax."

The next day many of the women in the audience were upset with St. John—to say the least. Katherine Pike was in a front-row seat. She would never have denigrated women alcoholics as St. John did, or agreed with the thrust of the message, but she was reportedly relieved that the speech at least wasn't feminist. Marty continued to be a middle-of-the-road anchor between the liberal younger activists like Jan and the seasoned diplomatic conservatives like Katherine Pike.

The third event of that mid-decade was an original public relations tour de force—Operation Understanding. On May 8, 1976, NCA sponsored a

Washington, D.C., gala featuring fifty-two prominent persons publicly
identifying themselves as recovered alcoholics. They did not, however, mention any affiliation with AA. Nevertheless, it was clear to many in the audience that AA was the primary mode of recovery from alcoholism for the
majority.

The purpose of the gala was to help further reduce the stigma surrounding alcoholism. If these famous individuals could be alcoholics and get well
despite their fame and public image, then maybe ordinary folks could, too.
Debbie and Walter Murphy coordinated the affair.

The roll call of participants was a star-studded cast from all the major
walks of life, including Buzz Aldrin, Harold Hughes, Dana Andrews, Garry
Moore, Dick Van Dyke, Mercedes McCambridge, Wilbur Mills[11]—and of
course, Marty. One newspaper editorial stated that "it was probably the
most dramatic mass attack on alcoholism stigma that we have seen in this
country."[12] *Newsweek,* in its "Review of the Decade (1970–1980)," identified Operation Understanding as one of the most important news stories of
the last ten years.

On the morning of the event, a news conference was held at the Shoreham Hotel. Press turnout was massive. Each celebrity was identified in
alphabetical order. All was quiet. But when the emcee, Dr. Luther Cloud,
announced, "This is Marty Mann," all those celebrities rose to their feet
and applauded and cheered Marty. She sat there in a state of shock. She
couldn't believe the ovation was for her.

"Then," said Walter Murphy, "something happened I have never witnessed in all the years I've been involved in press conferences, dating back
to my days with Arthur Godfrey and other celebrated people. Members of
the press joined in the ovation! Many of these folks understood that *they*
were there and sober as a result of the job Marty had performed in the area
of public education."

Marty was a celebrity's celebrity.

Murphy reported, "Following the banquet that evening, many of the
celebrities gathered in Marty's room. She spoke of the early days of NCA
and AA. They were spellbound. Finally, Garry Moore said, 'Marty, you
must write a book.' Marty responded that she and NCA could not afford
such an undertaking. Garry said he would pay for the recording equipment,

secretarial help, etc. Others agreed to share the expenses with Garry. However, Marty never accepted their offer." [13]

The following year, a second, also successful Operation Understanding II took place in San Diego as part of NCA's next annual meeting.

Few people at these grand events had any idea of the growing sorrow and stress in Marty's personal life. Priscilla was steadily and inexorably getting worse. Living with a person afflicted with Alzheimer's requires phenomenal fortitude and strength of character. When that person is your beloved lifetime partner, the issues of loss and grief are enormous. Priscilla seemed half-dead already. There was a pervasive sense of mourning among the Manns and all Priscilla's friends for this wonderful woman who had had so much self-esteem and liveliness and who now bore a failing mind and warped spirit.

Priscilla's loving nature often turned to irrational hate. Felicia found the change hard to take. Priscilla's memory was declining, and she would repeat herself over and over. Then she would angrily refuse to accept help but get furious when she forgot something—and worse, turn on Marty or others. For no reason, Priscilla would take offense at the slightest thing and "move up the big guns." She would make cruel jibes about Marty's eating slowly, but Marty had no choice. Her jaws had been patched up from the drunken suicide jump in England decades earlier. Frequent visits to the dentist for maintenance and repairs had been necessary ever since.

Periodically, Felicia would have Marty and Priscilla over for a good dinner in order to "feed up Marty," who worried Felicia because she looked so old and ill and thin. Felicia tried to "buck Marty up" when she saw her, but "it shreds me. I treat [pray for] Marty every day." Felicia sometimes fretted that Marty's accumulating physical problems were getting beyond the power of prayer to intercede and heal. [14]

Regardless, life had to go on. In late 1977, Marty's speaking tour took her to Santa Barbara, California. Friends threw a surprise birthday party for her. She had a wonderful time. Then early in 1978, Marty fell again, this time while leaving her apartment. She had no idea how she got to the Biltmore Hotel, where she was attending a medical convention. Somehow she crawled into bed. A group of doctors, all personal friends, came up to see her. Fortunately, no bones were broken, but she was severely bruised. The doctors shipped her off to the hospital for several days. Her nephew Tyler

Miller, who was in school at Harvard, visited her. Apparently, Marty had had a small stroke. Afterward she was temporarily confined at home in Easton with a nurse—all this while carrying the main responsibility for Priscilla.

In addition, Marty's emphysema was growing worse. Her brother said that she kept an oxygen tank at home from then on, but others who knew Marty very well say they never saw any evidence of such a device, nor did they see her need for one. Perhaps the oxygen tank was just a one-time, temporary prescription. Or maybe Marty chose to conceal this evidence of further deterioration of her physical condition.

A few months later, Marty was back in circulation and attended a dinner party at Felicia's. Priscilla could no longer accept such invitations. Another guest gave Marty a ride and drove her back later. When Marty arrived home after 10:00, Priscilla had vanished. Around 9:00 that evening, she'd taken the car and disappeared. Priscilla's attendant had already notified the police. Marty called Felicia in a panic. Had Priscilla gone there? No. At 1:00 A.M., four hours after she disappeared, Priscilla turned up. She said, "I got lost."

It's a miracle Priscilla ever did find her way home in the dark. Much as Felicia loved Priscilla, she couldn't help thinking, "It's too Goddamn bad that she didn't have a fatal accident. I hope this episode won't keep Marty from going out on her own." Felicia talked to Marty the next day, and Marty sounded pretty good. She seemed to have bounced back from the scare. And apparently there was now sufficient cause for Priscilla's driver's license to be cancelled.[15]

After the experience with Priscilla's nighttime escapade, Marty made some changes to give herself more freedom. She engaged a regular practical nurse for Priscilla for the 3:00–11:00 P.M. shift. And she bought a new color TV for Priscilla, who began watching soap operas for the first time in her life. To keep herself on a reasonably even keel, Marty was consulting with Dr. Carlotta Schuster, a Silver Hill psychiatrist and head of the alcohol unit.

Marty believed in being part of the solution instead of the problem. It occurred to her that care partners of Alzheimer's patients could benefit from a self-help group modeled on AA and Al-Anon. One day over lunch, she discussed the idea with her old friend LeClair Bissell.

LeClair was "sorry to see Marty so distressed." However, she discouraged Marty because, as LeClair wrote, "I did not want to see her lost to alcoholism and did not see how she'd get very far with a disease I was being taught was hopeless."[16]

Several Alzheimer's groups were already springing up around the country, and in October 1979, Robert Butler, M.D., director of the National Institute on Aging, convened a national meeting including representatives from these groups. The meeting, held in Minneapolis, was to provide a national focus for research and treatment of Alzheimer's disease. Through her many connections in the federal government, Marty would certainly have kept abreast of these developments. And if her health had held out, she might have played a significant role at least as a consultant in setting public health policy and implementing the formation of volunteer community groups concerned with Alzheimer's disease.

Instead, Marty's physical problems were increasing. Her balance wasn't always reliable. Her back and both hips pained her. Impaired lung capacity from a lifetime of heavy smoking had caught up with her. Increasingly, she used a cane, or a wheelchair if she had to go any distance, as in a large auditorium. Ten years of antidepressants had produced unpleasant side effects of dry mouth and eyes. The tear ducts in Marty's eyes weren't working, so she needed to use drops to provide moisture and lubrication. Marty, Felicia, and their friends in Religious Science concentrated on prayer to heal, or at least ease, Marty's many ailments.

Kathy McCarthy came into Marty's life about this time in 1978. Kathy, a sociology professor at Southern Connecticut State University, was among those able to give Marty rides to medical appointments. Kathy herself had grown up in the alcoholism movement. Her father, Ray McCarthy, was one of the early luminaries. An educator and lay therapist who got sober outside of AA, he was among the first invited to join the staff of the Yale Center of Alcohol Studies, where he introduced the concept of group therapy to the Yale Plan Clinics. He was a prolific writer and outstanding teacher at the Yale school. In retrospect, the connection with Kathy made for a poignant closing of this circle for Marty—Ray at the beginning of her great adventure in alcoholism education, his daughter at the end.

In addition to doctors' appointments, Kathy also sometimes chauffeured Marty to AA meetings. If Priscilla came along, they had to watch her when the basket was passed to pay for refreshments and rent. Priscilla would happily assume the money was for her and take it all.

As the Alzheimer's progressed, Priscilla became something of a kleptomaniac in other ways. When she would visit friends, she might help herself to any book or object that interested her. Marty had to monitor her closely and was sometimes in the embarrassing position of having to return items that Priscilla had lifted from the homes of their hosts.

Like others close to Marty during the 1970s, Kathy was deeply touched by Marty's devotion to Priscilla. She witnessed scenes "with Marty skillfully carrying on both sides of a conversation in front of strangers so that Priscilla's handicap would not embarrass her [Priscilla]." Kathy also saw the anguish and depression the situation brought Marty, yet Marty coped fairly well by applying the AA maxim to "Live one day at a time."

$\mathcal{T}$ranscendence

1979–80

IN 1979, MARTY FOUND HERSELF IN THE MIDDLE of an intense battle within NCA. For many years the wine, beer, and hard liquor interests had been represented on the board in accordance with Marty's determination not to play favorites between the wets and the drys. Alcohol per se was not the problem, the disease of alcohol*ism* was. Each of the three alcohol business interests also had a seat on NCA's Public Policy Committee. Dr. Max Weisman was chair of this committee, and Katherine Pike was vice chair. Marty was an ex officio member. Tom and Katherine Pike had recently completed terms on the main NCA board, where Tom had been board chair. The Pikes were Marty's close personal friends and long-standing, powerful supporters of her and NCA.

Another key player in the 1979 crisis was Sheila Blume, M.D., the president of the American Medical Society on Alcoholism (AMSA). (Later, AMSA became the American Society of Addiction Medicine—ASAM.) Sheila was on both the NCA board and Public Policy Committee and in 1982 was named NCA's medical director.

The U.S. Senate was considering warning labels for alcohol beverages. The alcohol industry was violently opposed. Senator Donald W. Riegle Jr. had prepared a series of questions related to the advisability of warning labels, which Blume mailed to the one thousand members of AMSA. The physicians voted strongly in favor of warning labels, as did Dr. Blume.

The Public Policy Committee met in a long, narrow hotel room to debate the issue of warning labels and what NCA's stance should be. Thirty members were men, three were women. It was a brutal meeting, filled with tension and high emotion. Dr. Blume presented the results of her survey. The beverage interests spoke heatedly against warning labels. The Wine Institute representative, John DeLuca, delivered a long, impassioned speech stating, among other things, that wine drinking is a mark of civilization. One of the women, Wanda Frogg, represented Native American concerns. She reminded the group that alcohol had had a very destructive influence on some civilizations.

Marty listened to the heated discussion but didn't speak a word. Finally, Katherine Pike called on her to say something. Marty slowly but forcefully answered, "The goal of NCA is three things—Reduce stigma. Reduce stigma. Reduce stigma."

The group interpreted this statement to mean that labeling was none of NCA's business. Katherine called for a vote. The three women voted for NCA to support labeling. All the men voted against it. Katherine was furious. When Marty approached her after the meeting with a conciliatory gesture, Katherine angrily pushed her arm away. Both Pikes resigned their national positions with NCA. However, Katherine stressed that she would remain active in California's state and local NCA affiliates.[1]

There was a huge upheaval in NCA. Within a few years, the alcohol industry was ousted from representation in NCA.

Brink Smithers played an important financial and strategic role behind the scenes in revamping the board. The incident led to a reevaluation of NCA's role in prevention through public policy and the influence of the alcohol industry in setting that agenda. By 1982, two years after Marty's death, NCA adopted a major new prevention position statement, calling for increased taxes on alcoholic beverages, a minimum national alcoholic beverage purchase age of twenty-one, curbs on alcohol advertising, and health warning labels on alcoholic beverages. NCA also adopted an education position statement "which recommends nonuse of alcohol by teenagers and provides other guidelines on alcohol education in both public- and private-school programs."[2]

A more cheerful occasion for Marty concerned a woman who subsequently became well known in the field of alcoholism and codependency, Sharon Wegscheider-Cruse. In 1979, Sharon proposed to NCA that she present at NCA's annual conference a talk on her research concerning alcoholic families. The topic was then new and controversial. The board had scarcely heard of Sharon, so they invited her to first attend a board meeting (at her own expense) and describe her material in person. Sharon passed scrutiny and was duly scheduled to speak at the conference.

When Sharon arrived at the Shoreham Hotel in Washington, D.C., she found her assigned lecture room was in the basement of the hotel, behind the furnace. The space could accommodate twenty-five persons. A wrecking ball next door nearly drowned out her voice. The presentation would be piped outside if additional people showed up. And did they! The room overflowed and two hundred more jammed the hall, pouring up the stairway to the floor above. One person ran upstairs and hastily negotiated a larger room.

After they all trooped up to the next floor, Sharon began over. Suddenly there was a knock on the door, and in came Marty. "I want to meet you," she said. "This is what I started." Marty stayed to listen and learn. From then on she endorsed and encouraged Sharon at a critical point in Sharon's work.

It so happened that Sharon's future husband, Joseph R. Cruse, M.D., was on NCA's board and dating Sharon. Like many physicians on and off the board, he believed that NCA should be more involved in medical research. Gradually, Sharon and Marty convinced him that hands-on research was better left to research institutions. NCA's mission was education to reduce stigma so that the public would support the research.

At this same conference, Marty was thrilled to be honored with a Marty Mann Day, culminating in "An Evening with Marty." More than a thousand persons attended the gala. Debbie Murphy wrote, produced, and emceed a lively, hilarious revue, in which various NCA leaders played instruments and sang popular tunes with lyrics adapted to tell something about Marty.

Marty told the audience that at one time she felt she was losing her strength from illness and had been fearful it might not return.

> I was kind of scared. But, you know, after tonight, I'm not one bit scared. Because if you're all out there, all over the country and outside of it, and you feel the way about me you've expressed tonight, I can't do wrong.[3]

Felicia heard all about it the next week when she had Marty over for lunch. Marty didn't feel well and just picked at her food except for enjoying the homemade soup. Felicia thought her dear friend looked better and

stronger, though, until Marty sat with the light on her face. Then Felicia
saw "that fatal shadow on her cheek."[4]

A few months later, in October, Marty celebrated her seventy-fifth birthday. Felicia threw a memorable party for her. Many AA friends were there,
including Susan B. Anthony. Susan spent much of the evening trying to persuade Marty to dictate her own autobiography. Marty dodged and de-
murred. She simply wasn't interested. In fact, Marty had long before
concluded in consultation with Bill Wilson that she could not write her full
story because then she would have to break her anonymity at the level of
the public press. Instead, at the request of Syracuse University, she arranged
to leave her NCA papers to its new archival library in the hope and expectation that one day someone would undertake a full account of NCA's remarkable history and accomplishments.

In the meantime, Priscilla's care was becoming more and more expensive. Marty decided they would have to sell the large Jackson Pollock painting that had been hanging in the New York apartment for nearly thirty
years. By 1979, Pollock was renowned as a leader of abstract expressionism. The value of *Number 15, 1949* had appreciated manyfold and would
bring a high price. Greg Miller, Betty's son, happened to visit New York one
week and as usual stayed at Marty and Priscilla's apartment. Marty asked
him to be there in her absence when a potential buyer from Europe came to
view the painting.

The painting was privately sold in 1979, but Marty had no record of the
private buyer or the sale price in her papers. The present owner remains
anonymous.

Winter passed without further crises. Marty continued to work at Silver
Hill and to make limited trips representing and speaking for NCA.

Marty also stayed close to AA. The longer she was in AA, the more precious the fellowship became to her. In the spring of 1980, she had just finished telling her story to a New Haven, Connecticut, group when a woman
approached with tears in her eyes and asked Marty to autograph *New
Primer on Alcoholism*.

"I've been waiting for twenty years to meet you," the woman said.
"Twenty years ago I heard you speak on a New York radio program, and I
decided it was all right to go to AA for help."

That same spring, intense excitement was building in the AA community, nationally and around the world. The forty-fifth anniversary of the founding of AA would be celebrated in New Orleans in July 1980. These international AA conventions occur only every five years. Attendance at this one was about twenty-five thousand. For the first time, women alcoholics would be featured, and Marty would be a major speaker. Of course, who else!

Bob Pearson, then the executive director of AA's General Service Office, had plotted for months to have Marty address the convention, but she kept resisting, making one excuse after another, saying her health really militated against such a commitment. Finally, by anticipating and meeting all her objections, he convinced her to accept. Every step of the way, from leaving Easton to returning home, Marty was protected and surrounded with all the support she knew she needed—and probably some she hadn't even imagined.

On the appointed day, the great hall was packed with both women and men. Marty arrived in a wheelchair, visibly impatient as always to go faster, go this way, go that way. Anyone pushing her chair could feel the energy. The lack of mobility frustrated her enormously. The city was steamy and hot, and the air-conditioning set high. Marty got a chill. But she was so excited she could hardly bear it, as on the way to the podium she constantly stopped her chair to greet large numbers of individuals she personally knew and each of whose name and significance she remembered.

After the introduction, Marty walked slowly to the podium. A rousing, prolonged ovation shook the rafters. "Her spine straightened, that gleam came back in her eye, and she really gave them what-for."[5] When the noise finally died down, Marty looked out over the audience, paused, and said, her voice breaking, "Talk about tears—I can't tell you what it feels like to be a great-great-great-great-grandmother to so many women. Because that's what you are, all of you. You're my children, and I'm so, so proud of you." The hall erupted in a roar. The prolonged applause gave Marty a few moments to collect herself. Her voice steadied and she was able to continue with her speech.

Marty was well aware of the controversy over whether women alcoholics were different from male alcoholics. Based on all the information available at the time, she unequivocally believed there was no fundamental difference except that the stigma was far greater for women. The disease acted the same in either sex. It affected them the same way. It gave them the same kinds of problems. Marty obviously didn't want women to be spoiled or their recovery retarded by excessive coddling. Judging from the loud ovation when she stated her convictions, the majority of her audience agreed.

Had Marty lived to know the later research on women alcoholics, she might have tempered her belief somewhat, at least with regard to treatment options. Today, for example, women alcoholics in *early* recovery tend to benefit if they are in treatment programs for women only. There are several reasons, but two stand out. A women's recovery group removes them from their traditional social role of taking care of others, especially men, before themselves. Second, because a majority of alcoholic women have been sexually or physically abused, or both, by males during their lives and thus often feel unsafe around men, a women's group offers a haven until recovery has stabilized.

From the standpoint of content and organization, this talk was not one of Marty's best. She was all over the map with themes and topics, as if she wanted to get on the record everything that was close to her heart about AA and women alcoholics. From the standpoint of emotional punch, the speech has no peer. A heartfelt connection is clear on the tape and was universally sensed by those fortunate to have been in the hall that day. With tears in their eyes, most of those present figuratively embraced Marty as a warm, caring mother who had given them new life.

Not only did the women respond with overwhelming love and appreciation for the bond they had with Marty. All of AA also knew that though Marty was not a literal cofounder of AA, she categorically belonged with the cofounders, Bill Wilson and Bob Smith, because of her immense contributions to AA and the alcoholism movement. Indeed, she was affectionately known as the "first lady" and the "queen" of Alcoholics Anonymous. At this gathering, AA recognized, honored, and celebrated her unique accomplishments

After her speech, two middle-aged women waited patiently in a long line of admirers. When their turn finally came, they were nearly overcome with emotion. Themselves living variations of a story Marty had been told thousands of times, the two women declared, "[As teenagers years ago] we heard you [speak] in the headmistress' sitting room in boarding school. We didn't know you could be talking about us, but you told us that there were women alcoholics, too. Now we are also sober in the program."[6]

At the New Orleans convention, Marty was also one of three speakers in a scheduled AA meeting. One of her important points was that she considered AA's official membership figures for women to be way too low. These figures and other data are gathered from random surveys conducted periodically by AA. However, because of the anonymity issue, the figures are approximations at best. The 1998 survey states that women comprise about one-third the total membership. Even in her day, Marty believed 50 percent was closer to the truth.

Despite her age, Marty continued to be a model for young women coming into recovery. As Susan B. Anthony said, "She is what I hoped to be when I was young—a liberated woman. She became a crusader, reformer, educator, organizer, agitator, lobbyist, a truly great speaker, a lucid writer, a great 12th stepper."[7]

The entire conference was a heady occasion for Marty. People who were there said she was stupendous, radiant, and looked and sounded better than she had in years. They also saw her frailty. Everybody, probably including Marty, sensed this was the last hurrah for the remaining member of the great triumvirate of Alcoholics Anonymous and the alcoholism movement—Bill Wilson, Bob Smith, and Marty Mann.

In a way, the conference closed another circle for Marty. She had been in New Orleans many times over the years on behalf of NCA. The relationship with the local affiliate hadn't always been smooth. There were some notable fights. Now the city was actually hosting AA's International Convention, and she was the honored speaker.

Even more mind-boggling, who would have thought fifty-three years before, when two alcoholics—Marty Mann and John Blakemore—eloped in New Orleans, that her life would be crowned with such triumph in a return to the scene of that disaster? AA members say that they "keep going around the block until they get it right"—*it* being how to live life. Marty had gotten it exactly right.

Marty came home from New Orleans elated. She bubbled over to everyone, "full of the old fire and enthusiasm and excitement."[8] Two weeks after Marty's return, Jane, one of her pigeons, was to pick her up in the morning and take her to the eye doctor at Yale. The night before, Marty made herself a snack of sliced tomatoes and a cup of tea. While sitting at the table and pouring hot water into the teacup, she suffered a massive cerebral hemorrhage and fell unconscious facedown onto the table. Probably she never knew what hit her.

Priscilla slept through it. Even if she'd wakened, she wouldn't have had the wits to cope with the emergency. The housekeeper found Marty comatose but still alive the next morning. Marty was rushed to St. Vincent's Medical Center in Bridgeport, Connecticut, where she died later that night, July 22, 1980, at 11:25 P.M.

Beloved by many AA members is the little daily meditation book *Twenty-Four Hours a Day*.[9] The meditation on the day of Marty's stroke was "Faith can move mountains." On the day of her death, it was "Greater works than these shall ye do." Both passages express exactly what Marty's life was about.

Though the handwriting had been on the wall, all of NCA, AA, and their many friends throughout the world were stunned. Jane couldn't believe it. Marty "was just so vital that even though she was older there was certainly nothing wrong with her mind, it was just that her body, which had taken such a battering, was gradually weakening. After a time I thought, you know, that was a terrific way to go."[10]

Felicia helped out with the telephoning that usually follows a death in the family. She called Liz Peck in Florida. Fortunately, Liz was sober and was willing to sign whatever papers were necessary. However, Liz had what amounted to a phobia about illness and death and declined to come north for the funeral.[11]

Felicia believed that Marty was ready to die and was grateful that "dear Marty—my most wonderful friend and my sponsor" had gone fast and was "now in a world with old friends."[12]

The *New York Times* ran a major obituary. Because of her extraordinary national and international impact and reputation, Marty's death was widely reported throughout the country, from little towns in rural America to the principal metropolitan newspapers. In the U.S. Senate, a long tribute to Marty was read into the *Congressional Record*. So widespread was her fame that even a noted religious journal, *The Christian Century*, printed an obituary. Condolences poured in from everywhere, including overseas. Marty might have been astonished at the loss felt by the nation and the world.

According to her wishes, Marty was cremated. Her ashes were transferred to the Mann family plot at Rosehill Cemetery in Chicago. Memorial services took place in many NCA and AA communities, including a touching private one at Silver Hill. Two official services were held. One was at the Saugatuck Congregational Church in Westport, Connecticut (near Easton), the other at St. Bartholomew's Episcopal Church in New York City. At St. Bartholomew's, several hundred, including state and national leaders, attended. Yev Gardner was once more called on to deliver the eulogy for an AA pioneer. One can imagine his emotions as he spoke of his beloved friend and colleague. For the first time, most of those attending either service met all of Marty's siblings and their families.

At the Saugatuck church, Felicia hugged and kissed Priscilla. Priscilla stared blankly at her and said, "Bang! Bang! Bang!" It was almost more than Felicia could bear, losing her two dearest friends. At the same time, she was paradoxically overcome with gratitude. To Marty and Priscilla, she owed her life plus long stretches of happy living.

Felicia recalled how Marty was "gifted with inexhaustible patience and wisdom." She gave Felicia "well-seasoned advice from time to time, but never unless I ask her." Marty would say, "When you don't know what to do, don't do anything. Just don't drink, and go to meetings. *Keep* going to meetings."

After the Saugatuck service, close friends and family retired to the Easton house to unwind and reminisce. Ted Mann, once the young boy intimidated by his aunt Marty, was now in his middle twenties. He'd never met Priscilla nor had he been in any of Marty's and her homes. In addition, he was just coming to terms with his own gay orientation and had no idea about Marty. His first realization that Marty was a lesbian came at this moment in Easton. To him, the whole home spoke of a loving relationship between two women. He picked up on it immediately and regretted that he'd never had the chance as an adult to talk with Marty and get to know her. Priscilla touched his heart when she confided, "I'm really glad I don't know what's been going on."

Marty lived long enough to see her wildest dreams well on the way to realization. She'd worked extremely hard and consistently for those dreams. As a result, her inner self had been transformed, and the outer world forever changed with relation to alcoholics and alcoholism.

One time, Marty was especially discouraged and depressed about the future because there was little money coming into NCA and growth was slow. She happened to be sitting in a meeting next to the chaplain at Fort Ord, California. He was the chairman of the Commanders' Council on Alcoholism. Marty recalled that when she had finished crying on his shoulder, he said, "Marty, I want to share with you something I was told early in my ministry. Never measure your accomplishments by how near you are to your goal. Measure your accomplishments by how far you have come." At the end of her life, Marty had come a huge distance indeed—and brought the whole country with her.

Any person's life should be so blessed!

Afterward

1980—93

MARTY AND PRISCILLA HAD PREPARED SIMILAR WILLS. (Priscilla's was dated 1968, Marty's 1979.) All their property was held in common. A surviving partner would inherit in full. Charles F. "Charlie" Smithers Jr., of Paine-Webber, a cousin of Brink's, was named as executor of Marty's estate, and Marty the executor of Priscilla's estate, with Marty's brother, Bill, as the backup. Bill, however, designated Smithers to replace him.

Upon the death of both women, the estate would be divided equally between Mann and Peck heirs. These heirs were specified as Christy (Mann) Doyle and Liz Peck. Marty apparently felt that on her side of the family, Betty and Bill were already well off, and Chris was the sister who could use some financial help. On Priscilla's side, her sister, Liz, was her only immediate family.

Marty's will stipulated that Priscilla continue to live in their Easton home with round-the-clock care as long as it was feasible for her to remain there. Charlie Smithers, Marty's executor, was very concerned about where funds adequate to support Priscilla would come from now that Marty's income was gone, so he moved quickly to liquidate what he could and still let Priscilla stay at home.

The lease on the New York apartment was given up and the furnishings disposed of. Marty had maintained a wardrobe there, because she stayed overnight in Manhattan when traveling and consulting for NCA. Mysteriously, her valuable outfits all disappeared. Bill Mann heard there had been a robbery.

Over the years, Marty and Priscilla had collected several modern paintings when the artists were still almost unknown. Also, Priscilla had inherited from her mother a still life by James Peale, *Fruit in a Chinese Basket.* These had all appreciated considerably in value. Smithers was not an art connoisseur, however, and didn't realize at first that this art collection was significant. Marty and Priscilla had in addition collected a number of rare books.

When a friend saw the paintings, he exclaimed, "Charlie, these are valuable!"

Smithers arranged for Christie's, a major New York auction house, to pick up the paintings for safekeeping and clean and appraise them for future sale. Some were sold at a big Christie's auction of American paintings on April 24, 1981. The James Peale went for $308,000 ($523,600 in year 2000 dollars). Several days later, an Edvard Munch, *Gothic Girl,* in another auction sold for $100,000 ($170,000 in year 2000 dollars). After taxes and auction fees, the Christie sales brought approximately $400,000 ($680,000 in year 2000 dollars) into the estate. To the relief of Charlie Smithers and the Mann siblings, Priscilla could be supported comfortably for the rest of her life.

Eventually, Priscilla needed to be hospitalized. Her last few months were spent in Carolton Convalescent Hospital, Fairfield, Connecticut, where she died of ovarian cancer on November 9, 1982, two years after Marty. Bill Mann tried to arrange for her burial next to Marty in Chicago, but Rosehill Cemetery ruled that the family plot was reserved for members of the family only, and Priscilla didn't qualify. A year after Priscilla's death, Bill was finally able to have Priscilla's cremains spread on the waters off the shore of Connecticut. In late October 1983, this was at last accomplished.

When the estate was finally settled after Priscilla's death, including sale of the house and cars and liquidation of investments, Liz Peck and Chris (Mann) Doyle each received around half a million dollars. Marty and Priscilla definitely belonged in the category of property-rich and relatively cash-poor. Liz, who still lived on very limited means in a trailer park in Bonita Springs, Florida, was stunned at her inheritance. Her spartan lifestyle remained the same, but she indulged herself with a boat and a beautiful old classic car.

Liz lived to be eighty-three. She died in 1993 in an auto accident that she caused. Her vision was extremely poor, and she shouldn't have been driving at all. Liz willed the bulk of her money to three veterinary hospitals. Priscilla, the animal lover, would have approved.

Liz's trailer home and personal belongings went to her neighbor and close friend across the street, Kim Kimberling, who had independent means and didn't need Liz's money. Kim rented out Liz's trailer to seasonal tenants until selling it in 1998.

From Priscilla, Liz had inherited the income from Marty's books. Liz willed the rights to Kim.

Epilogue

A SURPRISING FACT ABOUT MARTY even to people who knew her well is how compartmentalized her life may seem to have been. She had several primary families with whom she related closely, yet there was little cross-over between some of these groups—her natal family, AA, NCA and associated professional communities, the gay and lesbian community, her lifelong friends, and her later church community.

Marty herself, however, was anything but compartmentalized. She was a magnificently whole and self-realized woman. She simply chose to keep some aspects of her private life private during her lifetime. Some of those close to her honored that decision decades after her death, even up to the present, especially with regard to her lesbianism.[1]

Recovered alcoholics and their families have cause to be profoundly grateful to Marty Mann. She was truly effective in achieving her goal of reducing the stigma of alcoholism and creating a more enlightened climate for the treatment and prevention of the disease. She was the first to carry the message to the world at large, men *and* women, that alcoholism is a disease and is treatable. Her pragmatic emphasis on education, prevention, intervention, and treatment supported by science has proved successful. At her death, Americans by and large endorsed her basic precepts:

> Alcoholism is a disease and the alcoholic is a sick person.
> The alcoholic can be helped and is worth helping.
> This is a public health problem and therefore a public responsibility.

Marty's accomplishments on behalf of alcoholics and the alcoholism movement are irrefutable. Thanks to her remorseless forty-year crusade, America is no longer uninformed about alcoholism. She was a mover and a shaker, a charismatic leader who commanded attention and who received loyalty and love in return. Her strong ego didn't shrink from praise, but she sincerely and humbly believed that she functioned only as an instrument of a Higher Power. She frequently said this was what gave her strength.

Marty once wrote, "It hasn't been easy. It isn't easy now. But we believe in the power of prayer at the National Council Office and it has often worked miracles for us. We believe that our work is guided—that God works in many ways to help His children, and that our work is one of those ways."[2]

Jim Marsh, Marty's Montemare teacher who wrote her in 1963, was prescient when he quoted Robert Louis Stevenson to her, "It is better to travel hopefully than to arrive." Through suffering and disaster, Marty found herself in a mission that transformed her. As Jim Marsh said, "I cannot think of anything more fortunate happening to anyone. It does not matter how we come to ourselves, but only that we do come to ourselves."[3]

A liberated woman from the day she fell on her knees at Blythewood Sanitarium and felt her shackles drop away, Marty Mann belongs in the magnificent line of America's social and spiritual crusaders and reformers. Her pioneer work stands as a permanent legacy "that ranks as one of the most important contributions in this century to medicine, public health, and the nation's welfare."[4] Without question, Marty was one of the greatest figures of her time.

Yet Marty never forgot whence she came. With immense gratitude, she honored her second chance. She saw her life from a spiritual perspective, stripped to its essentials of redemption and grace. Her own eloquent words speak for themselves.

> The greatest gift of sobriety is the power to believe . . . the ability to recognize our Creator, to find our place in the universe, to have some notion of why we are here, to find some way of doing the things we were put here to do. . . . Sometimes those who are the poorest, the saddest, the most kicked-around, the most unloved, the most neglected

and the most forgotten are precisely the ones through whom a great message may be given. And I'm not sure it's an accident that this kind of message was given to alcoholics—people who were in the worst fix a human being can be in—people who had absolutely nothing more to lose, nowhere further to go, who were almost the pariahs of our day. (We have been called moral lepers, you know, very often.) These were the people who received a message that said, "If you will believe and if you will follow out and act on your belief in loving others and in wanting to help others, you will be healed." This is not the first time that this message has been given to the world . . . but this time it has been given in a way that many can use. . . . And in this program, each of these people is a living instrument of a Divine Power.[5]

$\mathcal{N}otes$

Prologue

1. Grace Grether, "Mrs. Mann's Own Story Aids Alcohol Victims," *Salt Lake Tribune*, 3 November 1947, p. 14.

Introduction

1. All these women blazed new trails in health care and contributed to the reduction of stigma in their special arenas. Margaret Sanger (1883–1966) was a birth-control pioneer. Jane Addams (1860–1935) was a social worker and founder of settlement houses in Chicago. Dorothea Dix (1802–87) was an advocate for adequate institutional treatment of the mentally ill.

2. Recent reports confirm that alcohol remains high on the list of causes of death. One article states that alcohol contributes to 100,000 deaths annually, making it the third leading cause of preventable mortality in the United States, after tobacco and diet or activity patterns. J. McGinnis and W. Foege, "Actual Causes of Death in the United States," *Journal of the American Medical Association* 270, no. 18 (10 November 1993): 2208. Another source reports that from 1985 to 1992, the economic costs of alcoholism and alcohol-related problems rose 42 percent to $148 billion. Two-thirds of the costs related to lost productivity are due to either alcohol-related illness (45.7 percent) or premature death (21.2 percent). Most of the remaining costs were in the form of health-care expenditures to treat alcohol-use disorders and the medical consequences of alcohol consumption (12.7 percent), property and administrative costs of alcohol-related motor vehicle crashes (9.2 percent), and various additional costs of alcohol-related crime (8.6 percent). National Institutes of Health (NIH) news release, 13 May 1998.

Stephanie Brown, Ph.D., author, clinician, and researcher in the field of adult children of alcoholics, is among those who believe that the population of alcoholics is underestimated. Her estimate is based on extrapolation from the large numbers of adult children of alcoholics (ACAs). She believes that alcoholics comprise close to 20 percent of the drinking population, not 7 to 10 percent as commonly stated. That translates into sixteen alcoholics per hundred Americans, compared with the "official" estimate of six to eight per hundred. See Stephanie Brown, *Safe Passage: Recovery for Adult Children of Alcoholics* (New York: John Wiley and Sons, 1992), 7.

3. Marguerite T. Saunders, "Congratulations from . . . ," fiftieth anniversary pamphlet (New York: National Council on Alcoholism and Drug Dependence, 1994).

4. Susan B. Anthony, "Memorial Tribute to Marty Mann," *Alcoholism: The National Magazine,* November–December 1980, 18.

5. Michael J. Stoll, "Behavioral Dollars: Who Got What from Whom," *Behavioral Health Management* 19, no. 1 (January/February 1999): 8–9.

6. See the report by Dean R. Gerstein, Robert A. Johnson, Henrick J. Harwood, Douglas Fountain, Natalie Suter, and Kathryn Malloy, *Evaluating Recovery Services: The California Drug and Alcohol Treatment Assessment (CALDATA)* (Sacramento: California Department of Alcohol and Drug Programs, April 1994) and the more recent Drug Abuse Treatment Outcome Study (DATOS) reported in a special issue of *Psychology of Addictive Behaviors,* eds. D. Dwayne Simpson and Susan J. Curry, 11, no. 4 (December 1997): 211–337.

Chapter 1: Roots

1. *Commemorative Biographical Record of the West Shore of Green Bay, Wisconsin, Including the Counties of Brown, Oconto, Marinette and Florence* (Chicago: J. H. Beers and Co., 1896), 486. Also see George S. Mann, *Genealogy of the Descendants of Richard Man of Scituate, Mass.* (Boston: Press of David Clapp and Son, 1884).

2. Fletcher Harper Swift, *Dictionary of American Biography,* vol. 12, part 2 (New York: Charles Scribner's Sons, 1933), 243.

3. *History of Northern Wisconsin* (Chicago: Western Historical Company, 1881), 590.

4. Marty Mann attributed these words to her grandfather, Dr. Horace Edwin Mann, in a speech at the Second Southeast Conference on Alcohol and Drug Abuse (SECAD), 1 December 1977 (Atlanta: Jermac Recordings), audiocassette.

5. *The Marinette Centennial Book* (Marinette, Wis.: Marinette County Historical Society, 1987), 32.

6. *History of Northern Wisconsin,* 590.

7. Albert Nelson Marquis, ed., *The Book of Chicagoans, a Biographical Dictionary of Leading Living Men of the City of Chicago* (Chicago: A. N. Marquis and Company, 1911), 103.

8. A nanny for the little twins was Fräulein Schwartz, a German-American

woman who also taught them German. They loved her. Sometimes she invited the children to her German-style apartment for a special treat. Fräulein Schwartz was followed by a French nanny and later by another German one.

9. St. Simon's Church is now defunct.

Chapter 2: Chicago!

1. Carl Sandburg, opening lines from "Chicago," *Chicago Poems* (New York: Holt, Rinehart and Winston, 1916), copyright 1916 by Holt, Rinehart and Winston; copyright 1944 by Carl Sandburg.

2. Thomas G. Aylesworth and Virginia L. Aylesworth, *Chicago, the Glamour Years (1919–1941)* (New York: Gallery Books, 1986), 103.

3. Charles J. Rolo, "Salons and Saloons," *Town and Country* 100, no. 4291 (December 1946): 90.

4. They ran their respective papers with a high hand. The distressing story of Felicia's upbringing can be read in Ralph G. Martin's biography, *Cissy* (New York: Simon and Schuster, 1979).

5. *90th Anniversary Celebration,* pamphlet (Chicago: The Latin School, 1978), 19.

Chapter 3: Through the Wringer

1. W. Robert Finegan, *The Barlow Story: An Illustrated History of Barlow Respiratory Hospital, 1902–1922* (Los Angeles: Barlow Respiratory Hospital, 1992), 3.

2. Ibid.

3. Ibid., 18.

4. Dorothy White Nicolson, *Twenty Years of Medical Research* (New York: National Tuberculosis Association, 1943), 54–56.

5. With the disease of tuberculosis in abeyance, Barlow Sanatorium has evolved into the Barlow Respiratory Hospital. A teaching hospital affiliated with the University of Southern California School of Medicine, it specializes in all kinds of chronic respiratory diseases and in weaning patients from ventilators. The great majority of patients is nontubercular.

6. Finegan, *The Barlow Story,* 22–23.

7. Ibid., 11.

8. Ibid., 22.

9. Ibid., 68.

10. "Transcript of Keynote Address by Mrs. Marty Mann, executive director, National Council on Alcoholism, at 57th Annual Meeting, National Tuberculosis Association, Cincinnati, Ohio, 22 May 1961" (New York: The National Council on Alcoholism, no date), 6.

11. Ann Scheid, *Pasadena: Crown of the Valley* (Northridge, Calif.: Windsor Publications, 1986), 69.

12. Ibid.

Chapter 4: School Days, School Days

1. The site is now occupied by the First Presbyterian Church.

2. *Lake Placid Club* (Fulton, N.Y.: Morrell Press, n.d.).

3. Ibid.

4. Ibid.

5. Floyd Miller, "What the Alcoholic Owes to Marty Mann," *Reader's Digest* 82, no. 489 (January 1963): 173.

6. Mrs. Marty Mann Papers, Box 2, Personal Correspondence, 1961–1964, letter from James R. Marsh to Marty Mann, 25 July 1963, Syracuse University Library, Department of Special Collections.

7. Bourbon may have first been distilled in America around 1789 by two Baptist preachers in Kentucky. By 1794 distilled liquor, not just wine, was so entrenched in society that President Washington had to call out the militia to put down an insurrection of western Pennsylvania farmers who rebelled at a tax on distilled spirits (the Whiskey Rebellion).

Young America was vulnerable to alcohol abuse. Vast distances and poor transportation facilities favored the shipping of high-proof distilled liquor over bulkier wine or beer. The lack of good soil for viticulture was counterbalanced by great resources for cereal products, the basis of distilled liquor. Whiskey became the preferred drink. The "triangle trade"—African slaves for West Indies molasses for New England rum—combined with a gradual breakdown of Old World customs, thereby contributing to increased alcohol abuse.

By the mid-1800s, alcoholism was rampant. Annual per capita consumption had risen to 7.1 gallons of pure alcohol per person. See William L. White, *Slaying the Dragon: The History of Addiction Treatment and Recovery in America* (Bloomington, Ill.: Chestnut Health Systems, 1998), 4. Also, Sally Brown, "Marty Mann: Alcoholism Pioneer" (unpublished seminary paper, Pacific School of Religion, Berkeley, Calif., 1985), 7–8.

8. For more information about the chemistry of the brain and its role in addiction, see chapter 2 of *Uppers, Downers, All Arounders,* 3d ed., by Darryl S. Inaba, William E. Cohen, and Michael Holstein (Ashland, Ore.: CNS Publications, 1997).

9. Martha E. Kendall, *Susan B. Anthony: Voice for Women's Voting Rights* (Springfield, N.J.: Enslow Publishers, 1997), 47.

10. For a fuller discussion of the Washingtonian movement, see William L. White, *Slaying the Dragon: The History of Addiction Treatment and Recovery in America* (Bloomington, Ill.: Chestnut Health Systems, 1998), 8–14.

11. Robbie Sharpe has described what alcoholism and the WCTU were like in her natal family. One cannot imagine a greater difference from the Manns and the way Marty was socialized.

Robbie's great-grandfather died in the mid-1850s from trying to jump aboard a ferryboat as it was "pulling away from the pier. He fell between the pier and the boat and drowned because he was too drunk to swim." Her "great-grandmother had died earlier of pneumonia because she would stand out in the snow in her shawl looking for her husband when he was drinking and didn't come home when she expected him to."

One of this unfortunate couple's daughters, Kate, was Robbie's grandmother. An orphan, Kate was passed around from relative to relative, treated much like an indentured servant. "Kate knew," said Robbie, "that she was the victim of alcoholism [simply called 'drinking' in those days]," so as an adult Kate became a Methodist, joined the Women's Christian Temperance Union, and made sure "that no one in our family drank." As a result, Robbie "was born into a teetotaling family when my mother married a teetotaling Methodist minister." Robbie's mother signed pledges (of abstinence) for her family, including the children with one exception, Robbie. That was because Robbie was a girl. Only males were considered vulnerable to alcohol. Her brother Billy was very proud of his pledge card. Robbie says she was resentful for years because she wanted a pledge card too. The white pledge cards were about the size of a three-by-five-inch card and had a white ribbon. To Robbie, "teetotaling meant . . . that we didn't drink but we talked about alcohol a lot and noticed other people's drinking." Roberta Sharpe, "Way Back in Those Days" (unpublished seminary paper, Pacific School of Religion, Berkeley, Calif., 1998).

12. Marty Mann, "Can We Conquer Alcoholism?" *Health* (Mountain View, California) 14, no. 7 (July 1947): 12–13, 29–30.

13. Family denial is a defense mechanism developed by family members, friends, and colleagues of an active alcoholic. It takes many forms, among them denial that anything is wrong, denial that addiction is the root of the problem, denial that alcoholism is a disease and a chronic one at that, and denial that there is a solution.

Chapter 5: The Sleeping Lion Stirs

1. The term *sleeping lion* is sometimes used by recovered alcoholics to describe the chronic nature of the disease of alcoholism. Even when the disease is in remission through abstinence, it can still roar back into life if the alcoholic resumes drinking.

2. Thomas G. Aylesworth and Virginia L. Aylesworth, *Chicago, the Glamour Years (1919–1941)* (New York: Gallery Books, 1986), 21.

3. George Marcelle held most of the positions in NCA's national office. During his last several years there, he was the public information officer, oversaw the

publications operations, and also managed the National Alcoholism Forum, which was NCA's annual conference.

4. Aylesworth and Aylesworth, *Chicago, the Glamour Years,* 22.

5. Because of the stigma and denial still surrounding alcoholism, many alcoholics remain hidden or unidentified.

6. Several people have commented that Marty may also have been feeling some anxiety over awakening sexual confusion.

7. Hal Higdon, *The Crime of the Century: The Leopold and Loeb Case* (New York: G. Putnam's Sons, 1985), 33.

Chapter 6: *The Glory Years*

1. The society editor of the *Chicago Tribune* reported on Thursday, 24 December 1925, that one debutante ball was attended by three hundred guests and described it as follows:

> The crystal ballroom of the Blackstone took on yet another guise last night for the third debutante ball of the week, that given by Mr. and Mrs. Louis R. Curtis for their daughter, Miss Anna Louise Curtis. Where garlands of poinsettias hung for Joan Chalmers' ball on Monday night, and where bunches of balloons floated Tuesday evening for Miss Emily Otis' party, huge clusters of real red poinsettias and artificial silver ones studded the rail of the balcony around the room for the Curtis' affair.

The *Tribune* reported on Thursday, Christmas Eve, a dinner dance "at the Casino for a little more than a hundred of the debutantes and their crowd." Also, on Christmas Day:

> The cotillion at Miss Catherine Crerar's debut ball at the Blackstone tonight was to have been a surprise for the young guests, but word of it seeped through the ranks of the debutantes and they're looking forward to a lively time with favors 'n' everything. Mr. and Mrs. John Crerar are to receive with their daughter and Mrs. Timothy B. Blackstone, the bud's grandmother, will probably be present for the earlier part of the affair.

2. This marriage of Katharine Seaburn Williams to Theodore Simmons was her first. She later divorced him and married James B. Tremaine of Santa Barbara, Calif. The Tremaines were influential supporters of Marty and the NCA.

3. Marty Mann, "Alcoholics Anonymous Official Tells of Life Plagued by Liquor," *Times Herald* (Washington, D.C.), 22 May 1945, p. 17. This was the first of a three-article series by Marty Mann. The two other articles were "Mrs. Mann Tells of Cheap Bar Life," 23 May, pp. 17–18, and "Mrs. Mann Tells about Final Victory over Alcoholism," 24 May, p. 25.

4. "Benefit Aid," *Chicago Tribune,* 26 March 1926, p. 26.

Chapter 7: The Merry Marriage-Go-Round

1. "Miss Margaret Mann Elopes at New Orleans," *Chicago Tribune,* 15 March 1927, p. 31.

2. Newspapers in New Orleans ran stories of the elopement on 15 March 1927, as follows: "Blakemore Weds Chicago Society Girl in Gretna," *Times Pica-yune,* p. 2; "John Blakemore and Chicago Girl Wedded Secretly," *Morning Tribune,* p. 9; "Elope to Gretna," *New Orleans Item,* p. 4.

3. Garry Barker, "Enter a Force," *Sun* (Melbourne, Australia), 18 February 1961, p. 23.

4. A nonalcoholic wife tends to stay around longer with an alcoholic husband than the reverse—a nonalcoholic husband with an alcoholic wife. Another scenario is if the alcoholic recovers during the marriage. Divorce still may occur because the sober partner no longer finds the still-active alcoholic a suitable partner, or the alcoholic partner leaves because he or she has lost a drinking partner. Or the recovered partner realizes that he or she wed a person he or she hadn't really known and would not choose now.

5. *Margaret Mann Blakemore v. John Blakemore,* fourth judicial district court, San Miguel County, N. Mex., case no. 10420 (20 June 1928).

6. National Council on Alcoholism and Drug Dependence (NCADD) Archives, Iron Mountain (Port Ewen, N.Y.), Carton no. 5, Marty Mann Personal Letters.

Chapter 8: Rising and Falling Stars

1. Alvin H. Goldstein, "Now She Can Leave It Alone," *St. Louis Post-Dispatch,* 26 November 1944, sec. H, p. 3.

2. Floyd Miller, "What the Alcoholic Owes to Marty Mann," *Reader's Digest* 28, no. 489 (January 1963): 176.

3. Goldstein, "Now She Can Leave It Alone."

4. Petition for bankruptcy no. 42836, filed 7 October 1929, in U.S. District Court, Northern District of Illinois.

5. Exfoliated vermiculite became a very useful product, used as insulation and as an additive to concrete products. Gayle Benefield, personal communication, 24 May 2000.

Chapter 9: The Sleeping Lion Awakes

1. Alvin H. Goldstein, "Now She Can Leave It Alone," *St. Louis Post-Dispatch,* 26 November 1944, sec. H, p. 3.

2. Leon Edel, *Bloomsbury: A House of Lions* (New York: J. B. Lippincott Company, 1979), 11–12.

3. Kate Summerscale, *The Queen of Whale Cay* (New York: Penguin Putnam, 1998), 1.

4. NCA's records are incomplete. Also, Joe Carstairs may have required her contributions to be confidential.

5. Passing out and blacking out are different. "Passing out" is falling asleep under the sedative influence of excessive drinking. "Blacking out" is forgetting what happened in the previous hours or days (sometimes weeks), although during that time the person is conscious and appears to others as functional, oriented, and more or less rational.

6. A "geographic" is an alcoholic's or addict's move from one locality to another, often far away, in hopes that a new environment will relieve the addiction, eliminate the problematic consequences, or both. Relief may indeed occur for a while, but the addictive disease will reassert itself in most cases if there is no treatment.

7. Goldstein, "Now She Can Leave It Alone."

Chapter 10: *In the Fury of the Storm*

1. Many times in telling her story, Marty Mann said she fell from the first floor, but in England the first floor is what Americans call the second floor.

2. William Seabrook, *Asylum* (New York: Harcourt, Brace and Company, 1935).

Chapter 11: *The Lion Roars*

1. In 1934, John Blakemore married his second wife, Elizabeth Ann Tucker of New York. They were divorced a year later. Then on 1 January 1938, Blakemore wed his third and last wife, Louise Chaffee from Rhode Island. They had two children, a daughter, Bruce, and a son, John.

2. Application for Social Security account number 114-01-3397 (Form SS-5), 3 February 1937.

3. "Women Suffer Too," *Alcoholics Anonymous*, 3d ed. (New York: Alcoholics Anonymous World Services, 1976), 222.

4. The progress of the disease is divided roughly into three stages, which overlap: early, middle, and late. The low-bottom alcoholic belongs in the late stage. Marty summed up the late stage as one where the alcoholic "lives to drink and drinks to live." He or she cannot function without alcohol and is nearly always drunk, even though not appearing so. This is the world's picture of the alcoholic. For a further discussion of these stages, see *Marty Mann's New Primer on Alcoholism* (New York: Holt, Rinehart and Winston, 1950), 19–57.

5. National Council on Alcoholism and Drug Dependence (NCADD) Archives, Iron Mountain (Port Ewen, N.Y.), Carton no. 5, Marty Mann Personal Letters.

6. Francis Schiller, *Dictionary of American Biography*, supplement 5 (New York: Charles Scribner's Sons, 1977), 383.

7. Grace Grether, "Mrs. Mann's Own Story Aids Alcohol Victims," *Salt Lake Tribune*, 3 November 1947, p. 14.

Chapter 12: Rebirth

1. On several occasions, Marty refers to Blythewood's five hundred acres. The actual number was fifty to eighty-six.

2. During the 1930s and 1940s, affluent alcoholics were routinely admitted to private sanitaria and hospitals that specialized in psychiatric care. There was also a scattering of alcoholic treatment facilities, but they accepted paying patients almost entirely.

3. National Council on Alcoholism and Drug Dependence (NCADD) Archives, Iron Mountain (Port Ewen, N.Y.), Carton no. 5, Marty Mann Personal Letters.

4. Recovered alcoholics in AA have adopted this saying as a shorthand way of saying that the disease is chronic and the compulsion will be reactivated by ingestion of the drug alcohol. The compulsion may not return immediately, but within a short time the person's drinking will once more be as uncontrollable as before, if not worse.

5. That coffee will sober a person up is a popular myth. The only nonmedical intervention is actually time—time for the liver to oxidize the toxin. Normally that is one hour per three-quarters ounce of pure alcohol (three-quarters ounce equals one shot of hard liquor, one four-ounce glass of wine, or one twelve-ounce can of beer).

6. See "The Twelve Steps" on page 364.

7. Marty had met the term *alcoholic* in Willie Seabrook's book *Asylum* when she was in Scotland in 1936. However, his definition of recovery was not abstinence but being able to drink normally. By 1938 the terms *alcoholic* and *alcoholism* had already appeared in American articles in a few popular magazines and medical journals. A handful of academic authors had written books using the terms. Marty may or may not have been familiar with these resources. She was in the last stages of drinking and in no shape mentally or physically to be reading much of anything. The psychiatrists she consulted didn't seem to be informing her, either. Even if she had encountered the words *alcoholic* and *alcoholism* before Blythewood, the significance had obviously escaped her (or been denied) until she encountered *Alcoholics Anonymous.* It is a common human experience that when the student is ready, the teacher will appear. Marty's ears were finally open to the terminology and message of fellow alcoholics when she was at Blythewood. Dr. Foster Kennedy later recognized the importance to an alcoholic of hearing about his affliction from another alcoholic "who'd been there."

8. "Remittance man" is an English term for an undesirable younger son of a good family who has been sent abroad and paid a remittance to stay away.

9. Another reason for the connection with Chris may have been that Chris and Grennie Curtis, one of the patients, had already fallen in love and were behaving inappropriately, in the staff's judgment. If Chris were banned from Blythewood as a "bad influence," Marty may indeed have seen red yet blamed herself for introducing the two and even abetting the romance. (See chapter 13 for an account of Chris and Grennie.)

10. This sentence, "We cannot live with anger," does not appear in the multi-lith manuscript of *Alcoholics Anonymous.* The sentence closest to the one to which Marty referred says, "If we are to live, we must be free of anger." *Alcoholics Anonymous,* multilith edition (New York: Alcoholics Anonymous World Services, 1938), 63.

11. "Women Suffer Too," *Alcoholics Anonymous,* 3d ed. (New York: Alcoholics Anonymous World Services, 1976), 228.

12. NCADD Archives, Marty Mann Personal Letters.

Chapter 13: A Pioneer in the Making

1. "Women Suffer Too," *Alcoholics Anonymous,* 3d ed. (New York: Alcoholics Anonymous World Services, 1976), 228.

2. "For Men Only?" *AA Today: A Special Publication by the AA Grapevine Commemorating the 25th Anniversary of Alcoholics Anonymous* (New York: AA Grapevine, 1960), 33.

3. Robert Thomsen, *Bill W.* (New York: Harper and Row, 1975), 280.

4. Katherine McCarthy, "Memorial Tribute to Marty Mann," *Alcoholism: The National Magazine,* November–December 1980, 15.

5. Today an AA sponsor is nearly always someone of the same gender, who usually has more sobriety than the sponsee, or "pigeon." The reason for "same sex" is to eliminate the potential for a romantic attachment, which would interfere with a sponsor's objectivity and a sponsee's recovery. The sponsor functions as a "big sister/big brother" guide, coach, confidant, support, and friend. It is recommended that a sponsor have completed Steps Four and Five (personal-inventory Steps) to be free of "baggage" that might inhibit the growth of a sponsee. AA members are advised to choose sponsors whom they like and who "walk the talk"—people whose behavior and attitudes exemplify the Twelve Steps.

In Marty's early sobriety, of course, and for some years thereafter, a woman often had no other recovered woman around and so had to select a male sponsor. Grandfatherly older men were frequently chosen or might volunteer themselves, because they tended to be "safe." As time went on, Marty often sponsored men. A gay woman was not a romantic threat. The opposite also occurred, with a gay man sponsoring a straight woman.

6. Marty disagreed with the word *moral* in Step Four: "Made a searching and fearless moral inventory of ourselves." She preferred, "Made a searching and fearless inventory of ourselves—of our assets and liabilities."

7. "For Men Only?" 33.

8. "Bill's Story," *Alcoholics Anonymous,* 3d ed. (New York: Alcoholics Anonymous World Services, 1976), 13–14.

9. *'Pass It On,' The Story of Bill Wilson and How the A.A. Message Reached the World* (New York: Alcoholics Anonymous World Services, 1984), 213.

10. *Alcoholics Anonymous Comes of Age: A Brief History of A.A.* (New York: Alcoholics Anonymous World Services, 1957), 3.

11. Ibid., 3–4.

12. "Book Notices," *Journal of the American Medical Association* 113, no. 16 (14 October 1939): 1513.

13. *Digest of Proceedings at Dinner Given by Mr. John D. Rockefeller, Jr., in the Interest of Alcoholics Anonymous, at Union Club, New York City, February 8, 1940* (New York: Alcoholics Anonymous, 1941), 9.

14. National Council on Alcoholism and Drug Dependence (NCADD) Archives, Iron Mountain (Port Ewen, N.Y.), Carton no. 5, Marty Mann Personal Letters.

15. Marriage license no. 6352, Borough of Manhattan, New York, N.Y., 15 May 1940.

16. Stepping Stones was the first home Lois and Bill had to themselves after twenty-three years of marriage. A brochure by the Stepping Stones Foundation describes the place as follows:

> Lois and Bill kept hearing about a house that a friend of someone in AA wanted to sell them in Bedford Hills, about 40 miles north of New York City. But buying the property, especially in affluent Westchester County, was so out of their means, they dismissed it.
>
> But one March day in 1941, Bill and Lois were nearby and visited the site. They were immediately enchanted by what was, and continues to be, a very special place.
>
> "The interesting, brown-shingled, hip-roofed dwelling stood among trees on a hill overlooking a valley," Lois remembered. "We were charmed by its secluded location and wanted to see the interior. A window was unlocked and we clambered in. Bill was crazy about the large living room with its huge stone fireplace . . . which implied cheer and friendship and hominess." There also was a fireplace on the second floor which housed the master bedroom, and a long room flanked with shelves for them to place their considerable library.
>
> Bill was unemployed, and Lois provided only a small income as a store saleswoman. Buying a house seemed impossible. But they loved the house, and the owner wanted them to have it. A plan was devised to finance the $6,500 house and 1.7 acres of property at $40 a month with no down payment or interest for the first year. "Since the $20 a month storage charge on our furniture would be eliminated when we moved," Lois wrote, "we could easily raise another twenty," which they did through the generosity of a friend. Bill and Lois nicknamed the place "Bil-Lo's Break."

Not long after the Wilsons moved in, they changed the name to Stepping Stones, because the access from the original garage and driveway for many years was up rugged stone steps. Over the years Lois, who was shrewd about real estate, managed to buy up adjacent land as it became available. Bill, always handy with tools, built a comfortable one-room studio (with fireplace) called "Wit's End," where he did most of his writing, reading, and meditating. He also built the garage up by the house. He refused, however, to pave the long dirt driveway—said it brought happy memories of his Vermont boyhood. Soon after he died in 1971, Lois had it paved!

The downstairs at Stepping Stones has a large living room with a dining area, a small studio (which Bill used for his spiritual explorations, e.g., séances and Ouija board sessions—Lois called it the "spook room"), two bedrooms (each with a bath), a small kitchen/dinette, and a large outdoor porch. Upstairs were Bill and Lois's bedroom and bath and a long rectangular room with a fireplace, which is now a museum/gallery. Lois's sewing corner is also here.

The whole house is furnished with beautiful antiques, china, etc., that Lois inherited from her parents. It's maintained as a museum, exactly as Lois left it. She was a very organized woman—also a skilled interior decorator. She made the slipcovers, curtains, etc. After she became elderly and frail, Lois installed a little elevator so she could get to her bedroom on the second floor. She refused to use one of the pleasant downstairs bedrooms.

Today, volunteers conduct regular tours of Stepping Stones by appointment.

Chapter 14: The Learning Curve Steepens

1. See Step Twelve on page 364. AAs are "carrying the message" of recovery when they are asked to call on a still-suffering alcoholic.

2. Mary Baker Eddy was the founder of Christian Science.

3. Lyn Hartridge Harbaugh, "Sister Francis and the Ministry of the High Watch: From the Principles of New Thought to the Principles of Alcoholics Anonymous" (BA thesis, Smith College, April 1995).

4. Ibid., 8.

5. Lois Wilson, *Lois Remembers* (New York: Al-Anon Family Group Headquarters, 1994), 139.

6. Ty Miller's first wife, Kaye, not an alcoholic, started AA in Los Angeles. See *Alcoholics Anonymous Comes of Age: A Brief History of A.A.* (New York: Alcoholics Anonymous World Services, 1957), 91–92.

7. Alcoholics in the first year or so of recovery tend to be emotionally unstable, as long-repressed feelings begin to surface. Sex drives, as with adolescents, are often misinterpreted. In addition, alcoholics typically have poor relationship skills. When two newcomers start acting out these originally unruly feelings, someone usually gets hurt and may return to drinking or using. When an AA with some degree of sobriety participates in seducing a newcomer, that is rightly viewed as an unethical use

of power. For all these reasons, AAs are usually advised not to seek or take a new partner for the first year of their own recovery.

8. Sylvia Kaufman, "The Keys of the Kingdom," *Alcoholics Anonymous,* 3d ed. (New York: Alcoholics Anonymous World Services, 1976), 304–12.

9. Wilson, *Lois Remembers,* 123–24.

10. Katherine Caragol was one of Kennedy's medical students. She was twenty-three; he was fifty-six. It was the second marriage for both. The nuptials took place on 9 August 1940, at Pendleton Hill Baptist Church in North Stonington, Connecticut, Katherine's hometown. The hour, 9:30 P.M., was unusual but was perhaps dictated by the busy schedules of the bride and groom. Katherine's parents were divorced. Her mother was bitterly opposed to the match and was not invited to the wedding.

The best man was John Rae. Helen and John Rae lived in North Stonington and were dear friends of Katherine's father, Jo. The three arranged a small, private wedding. Marty may already have known the Raes, and it is probable she did know Jo Caragol and perhaps Katherine's mother also. The Kennedys' daughter, Hessie Kennedy Rubin, suggested that Marty and Jo may have been the Raes' houseguests the weekend of the wedding.

Hessie Kennedy Rubin, personal communication, 9 May 2000.

11. National Council on Alcoholism and Drug Dependence (NCADD) Archives, Iron Mountain (Port Ewen, N.Y.), Carton no. 5, Marty Mann Personal Letters.

Chapter 15: Priscilla

1. Carl W. Mitman, *Dictionary of American Biography,* vol. 7 (New York: Charles Scribner's Sons, 1934), 382–83.

2. Was Tracy Peck Jr. an alcoholic? Possibly, given his early death. Also, while his employment seems undemanding of his obvious intelligence, it could provide privacy for daytime drinking. Finally, Priscilla and Liz Peck probably inherited a genetic predisposition for addictive disease. Their father, Tracy, could have been the source. Even today, stigma prevents noting alcoholism as the primary cause of death on a person's death certificate.

3. Esther Newton, *Cherry Grove, Fire Island* (Boston: Beacon Press, 1993), 207.

4. The Third Tradition, see page 365.

5. LeClair Bissell, personal communication, 1998.

6. Dakin Williams and Shepherd Mead, *Tennessee Williams: An Intimate Biography* (New York: Arbor House, 1983), 300.

7. One of Priscilla's paintings has been located. It belonged to Felicia Magruder and was generously given to the authors by Felicia's grandson, Joe Arnold,

after Felicia's death. A thirteen-by-nineteen-inch watercolor, the painting features a lifeguard in a lighthearted beach scene.

8. Steven Naifeh and Gregory White Smith, *Jackson Pollock: An American Saga* (New York: Clarkson N. Potter; Distributed by Crown Publishers, 1989), 670.

9. Antabuse was discovered in Europe in 1946. Dr. Ruth Fox brought it to the United States in 1948, and the drug became widely available by prescription by 1950.

10. Mrs. Marty Mann Papers, Box 12, General Files, Address and Telephone Books, Syracuse University Library, Department of Special Collections.

11. Felicia, born Countess Felicia Gizycka in 1905, was the daughter of Count Josef Gizycki and Eleanor Medill Patterson. She married Drew Pearson in 1925 and divorced him three years later. She married Dudley de Lavigne in 1934, but the marriage lasted less than a year. In 1958, she married John Kennedy Magruder and divorced him in 1964. For most of her professional career, she went by the name Felicia Gizycka.

12. "Stars Don't Fall," *Alcoholics Anonymous,* 3d ed. (New York: Alcoholics Anonymous World Services, 1976), 413–14. The cousin to whom Felicia referred may have been Alicia Patterson, the daughter of publisher Joseph Medill Patterson. Marty's and Alicia's Chicago debuts were in the same 1925–26 season. Also, Alicia's first marriage was to Jim Simpson, the son of James Simpson Sr., the president of Marshall Field and Will Mann's friend and boss. Alicia and Jim were married in 1927 and divorced a year later.

13. Ibid., 414

14. Ibid., 415.

15. Felicia Gizycka, "To Those Who Didn't Make It," pp. 5–6, a loose manuscript in carton of Felicia Gizycka's 1950 journals. Courtesy of Joseph Arnold, Laramie, Wyo.

16. This is an Al-Anon principle that applies to a nonalcoholic's relationship with an alcoholic.

17. Gizycka, "Marty-Priscilla," a loose manuscript in carton of Felicia Gizycka's 1950 journals.

Chapter 16: Dawn of a Vision

1. See Tradition Eleven on page 365.

2. For a discussion of this meeting, see Bruce Holly Johnson, "The Alcoholism Movement in America" (Ph.D. dissertation, University of Illinois at Urbana-Champaign, 1973), 244–47.

3. Howard W. Haggard and E. M. Jellinek, *Alcohol Explored* (Garden City, N.Y.: Doubleday, Doran and Co., 1942), 175.

4. Jack Alexander, "Alcoholics Anonymous," *Saturday Evening Post,* 1 March 1941, 9–11, 89–90, 92.

5. The membership records of the National Association of Publicity Directors do not go back to the 1940s.

6. Dwight Anderson, "Alcohol and Public Opinion," *Quarterly Journal of Studies on Alcohol* 3, no. 3 (December 1942): 376–92.

7. Ibid., 393.

8. Based on a poem by Reinhold Niebuhr (1872–1971), an American theologian.

9. Dwight Anderson (with Page Cooper), *The Other Side of the Bottle* (New York: A. A. Wyn, 1950), 215.

10. It has recently been published in a third edition under the revised title *Understanding and Counseling Persons with Alcohol, Drug, and Behavior Addictions* (Nashville: Abingdon Press, 1998).

Chapter 17: The Entrepreneur

1. Mary Pickford and Dorothy Parker were both alcoholics who served on the advisory board of Marty Mann's organization. Scott Eyman's biography, *Mary Pickford: America's Sweetheart* (New York: Donald L. Fine, 1990), includes a 1955 quote by Mary Pickford in the opening to chapter 13: "I'm grateful that the world is beginning to look upon alcoholism as a disease." In a personal communication, Scott Eyman said that Mary Pickford could have dabbled in AA, but she kept it very quiet if she did so. All of her friends said she drank very openly and didn't seem in the least guilty or conflicted about it. She was insulated by her money and a nest of people who were afraid that confronting her would endanger their meal tickets.

2. Things really changed when Harold Hughes offered an amendment to the Selective Service Act requiring the military to offer treatment and rehabilitation to its alcoholics.

3. William E. Swegan, *The Life of an Air Force Sergeant and His Recovery from Alcoholism* (Sonoma, Calif.: self-published, no date), 61–62.

4. William L. White, personal communication, 28 December 1998.

5. Mrs. Marty Mann Papers, Box 1, Speaking Dates Records, 1947–1948, Syracuse University Library, Department of Special Collections.

6. *Santa Barbara News-Press*, 26 March 1949, D-10.

7. Dean R. Gerstein, Robert A. Johnson, Henrick J. Harwood, Douglas Fountain, Natalie Suter, and Kathryn Malloy, *Evaluating Recovery Services: The California Drug and Alcohol Treatment Assessment (CALDATA)* (Sacramento: California Department of Alcohol and Drug Programs, April 1994) and the more recent *Drug Abuse Treatment Outcome Study (DATOS)* reported in a special issue of

Psychology of Addictive Behaviors, eds. D. Dwayne Simpson and Susan J. Curry, 11, no. 4 (December 1997): 211–337.

8. Begun in Miami, Fla., in 1989, the purpose of drug courts is to offer the option of treatment to selected felons who have already been convicted and who have been identified as having problems resulting from alcohol and/or drug use. Excluded are candidates with a history of violence, sex crimes, or drug sales. The court-ordered treatment is closely supervised by a team that is knowledgeable about addictive disease. A judge heads the team, which includes a district attorney, public defender, probation officer, and appropriate counselor(s). Treatment is intensive and at least a year in length. AA is an important element of the treatment program.

9. "Problem Drinkers," *The March of Time,* 1946 by Time, Inc., videocassette. (Distributed by Turner Home Entertainment.)

10. John Keats, *You Might as Well Live: The Life and Times of Dorothy Parker* (New York: Simon and Schuster, 1970), 161.

Chapter 18: Rocking the Boat

1. Today the ratio of open to closed AA meetings has shifted in many areas so that most meetings are open and only a few are closed.

2. Yvelin Gardner, "Alcoholism—Out of the Shadows: A History of the Development of the Modern Approach to Alcoholism" (unpublished paper, no date), 68. Courtesy of George C. Dimas, Salt Lake City.

3. "Women Suffer Too," *Alcoholics Anonymous,* 3d ed. (New York: Alcoholics Anonymous World Services, 1976), 229.

4. National Council on Alcoholism and Drug Dependence (NCADD) Archives, Iron Mountain (Port Ewen, N.Y.), Carton no 1, "Bill at the Banquet," Yale University, 4 August 1948.

5. Ernest Kurtz, *Not-God: A History of Alcoholics Anonymous* (Center City, Minn.: Hazelden, 1979), 119.

6. Bill W., "Let's Be Friendly with Our Friends: Friends on the Alcoholism Front," *AA Grapevine* 14, no. 10 (March 1958): 8.

7. See the Twelve Steps and Twelve Traditions on pages 364 and 365.

8. A talk by Bill Wilson at the annual meeting of NCA, New York, 30 March 1956, audiocassette. Courtesy of Jim Blair, Montreal.

Chapter 19: Sowing the Future

1. Emma Bugbee, "Mrs. Marty Mann, Ex-Alcoholic, Explains How She Was Cured," *New York Herald Tribune,* 9 October 1944, p. 9.

2. John Blakemore (son of Marty Mann's ex-husband), personal communication, 30 April 2000.

3. About three years after Blakemore's death, his third wife's drinking got out

of control—similar to Marty's in 1937. Louise Blakemore finally drank herself to death of a cerebral hemorrhage in 1975. "What a terrible waste of two delightful, funny, talented, and much loved people," wrote Bruce Blakemore, John and Louise's daughter, in a letter to Sally Brown, 5 January 2000.

4. Bruce Blakemore, personal communication, 5 January 2000.

5. Ruth O., personal communication, 13 February 1998.

6. Ron Roizen, "The American Discovery of Alcoholism, 1933–1939" (Ph.D. dissertation, University of California, Berkeley, 1991).

7. William L. White, *Slaying the Dragon: The History of Addiction Treatment and Recovery in America* (Bloomington, Ill.: Chestnut Health Systems, 1998).

8. Some alcoholism appears to be induced by prolonged heavy drinking that seems to trigger a permanent change in the body's biochemistry. This may be what happens in that fraction of alcoholics who do not appear to have any familial history of the disease.

9. See *Alcoholics Anonymous*, 3d ed. (New York: Alcoholics Anonymous World Services, 1976), xxiv. The physiological basis of the disease of alcoholism is often genetic.

Chapter 20: Life Happens

1. Dodie Kazanjian and Calvin Tomkins, *Alex: The Life of Alexander Liberman* (New York: Alfred A. Knopf, 1993), 161–62.

2. Ibid., 162.

3. Ibid., 170.

4. Emma Bugbee, "Mrs. Marty Mann, Ex-Alcoholic, Explains How She Was Cured," *New York Herald Tribune*, 9 October 1944, p. 9.

5. National Council on Alcoholism and Drug Dependence (NCADD) Archives, Iron Mountain (Port Ewen, N.Y.), Carton no 1, transcript of remarks by Forbes Cheston, 15 July 1948.

6. Bill Mann, personal communication, 2 April 1998.

7. Mrs. Marty Mann Papers, Box 2, Personal Correspondence, 1949–1950, Syracuse University Library, Department of Special Collections.

8. Robert Foster Kennedy, "Discussion Before the Medical Society of the State of New York," *Alcoholics Anonymous Comes of Age: A Brief History of A.A.* (New York: Alcoholics Anonymous World Services, 1957), 320.

Chapter 21: Yale Files for Divorce

1. Mrs. Marty Mann Papers, Box 5, Severance of NCA and Yale, Minutes, 28 December 1949, Syracuse University Library, Department of Special Collections.

2. Ibid.

3. *Pioneers We Have Known in the Field of Alcoholism* (Mill Neck, N.Y.: Christopher D. Smithers Foundation, 1979), 16–17.

4. Alcoholics Anonymous, General Service Office, Archives, New York.

5. Mrs. Marty Mann Papers, Box 2, Personal Correspondence, 1949–1950, Letter from William G. Wilson, 6 July 1949.

6. Neither Haggard nor Bacon continued on NCEA's board of directors past 1949. Jellinek, too, resigned in 1949 but returned in 1951 for the first of two terms.

7. Mrs. Marty Mann Papers, Box 2, Personal Correspondence, 1949–1950, Letter to Franklin Huston, 8 December 1949.

Chapter 22: Unsettled Weather

1. Scott Eyman, author of *Mary Pickford: America's Sweetheart* (New York: Donald L. Fine, 1990), said in a personal communication that it is entirely possible that Mary Pickford could have been helping Marty and her organization out of memory of her sister Lottie, her brother Jack, or her mother—all of whom were heavy drinkers—without ever thinking of herself as an alcoholic.

2. Yvelin Gardner, "Alcoholism—Out of the Shadows: A History of the Development of the Modern Approach to Alcoholism" (unpublished paper, no date). Courtesy of George C. Dimas, Salt Lake City.

3. Mrs. Marty Mann Papers, Box 2, Personal Correspondence, 1951–1952, letter from Marty Mann to John Lamont, Syracuse University Library, Department of Special Collections.

4. At the age of twenty-two, Carson burst onto the literary scene with *The Heart Is a Lonely Hunter*. Before she was thirty, she had produced several other major works: *Reflections in a Golden Eye*, *The Member of the Wedding* (novel and play), and numerous short stories and articles. Despite increasingly severe handicaps from a series of strokes, she continued to write until she died in 1967 at the age of fifty; her works include *The Ballad of the Sad Café*, *The Square Root of Wonderful* (play), *Clock without Hands*, *Sweet as a Pickle* and *Clean as a Pig* (poems), and *The Mortgaged Heart*.

5. Mrs. Marty Mann Papers, Box 2, Personal Correspondence, Carson McCullers.

6. Virginia Spencer Carr, *The Lonely Hunter: A Biography of Carson McCullers* (New York: Doubleday and Company, 1975).

7. Virginia Carr interviewed Marty in her NCA office when Carr was writing *The Lonely Hunter*. They talked more about Reeves than Carson because of his extreme alcoholism. Marty asked Carr not to contact Priscilla. Virginia Carr, personal communication, 30 July 1998.

8. Carr, *The Lonely Hunter*, 361.

9. Jane Bowles suffered from writer's block. Several of her short stories were published, but only three longer works: *Two Serious Ladies*, a novel; *In the Summer House*, a play; *My Sister's Hand in Mine*, a collection of Jane's works. *Out in the World*, another novel, is incomplete and unpublished.

10. Truman Capote, *The Dogs Bark: Public People and Public Places* (New York: Random House, 1973), 381–82.

11. Ibid., 382, 384.

12. Ibid., 385.

13. Jane Bowles, *Out in the World: Selected Letters of Jane Bowles 1935–1970*, ed. Millicent Dillon (Santa Barbara, Calif.: Black Sparrow Press, 1985), 167.

14. Paul Bowles, personal communication, 29 May 1999.

15. Bowles, *Out in the World*, 166.

16. Ibid., 167–69.

17. Ibid., 181. Millicent Dillon spoke on the phone in 1977 with Marty when Dillon was writing *A Little Original Sin: The Life and Work of Jane Bowles*. Marty "had some reluctance about talking to me of her relationship to Jane Bowles. Naturally, I did not press her." Millicent Dillon, personal communication, 8 August 1998.

18. See Step Twelve on page 364.

19. Felicia Gizycka, *Journals,* 1950–1951, October 27. Courtesy of Joseph Arnold, Laramie, Wyo.

20. National Council on Alcoholism and Drug Dependence (NCADD) Archives, Iron Mountain (Port Ewen, N.Y.), Carton no. 10, Marty Mann, Religious Items.

21. Gizycka, *Journals,* 5 April 1957.

22. Ibid.

23. Ibid., August 1954.

24. Ibid.

25. Walter J. Murphy, "A Tribute to Mrs. Marty Mann" (speech delivered at the fiftieth anniversary celebration of NCADD, Washington, D.C., 28 October 1994). Courtesy of Walter J. Murphy, Vero Beach, Fla.

Chapter 23: The Sun Breaks Through

1. Neil Scott, "R. Brinkley Smithers: 35 Years of Leadership," *Alcoholism and Addiction* 9, no. 1 (October 1988): 17.

2. William L. White, *Slaying the Dragon: The History of Addiction Treatment and Recovery in America* (Bloomington, Ill.: Chestnut Health Systems, 1998), 190.

3. LeClair Bissell, personal communication with Sally Brown, 12 February 1999.

4. Walter J. Murphy, "A Tribute to Mrs. Marty Mann" (speech delivered at the fiftieth anniversary celebration of NCADD, Washington, D.C., 28 October 1994). Courtesy of Walter J. Murphy, Vero Beach, Fla.

5. Adele Smithers-Fornaci, personal communication with Sally Brown, 6 January 1999.

6. Ibid., 1 June 1998.

Chapter 24: The Clouds Lift

1. Jane, "Marty Mann," *Nice Girls Don't Drink: Stories of Recovery,* ed. Sarah Hafner (Westport, Conn.: Bergin and Garvey, 1992), 214.

2. Yvelin Gardner, "Memorial Tribute to Marty Mann" (eulogy delivered at a memorial service for Marty Mann, St. Bartholomew's Episcopal Church, New York City, 14 September 1980), *Alcoholism: The National Magazine,* November–December 1980, pp. 13–14.

3. Adele Smithers-Fornaci, personal communication, 11 January 1999.

4. Physicians with a specialty in addiction medicine are called addictionists.

5. The pioneering New York City Medical Society on Alcoholism was founded by Drs. Ruth Fox, Percy E. Ryberg, Stanley E. Gitlow, Harold W. Lovell, Frank A. Seixas, and James E. Shea.

6. "Resolved, That the American Medical Association identifies alcoholism as a complex disease and as such recognizes that the medical components are medicine's responsibility. Such recognition is not intended to relieve the alcoholic of moral and legal responsibility, as provided by law, for any acts committed when inebriated; nor does this recognition preclude civil arrest and imprisonment, as provided by law, for antisocial acts committed when inebriated." American Medical Association, *Proceedings of the House of Delegates,* Twenty-first Clinical Convention (Chicago: American Medical Association, 1967), 211.

7. This definition was approved by the board of directors of the National Council on Alcoholism and Drug Dependence on 3 February 1990 and by the board of directors of the American Society of Addiction Medicine on 25 February 1990.

8. American Medical Association, *Policy Compendium* (Chicago: American Medical Association, 1999), 226. Also "Role of Self-Help in Addiction Treatment," American Medical Association House of Delegates Resolution 713-A-98; adopted June 1998.

9. Mrs. Marty Mann Papers, Box 2, Personal Correspondence 1953–1957, Syracuse University Library, Department of Special Collections.

10. Marty Mann, "European Trip, April 26–June 2, 1956," Rockefeller Archive Center, Rockefeller Family Archives, Record Group 2-OMR, Welfare-General, Box 42, Folder 460, p. 2.

11. Ibid., 3.

12. William L. White, *Slaying the Dragon: The History of Addiction Treatment and Recovery in America* (Bloomington, Ill.: Chestnut Health Systems, 1998), 187.

13. Mrs. Marty Mann Papers, Box 2, Personal Correspondence, 1953–1957.

14. Although Lill, Marty and her siblings, and Lill's doctor all knew that metastatic cancer was killing her, cancer is not listed on Lill's death certificate as a primary or even a secondary cause of death. Stigma toward this disease still prevailed.

15. Walter J. Murphy, personal interview, 6 April 1998.

16. "Marty Mann Accomplished Understanding of Alcoholism," *Suburban and Wayne Times* (Pennsylvania), 31 January 1974, 8-B.

17. Mrs. Marty Mann Papers, Box 1, Marty Mann Files, Surgery, 1958.

Chapter 25: Leo Redux

1. Mrs. Marty Mann Papers, Box 2, Personal Correspondence, 1961–1964, Syracuse University Library, Department of Special Collections.

2. Dodie Kazanjian and Calvin Tomkins, *Alex: The Life of Alexander Liberman* (New York: Alfred A. Knopf, 1993), 238.

3. Ibid.

4. Ibid., 282.

5. Mrs. Marty Mann Papers, Box 12, General Files, Address and Telephone Books (28 June 1963).

6. Dr. Blackwell graduated at the head of her class of all men. She went on to found the New York Infirmary for Women and Children and had a role in the creation of its medical college. She then returned to her native England, helped found the National Health Society, and taught at the first college of medicine for women to be established there.

7. *The Elizabeth Blackwell Award* (official publication), Hobart and William Smith Colleges, 63, no. 3 (August 1963).

8. "Mrs. Marty Mann: Alcoholism Head at Pebble Beach," *Monterey Peninsula Herald* (Monterey, Calif.), 11 March 1964, p. 6. Also, letter of confirmation of the award from the American Psychiatric Association. National Council on Alcoholism and Drug Dependence (NCADD) Archives, Iron Mountain (Port Ewen, N.Y.), Carton no. 1, 25 May 1964.

9. E. M. Jellinek, *The Disease Concept of Alcoholism* (New Brunswick, N.J.: New College and University Press with Hillhouse Press, 1960), 10.

10. In the first two cases (Driver v. Hinnant and Easter v. District of Columbia), Joe Driver and DeWitt Easter were indigent public inebriates convicted for public intoxication. This was the standard approach in most U.S. communities. A U.S. court of appeals reversed both convictions, thereby setting a precedent that public intoxication was the involuntary result of chronic alcoholism and thus not criminal behavior (1966).

Leroy Powell was another indigent public inebriate. His conviction for public intoxication was appealed to the Supreme Court on the same grounds as Easter and Driver two years before—that public intoxication was the involuntary result of chronic alcoholism and thus not criminal behavior. The Supreme Court, however, by a one-vote margin decided against Powell, saying that involuntary behavior was not the issue (1968). The justices in fact feared that most communities lacked hospital facilities to treat inebriates diverted to them by the criminal justice system.

The NCA Washington affiliate and others believed the Supreme Court opinion would have gone the other way if the national NCA office had joined the case. However, the three decisions and the publicity surrounding them generated momentum for decriminalizing chronic alcoholism.

For a full treatment of this important development, see Bruce Holly Johnson, *The Alcoholism Movement in America* (Ph.D. dissertation, University of Illinois at Urbana-Champaign, 1973), 113–16.

11. "Transcript of Keynote Address by Mrs. Marty Mann, executive director, National Council on Alcoholism, at 57th Annual Meeting, National Tuberculosis Association, Cincinnati, Ohio, May 22, 1961" (New York: The National Council on Alcoholism, no date).

12. These are words Marty Mann heard from her grandfather. See note 4, chapter 1.

13. Sam Houston, the liberator of Texas from Mexico, was a chronic alcoholic. Marty reported that at one time Houston was hopelessly drunk among the Cherokees for many years. She said that he got sober when friends found him and told him there was a job only he could do—implying that a sense of mission accounted for his sobriety ever after.

The truth is that marriage to his adored second wife, Margaret Lea, in 1840, was what toned down his drinking. He tried hard to control his excesses for the rest of his life. In fact, he took the pledge and joined the Houston Sons of Temperance. However, he switched to a continual sipping of bitters (then 40 percent alcohol, about the same as whiskey), telling his wife that the old Texas recipe of bitters with orange peel was good for you.

14. At this late date, nearly forty years after the fact, the three reporters of Marty's relapse cannot pinpoint the year, except that it was in the early 1960s and possibly even 1959.

15. The young AA woman from Bronxville moved away, perhaps to Florida, within a year or two. Her name has been lost, but the event remains vivid in the memories of those Bronxville AAs who knew.

16. Mrs. Marty Mann Papers, Box 12, General Files, Address and Telephone Books, Warren Chemists prescription label for Antabuse, 13 October 1964, for Marty Mann, prescribed by Dr. Fox. The date on the label is not evidence of *when* Marty relapsed. The prescription may be a renewal of others written over the years for her. Nor is a prescription for Antabuse necessarily evidence of a person's having relapsed at all, nor even being in danger of relapsing. Some recovered alcoholics keep such a prescription on hand in case they ever need it. Others may have a supply of the medication already filled for the same reason. Given the reported accounts of Marty's relapse, however, and the date of this particular prescription, it can be assumed that Marty's was written for a reason.

17. The authors will always be grateful to Dr. Rosenblum. She knew Marty

well in both AA and the lesbian community. She was very helpful with her many recollections of Marty and with referrals to other resources. After an extended illness,
Dr. Rosenblum died on 19 January 2000.

18. Ernest Kurtz, personal communication, 11–12 June 1998. Also see Ernest
Kurtz, *Not-God: A History of Alcoholics Anonymous* (Center City, Minn.: Hazelden, 1979), 345. Marty was a minor character in Kurtz's history, being briefly important for his purposes because of her role in AA's anonymity developments of the
middle 1940s. Consequently, Kurtz had no reason to single out her sobriety for special discussion. His information is contained in an appendix: "Because of a later
'slip' by Marty, there was at the time of this research at least one woman claiming
longer continuous sobriety in A.A."

19. Mrs. Marty Mann Papers, Box 2, Personal Correspondence, 1951–1952.

20. Many helpful books and pamphlets on relapse are available. For a good
introduction, see Terence T. Gorski and Marlene Miller, *Staying Sober: A Guide for
Relapse Prevention* (Independence, Mo.: Independence Press, 1986).

21. Marty Mann, "10-Year Plan for NCA," 10 June 1965. Courtesy of the
Christopher D. Smithers Foundation, Mill Neck, N.Y.

22. Felicia Gizycka, *Journals*, 11 May 1969. Courtesy of Joseph Arnold, Laramie, Wyo.

23. Nancy Olson, personal communication, 13 August 1998.

Chapter 26: Letting Go

1. Mrs. Marty Mann Papers, Box 3, Field Memo 10, Lyndon B. Johnson letter
to Thomas Carpenter, 7 April 1967, Syracuse University Library, Department of
Special Collections.

2. The Houston NCA affiliate was established in 1946. Five years later, it was
discontinued due to lack of funds, then was resurrected in 1952 and has been a
strong, active center since. Frances A. Robertson was its founding executive director in 1952. She was a close friend of Marty's. For a history of the Houston affiliate, see James Gregory Goodwin, "The Origins, Development and Significance of
the Houston Council on Alcoholism and Drug Abuse (NCADA) of Houston,
Texas: The First Twenty-Five Years 1946–1971" (M.A. thesis, University of Houston, 1971).

3. Mrs. Marty Mann Papers, Box 12, General Files, Address and Telephone
Books, Warren Chemists prescription label for Elavil, 7 July 1969, for Marty Mann,
prescribed by Dr. Gitlow.

4. Felicia Gizycka, *Journals,* 1 October 1967. Courtesy of Joseph Arnold,
Laramie, Wyo. Also see Victoria Glendenning, *Elizabeth Bowen* (New York: Alfred A. Knopf, 1978), 236–38.

5. Virginia Spencer Carr, *The Lonely Hunter: A Biography of Carson
McCullers* (Garden City, N.Y.: Doubleday and Company, 1975), 355.

6. Gizycka, *Journals.*

7. NCA talk, Cincinnati, Ohio, 24 January 1968 (Chattanooga, Tenn.: Bill's Tapes), audiocassette.

8. The two classic books on intervention are Vernon E. Johnson, *I'll Quit Tomorrow* (San Francisco: Harper and Row, 1980), and *Training Families to Do an Intervention* (Minneapolis: Johnson Institute, 1996).

9. "Mrs. Marty Mann's Role as NCA Founder Consultant," *NCA Newsletter,* Spring 1968, p. 4 (Marty Mann letter to Thomas Carpenter, 20 January 1967).

10. Ibid., 5 (Thomas P. Carpenter letter to Marty Mann, 1 March 1967).

11. National Council on Alcoholism and Drug Dependence (NCADD) Archives, Iron Mountain (Port Ewen, N.Y.), Carton no. 10, R. Brinkley Smithers letter to Thomas P. Carpenter, 22 March 1967.

12. "Mrs. Marty Mann's Role as NCA Founder Consultant," p. 5 (NCA board action, 13 April 1967).

13. NCADD Archives, Carton no. 10, R. Brinkley Smithers letter to David Janavitz, 26 May 1967.

14. Ibid., final contract between Marty Mann as founder-consultant and NCA, 8 June 1967.

15. Ibid., memo from William W. Moore Jr. to Marty Mann, 10 May 1968, and memo from Thomas Carpenter, 10 June 1968.

16. Ibid., Tom Pike letter to William W. Moore Jr., 25 July 1969.

17. Nancy Olson, an unpublished history-in-progress of the Hughes Act (Comprehensive Alcohol Abuse and Alcoholism Prevention, Treatment, and Reha-bilitation Act of 1970), Senator Harold Hughes and others, Kingston, Pa., 1998.

18. William L. White, *Slaying the Dragon: The History of Addiction Treatment and Recovery in America* (Bloomington, Ill.: Chestnut Health Systems, 1998), 266.

19. The "Findings" section of the Senate-passed bill, which included a state-ment that alcoholism is a disease, was removed by the House committee before it re-ported the bill to the full House of Representatives. However, both the House and Senate committee reports on the legislation contained language declaring that alco-holism is a disease. These reports are an important part of the legislative history taken into account when legislation is implemented by the administrative branch of government. Nancy Olson, personal communication, 25 September 1999.

20. William L. White, personal communication, 14 May 2000.

Chapter 27: A New Path

1. *Cousin* or *friend* were the euphemisms used by gay men and lesbians to de-scribe their partners.

2. Mrs. Marty Mann Papers, Box 14, Miscellaneous, Letters re: Hip 1970, Syracuse University Library, Department of Special Collections.

3. Ibid.

4. Felicia Gizycka, *Journals*, March 1970. Courtesy of Joseph Arnold, Laramie, Wyo.

5. Ibid.

6. Ibid.

7. Letter from Edward L. Johnson to Mel Barger, 10 June 1981. Courtesy of Mel Barger, Toledo, Ohio.

Chapter 28: Sorrow and Serenity

1. Paul L. Montgomery, "500 Meet at St. John's to Mourn Loss of Bill W.," *New York Times*, 15 February 1971, p. 32.

2. See list of audiotapes on pages 359–61.

3. John Malcolm Brinnin, *Truman Capote: Dear Heart, Old Buddy* (New York: Delacorte Press/Seymour Lawrence, 1986), 82.

4. Gerald Clarke, *Capote: A Biography* (New York: Simon and Schuster, 1988), 504.

5. Ibid.

6. John Blakemore, personal communication, 29 January 2000.

7. Ibid.

8. Dr. Weisman was an important resource in the authors' research. They are very grateful to have met and known him. He died on 5 January 2000.

9. Marty Mann, "America's 150 Year War: Alcohol vs. Alcoholism" (typescript of a paper presented at the Thirtieth International Congress on Alcoholism and Drug Dependence, 4–9 September 1972, Amsterdam). Courtesy of Archer Tongue, Lausanne, Switzerland. A slight revision of this paper was published in *Alcohol Health and Research World*, Spring 1973, pp. 5–7.

10. One multifaceted topic that women seldom mention in mixed meetings relates to reproductive issues that affect a woman's recovery, such as PMS, menstruation, pregnancy, birth, children, menopause, and abortion to name a few. Women also tend to feel more secure in women's meetings in early sobriety, because a majority of alcoholic women have been sexually traumatized by men through incest as children or rape later on.

11. Buzz Aldrin was an astronaut, famous for walking on the moon with Neil Armstrong. Senator Harold Hughes was the author of the congressional bill establishing NIAAA. Wilbur Mills was chair of the powerful Ways and Means Committee of the House of Representatives. Andrews, Moore, Van Dyke, and McCambridge were all famous movie and TV actors.

12. National Council on Alcoholism, "40th Anniversary Commemorative Journal, 1944–1984," p. 19.

13. Walter Murphy, personal communication, 31 December 1998.

14. Felicia Gizycka, *Journals*, 24 July 1976. Courtesy of Joseph Arnold, Laramie, Wyo. Also see "Marty-Priscilla," a loose manuscript in carton of Felicia Gizycka's 1950 journals.

15. Ibid., 13 May 1978.

16. LeClair Bissell, personal communication, 2 September 2000.

Chapter 29: Transcendence

1. Jay Lewis, "Following the NCA Action on the Labeling Issue . . ," *The Alcoholism Report* 8, no. 4 (14 December 1979): 5–6.

2. National Council on Alcoholism, "40th Anniversary Commemorative Journal, 1944–1984," p. 21.

3. Nancy Olson, an unpublished history-in-progress of the Hughes Act (Comprehensive Alcohol Abuse and Alcoholism Prevention, Treatment, and Rehabilitation Act of 1970), Senator Harold Hughes and others, Kingston, Pa., 1998.

4. Felicia Gizycka, *Journals,* 18 May 1979. Courtesy of Joseph Arnold, Laramie, Wyo.

5. Ms. Pat W., personal communication, 24 August 1998.

6. Katherine McCarthy, "Memorial Tribute to Marty Mann," *Alcoholism: The National Magazine,* November–December 1980, p. 15.

7. Susan B. Anthony, "Memorial Tribune to Marty Mann," *Alcoholism: The National Magazine,* November–December 1980, p. 18.

8. Jane, "Marty Mann," *Nice Girls Don't Drink: Stories of Recovery,* ed. Sarah Hafner (Westport, Conn.: Bergin and Garvey, 1992), 229.

9. *Twenty-Four Hours a Day* (Center City, Minn.: Hazelden, 1954).

10. Jane, "Marty Mann," 229.

11. Kim Kimberling, Liz Peck's Florida neighbor and friend, said that Liz's phobia was so extreme that she refused to visit anyone who was ill, especially if the person was hospitalized. Liz would wait in the car while Kim went inside to visit.

12. Gizycka, *Journals,* 24 July 1980.

Epilogue

1. Marty gave a major portion of her papers to the Syracuse University Library, Department of Special Collections. Included were letters and other materials that specifically indicated her sexual orientation, to be available to historians after her death.

2. Marty Mann, "The Public Journal of the National Council on Alcoholism," *Alcoholism: The National Magazine,* November–December 1980, p. 63.

3. Mrs. Marty Mann Papers, Box 2, Personal Correspondence, 1961–1964, 25 July 1963, letter from James R. Marsh to Marty Mann, Syracuse University Library, Department of Special Collections.

4. "Memorial Tribute to Marty Mann," *Alcoholism: The National Magazine,* November–December 1980, p. 12.

5. Mann, "The Public Journal of the National Council on Alcoholism," 63.

Selected Bibliography

AA Grapevine, Inc. *Best of the Grapevine.* New York: AA Grapevine, Inc., 1985.
Al-Anon Family Group Headquarters, Inc. *First Steps: Al-Anon—35 Years of Beginnings.* New York: Al-Anon Family Group Headquarters, Inc., 1986.
———. *Lois Remembers.* New York: Al-Anon Family Group Headquarters, Inc., 1987.
Alcoholics Anonymous World Services, Inc. *Alcoholics Anonymous Comes of Age.* New York: Alcoholics Anonymous World Services, Inc., 1957.
———. *Alcoholics Anonymous.* 3d ed. New York: Alcoholics Anonymous World Services, Inc., 1976.
———. *As Bill Sees It.* New York: Alcoholics Anonymous World Services, Inc., 1967.
———. *Dr. Bob and the Good Oldtimers.* New York: Alcoholics Anonymous World Services, Inc., 1980.
———. *'Pass It On': The Story of Bill Wilson and How the A.A. Message Reached the World.* New York: Alcoholics Anonymous World Services, Inc., 1984.
———. *Twelve Steps and Twelve Traditions.* New York: Alcoholics Anonymous World Services, Inc., 1952.
The American Historical Society, Inc. *American Biography: A New Cyclopedia.* New York: The American Historical Society, Inc., 1923.
Anderson, Dwight. "Alcohol and Public Opinion." *Quarterly Journal of Studies on Alcoholism* 3, no. 3 (December 1942): 376–92.
Anderson, Dwight, with Page Cooper. *The Other Side of the Bottle.* New York: A. A. Wyn, Inc., 1950.
Andrews, Deborah, ed. *The Annual Obituary 1989.* Chicago: St. James Press, 1990.
Aylesworth, Thomas G., and Virginia L. Aylesworth. *Chicago, the Glamour Years (1919–1941).* New York: Gallery Books, 1986.

B., Dick. *Hope!: The Story of Geraldine D., Alina Lodge and Recovery.* Kihei,
    Hawaii: Tincture of Time Press, 1997.
B., Sally, and David B. *Our Children Are Alcoholics: Coping with Children Who
    Have Addictions.* Dubuque, Iowa: Islewest, 1997.
Bell, Anne Olivier, ed. *The Diary of Virginia Woolf, Vol. 5. 1936–1941.* New York:
    Harcourt Brace Jovanovich, 1984.
Bell, R. Gordon. *A Special Calling.* Toronto, Canada: Stoddart, 1989.
Bordin, Ruth. *Woman and Temperance.* Philadelphia: Temple University Press, 1981.
Brinnin, John Malcolm. *Truman Capote: Dear Heart, Old Buddy.* New York:
    Delacorte Press/Seymour Lawrence, 1986.
Brown, Sally. "Marty Mann, Alcoholism Pioneer." Unpublished seminary paper,
    Pacific School of Religion, Berkeley, Calif., 1985.
Brown, Stephanie. *Safe Passage: Recovery for Adult Children of Alcoholics.* New
    York: John Wiley and Sons, Inc., 1992.
Capote, Truman. *The Dogs Bark: Public People and Private Places.* New York:
    Random House, 1973.
Carr, Virginia Spencer. *The Lonely Hunter: A Biography of Carson McCullers.*
    New York: Doubleday and Co., 1975.
Christopher D. Smithers Foundation. *Pioneers We Have Known in the Field of
    Alcoholism.* Mill Neck, N.Y.: Christopher D. Smithers Foundation, 1979.
Clarke, Gerald. *Capote: A Biography.* New York, Simon and Schuster, 1988.
Clinebell, Howard. *Understanding and Counseling Persons with Alcohol, Drug,
    and Behavioral Addictions.* 3d ed. Nashville, Tenn.: Abingdon Press, 1998.
Colvin, David L. *Prohibition in the United States.* New York: Geo. H. Doran Co.,
    1926.
Conley, Paul C., and Andrew A. Sorensen. *The Staggering Steeple.* Philadelphia:
    Pilgrim Press, 1971.
Dillon, Millicent. *Out in the World: Selected Letters of Jane Bowles 1935–1970.*
    Santa Barbara, Calif.: Black Sparrow Press, 1991.
Edel, Leon. *Bloomsbury: A House of Lions.* New York: J. B. Lippincott Co., 1979.
Eyman, Scott. *Mary Pickford: America's Sweetheart.* New York: Donald L. Fine,
    Inc., 1990.
Faderman, Lillian. *Odd Girls and Twilight Lovers.* New York: Columbia
    University Press, 1991.
———. *To Believe in Women.* Boston: Houghton Mifflin, 1999.
Finegan, W. Robert. *The Barlow Story: An Illustrated History of Barlow
    Respiratory Hospital.* Los Angeles: Barlow Respiratory Hospital, 1992.
Gardner, Yvelin. "Alcoholism—Out of the Shadows: A History of the Development
    of the Modern Approach to Alcoholism." Unpublished paper, in the possession
    of George C. Dimas, Salt Lake City, Utah, n.d.

Gerstein, Dean R., Robert A. Johnson, Henrick J. Harwood, Douglas Fountain, Natalie Suter, and Kathryn Malloy. *Evaluating Recovery Services: The California Drug and Alcohol Treatment Assessment (CALDATA).* Sacramento: California Department of Alcohol and Drug Programs, 1994.

Gizycka, Felicia. Unpublished journals, 1950–1991.

Glendinning, Victoria. *Elizabeth Bowen.* New York: Alfred A. Knopf, 1978.

Gorski, Terence T., and Merlene Miller. *Staying Sober: A Guide for Relapse Prevention.* Independence, Mo.: Independence Press, 1986.

Hafner, Sarah, ed. *Nice Girls Don't Drink: Stories of Recovery.* Westport, Conn.: Bergin and Garvey, 1992.

Haggard, Howard, and E. M. Jellinek. *Alcohol Explored.* Garden City, N.Y.: Doubleday, Doran, 1942.

Hartigan, Francis. *Bill W.: A Biography of Alcoholics Anonymous Cofounder Bill Wilson.* New York: St. Martin's Press, 2000.

Healy, Paul F. *Cissy: The Biography of Eleanor M. "Cissy" Patterson.* Garden City, N.Y.: Doubleday, 1966.

Higdon, Hal. *The Crime of the Century: The Leopold and Loeb Case.* New York: G. P. Putnam's Sons, 1975.

J. H. Beers and Co. *Commemorative Biographical Record of the West Shore of Green Bay, Wisconsin.* Chicago: J. H. Beers and Co., 1896.

Jellinek, E. M. *The Disease Concept of Alcoholism.* New Brunswick, N.J.: New College and University Press with Hillhouse Press, 1960.

Johnson, Bruce Holley. "The Alcoholism Movement in America." Ph.D. diss., University of Illinois, 1973.

Johnson Institute. *Training Families to Do a Successful Intervention.* Minneapolis, Minn.: Johnson Institute–QVS, 1996.

Johnson, Vernon E. *I'll Quit Tomorrow.* San Francisco: Harper and Row, 1980.

Kazanjian, Dodie, and Calvin Tomkins. *Alex: The Life of Alexander Liberman.* New York: Alfred A. Knopf, 1993.

Keats, John. *You Might as Well Live: The Life and Times of Dorothy Parker.* New York: Simon and Schuster, 1970.

Kendall, Martha E. *Susan B. Anthony: Voice for Women's Voting Rights.* Springfield, N.J.: Enslow Publishers, Inc., 1997.

Ketcham, Katherine, William F. Asbury, Mel Schulstad, and Arthur P. Ciaramicoli. *Beyond the Influence: Understanding and Defeating Alcoholism.* New York: Bantam Books, 2000.

Kurtz, Ernest. *Not-God: A History of Alcoholics Anonymous.* Expanded ed. Center City, Minn.: Hazelden, 1991.

———. "Twelve Step Programs," in *Spirituality and the Secular Quest.* Peter H. VanNess, ed. New York: Crossroad Publishing Co., 1996.

Lender, Mark Edward. *Dictionary of American Temperance Biography.* Westport, Conn.: Greenwood Press, 1984.

Leonard, John W., ed. *The Book of Chicagoans.* Chicago: A. N. Marquis and Co., 1905.

Mann, Marty. *Marty Mann Answers Your Questions about Drinking and Alcoholism.* New York: Holt, Rinehart and Winston, 1970.

————. *Marty Mann's New Primer on Alcoholism.* New York: Holt, Rinehart and Winston, 1958.

Martin, Ralph G. *Cissy.* New York: Simon and Schuster, 1979.

Mayer, Harold, and Richard C. Wade. *Chicago, The Growth of a Metropolis.* Chicago: University of Chicago Press, 1969.

McCrady, Barbara S., and William R. Miller. *Research on Alcoholics Anonymous.* New Brunswick, N.J.: Rutgers Center of Alcohol Studies, 1993.

McFarland, Barbara. *Women in Treatment.* Center City, Minn.: Hazelden, 1984.

McGrew, Patrick, and Robert Julian. *Landmarks of Los Angeles.* New York: Harry N. Abrams, 1994.

Murray, Natalia. *Darlinghissima.* New York: Random House, 1985.

Naifeh, Steven, and Gregory W. Smith. *Jackson Pollock: An American Saga.* New York: Clarkson N. Potter, Inc., 1989.

National Council on Alcoholism. *40th Anniversary Commemorative Journal, 1944–1984.* New York: National Council on Alcoholism, 1984.

National Council on Alcoholism and Drug Dependence (NCADD). *50th Anniversary, 1944–1994.* New York: NCADD, 1994.

National Institute on Drug Abuse (NIDA). *Drug Abuse Treatment Outcome Study (DATOS).* Washington, D.C.: National Institute on Drug Abuse (NIDA), 1998.

Newton, Esther. *Cherry Grove, Fire Island.* Boston: Beacon Press, 1993.

Nicolson, Dorothy White. *Twenty Years of Medical Research.* New York: National Tuberculosis Association, 1943.

Olson, Nancy. *With a Lot of Help from Our Friends: The Politics of Alcoholism.* Forthcoming.

Page, Penny Booth. "E. M. Jellinek and the Evolution of Alcohol Studies: A Critical Essay." *Addiction* 92, no. 12 (1997): 1619–37.

Peluso, Emanuel, and Lucy Peluso. *Women and Drugs.* Minneapolis, Minn.: CompCare Publications, 1988.

Pike, Thomas P. *Memoirs.* San Marino, Calif.: self-published, 1979.

Potter, Jeffrey. *To a Violent Grave: An Oral Biography of Jackson Pollock.* New York: G. P. Putnam's Sons, 1985.

Raphael, Matthew J. *Bill W. and Mr. Wilson.* Amherst, Mass.: University of Massachusetts Press, 2000.

R. R. Bowker Co. *Biographical Directory of Fellows and Members of the American Psychiatric Association.* New York: R. R. Bowker Co., 1968, 1973, 1977.

Raymond, Irving Woodworth. *The Teaching of the Early Church on the Use of Wine and Strong Drink*. New York: AMS Press, 1927.

Rich, Doris L. *Amelia Earhart*. Washington, D.C.: Smithsonian Institute Press, 1989.

Robe, Lucy. *Co-starring Famous Women and Alcohol*. Minneapolis, Minn.: CompCare Publishers, 1986.

Robertson, Nan. *Getting Better*. New York: William Morrow and Co., Inc., 1988.

Roizen, Ron. "The American Discovery of Alcoholism, 1933–1939." Ph.D. diss., University of California Berkeley, 1991.

Rolo, Charles J. *Town and Country, 100 Years of Publication*. New York: Hearst Magazines, Inc., 1946.

Roth, Paula, ed. *Alcohol and Drugs Are Women's Issues*. Metuchen, N.J.: The Scarecrow Press, 1991.

Sandmaier, Marian. *The Invisible Alcoholics: Women and Alcohol Abuse in America*. 2d ed. Blue Ridge Summit, Pa.: TAB Books, 1992.

Scheid, Ann. *Pasadena: Crown of the Valley*. Northridge, Calif.: Windsor Publications, 1986.

Sharpe, Roberta. "Way Back in Those Days." Unpublished seminary paper, Pacific School of Religion. Berkeley, Calif., 1998.

Stanton, Elizabeth Cady. *Eighty Years and More*. New York: Schocken Books, 1971.

Strachan, J. George. *Practical Alcoholism Programming*. Vancouver, Canada: Mitchell Press Ltd., 1971.

Summerscale, Kate. *The Queen of Whale Cay*. New York: Viking, 1997.

Swegan, William E. *The Life of an Air Force Sergeant*. Sonoma, Calif.: self-published, n.d.

Tharp, Louise Hall. *The Peabody Sisters of Salem*. Boston: Little, Brown and Co., 1950.

Thomsen, Robert. *Bill W*. New York: Harper and Row, 1975.

Tremaine, Kit. *Fragments—My Path through the Twentieth Century*. Grass Valley, Calif.: Blue Dolphin Publishing, 1992.

Trice, Harrison M., and Janice M. Beyer. "Charisma and Its Routinization in Two Social Movement Organizations," *Research in Organizational Behavior* 8 (1986): 133–64.

V., Rachel. *A Woman Like You*. San Francisco: Harper and Row, 1985.

Vaillant, George E. *The Natural History of Alcoholism Revisited*. Cambridge, Mass.: Harvard University Press, 1995.

Vaughan, Clark. *Addictive Drinking*. New York: Penguin Books, 1984.

Western Historical Co. *History of Northern Wisconsin*. Chicago: Western Historical Co., 1881.

White, William L. *Slaying the Dragon: The History of Addiction Treatment and Recovery in America*. Bloomington, Ill.: Chestnut Health Systems/Lighthouse Institute, 1998.

Whitfield, Eileen. *Pickford: The Woman Who Made Hollywood*. Lexington, Ky.:
    University Press of Kentucky, 1997.
Williams, Dakin, and Shepherd Mead. *Tennessee Williams: An Intimate Biography*.
    New York: Arbor House, 1983.
Williams, John Hoyt. *Sam Houston: A Biography of the Father of Texas*. New
    York: Simon and Schuster, 1993.
Wilson, J. G., and John Fiske, eds. *Appleton's Cyclopaedia of American Biography*.
    New York: D. Appleton and Co., 1898.
Wineapple, Brenda. *Genet*. New York: Ticknor and Fields, 1989.
Wing, Nell. *Grateful to Have Been There*. Park Ridge, Ill.: Parkside Publishing
    Corp., 1992.

Audiotapes

1. 12/11/46	San Francisco	"What AA Means to Me"
2. early 1947		"AA at Large"
3. 8/23/56	Albany, New York	AA Meeting
4. 6/8/57	Watsonville, California	AA Meeting
5. c. 1959		"The Changes Regarding Women in AA" (At Felicia's sixteenth AA anniversary)
6. 1960	New York City	National Council AA GSO
7. c. 1960	Long Beach, California	AA Third International Convention
8. 9/22/60	Jacksonville, Tennessee	AA Southeastern Conference
9. 5/22/61	Cincinnati (transcript)	National TB Association (keynote speech)
10. 6/2/61	Austin, Texas	Institute at University of Texas
11. 12/1/64	Hobbs, New Mexico	NCA ("Organizing an Affiliate")
12. 1/1/65	Hot Springs, Arkansas	Arkansas State Convention
13. 1965	Kent, Connecticut	High Watch Twenty-Fifth Anniversary
14. 7/3/65	Toronto, Canada	AA Fourth International Convention
15. 2/20/66	Louisville, Kentucky	Fifteenth Kentucky State Convention
16. 10/25/66	Jamestown, North Dakota	
17. 5/67	Hartford, Connecticut	"Marty's Story"
18. 9/30/67	Wichita, Kansas	
19. 1/24/68	Cincinnati, Ohio	NCA

20. 8/15/68	Charlotte, North Carolina	
21. 10/4/68	San Francisco	
22. 11/68	Cleveland, Ohio	Northeast Group Twenty-Ninth Anniversary
23. 1970	New Brunswick, New Jersey	Rutgers School of Alcohol Studies "History of Alcohol Use and Alcoholism"
24. 1971	Monteagle, North Carolina	
25. 3/22/72	Saint Louis, Missouri	

Silver Hill—Inpatient Lectures/Discussion in New Canaan, Connecticut

26. 2/9/74	The Gentle Art of Conning
27. 3/1/74	The Prison of Perfectionism
28. 3/15/74	The First Step
29. 3/25/74	Hazards of Sobriety
30. 4/5/74	Stigma and Disease
31. 5/17/74	Families of Alcoholics
32. 6/7/74	The Three Rs
33. 6/28/74	Acceptance
34. 7/12/74	Special Meaning of Honesty
35. 7/19/74	Sensitivity
36. 8/8/74	Self-Discipline
37. 10/4/74	Isolation
38. 11/8/74	Wall of Defiance
39. 11/15/74	Dry or Sober
40. 11/22/74	Slips or Relapse

41. 5/8/76	Washington, D.C.	Interview by Neil Scott
42. 7/13/76	New York City	Interview by Geo. Gordon (two tapes)
43. 11/9/76	Houston	Houston Regional Council on Alcoholism
44. 12/1/77	Atlanta	SECAD II—Overview on Alcoholism
45. 12/3/77	Atlanta	Peachford Hospital
46. 4/13/79	Fairfield, Connecticut	MM Fortieth Anniversary
47. 4/25/80	Fairfield, Connecticut	MM Forty-first Anniversary
48. 5/17/80	Easton, Connecticut	Interview by Mel Barger
49. 7/3–6, 1980	New Orleans	AA Seventh International Convention (major address)

50. 7/3–6, 1980 New Orleans AA Seventh International Convention (AA Meeting)

51. date unknown Al-Anon Eleventh Annual Wisconsin Conference

52. 8/14/87 Omaha, Nebraska Bob Smith Jr., Cornhuskers' Roundup

53. c. 1989 Eatonton, Georgia Mary Campbell, "The Magic and the Power of the Twelve Steps" (AA Women's Workshop, Rock Eagle—mentions Marty and early AA)

Interviews

Anderson, Lucia R.
Arnold, Joseph P.
Barger, Melvin
B., Cora Louise
Benefield, Gayle
Bissell, LeClair, M.D.
Blake, Lizabeth
Blakemore, Bruce L.
Blakemore, John
Blume, Sheila, M.D.
Brown, Stephanie
Buckingham, William, M.D.
Burns, Dick
Caragol, Wilfrid
Carr, Virginia Spencer
Clinebell, Howard
Cruse, Joseph, M.D.
Darling, Diane
Dillenberger, Jane
Dillon, Millicent
Dimas, George
Dirlam, Joel
Dodd, Martin
Du Plain, Jan
Eyman, Scott
Fillmore, Kaye
Garland, Dorothy

Gitlow, Stanley, M.D.
Gomberg, Edith
Gregerson, Barbara
Harbaugh, Lyn
Hartigan, Francis
Havens, Thwing
Hayse, Helen Ware
Hunter, Conway, M.D.
Jenks, Katie
Katis, James, M.D.
Kennedy, Ian
Kennedy, Linda
Kimberling, Kim
Kline, David
Krouch, Dan
Kurtz, Ernest
Long, Gaylord
Long, Joreen
Lubinski, Christine
MacFarlane, Ann
MacKay, Marianne
Magruder, Felicia
Mann, Ted
Mann, William
Mannes, Elena
Marcelle, George
Marley, Hal

Marsh, Earl, M.D.
Martin, Joseph
Martin, Peggy
Mauch, Bea
McCarthy, Katherine
Miller, Gregory
Miller, Tyler
Murphy, Debbie
Murphy, Walter
Murray, Clark
Newton, Esther
Noll, Ann
O., Ruth
Ohliger, Paul, M.D.
Olson, Nancy
Osman, Claire
Parkerson, Joan
Patterson, Betty
Patterson, Pat
Paullus, Mary Joyce
Pearson, Betsy
Pearson, Bob
Phillips, Donald A.
Pittman, Bill
Pointevent, Bruce
Pope, Marjorie
R., Bonnie
Reida, Marge
Riordan, Dave
Roizen, Ron
Rosenblum, Lila

Ross, Mary
Rubin, Hessie Kennedy
Ryberg, Percy, M.D.
Santon, Judit
Schafer, Eleanor
Schneider, Max, M.D.
Schuckit, Marc, M.D.
Schulstad, Mel
Schuster, Carlotta, M.D.
Scott, Neil
Sharpe, Roberta
Sherman, Paul
Skinner, Jeanne
Smith, Robert, Jr.
Smithers, Charlie
Smithers-Fornaci, Adele
Steinhauer, Gordon
Swegan, Bill
Takamine, Joseph, M.D.
Tanzola, Kay
Violett, Ellen
Walker, Pat
Wegscheider-Cruse, Sharon
Weisman, Maxwell, M.D.
Whaley, Searcy
White, William L.
Whitfield, Eileen
Wickman, Mary
Wing, Nell
Wright, George
Zuska, Joseph, M.D.

The Twelve Steps of Alcoholics Anonymous*

1. We admitted we were powerless over alcohol—that our lives had become unmanageable.
2. Came to believe that a Power greater than ourselves could restore us to sanity.
3. Made a decision to turn our will and our lives over to the care of God *as we understood Him.*
4. Made a searching and fearless moral inventory of ourselves.
5. Admitted to God, to ourselves, and to another human being the exact nature of our wrongs.
6. Were entirely ready to have God remove all these defects of character.
7. Humbly asked Him to remove our shortcomings.
8. Made a list of all persons we had harmed, and became willing to make amends to them all.
9. Made direct amends to such people wherever possible, except when to do so would injure them or others.
10. Continued to take personal inventory and when we were wrong promptly admitted it.
11. Sought through prayer and meditation to improve our conscious contact with God *as we understood Him,* praying only for knowledge of His will for us and the power to carry that out.
12. Having had a spiritual awakening as the result of these steps, we tried to carry this message to alcoholics, and to practice these principles in all our affairs.

---

* The Twelve Steps of AA are taken from *Alcoholics Anonymous,* 3d ed., published by AA World Services, Inc., New York, N.Y., 59–60. Reprinted with permission of AA World Services, Inc. (See page x.)

The Twelve Traditions of Alcoholics Anonymous*

1. Our common welfare should come first; personal recovery depends upon A.A. unity.
2. For our group purpose there is but one ultimate authority—a loving God as He may express Himself in our group conscience. Our leaders are but trusted servants; they do not govern.
3. The only requirement for A.A. membership is a desire to stop drinking.
4. Each group should be autonomous except in matters affecting other groups or A.A. as a whole.
5. Each group has but one primary purpose—to carry its message to the alcoholic who still suffers.
6. An A.A. group ought never endorse, finance, or lend the A.A. name to any related facility or outside enterprise, lest problems of money, property, and prestige divert us from our primary purpose.
7. Every A.A. group ought to be fully self-supporting, declining outside contributions.
8. Alcoholics Anonymous should remain forever nonprofessional, but our service centers may employ special workers.
9. A.A., as such, ought never be organized; but we may create service boards or committees directly responsible to those they serve.
10. Alcoholics Anonymous has no opinion on outside issues; hence the A.A. name ought never be drawn into public controversy.
11. Our public relations policy is based on attraction rather than promotion; we need always maintain personal anonymity at the level of press, radio, and films.**
12. Anonymity is the spiritual foundation of all our traditions, ever reminding us to place principles before personalities.

---

* The Twelve Traditions of AA are taken from *Twelve Steps and Twelve Traditions*, published by AA World Services, Inc., New York, N.Y., 129–87. Reprinted with permission of AA World Services, Inc. (See page x.)

** In 1960, prior to a World Service Conference, Lois Wilson added "TV" to Al-Anon's Eleventh Tradition, which until then had been identical to AA's wording. So the Al-Anon version now reads: "Our public relations policy is based on attraction rather than promotion; we need always maintain personal anonymity at the level of press, radio, TV, and films. We need guard with special care the anonymity of all AA members."

Index

A

A. Bishop and Company, 16

AA. *See* Alcoholics Anonymous (AA)

AA Grapevine, 150, 165–66, 182, 185

AAAS. *See* American Association for the Advancement of Science (AAAS)

abolition, and temperance, 42

abstinence, 200

    as corrective, 160

    as necessary for alcoholics, 102

    and relapses, 136

    and temperance, 42, 43

    and treatment, 154

    and Washingtonian movement, 44

abstract expressionism, 198–99

ACAs. *See* adult children of alcoholics (ACAs)

acrophobia, 291

activism, vs. hedonism, 252

Addams, Jane, 6, 20, 157, 327n1

addiction, cross-fertilization of ideas about, 244

addictionists, 346n4

addictive behavior, 56–57

addictive disease, 275

addicts, use of term, 274

Ade, George, 19

Adelphi College/University, 141, 303

Adler, Julius Ochs, Mrs., 191–92

adult children of alcoholics (ACAs), 298, 327–28n2

Aeolian Hall, 121, 127

AHA. *See* American Heart Association (AHA)

Al-Anon, 150, 221–22, 280

Alateen, 280

alcohol

    as anesthetic and medicine, 40

    high tolerance for, 4

    as psychoactive drug, 195, 275

Alcohol Explored (Haggard and Jellinek), 154

alcoholic(s)

    defined, 244

    use of term, 7, 82, 105, 160, 179, 193, 274, 335n7

    See also alcoholism

alcoholic neuritis, 93

Alcoholics Anonymous (AA)

    beginning of, 104–5, 107, 111, 115

    empirical tools, 193

    forty-fifth anniversary, 315–17

    meetings, 342n1

organization of, 44
power of, 206
precursor of, 44
See also sponsors; Twelve Steps;
    Twelve Traditions
Alcoholics Anonymous (Big Book), 8–9,
    104, 105, 107, 108, 111, 112,
    114–15, 116, 118, 125, 129, 131,
    148, 158–59, 194, 304
Alcoholics Anonymous Comes of Age,
    205–6
alcoholism
    broad negative social impact of, 6–7
    chronic nature of, 331n1, 331n13,
        335n4
    defined, 192–93, 244–45
    as disease, xiii–xiv, 4, 7, 8, 10, 34,
        75–76, 91, 105, 124, 135,
        155–56, 159, 162–63, 171,
        194–95, 213, 243, 244–45,
        255, 324, 346n6, 350n19
    occupational, 235
    as progressive, 74, 160
    as religious sin, 41, 42, 161, 194
    stages of, 334n4
    study of, 192–93
    use of term, 7, 102, 105, 160, 193,
        335n7
alcoholism movement, vii, xi, 7, 11, 33,
    235, 243–44, 301, 316
Alcoholism, the National Magazine,
    165
Aldrin, Buzz, 306, 351n11
Alexander, Jack, 154
allergy, defined, 105
ALMACA, 300–301
Alzheimer's disease, 276, 286, 291,
    307–10
AMA. *See* American Medical
    Association (AMA)

American Association for the Advance-
    ment of Science (AAAS), 254
American Group Therapy Association,
    38
American Heart Association (AHA), 279
American Institute of Psychotherapy
    and Psychoanalysis, 291
American Lung Association, 34, 256
American Medical Association (AMA),
    118–19, 245, 255, 346n6
American Medical Society on
    Alcoholism (AMSA), 311
American Psychiatric Association
    (APA), 170, 255
American Public Health Association
    (APHA), 229, 254
American Society of Addiction
    Medicine (ASAM), 244–45
American Society of Composers,
    Authors, and Publishers (ASCAP),
    152, 156, 157, 160
American Society of Mexico, 203
amnesiac episodes, 74
amphetamines, 120
AMSA. *See* American Medical Society
    on Alcoholism (AMSA)
Anderson, Dwight, 155–56, 158, 159,
    166, 171, 210, 212
Anderson, Margaret, 19
Anderson, Sherwood, 19
Andrews, Dana, 306
anger, 107
Angostura Bitters, 262
anonymity, as AA issue, 128, 179–83,
    185–86, 220, 263, 280
Antabuse, 147, 263, 340n9
Anthony, Susan B., 43, 189
Anthony, Susan B., II, 9, 43, 189, 304,
    314, 317
antidepressants, 272

Antioch College, 13
APA. *See* American Psychiatric
  Association (APA)
APHA. *See* American Public Health
  Association (APHA)
Armour, Philip, 68–69
Arnold, Joe, 286–87
Art Directors' Association, 122
ASAM. *See* American Society of
  Addiction Medicine (ASAM)
ASCAP. *See* American Society of
  Composers, Authors, and
  Publishers (ASCAP)
asceticism, 41
Asylum (Seabrook), 82
atheism, 23–24, 105–6
Auden, W. H., 143
audiotapes, of Mann, 10–11, 176,
  359–61
Auer, Leopold, 127
Austen Riggs Foundation for the Study
  and Treatment of Neuroses, 294
Austen Riggs Psychiatric Hospital, 90, 94
avant-garde expressionism, 19–20, 198

B
Bacon, Selden D., 154, 166, 174, 196,
  207, 210–12, 242
Baird, Edward G., 166
Bangs, Grace Allen, 87, 156, 159, 166,
  168
Barker, Raymond (Ray) C., 228–30
Barkley, Roger, Rev., 95
Barlow Respiratory Hospital, 329n5
Barlow Sanatorium, 29–35, 329n5
Barlow, W. Jarvis, 29–31, 34–35
Barney, Natalie, 73
Beaton, Cecil, 199
Beecher, Lyman, on temperance, 42
Belden Stratford Hotel, 62

Bellevue Hospital, 91, 92–94, 97, 127,
  131–32, 226, 250
Benchley, Robert, 177
Benzedrine, 120
Bergman, Ingrid, 202
Betty Ford Center, 296
Big Book. *See Alcoholics Anonymous*
  (Big Book)
Bill W. *See* Wilson, Bill (Bill W.)
biochemistry, 193, 196, 343n8
Bissell, LeClair, xi, 36, 134, 236–37,
  265, 296, 308–9
bitters, 262
blackouts/blacking out, 74, 84, 89, 334n5
Blackwell, Elizabeth, 254, 347n6
Blakemore, Bruce, 188
Blakemore, John, xii, 55–56, 58–60, 87,
  167, 188–89, 298, 317, 334n1,
  342–43n3
Bloomsbury Group, 72
Blume, Sheila, 166, 311–12
Blythewood Sanitarium, 94, 97–110,
  119, 120, 121, 124–25, 325
Bob, Dr. *See* Smith, Bob
bohemianism, 19
Bowen, Elizabeth, 272–73
Bowles, Jane, 143, 223–26, 262, 295,
  344n9, 345n17
Bowles, Paul, 143, 223, 224
Brier Place, 67
Britten, Benjamin, 143
Broadway inn, 77–79
Brown, Stephanie, 327–28n2
Buddhism, 140, 259, 268
Burger, Bobby, 127
Butler, Robert, 309

C
Calvin, D. Leigh, Mrs., 163, 165
Campbell, Mary, 114

CAP. *See* Civil Air Patrol (CAP)
Capote, Truman, 143, 223, 253, 295–96
Carpenter, Tom, 277, 292
Carr, Virginia Spencer, 222
Carstairs, Marion (Joe), 73, 202, 209
Cathedral of the Incarnation, 246–47
Cavett, Frank, 177
Center of Alcohol Studies. *See* Yale
  Center of Alcohol Studies
Chafetz, Morris, 282–83
Chase, Edna, 198
Cherry Grove, Fire Island (Newton),
  143
Cherry Grove, on Fire Island, 142–44,
  146, 226
Cheston, Forbes (Chesty), 202–3
Chicago, influence on Mann, 18–25
Chicago Tribune, 20, 56, 59
Chicago World's Exposition of 1893, 68
Christian Century, The, 318
Christian Science, 126
Christy, Margaret (Deming), maternal
  grandmother, 15–16, 17, 23, 68, 71
Christy, Robert Curtis, maternal grand-
  father, 15–16, 17, 23, 33, 67–68
chronic inebriety, 3, 5, 154, 163
Church of Religious Science, 227–30,
  254
Church of the Atonement, 23
cigarette smoking, 46–47, 81, 146. *See
  also* nicotine; tobacco cessation
Civil Air Patrol (CAP), 120
Civil Rights Act, 252
class norms, 40–44
Clay, Barbara, 71, 83
Cleveland *Plain Dealer*, 127–28, 131
Cleveland University Hospitals, 286–87
Clinebell, Howard, 162
Cloud, Luther, 290, 306
cocktail parties. *See* social drinking
coffee, for sobering up, 335n5

Commander's Council on Alcoholism,
  320
Comprehensive Alcoholism Prevention
  and Treatment Act of 1970
  (Hughes Act), 282
compulsion, uncontrolled, 83–84, 102
Concerning the Spiritual in Art
  (Kandinsky), 198
Congressional hearings, on women and
  alcoholism, 304
Congressional Record, tribute in, 318
consumerism, 217
Continental Iron Works, 141
convalescence, 124, 130–31
Cornell University, 235
Cornell University Medical School, 91
Crawford, Cheryl, 143
criminalization, of alcoholism, 10
Croci, Adele, 235
Cruse, Joseph R., 313
cultural norms and influences, 18–20,
  40–44
Cunard, Elizabeth, 72
Curtis, Grenville (Grennie) Francis, 120

D
Damrosch, Leopold, 61
Darrow, Clarence, 50
death rates, of alcoholism, 6, 327n2
Defense Department (U.S.), 170
de la Terga, Katherine Caragol, xii, 135,
  339n10
delirium tremens (d.t.'s), 89, 132
DeLuca, John, 312
denial, 4, 44, 46, 147, 274–75, 331n13,
  332n5
depression, 119, 131, 174, 271–72
Depression. *See* Great Depression
detoxing, 77–78, 122, 131–32, 150, 233
Dickinson, LaFell, Mrs., 166–67
Dimas, George C., 302, 304

Disease Concept of Alcoholism, The (Jellinek), 255
Disney, Roy, 157
distilled liquor, 330n7
Divine Power, 326. *See also* Higher Power
divorce, and alcoholism, 60
Dix, Dorothea, 6, 157, 248, 327n1
Dr. Bob. *See* Smith, Bob
Doctors Hospital, 90, 204
Doyle, Jesse (Jess), 201
Dreiser, Theodore, 19
Driver, Joe, 347n10
drugs. *See* hard drugs; street drugs; specific drugs
drunkenness, 3, 41, 75. *See also* inebriation
d.t.'s. *See* delirium tremens (d.t.'s)
Du Plain, Jan, 303–5
Durand, Henry Calvin, 33

E
EAPA. *See* Employee Assistance Professionals Association (EAPA)
Earhart, Amelia, 60
Easter, DeWitt, 347n10
Eddy, Mary Baker, 126
Edgehill-Newport, 237
Edgewater Beach Hotel, 17
education and outreach, 8–9, 13, 42, 122, 146, 153–63, 171, 188, 259, 261, 281–82, 306
Eighteenth (18th) Amendment. *See* Prohibition
Elavil, 272
Elizabeth Blackwell Award, 254, 347n6
Elman, Mischa, 127
Emerson, Kendall, 166
emotional growth, stopped by alcoholic drinking, 48, 131
empathy, 121

Employee Assistance Professionals Association (EAPA), 300–301
environmental issues/factors, 196, 245
Episcopal church, 17, 23–24, 246
Ericsson *Monitor*, 141
ethanolism, 160
ethical norms, 40–44
evangelism, 153
Evening Standard, 203
exorcisms, 200

F
families, and alcoholism, 4, 194–95, 221–22, 245
family denial, 44, 331n13
Farrell, James T., 19
Fastzkie, Linda, 286–87
fear, 7, 27
fellowship, of AA, 117, 130–31
Fillmore, Kaye, 242
Fitzgerald, F. Scott, and Prohibition, 46
Flanner, Janet (Genet), 73, 143, 202
flawed personality, 297
Ford, Betty, 47, 181
Fosdick, Harry Emerson, 166
Fox, Ruth, xiii, 6, 147, 154–55, 159, 205, 244, 249–51, 263, 265
Frank A. Munsey Company, 20
Franks, Bobby, 50–51
Franks, Jacob, 50–51
freedom, 108
Frogg, Wanda, 312
Funeral Church, 249

G
Gardner, John W., 270
Gardner, Yvelin (Yev), 203, 219, 231–33, 240, 246–47, 275, 293, 319
General Service Office, 240

genetics, and alcoholism, 194–95, 245,
  339n2
geographic, defined, 334n6
Gershwin, Frances, 61
Gitlow, Stanley, 60, 249–50, 272
Gizycka, Felicia, 20, 148–51, 226–31,
  271–73, 276, 280, 286, 288–92,
  307–8, 313–14, 318–19, 329n4,
  340n11
God, 105–6, 108. *See also* Higher
  Power
Godfrey, Arthur, 306
Godowsky, Leopold, 61
Gold, Betty, 203
Gold Key Award, 288, 290–91
gold mining, 67–68
Golden Rule, 225
Gomberg, Edith, 161
Great Depression, 67, 85, 124
Greenberg, Clement, 198
Greenwich, Connecticut, 94, 99
Greenwich Time, 99
group therapy, AA as, 117–18
Gulick, Merle A., 255

H
Haggard, Howard W., 154, 159, 163,
  166, 174, 196, 212
hair of the dog, 74
halfway houses, 273, 299
hallucinations. *See* delirium tremens
  (d.t.'s)
hangovers, 73–74
hard drugs, 284
hard liquor, 42
Harper's Bazaar magazine, 197
Havens, Joseph, 140
Hayward, Susan, 177
healing, 119
Hearst, William Randolph, 65
Hecht, Ben, 19

hedonism, vs. activism, 252
Held, John, Jr., 46
Hemsley, Rollie, 180–81
Hemingway, Ernest, 19
Hess, Thomas B., 198
High Watch Farm, 125–26, 135, 149,
  190
Higher Power, 109, 183, 325. *See also*
  God
Highland Park, 54
Highsmith, Patricia, 143
Hill, Warren E., 141
Hiss, Alger, 230
historical influences and traditions,
  40–45
Hitler, Adolf, 124
Holman, Libby, 224
Holmes, Ernest, 227
homophobia, 217–18
homosexuality, 50
hopelessness, 75, 217
Hopkins, Emma Curtis, 126
horse's neck, 200
Houston, Sam, 261, 348n13
Hudson, Barclay, 90
Hudson, Janie, 90
Hughes Act, 282, 284, 294, 302
Hughes, Harold, Senator, 47, 281–82,
  283, 306, 341n2, 351n11
Huss, Magnus, 160
Huston, Franklin, 167, 210
hypersensitivity, 112

I
IBM. *See* International Business
  Machines (IBM)
ignorance, 7, 27, 46, 153
incarceration, vs. treatment, 174–75
industry, 188, 235
inebriate, 7, 45, 193. *See also* chronic
  inebriety

Inebriate, The, 252
inebriation, as religious violation, 41.
    See also chronic inebriety; drunk-
    enness
Ingram, Jonas H., 189
inpatient treatment, 296, 299
Institute for Alcoholism Prevention and
    Workplace Problems, 235
Institute of Alcohol Studies, University
    of Texas, 261–62
Institute of Rehabilitation Medicine,
    286–87, 290–92
International Business Machines (IBM),
    233–34, 236
International Conference on
    Alcoholism, 201–2
International Congress on Alcoholism
    and Drug Dependence, 301
International Institute for Research on
    Problems of Alcohol, 247
International Studio Magazine, 65–66
International Telephone and Telegraph
    (ITT), 300
International Union for Health
    Education of the Public, 247
intervention, 259
interviews, about Mann, 362–63
isolation, 89, 100. *See also* loneliness
ITT. *See* International Telephone and
    Telegraph (ITT)

J
James, William, 108
Jellinek, Elvin M. (Bunky), 154,
    159–60, 161, 163, 166, 174, 196,
    212, 244–245, 247, 255, 266
Johnson, Edward L., 290
Johnson, Lyndon B., 252, 270
Johnstone, Alan (Johnny), 69, 85, 120
Jordan, Barbara, 255
Juilliard School of Music, 61

Junior League, 56, 167
justice, sense of, 25

K
Kandinsky, Wassily, 198
Katis, James, 295
Kaufman, Sylvia, 129
Kendall, Don, 282
Kenmore Park, 17, 26, 33, 54
Kennedy, John F., 252, 256–57, 261, 270
Kennedy, Robert Foster, xii, 91–94,
    118–19, 121, 135, 205–6, 218,
    226, 271
Kimberling, Kim, 323, 352n11
King, Martin Luther, Jr., 252
Knickerbocker Hospital, 187
Knowlson, Lois, 210, 212
Koch, Robert, 28
Kodachrome, invented, 61
Kodak, 61
Kreisler, Fritz, 127
Kurtz, Ernest, 181, 263, 348–49n18

L
Lackland Air Force Base, 170
Lake Placid Club, 37
Lardner, Ring, 19
Latin School for Boys, 22
Latin School for Girls, 22, 23
Layton, Thomas, 1
Leadership Training Institute on
    Women and Alcoholism, 304
Lear, Norman, 255
learning curve, 135
legal issues, 256
legislation, 188, 248
Leopold-Loeb case, 51, 217–18
lesbianism, 66–67, 71, 73, 138,
    142–46, 199, 218, 222–25, 324
Liberman, Alexander (Alex), 197–99,
    219, 253, 293

Limur, Ethel Mary de, 247, 249

Lincoln Storage Warehouse Company,
    140

Lindsay, Vachel, 19

Little Review magazine, 19–20

Lockwood, Edgar, 166

Lolli, Giorgio, 154

loneliness, 124. *See also* isolation

Long Beach Naval Hospital, 47

Long Island Hospital Medical College,
    14

Lord's Prayer, 115, 272

Los Angeles Orthopedic Hospital, 63

Lost Weekend, The (film), 176, 177

Louchheim Aline B., 198

Lovell, Harold W., 248

lysergic acid diethylamide (LSD), 271

M

MacCormick, Austin, 159, 166, 210–12

Macy's, R. H., 137–38

Maher, Horace R. "Popsy," 111

Man, Richard, paternal ancestor, 12

Mann, Edward K. (Ted), nephew, 204,
    286, 319

Mann, Elisha, paternal great-grand-
    father, 13

Mann, Flora Ann (Tracy), paternal
    grandmother, 14

Mann, Fred Eugene, paternal uncle, 15

Mann, Horace, paternal ancestor, 13

Mann, Horace Edwin, paternal grand-
    father, 13–15, 328n4

Mann, J. Stephen (Steve), nephew, 204–5

Mann, Lillian Christy (Chris), sister, 16,
    26–27, 62–64, 70, 85, 89, 101,
    106–7, 120–21, 137, 156, 201,
    205, 219, 321–22

Mann, Lillian (Lill) Christy, mother, 16,
    26–27, 67–70, 85, 120, 190–91,
    218, 221, 229, 248–50

Mann, Marty (Margaret)
    in AA, 7, 8–10, 44–45, 109–23,
        136, 297, 314
    abstinence, 200
    as advocate and lobbyist, 174
    alcohol use, her family's, 39–41,
        44, 56–57
    alcohol use, her own, 35, 39–40,
        41, 47–50, 59–60, 71, 73–80,
        82–84, 86–91
    alcoholism, 73–84
    anonymity, 9
    as atheist, 23–24, 105–6
    as author, 8, 219–21, 285
    birth and baptism, 16, 17
    in California, 29–35, 36–37
    cancer, 203–5, 207, 253
    careers, 20–21, 65–67, 71, 74,
        137–38, 152
    as catalyst, 8
    charisma, 4, 163, 176, 325
    in Chicago, 18–25, 53–57, 67
    competitive spirit, 22
    in Connecticut, 226–27
    as courageous, 218
    crusading spirit, 12
    cultural influences, 18, 19–20, 40
    death, 7, 47, 317–18
    as debutante, 53–55, 332n1
    depression, 131, 174, 271–72
    determination of, 127
    as educator, 8, 9, 13, 146, 153–63,
        171
    emphysema, 308
    enduring national impact, 13
    as entrepreneur, 164–78
    as expatriate, 84
    in Europe, 50, 51–52, 58, 71–72,
        73, 77, 79–83, 202, 247–48,
        266, 272
    extracurricular activities, 23, 24

family philosophy, 13, 14
family relationships, 12–17, 26–27, 191
in Florida, 37
gallbladder attack, 133–34, 266
gender as barrier/stigma, 10, 115–16, 122
hip fracture, 285–86, 290
historical influences, 40–41
illnesses, 27–35, 60, 75–76, 133–34, 203–5, 207, 253, 266, 276, 308–9
justice, sense of, 25
leadership qualities, 240
lesbianism, 66–67, 71, 73, 138, 142–46, 199, 218, 222–25, 324
marriage and divorce, 58–60
in Massachusetts, 90
nannies, 17
in New Mexico, 21, 24–25, 60–61, 62
in New Orleans, 55, 58–59, 315–17
in New York, 37–39, 65–67, 71, 84, 85, 199–200
obituary, 318
personal courage, 7
as pioneer, vii, 9, 111–23
political influences, 18, 20
as pragmatist, 117
prerecovery attitudes, 42
pseudonym, 154
as public health care reformer, 6, 165, 229
in recovery, 124–37
relapses, 131–36, 262–69
religious influences, 17, 23–24, 40–42
retirement, 277–83, 302
schooling, 22, 36–40, 50–51
seeks help, 76–77, 88, 91–94

self-image, 242
seventy-fifth birthday celebration, 314
as smoker, 46, 81, 146
sobriety and learning curve, 124–37
sobriety and rebirth, 97–110
social influences, 18–25, 40–44, 47–48, 66
as social reformer, 6
as speaker, 3–5, 8, 22, 31–32, 121–22, 154, 162–63, 171–76, 194, 257–62, 265, 273–74
spirit of triumphant individualism, 13
spiritual experience, 107–8, 115
spiritual nature, 24
suicide attempts, 80, 90, 108
sympathetic nature, 25
teenage years, 26–40, 46, 47–50
temperament and character, 18, 27
travel and vacations, with family, 24, 54
tuberculosis, 27–35, 60
upbringing in Chicago, 18–25
as urbanite, 85
as vain, 241–42
as visionary, vii, 8, 152–63
in Washington, D.C., 86–87
willpower, 26, 76, 136
as writer, 22–23
Mann, Mary Elizabeth (Betty), sister, 23, 26, 69, 86, 101, 121, 128–29, 156–57, 226, 285
Mann, William (Bill) Henry, brother, xi, 23–24, 26–27, 68–69, 85–86, 120–21, 138, 148, 156, 165, 190, 204–5, 219–20, 223, 229, 321–22
Mann, William (Will) Henry, father, 13, 15–17, 24

as alcoholic and compulsive gambler, 38–40, 44, 51, 56–57
career, 16, 20–23, 27, 50–51, 54, 56
death, 218, 229
financial problems, 67–70, 86, 191
gold mining in Montana, 67–69
marriage, 16
retirement, 58
sobriety, 69
temperament and character, 27
will, 321
Mann, William J. C. (Bill), nephew, 204
Mannes, Leopold, 60–62, 66, 90, 100, 109, 119–20, 137
Mannes School of Music, 61, 66
Marcelle, George, 47, 146, 303, 331–32n3
March of Time, The, 176
marriage, and alcoholism, 333n4
Marsh, Jim, 38–39, 325
Marshall Field and Company, 20–22, 23, 54, 56
Martin, Sarah, pseudonym, 154
Marty Mann Answers Your Questions about Drinking and Alcoholism, 220, 280, 285
Marty Mann's New Primer on Alcoholism (Mann), 8, 220, 285, 300, 314
Marty Mann's Primer on Alcoholism (Mann), 8, 219–20
McCambridge, Mercedes, 306
McCarthy, Kathy, 309–10
McCarthy, Ray, 154, 309
McCarthyism, 217–18
McCormick, Robert, 20
McCullers, Carson, 143, 222–23, 225, 226, 272–73, 344n4
McCullers, Reeves, 222

McNally, Andrew, 33
medical profession, 4, 118–19, 184, 187, 245, 255, 298, 346n6
meditation, 268
Menninger Clinic, 246
Menninger, Karl A., 167, 246
Menominee River Hospital, 14
military, alcohol programs, 170–71, 341n2
Miller, Greg, nephew, 128, 226, 286, 314
Miller, R. Tyler (Ty), nephew, 128, 226, 286, 307–8
Millet, John A. P., 294
Mills, Wilbur, 306, 351n11
Miss Nixon's School, 52
moderation, 41, 42
Moholy-Nagy, Laszlo, 198
Monitor (iron ship), 141
Montemare School, 37–39, 65
Moore, Garry, 306–7
Moore, William (Bill) W., Jr., 279, 280, 302
moral character, lack of, 7
mortality, 6, 327n2
Mulcahy, Henry, 212
Munch, Edvard, 322
Municipal Tuberculosis Sanatarium, 28
Murphy, Debbie, 306, 313
Murphy, Stacia, vii, 281
Murphy, Walter, 176, 237, 239, 250, 254, 255–56, 306
Murray, Natalia, 143, 202
Murrow, Edward R., 246
mysticism, 268
myth, vs. facts, 7

N
narcissism, 121
National Alcoholism and Family Congress, 165
National Alcoholism Forum, 331–32n3

National Association of Publicity
    Directors, 155
National Clearing House for Alcohol
    and Drug Information, 304
National Committee for Education on
    Alcoholism (NCEA), 164–96, 203,
    207–13, 235, 244, 246, 283
National Committee for the Homeless
    and Institutional Alcoholic, 246
National Committee on Alcoholism
    (NCA), 213, 248
National Council on Alcoholism
    (NCA), 8, 9, 11, 33, 35, 42, 73,
    128, 166, 185, 213, 217–22,
    228–35, 237–38, 241–56, 264,
    266, 274–83, 288, 300–304,
    311–14, 347n10, 349n2
National Council on Alcoholism and
    Drug Dependence (NCADD), xii,
    8, 9, 11, 220, 235, 275, 325
National Institute of Mental Health
    (NIMH), 256
National Institute on Aging, 309
National Institute on Alcohol Abuse
    and Alcoholism (NIAAA), 282–83
National Institutes of Health (NIH),
    327n2
National Mental Health Act, 201–2
National Organization of Women
    (NOW), 304
National Tuberculosis Association
    (NTA), 31–32, 34, 153, 156, 166,
    254, 256–58, 260
NCA. *See* National Council on
    Alcoholism (NCA)
NCADD. *See* National Council on
    Alcoholism and Drug Dependence
    (NCADD)
NCEA. *See* National Committee for
    Education on Alcoholism (NCEA)
NCEA Public Journal, 165

neuroscience/neurochemistry, 193, 196
New York Academy of Medicine, 164
New York Herald Tribune, 200
New York Herald Tribune Club
    Women's Service Bureau, 87, 156
New York Hospital, Westchester
    Division, 82
New York City Medical Society on
    Alcoholism, 244–45, 249
New York State Medical Society, 155,
    159, 166, 205–206
New York Times, 191, 318
New Yorker magazine, 114, 202
Newman, Barnett, 198
Newsweek magazine, 306
Newton, Esther, 143
NIAAA. *See* National Institute on
    Alcohol Abuse and Alcoholism
    (NIAAA)
niacin (nico), 271
nicotine, 6, 47, 81, 195. *See also* ciga-
    rette smoking; tobacco cessation
nicotinic acid, 271
NIH. *See* National Institutes of Health
    (NIH)
NIMH. *See* National Institute of
    Mental Health (NIMH)
Nineteenth (19th) Amendment, 44
Nixon, Richard, 282, 284
North Shore, of Chicago, 16
Not-God (Kurtz), 283
NOW. *See* National Organization of
    Women (NOW)
NTA. *See* National Tuberculosis
    Association (NTA)
NYSMS. *See* New York State Medical
    Society (NYSMS)

O
occupational alcoholism, 235
O'Connor, Sandra Day, 255

Olson, Nancy, 239, 281
Operation Understanding, 305–7
outreach. *See* education and outreach

P
Parker, Dorothy, 167, 176–77, 341n1
Parsons, Betty, 147, 198–99
passing out, defined, 334n5
Patterson, Eleanor (Cissy), 20
Payne Whitney Outpatient Clinic, 90
Peace Corps, 257
Peace of Mind, 130
Peale, James, 141, 322
Pears, Peter, 143
Pearson, Bob, 315
Peck, Elizabeth (Lillie), 139
Peck, Elizabeth (Liz), 139, 140–42, 172,
    219, 228–29, 237, 271, 288–90,
    292, 318, 321–23, 352n11
Peck, Ethel Hill, 139, 141
Peck, Priscilla, 127, 137–51, 156, 159,
    165–66, 177, 197–200, 203, 219,
    222–24, 227–31, 253–54, 263,
    265, 271–73, 276, 280, 286–87,
    289, 291–94, 297, 303, 307–10,
    314, 319, 321–22
Peck, Teresina, 139–40
Peck, Teresina II (Terry), 140
Peck, Tracy, 139
Peck, Tracy, Jr., 139–40, 339n2
Penitentes, 24
personality, and alcoholism, 296–97
Peshtigo Company, 14
Phillips, Ila, 127, 172
Pickford, Mary, 167, 219, 341n1,
    344n1
Pike, Katherine K., 33, 167, 242–43,
    305, 311–12
Pike, Tom, 33, 167, 242–43, 280, 282,
    311–12
polio epidemics, 62–64, 201

politics, 18, 20, 42, 270. *See also* legis-
    lation
Pollock, Jackson, 147–48, 198–99, 200,
    314
polyaddiction, 275
polyneuritis, 93
Pope, Marjorie Reid, 240–41
post-traumatic stress disorder (PTSD),
    92
Powell, Leroy, 347n10
pragmatism, 117
prayer, 107–8, 228–30, 325
Presence. *See* God
Presnall, Lewis F., 300
prevention, 259
*Primer on Alcoholism. See Marty
    Mann's Primer on Alcoholism*
Prohibition, 8, 20, 39, 42, 43, 44, 46,
    48, 158, 163. *See also* temperance
    movement
Protestant culture, 40
psychiatry, 76–77, 88, 91–94, 118, 119,
    192–93
psychoactive drugs, 195, 275
psychoanalysis, 298
psychology, 196
psychosocial factors, 245
psychotherapy, 134
PTSD. *See* post-traumatic stress disor-
    der (PTSD)
public health movement, vii, 1, 6–7, 10,
    34, 40, 165, 217, 229
public opinion, changing, 7–8, 175, 243
public policy, 311–12
Pullman, George M., Mrs., 33
punishment, vs. intervention and treat-
    ment, 10
Puritan ethic, 40

Q
Quakers, 140

Quarterly Journal of Studies on Alcohol, 155
Queen Mary, 83–84, 126

R
rationalization, 46
RCPA. *See* Research Council on Problems of Alcohol (RCPA)
recidivism, 175–76
recovered, use of term, 183, 194
recovery, 134–35, 338–39n7
Regan, Riley, 299
Regent Hospital, 250
Reinhardt, Ad, 198
relapses, 131–36, 262–69
religion, 17, 23–24, 40–44, 161, 187, 194
Religious Science, 227–30, 254, 267, 309
Religious Society of Friends, 140
remittance man, defined, 335n8
Research Council on Problems of Alcohol (RCPA), 154, 155, 159
resentment, and addiction, 56–57, 107, 117, 119
Richardson, Elliot, 282
Riegle, Donald W., Jr., Senator, 311
Riggs, Austen, 294
Robertson, Frances A., 349n2
Rockefeller Institute, 120
Rockefeller, Nelson, 128
Rockland Hospital, 133
Roizen, Ron, 192
Roosevelt, Eleanor, 209
Roosevelt Hospital, 236–27
Rosehill Cemetery, 319
Rosenberg, Harold, 198
Rosenblum, Lila, 229, 263, 291, 348n17
Ross, Mary Clark, 241
Rothko, Mark, 198

Rowell, Wilfrid A., 140
Royal National Orthopaedic Hospital, 81
Rush, Benjamin, 160
Rush Medical College, 14
Rusk, Howard, 287–88
Rutgers University, 235, 304

S
Saarinen, Aline, 198
Sackville-West, Vita, 72
St. Bartholomew's Episcopal Church, 24, 319
St. Francis Hospital, 187
St. John, Adela Rogers, 305
St. John the Divine, 293
St. Simon's Church, 17
St. Vincent's Medical Center, 318
Saks Fifth Avenue, 197
salvation, 113
San Fernando Valley, California, 99
Sandburg, Carl, 18, 19
Sanger, Margaret, 6, 327n1
sanitariums, 11, 21, 28
Santa Barbara Council on Alcoholism, 167
Santa Barbara Girls' School, 36
Saturday Evening Post, 154, 181
Saugatuck Congregational Church, 319
School of Alcohol Studies, 299
schools, alcohol education in, 169
Schultz, Charles, 282
Schuster, Carlotta, 308
Schwartz, Fräulein, 328–29n8
Schweitzer, Albert, 240
Scott, Neil, 167
Seabrook, William (Willie), 82–83, 87, 335n7
Selective Service Act, amendment, 341n2
self-centeredness, 112

self-confidence, 102
self-control, 76
self-education, 154
self-esteem, 102, 123
self-help, 44, 105, 245
self-hypnosis, 106
self-image, 242
self-knowledge, 268
self-will, 76
Serenity Prayer, 157
Sewall, Pat, 205
sexual orientation, 145, 217–18. *See also* lesbianism
sexual revolution, 47
Shaker Heights Nature Center, 128
Sharpe, Roberta (Robbie), 331n11
Shaskan, Donald A., 38
Sheridan Park, 16, 17
Sherman, Paul, 300–301
Silkworth, William D., 190, 205
Silver Hill Hospital, 294–97, 308, 314, 319
Simpson, James (Jim), 23, 56, 250
Simpson, Jessie, 23, 250
Sinclair, Upton, 19
Slaying the Dragon (White), 193, 248
sleeping lion, 46, 71, 331n1
Smash Up (film), 177
Smith, Anne, 129
Smith, Bob, Dr., AA cofounder, 9, 10, 104–5, 115, 129, 162, 167, 180–81, 185–86, 218
Smith (Hobart and William) Colleges, 254
Smith, Margaret Chase, 255
Smith, Margarita (Rita), 225
Smith, Oliver, 143
Smithers Alcoholism Treatment and Training Center, 236–27, 265, 296
Smithers, C. Francis, 234

Smithers, Charles (Charlie) F., Jr., 321–22
Smithers, Christopher D., 233
Smithers (Christopher D.) Foundation, 234, 235, 300
Smithers-Fornaci, Adele, 235, 238
Smithers, R. Brinkley (Brink), 233–38, 251, 276, 277–79, 282, 300, 302, 312
smoking. *See* cigarette smoking
social drinking, 40–42, 44, 47, 102
Social Security Act, 88
social issues and influences, 6–7, 18–25, 40–44, 47–48, 66, 196, 217
social welfare, and temperance, 42
societal denial, 274–75
Society for the Study of Addiction to Alcohol and Other Drugs, 254
Society of Public Health Educators, 254
Speiser, Mortimer D., 204
spirituality, 107–9, 115, 268
sponsors, 336n5
Standard Oil, 73, 114
Stars and Stripes, 165
statistics, related to alcoholism, xiii, 6–7, 48, 327–28n2, 330n7
Stein, Gertrude, 73
Stepping Stones, 121, 337–38n16
Stevenson, Robert Louis, 325
stigma
    of addiction/alcoholism, vii, 4, 5, 7, 153, 157, 217, 246, 324, 332n5, 339n2
    of diseases, 27–28, 29, 34, 346n14
    reducing, 261, 312
Still, Clyfford, 198
Strachey, Alex, 72
Strachey, Lytton, 72
Straight (Mrs. Willard) Foundation, 197
street drugs, 6, 195, 274–75
Strong, Leonard, 288

Studdiford, William, 204
substance abuse, 160
suffrage movement, 43, 44
suicide, 80, 87, 90, 108
Summer School of Alcohol Studies, Yale
  University, 161–62, 170, 235
Susskind, David, 38
Swafford, Tom, 255
Swegan, Bill, 170–71
Swinyard, Chester A., 287–88
Syracuse University Library, 352n1

T

tai chi, 268
Tanzola, Kay, 299
Taylor, Bert, 121
Taylor, Elizabeth, 181
TB. *See* tuberculosis (TB)
teetotaling, 44–45, 331n11. *See also* ab-
  stinence
television, 243, 281–82
Temenos, 140
temperance movement, 8, 40, 41–44,
  163. *See also* Prohibition
therapy. *See* group therapy; psycho-
  therapy
Thirteenth-stepping, 129
Thomsen, Robert, 113, 336n3
Throop, Amos G., 33
Tiebout, Harry, 94, 98, 100–106, 108,
  109, 111, 118, 119, 121, 130–31,
  167, 205, 210, 212, 250, 270
TM. *See* transcendental meditation (TM)
tobacco cessation, and treatment, 47.
  See also cigarette smoking; nicotine
tolerance, for alcohol, 4
Towertown, 19
Town and Country magazine, 71, 197
Towns Hospital, 115, 132, 190, 233,
  250
transcendental meditation (TM), 268

treatment
  and abstinence, 154
  drug courts, 342n8
  inpatient, 296, 299
  medical, 184
  and tobacco cessation, 47
Tremaine, Kit, 167
Trinity Church, 59
tuberculosis (TB), 27–35, 60
Tweed, Boss, 97
Twelve Steps, of AA, 105, 117, 119,
  124, 128, 130, 134, 136, 183, 190,
  228, 298, 364
Twelve Traditions, of AA, 145, 186, 365
twenty-four-hour program, 134
Twenty-Four Hours a Day, 318

U

United Fund, 284
University of Wisconsin, 15

V

Van Dyke, Dick, 306
Varieties of Religious Experience
  (James), 108
Vestermark, A. V., 201–2
Vietnam War, 252, 284
Vision in Motion (Moholy-Nagy), 198
vitamin B$_3$, 271
Vogue magazine, 146, 148, 177,
  197–99, 203, 219, 253, 276, 293
voluntarism, 40, 256–58
Voluntary Health Movement, 257–58,
  260–61
Vreeland, Diana (Dee-Anne), 253–54,
  293

W

Walt Disney Studios, 157
war zone trauma, 92
Washington, D.C., *Times*, 20

Washingtonian Society, as AA pre-
    cursor, 44
WCTU. *See* Women's Christian
    Temperance Union (WCTU)
Wegscheider-Cruse, Sharon, 312–13
Weisman, Maxwell (Max) N., 172,
    298–99, 311
welfare, social. *See* social welfare
West, Louis J., 170
Whale Cay island retreat, 73, 209, 266
Whiskey Rebellion, 330n7
White, B. D., 69
White, William (Bill) L., 171, 193, 235,
    248, 283
WHO. *See* World Health Organization
    (WHO)
Wiley, Anna C., 94, 97, 106, 121
Willard, Francis E., 44
Williams, Dakin, 146
Williams, Jack, 128
Williams, Jean, 128
Williams, Katharine (Kit) Seaburn, 55
Williams, Tennessee, 143, 146, 223
willpower, 7, 26, 44, 76, 136
Wilson, Bill (Bill W.), AA cofounder,
    9–10, 47, 104–5, 109, 112–19,
    121–22, 125–26, 128–29, 132–33,
    148–49, 154, 156, 158–60, 162,
    167, 180–82, 184–86, 190, 194,
    205, 209–10, 218, 228, 239, 263,
    267, 271, 281–82, 288, 290–93,
    314
Wilson, Lois, 112–13, 116, 119,
    121–22, 125, 128, 132–33, 145,
    210, 218, 267, 290
women
    in AA, 10, 113–16, 122–23, 127,
        129–30, 151, 264, 304–5,
        351n10
    as alcoholics, 243, 264, 303–5,
        315–16

drinking habits of, 40
gender as barrier/stigma, 10,
    115–16, 122
in temperance movement, 42–44
voting rights, 44
Women's Christian Temperance Union
    (WCTU), 44, 163, 270, 331n11
women's movement, and temperance, 42
Women's State Temperance Society
    (WSTS), 43
Woolf, Virginia, 72, 272
World and Alcoholism, The (Mann),
    221
World Health Organization (WHO),
    221, 244–45, 247
World War I, 26, 31
World War II, 83, 120, 122, 124, 142,
    156, 188, 217
World's Columbian Exposition (1893),
    19
World's Fair (1933), 68
Wright, Richard, 19
Wrigley, William J., 33
WSTS. *See* Women's State Temperance
    Society (WSTS)
Wyman, Nona, 99, 124–25, 227

Y
Yale Center of Alcohol Studies, 154,
    160–64, 183–84, 192, 196,
    207–13, 235, 309
Yale College, 162
Yale Plan Clinics, 154, 193, 309
Yale University, 3, 170–71, 174, 175,
    180, 191
Young, Betty, 255
Young, Robert (Bob), 255

Z
Zonolite company, 68–69
Zuska, Joseph, 47

About the Authors

The Reverend Sally Brown is an ordained minister in the United Church of Christ and a board-certified clinical chaplain. In 1998, she retired from hospital chaplaincy at the Palo Alto VA Health Care System (California) to help research and write the biography of Marty Mann. Her chaplaincy specialties were hospice inpatients, women veterans, and alcohol and drug patients. She was recognized at the VA and by regional and national awards from the United Church of Christ for her leadership and work as a chaplain. She continues to be active in her denomination and community.

Sally's first degrees were a bachelor of arts in English from the University of Washington (Seattle) and a master of science in recreation from San Jose State University (California). Prior to her master of divinity degree from the Pacific School of Religion (California) and entry into the ministry, Sally was a professionally certified recreational therapist, specializing in the older adult population. She developed and taught California's first community college courses in gerontology and in adapted recreation, and consulted in convalescent hospitals. Her lifelong avocation has been dance.

David R. Brown attended graduate school at the Massachusetts Institute of Technology where he received his master's degree and worked on one of the earliest electronic computers: the Whirlwind. After graduate school, he worked at MIT and an MIT spin-off, the Mitre Corporation. In 1963, when he moved with his family to California, he worked at the Stanford Research Institute, mostly as a manager of computer research, until his retirement in 1991. In 1968, he was honored as a Fellow of the Institute of Electrical and Electronics Engineers in recognition of his contributions to computer development.

At Stanford Research Institute (now SRI International), he was involved in contract research for both government and industry. He was associated with many developments, including interactive computer terminals, the ARPA network (now the Internet), and artificial intelligence. A project in the 1970s was concerned with the processing of data from Alcoholism Treatment Centers of the NIAAA.

In 1982, he was appointed to the Alcoholism Advisory Board of Santa Clara County where he served until 1990, including three terms as chairperson. While there, he helped form the Long-Range Planning Committee of the Alcoholism Advisory Board, a committee designed to anticipate future needs of the county in alcohol prevention, intervention, and treatment.

In retirement, he is active in his church and denominational affairs. In connection with his avocation, genealogy, he works part time as a librarian at the local Family History Center of the Church of Jesus Christ of Latter-day Saints.

He is a member of the board of directors of the National Council on Alcoholism and Drug Dependence of Silicon Valley.

Sally and David were married in 1944. She recovered from alcoholism in 1977. They have four grown children and a granddaughter.

HAZELDEN PUBLISHING AND EDUCATIONAL SERVICES
is a division of the Hazelden Foundation, a not-for-profit organization.
Since 1949, Hazelden has been a leader in promoting the dignity and treatment of people afflicted with the disease of chemical dependency.

The mission of the foundation is to improve the quality of life for individuals, families, and communities by providing a national continuum of information, education, and recovery services that are widely accessible; to advance the field through research and training; and to improve our quality and effectiveness through continuous improvement and innovation.

Stemming from that, the mission of this division is to provide quality information and support to people wherever they may be in their personal journey—from education and early intervention, through treatment and recovery, to personal and spiritual growth.

Although our treatment programs do not necessarily use everything Hazelden publishes, our bibliotherapeutic materials support our mission and the Twelve Step philosophy upon which it is based. We encourage your comments and feedback.

The headquarters of the Hazelden Foundation are in Center City, Minnesota. Additional treatment facilities are located in Chicago, Illinois; Newberg, Oregon; New York, New York; Plymouth, Minnesota; and St. Paul, Minnesota. At these sites, we provide a continuum of care for men and women of all ages. Our Plymouth facility is designed specifically for youth and families.

For more information on Hazelden, please call 1-800-257-7800. Or you may access our World Wide Web site on the Internet at www.hazelden.org.